W9-CBH-920

Better Homes and Gardens®

ENTERTAINING
·WITH·EASE·
—COOK BOOK—

© 1984 by Meredith Corporation, Des Moines, Iowa.
All Rights Reserved. Printed in the United States of America.
First Edition. First Printing.
Library of Congress Catalog Card Number: 83-61316
ISBN: 0-696-00895-5

Better Homes and Gardens® Books
Editor: Gerald M. Knox
Art Director: Ernest Shelton
Managing Editor: David A. Kirchner

Food and Nutrition Editor: Nancy Byal
Department Head, Cook Books: Sharyl Heiken
Associate Department Heads: Sandra Granseth, Rosemary C. Hutchinson,
  Elizabeth Woolever
Senior Food Editors: Julie Henderson, Julia Malloy, Marcia Stanley
Associate Food Editors: Jill Burmeister, Molly Culbertson, Linda Foley,
  Linda Henry, Lynn Hoppe, Mary Jo Plutt, Maureen Powers, Joyce Trollope
Recipe Development Editor: Marion Viall
Test Kitchen Director: Sharon Stilwell
Test Kitchen Home Economists: Jean Brekke, Kay Cargill, Marilyn Cornelius,
  Maryellyn Krantz, Dianna Nolin, Marge Steenson

Associate Art Directors: Linda Ford Vermie, Neoma Alt West, Randall Yontz
Copy and Production Editors: Marsha Jahns, Mary Helen Schiltz, Carl Voss,
  David A. Walsh
Assistant Art Directors: Harijs Priekulis, Tom Wegner
Senior Graphic Designers: Alisann Dixon, Lynda Haupert, Lyne Neymeyer
Graphic Designers: Mike Burns, Mike Eagleton, Deb Miner, Stan Sams,
  D. Greg Thompson, Darla Whipple, Paul Zimmerman

Vice President, Editorial Director: Doris Eby
Executive Director, Editorial Services: Duane L. Gregg

General Manager: Fred Stines
Director of Publishing: Robert B. Nelson
Vice President, Retail Marketing: Jamie Martin
Vice President, Direct Marketing: Arthur Heydendael

Entertaining with Ease Cook Book
Editors: Sandra Granseth, Julia Malloy, Joyce Trollope
Copy and Production Editor: David A. Walsh
Graphic Designer: Mike Eagleton
Electronic Text Processor: Jacquin I. Bodensteiner

Our seal assures you that every recipe in the *Entertaining with Ease Cook Book* has been tested in the Better Homes and Gardens® Test Kitchen. This means that each recipe is practical and reliable, and meets our high standards of taste appeal.

On the cover:
Vichyssoise
Chicken Marsala
Almond and Plum Tart
Homemade Herb Linguine with Cheesy Sauce
(See Index for page numbers.)

People enjoy nothing more than going to a good party—unless it's hosting a great party. Yet some people hesitate to entertain. They may be experienced cooks, but are uncomfortable giving a party. If you're that way, the *Entertaining with Ease Cook Book* will help you conquer your fears. And if you're a confident host already, it will help you enjoy entertaining even more.

A look through this book will inspire you to have a party soon! Delicious recipes and delightful ideas abound. The *Entertaining with Ease Cook Book* does more than inspire, however. It also explains the big— and little—details that make a party great.

True to its title, this book is easy to use. For a dinner party, for example, you'll find all the recipes you need— even complete menus—in one section. The same is true for brunch, lunch, and supper parties, and special celebration parties.

The *Entertaining with Ease Cook Book* offers complete parties ranging from a candlelight dinner for four to a holiday open house for 25. Each party has a menu and instructions that take you from party concept to party time, ensuring you omit no steps and you always have success—even the first time around.

Even the recipe design makes things easier for you. You'll see that the recipes are simple to follow and that they all come with a timetable. A glance at the timetable tells you when you must start preparing a recipe.

Also, throughout the book you'll find helpful technique hints, fascinating recipe information, and pronunciation guides to names of foreign recipes. These make entertaining not only easy, but also interesting.

Finally, we at Better Homes and Gardens® Books hope that the *Entertaining with Ease Cook Book* makes entertaining fun and exciting and that you enjoy using this book as much as we enjoyed creating it for you.

CONTENTS

CHAPTER 1

PARTY PLANNING

CHAPTER 2

DINNER PARTIES

CHAPTER 3

BRUNCH, LUNCH, AND SUPPER PARTIES

CHAPTER 4

SPECIAL CELEBRATION PARTIES

CHAPTER 5

BARMANSHIP

PLANNING A PARTY

Good hosts enjoy their own parties. How do they do it? Like good cooks, good hosts take the basics, then add a personal touch. Also, they're well organized. In this chapter we offer you ideas to help make you a good host and to let you have as much fun, perhaps even more, at your next party as your guests have.

What's the Occasion? Any reason for a party is a good reason! Celebrate your parents' wedding anniversary in grand fashion. Share your excitement about a new home by hosting a housewarming party. Gather people together for a special television show. Or, if you're just in the mood to entertain, go ahead—without a special reason.

If you're a first-time host, start with an easy party. Have friends over for dessert and coffee. Or, try a picnic. Either way is a good way to begin gaining experience at entertaining.

If you're experienced, however, host a formal dinner or a fancy cocktail party to celebrate an extra-special occasion.

Whatever the occasion, remember: first things first. And the first thing to decide when entertaining is your budget.

The Budget. When it comes to parties, "time is money" applies doubly. What you lack of one you can make up with the other —if you like. You will need to decide just how much money and time you're willing to spend. Remember this, however: Don't overspend, or you won't enjoy your own party. Besides, to have a great party you don't need to overindulge in time or money. After all, it is the impression—not the cost— that counts. By adding personal touches to even the most casual party theme, you can entertain with style. Just let guests know how really special they are; that is what they will remember most.

When figuring your party budget, try to think of all expense items, such as food, decorations and flowers, invitations, any rentals required (chairs, tables, so on), and baby-sitter's fee. However much you decide to spend, it's a good idea to reserve 10 percent for unforeseen items.

To entertain with elegance, not extravagance, try these suggestions. Host a participation party. (This book offers you menus for four participation parties.) Everyone will enjoy joining in. Or, plan a single-course party such as a dessert party. People will love you for giving them the chance to be just a bit indulgent!

To keep decoration cost manageable, use a single flower on each plate instead of filling your home with bouquet upon bouquet of flowers. (For the party shown here, a single anthurium bedecks each plate. It's simple, yet the flower's shape and color add to the evening's festive spirit.) Or, for a more casual feeling, use your potted plants as centerpieces.

With your budget decided, figure how many guests to invite. If the occasion leaves you free to determine the crowd size, decide whether to invite a few guests and treat them lavishly, or many and keep the cost per person low.

The Guest List. The right mix of people at a party is as important as the right mix of food and drinks. Invite a good blend of listeners and talkers. Select guests with a common interest or bring together a group of people with wide-ranging interests. Mix ages, too, for a marvelous medley guaranteed to spark lively conversation.

Whom you decide to invite depends on the occasion, how many people your house can hold, and—perhaps most important—the crowd size you feel comfortable hosting. Inexperienced hosts should keep the party size down—six or so. Your parties can get bigger as you gain more hosting experience.

Remember to keep in mind the likes and dislikes of guests. Also, don't try to repay all your social obligations with one party. It never succeeds.

Invitations. Either telephoned or mailed invitations are acceptable. Make sure your invitation contains all specific information: date, time, place, type of party, attire (if special), address, phone number, and a RSVP request to be sure you know how many guests to expect.

If you mail the invitations, include a map showing how to get to your home. Your guests will appreciate the thoughtfulness.

For telephone invitations, try to call everyone on the same day. That way no one will feel he's an afterthought.

MENU PLANNING

■ Grand entertaining doesn't have to mean long hours in the kitchen—if you come up with the right menu. Although you want to show guests how special they are, you don't want to be chained to your kitchen counter tops before or—even worse—during your party. Planning the party menu takes the same care and thought as planning your guest list. To help you select your menu, consider these suggestions.

The First Step. When planning your menu, think as if you were painting the meal. Visualize the parts that will make up the whole. Imagine how the foods will look and taste together. Select foods and garnishes (always remember the garnishes; they're the subtle strokes that highlight the meal!) that complement or contrast provocatively, yet pleasingly—the way colors and techniques work together in a good painting.

If you take a culinary artist's approach to menu planning, you're bound to end up with a menu that's creative, exciting, fun, and delicious. Of course, even the greatest artists have guidelines they follow when painting. So, too, do good chefs. Here are a few to help you plan your menu.

Guidelines for Great Menus.
■ Consider first the occasion. What's spectacular for one occasion may be inappropriate for another. A party menu that works wonderfully for a formal dinner, for example, just won't work for a dinner where the main focus is a special TV show.
■ Plan menus around dishes you're comfortable with, but don't be afraid to add one or two new dishes. (Our party menus and timetables will help you immensely when striking out to new food horizons, especially when preparing recipes you've never tried before.)
■ Combine interesting, contrasting colors in foods. Avoid foods all of the same color. Although monochromatic schemes work well in interior decorating, with foods they give diners the visual blahs. By the same token, serve foods that have different textures. A carrot-potato puree, for example, makes an excellent dinner companion for

crisp, fried chicken, but wouldn't pair well with creamed seafood.
■ Consider how you'll present the foods. Think of everything—even your tablesetting—when planning a menu.
■ Make one dish a splashy one. Let the others play minor, but still important, roles. Nothing upstages a menu's star more than too many showy competitors.
■ Serve any one type of food only once during a meal.
■ Avoid any food with an overpowering smell. Otherwise, the other dishes—no matter how delicious—simply will not be fully appreciated.
■ Plan as many make-aheads as will work well in your menu. Easy-to-prepare and easy-to-serve foods work wonders in helping hosts enjoy their own parties.
■ Know your guests' restrictions. If a good friend is on a diet or needs to follow a strict, special diet, it may be better for all if you

invited that person at a time when you could tailor the menu to his restrictions.

Coming up with just the right menu will help your party succeed—and go smoothly. To help you become organized and make things go even more smoothly, take a look at our party-countdown schedule, then adapt from it to fit your style.

Countdown to the Party.

- *One month ahead*: For very formal parties plan the menu, make up your guest list, and mail invitations. If your party is casual, then make your arrangements about two weeks ahead.
- *Two weeks ahead:* Telephone guests who have yet to respond to your written invitations. (Make substitutions, if necessary.) For casual parties, telephone your invitations. Order any special flowers.
- *One week ahead:* Do preliminary housecleaning, especially any time-consuming tasks. Check your tablesettings to see that they're spotless. Order special meats or cuts of meat. Inventory items such as matches, place cards (if you're using them), candles, and liquor, and make a list of things you need.

- *Two to three days before:* Shop for everything but highly perishable items. Thoroughly reclean the house, if necessary.
- *Day before:* Arrange and set your tables. Recheck your recipes to ensure you have all the ingredients needed. Buy highly perishable items. Plan your timetable for cooking the foods. Prepare as many foods as

possible. (For example, chop vegetables you'll cook, but wait until the party day to cut salad vegetables.)
- *Party day:* Go over the house again in the morning. Prepare food according to your timetable so everything will finish at the same time. (Wash dishes as you go along to save clean-up time later.) Make sure everything that needs chilling will be well chilled by party time. Finally, save an hour for yourself, if possible, to relax before guests arrive.

A marvelous menu and a well-conceived pre-party schedule go a long way toward making a party successful. To make your party really special, however, you have to add some distinctive touches—the icing on the cake, so to speak. To find out how to put real personality in your party, read on.

MAKING A PARTY SPECIAL

Long after your party ends, thoughts of its amiable atmosphere will linger. Your guests will remember how well they enjoyed themselves. And what helped to make your party unique were all those little things you did—the extras you really didn't have to do—to help people have a wonderful time. When it comes to parties, the little things are what make a party exceptional. They are what create the lasting impression that yours was a very special party.

Make Your House Look Special. With parties—just as with people—first impressions really count. So make your house exude the feeling of fun. Go all out with decorations—if the occasion calls for it; or keep the trimmings simple, if the evening is to be a quiet, elegantly simple one. For a Christmas party, for example, deck the halls—and the living room, and the dining room, and the kitchen, and everywhere else your merry heart wishes. On the other hand, for a quiet evening of tea and cake after the theater, a simple arrangement of flowers—from your own garden, perhaps—and quiet music are appropriate. For other occasions, decorations can run the full gamut in between.

If you like, set the party's stage even before guests arrive at your door. Adorn the front lawn or driveway with the right touches. For example, line the driveway and walkway with bag lights or torches to give guests the feel of a grand entrance. Everyone will enter your house feeling more splendid. For a Halloween party, a few well-positioned ghosts and goblins will help raise goosebumps even the chilly autumn air couldn't account for. Inside, carry the theme throughout your house.

If you're hosting a dinner party, you certainly don't need both candles and a centerpiece—but together they do add elegance. And today the only restrictions on centerpieces are those imposed by your own imagination. No longer are centerpieces limited to expensive and intricate flower arrangements—although those still are an excellent choice. Now, however, a bowl or cornucopia of fresh fruits can make a charming centerpiece, as well as a grand finale for your meal.

Other indoor ideas include brightly colored fall leaves and ornamental corn for the Thanksgiving table, a single red carnation on each Valentine's place setting, and a turn-the-tables surprise gift for the birthday well-wishers. When it comes to decorations, let your imagination go.

Make Your Food Look Special. To lend sparkle to your party's atmosphere, your food needs to do more than taste great. It must look the part, too—which is really quite easy to achieve. Just a few, simple garnishes added to your dishes, and they'll be dressed to fit the occasion.

On these two pages we give some simple ideas. Chocolate leaves will delight and amaze everyone. Orange strips add color as well as flavor to the *Citrus Mousse*. Thin carrot strips adorn *Dill Vinaigrette Salad* like folded ribbons. And the *Pizzelle* dessert cup provides the perfect way to present the *Citrus Mousse* (see the recipe and garnish indexes for page references).

These, of course, are just a few ideas for garnishes. Other ideas include fresh parsley sprigs (old standbys, yes, but still as delightful as ever), citrus fruit wedges, tomato or radish roses, green onion brushes, and decorative mushrooms (see the garnish index for page references).

An additional way to dress up your food is to give special treatment to your place settings. Especially carefully folded cloth dinner napkins and properly placed plates and glasses will lend a ceremonial air to a formal dinner, for example.

Make Your Guests Feel Welcome. Another important final touch to a good party is a warm feeling of hospitality. A cheerful welcome at the door surely will put guests in the right mood and let them know how much you value their coming. Introductions, when necessary, also will make sure your guests feel at ease.

Think of guests' comfort when you set up for your party. Have refreshments on tables that are easy to get to. If you allow smoking in your house, provide plenty of ashtrays.

Light a few candles to clear the air for nonsmokers and perhaps crack a window to allow in some fresh air. In the guests' restroom place a single fresh flower and a lighted candle to show the extra consideration you have for them.

Touches like these help make guests feel especially welcomed, but the most important touch is you. Spend as much time as you can with your guests (this is where good menu planning helps), and they'll really know you value their company. After all, nothing makes a party more special than good company.

SETTING THE SCENE

By now, you've imagined lots of new, exciting ideas to make your next party really *your* party. You know how to make your food look stunning and your guests feel welcomed. Time, however, to think about the nitty-gritty how to serve the food? Don't let this bring your imagination to a screeching halt. In fact, put it in overdrive. No matter what else you've done to set the party's atmosphere, if you don't make your table its loveliest and serve food without a fuss, your party just won't delight as it should.

Serving the Food. When it comes to serving the food, the right way is the convenient way. Some occasions dictate the style of serving food. A gathering of 30 relatives and friends, for example, would be hard to manage any way but buffet style. And Thanksgiving dinner for four served any way but semiformal or formal just wouldn't seem right. Still, within those distinct styles you can have many variations on a theme.

For example, for sit-down dinners the hosts can fill guests' plates and pass them, or the food itself can make the rounds. Buffets can be so casual that guests seat themselves in any comfortable spot, or a bit less casual and have seats assigned at preset tables.

If you choose buffet style, be sure to set the serving table so guests can help themselves easily. You don't want anyone holding up the line when all are eager to try your culinary treats! To keep guests moving smoothly around your buffet table arrange the food logically: main dish, vegetables, salad, relishes, rolls, and beverages.

Setting the Table. The attire of your table can range from high style, black tie to down-home, kick-off-the-shoes-and-sit-a-spell. Both can work equally well. How you top your table depends on the occasion—and what you like.

Keep your eyes open for items that will reflect your style. If you prefer a natural centerpiece, collect from nature on your next walk in the woods. Look for interesting branches, cones, rocks, and reeds that will make a charming centerpiece. Or, if you like nostalgia, visit antique shops and come away with knickknacks from another era for use on another night. Anything goes when it comes to setting your table, and usually the more remarkable the better. The thing to remember is that unique table toppings and

centerpieces don't come together overnight. They take slow acquisition.

The same goes for serving pieces and place settings. You may not have a complete set (or even one place setting!) of the finest china, but don't let that stifle your serving style. Take another look at your everyday objects. Put in a different perspective they'll serve a different purpose. Large bowls, baskets, and clear plastic buckets work well as serving pieces. Ceramic tiles can become Art Deco coasters. For place mats use large printed handkerchiefs. Or try bamboo mats to help set the stage when serving Far Eastern cuisine. Tablecloths can be anything from quilts to crepe paper. When setting your table the trick is to keep both your mind and eyes wide open.

When It All Comes Together. As you can see on these two pages, when everything comes together just so, the results are spectacular! Here *Dill Vinaigrette Salad, Brown-and-Serve Whole Wheat Rolls,* and *Cock-a-Leekie Soup* (see the recipe index for page references)—served in a simple,

yet festive setting—would make a showy beginning for any dinner party. Shown opposite are two more striking dishes: *Artichokes Continental* and *Citrus Mousse* (see the recipe index for page references). Either would add an exotic touch to a party.

The recipes shown here give you an idea of just how delightful the food at your next party can look. For still more ideas and recipes, browse through the rest of this book. Remember the party suggestions offered, and modify them to suit *your* needs. Most of all, enjoy entertaining!

CANDLELIGHT DINNER

Frosty Fruit Delight

Marinated Avocado-Mushroom Salad

Crab-Stuffed Steaks

Parslied Carrots

Easy Brioche with Butter Curls

Upside-Down Chocolate Pie

If you're looking for a way to make friends feel very special, invite them to a spectacular dinner party. It's a great excuse to use your best dishes, glasses, and cloth napkins. Then, show off and give that extra touch to your table setting by folding the napkins attractively.

The menu for this formal, sit-down dinner for four is a sophisticated version of the familiar steak and salad dinner. It's sure to appeal to almost everyone's taste and is well worth the expense. You'll find that these classy-looking foods are not difficult to prepare and allow you to do much of the work before your guests arrive.

When you and your guests finish the appetizer, *Frosty Fruit Delight*, remove the dishes to make way for *Marinated Avocado-Mushroom Salad*. Make this course special by arranging the salad attractively on individual salad plates. Chill in the refrigerator until ready to serve.

Pace the dinner courses so you'll be ready for the steaks when they are finished broiling. If guests linger more than expected over the appetizer course, serve the salad with the main course.

For a beautiful presentation and easier serving, arrange the *Parslied Carrots* on the same heated platter with the broiled *Crab-Stuffed Steaks*. Garnish with fresh mushrooms, if you like, and use watercress or parsley for extra color.

Pass the *Easy Brioche* rolls with both the salad and the main courses.

TIMETABLE

The day before: Start the dinner by preparing the *Easy Brioche*. Chill dough in the refrigerator until the next day. Next, make *Upside-Down Chocolate Pie* (save making the chocolate curl garnish until the next day). Freeze slush mixture for *Frosty Fruit Delight*.

4 to 6 hours before: Shape the dough for the *Easy Brioche* and use either individual brioche pans or muffin pans for baking. Let rolls rise; then bake.

Set the table and arrange the centerpiece. You can use an assortment of candles, flowers, fruit, or whatever you wish. If you don't use flowers for the centerpiece, consider adding a fresh flower to each guest's place setting just before dinner. Check page 18 for illustrated directions on folding the napkins.

Prepare the fruit combination for *Frosty Fruit Delight*. Be sure to treat with ascorbic acid color keeper any fresh fruit that will darken. Cover and chill fruit.

Wash the lettuce for the salad. Drain the greens thoroughly on paper toweling and chill in refrigerator.

2 to 3 hours before: Prepare salad dressing and marinate vegetables. Keep salad ingredients chilled.

Make butter curls for the rolls and chocolate curls.

Start the *Crab-Stuffed Steaks*—assemble stuffing, then prepare and stuff steaks. Cover and chill meat.

1 hour before: Chill the wine glasses and the dishes you plan to use for the fruit mixture. If using mushrooms for the steak platter garnish, wash them.

Prepare *Parslied Carrots*; set aside in saucepan until ready to cook. (Start cooking carrots at the appropriate time so they are ready for the main course.)

Arrange the *Marinated Avocado-Mushroom Salad* on the individual salad plates; cover and chill.

At serving time: Fill the water goblets. Place the rolls in a basket, if desired, and butter curls in bowl. Finish *Frosty Fruit Delight*, spooning it into individual dishes. Start broiling steaks and fix mushroom garnish. After guests are seated, pour wine and serve fruit cup.

Folding napkins: An attractively folded napkin adds a graceful, elegant look to your dining table. Try this technique for folding a napkin: Start by folding a large square napkin (lightly starched or made of stiff fabric) into quarters. (**1**) Arrange all four open corners at the upper right. Fold one layer back to the opposite corner, forming a triangle with this layer. (**2**) With the napkin point toward outside, make accordion pleats with this layer until you reach the center fold. Press center lightly. Hold in place while pleating the next single layer; accordion-pleat just to the center, having napkin point toward outside. (**3**) Pleated sections should be next to one another. Press center lightly. (**4**) Holding the pleated sections, fold napkin across both pleated sections to form a triangle with pleated sections on the outside. Arrange the napkin at place setting with point of triangle away from guest.

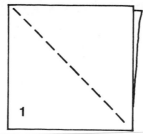

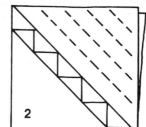

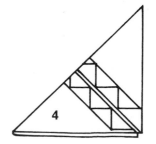

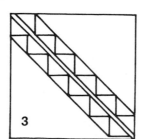

After the dessert course, move into the living room. Here you can sit back and enjoy more coffee and conversation. If you like, offer your guests after-dinner drinks (see page 309 for suggestions).

Easy Brioche

1 13¾-ounce package hot roll mix
¾ cup warm milk (110° to 115°)
3 eggs
¼ cup butter *or* margarine, softened
½ cup all-purpose flour
¼ cup sugar
1 tablespoon water

▬ Remove yeast packet from hot roll mix package. In large mixing bowl dissolve yeast in the warm milk.

▬ Separate *one* of the eggs; set egg white aside in refrigerator. Stir egg yolk, the remaining 2 eggs, and the softened butter or margarine into yeast-milk mixture. Stir together the flour from the hot roll mix, the ½ cup flour, and sugar. Add to yeast mixture; mix well. Scrape down sides of bowl.

▬ Cover dough; store in the refrigerator for 3 to 24 hours. Stir dough down; turn out onto lightly floured surface. Divide into 4 equal portions; set one portion aside. Divide each remaining portion into 5 pieces, making a total of 15. Form each piece into a ball. Place each in a greased individual brioche pan. Divide reserved dough into 15 pieces; shape into balls. Make an indentation in each large ball. Press a small ball into each indentation. (*Or*, if desired, use muffin pans instead of individual brioche pans. Prepare dough and divide into 4 equal portions; set one portion aside. Divide each remaining portion into *6* pieces, making a total of *18*. Form each piece into a ball; place in *18* greased muffin cups. Divide reserved dough into *18* pieces; shape into balls. Press each into indentation in large ball.)

▬ Combine reserved egg white and the 1 tablespoon water; brush over rolls. Cover; let rise in warm place till nearly double (40 to 45 minutes). Bake in a 375° oven for 7 minutes; brush again with egg white mixture. Bake 8 to 11 minutes longer. Makes 15 or 18.

▬ Preparation time: 30 minutes
▬ Chilling time: at least 3 hours
▬ Rising time: 40 to 45 minutes
▬ Cooking time: 15 to 18 minutes

Frosty Fruit Delight

1 8-ounce can pineapple chunks (juice pack)
1 12-ounce can ginger ale
½ of a 6-ounce can (⅓ cup) frozen orange-grapefruit juice concentrate, thawed
1½ cups desired fresh fruit
     (see column at right)

▬ Drain pineapple, reserving 3 tablespoons juice. Combine reserved pineapple juice, ginger ale, and the thawed concentrate. Pour into a 9x5x3-inch loaf pan. Cover pan with foil; freeze for 4 hours or till firm. Combine the pineapple chunks and desired fresh fruit. Cover; chill. To serve, break up juice mixture with a spoon till slushy. Spoon chilled fruit mixture into 4 well-chilled sherbet glasses. Top with frozen juice mixture. Garnish with fresh mint, if desired. Serves 4.

▬ Advance preparation time: 35 minutes
▬ Freezing time: at least 4 hours
▬ Final preparation time: 10 minutes

Parslied Carrots

1 pound carrots (6 medium), cut into julienne strips
2 tablespoons lemon juice
2 tablespoons butter *or* margarine
1 tablespoon sugar
2 tablespoons snipped parsley

▬ In a saucepan combine carrots, lemon juice, butter or margarine, sugar, ½ cup *water*, ¼ teaspoon *salt*, and ⅛ teaspoon *pepper*. Bring to boiling; reduce heat. Cover; cook over low heat for 15 minutes or till carrots are tender. Uncover; continue to cook 10 minutes more or till the liquid has evaporated, carefully stirring occasionally to prevent carrots from sticking. To serve, sprinkle with parsley. Makes 4 servings.

▬ Preparation time: 20 minutes
▬ Cooking time: 25 minutes

Fresh fruit suggestions for the *Frosty Fruit Delight* include: cantaloupe or honeydew melon cubes or balls; orange sections; seedless grapes; blueberries; strawberries (halve large berries); peeled and sliced kiwifruit, mangoes, papayas, or peaches; sliced or cut-up nectarines, plums, or pears; and halved and pitted dark sweet cherries.

Restaurant menus sometimes offer a "surf-and-turf" combination—seafood and beef. If you've ever sampled that combination, then you'll be especially interested in trying *Crab-Stuffed Steaks*.

It's easy to make this delicious recipe. First, stuff the steaks in advance and store, covered, in the refrigerator. When dinnertime arrives, you need only to broil the meat. Set a timer so you'll get an accurate broiling time for the doneness you prefer.

Quickly finish the mushroom garnishes and trim the platter.

Crab-Stuffed Steaks

    2 tablespoons finely chopped celery
    2 tablespoons finely chopped onion
    1 clove garlic, minced
    1 tablespoon butter *or* margarine
    1 5½-ounce can crab meat, drained, flaked, and cartilage removed
    3 tablespoons fine dry bread crumbs
    2 tablespoons dry white wine
    ½ teaspoon Worcestershire sauce
    ¼ teaspoon salt
    ⅛ teaspoon pepper
    4 beef top loin steaks, cut 1 to 1¼ inches thick
       Watercress *or* parsley
       Whole fresh mushrooms (optional)

▬▬ For the stuffing, in a saucepan cook celery, onion, and garlic in butter or margarine till tender but not brown. Remove from heat. Add crab meat, bread crumbs, wine, Worcestershire, salt, and pepper.

▬▬ Slash fat edge of steaks at 1-inch intervals (don't cut into meat). Slice a pocket in the other side of each steak; stuff pockets with crab mixture. Place steaks on the rack of an unheated broiler pan. Broil about 3 inches from heat to desired doneness, turning once. Allow about 10 minutes total for rare, 12 to 14 minutes total for medium, and about 20 minutes total for well done. Transfer steaks to heated serving platter. Garnish with watercress or parsley and mushrooms, if desired. Makes 4 servings.

▬▬ Preparation time: 25 minutes
▬▬ Cooking time: 10 to 20 minutes

Marinated Avocado-Mushroom Salad

    ¼ cup salad oil
    ¼ cup dry white wine
    2 tablespoons vinegar
    1 tablespoon snipped parsley
    ½ teaspoon sugar
    ¼ teaspoon salt
    ¼ teaspoon dried basil, crushed
    1 medium avocado, seeded, peeled, and sliced
    1 cup sliced fresh mushrooms
    2 thin slices onion, separated into rings
    3 cherry tomatoes, quartered
       Bibb lettuce

▬▬ To make dressing, in a screw-top jar combine oil, wine, vinegar, parsley, sugar, salt, and basil. Pour dressing over avocado, mushrooms, onion rings, and cherry tomatoes in a shallow dish. Cover and chill for 2 to 3 hours; occasionally spoon dressing over the vegetables. Drain vegetable mixture. Arrange vegetables on Bibb lettuce leaves. Makes 4 servings.

▬▬ Preparation time: 30 minutes
▬▬ Marinating time: at least 2 hours

These whole mushroom garnishes are a snap to make. After carefully washing the mushrooms, use a punch-type can opener to make a series of slight indentations on the mushroom caps, as shown. The number of marks you make depends on the size of each mushroom.

Upside-Down Chocolate Pie

Pastry for Pecan Single-Crust Pie
- 3 **egg whites**
- ½ **teaspoon vinegar**
- ¼ **teaspoon ground cinnamon**
- ½ **cup sugar**
- 1 **6-ounce package (1 cup) semisweet chocolate pieces**
- 3 **egg yolks**
- ¼ **cup water**
- 1½ **cups whipping cream**
- ¼ **cup sugar**
  Chocolate curls (see photograph, page 164)

■ Prepare Pastry for Pecan Single-Crust Pie. On a lightly floured surface roll pastry from center to edge, forming a circle about 12 inches in diameter. Line a 9-inch pie plate with pastry. Trim to ½ inch beyond edge. Flute edge high. Prick bottom and sides with the tines of a fork. Bake in a 450° oven for 10 to 12 minutes or till golden. Cool on a wire rack.

■ For the meringue layer, in a small mixer bowl combine egg whites, vinegar, and cinnamon. Beat with electric mixer till soft peaks form (tips curl over). Gradually add the ½ cup sugar, beating till stiff peaks form (tips stand straight). Spread meringue over the bottom and up the sides of the baked pastry shell. (If desired, use decorating bag with tip and pipe about ¼ of the meringue around top edge of meringue spread in pastry shell). Bake in a 325° oven for 15 minutes. Remove from oven and cool on wire rack.

■ Meanwhile, for the chocolate filling, melt semisweet chocolate in a saucepan over low heat; cool to room temperature. In a bowl beat together egg yolks and water till combined. Gradually stir in the melted and cooled chocolate. Lightly spread *¼ cup* of the chocolate mixture over the meringue. Chill 1 hour.

■ Beat whipping cream and ¼ cup sugar till soft peaks form. Fold *half* of the whipped cream into the remaining chocolate mixture. Carefully spread over chilled pie. Spread remaining cream in a 6-inch circle in center atop chocolate mixture. Chill for 4 to 24 hours. Top with chocolate curls. Makes 8 servings.

Pastry for Pecan Single-Crust Pie: Stir together 1¼ cups all-purpose *flour* and ½ teaspoon *salt*. Cut in ⅓ cup *shortening* till pieces are the size of small peas. Stir in 3 tablespoons finely chopped *pecans*. Sprinkle 3 to 4 tablespoons cold *water* over the mixture, one tablespoon at a time; toss gently with a fork till mixture is moistened. Form dough into a ball.

■ Preparation time: 1 hour
■ Cooking time: 25 to 27 minutes
■ Chilling time: at least 5 hours

After *Upside-Down Chocolate Pie* chills for several hours, the meringue under the rich chocolate filling becomes soft and marshmallowy.

Cover and store any remaining pieces of pie in the refrigerator. They will taste just as delicious the next day as they did at your dinner party. (We doubt you'll have any leftovers, however!)

Progressive Dinner

Salad Course
Tabouleh Bread
Moroccan Orange Salad
Artichoke-Mushroom Salad
Mideastern Green Salad
Iced Tea and Rosé Wine

Main Course
Indonesian Sâté with Peanut Sauce
Turmeric Rice
Iced Tea and Red Wine

Dessert Course
Gugelhupf with Apricot Sauce
Baklava Tarts
Pizzelles
Variety of Coffees

A three-course international dinner for eight people may sound a bit overwhelming even for experienced hosts. However, if you invite three other couples to help you stage a progressive dinner, work is kept to a minimum. At a progressive dinner each course is served at a different home, and everyone travels from one house to the next. Since the cost and work are shared, you'll find that it's an inexpensive and easy and fun way to entertain. Because four couples pitch in and there are only three courses, the fourth couple (perhaps apartment dwellers) can "sign up" for food preparation only.

Salad Course

Start the progressive feast with an ethnic salad bar where guests serve themselves buffet style. One couple prepares all of the salads, and then serves the food outside on the patio or inside (depending on the weather). They also prepare the cold beverages—iced tea and rosé wine make tasty accompaniments for this course. Another couple makes the bread, since it's an item that's easy to transport.

If you're bringing the *Tabouleh Bread,* bake it the day before and bring along a small container of butter. Since this bread is based on thawed, frozen bread dough, remember to allow enough time for thawing of the dough (about 2 hours at room temperature).

The baked bread keeps overnight if tightly wrapped in foil and stored in the refrigerator. Carry it to the party in the foil wrappings. Then, unwrap the bread, place it on a wooden cutting board, and slice to serve.

The day before: Start preparing the *Artichoke-Mushroom Salad* except for adding the mushrooms. Cover and chill. Shake together the dressing for *Mideastern Green Salad* and chill.

6 to 8 hours before: Arrange the *Moroccan Orange Salad* on the serving platter; cover and chill until serving time. Wash and drain the greens for the *Mideastern Green Salad* and store greens in plastic bags or containers in the refrigerator. Crumble the feta cheese and shred the cucumber; cover and chill in separate containers. Prepare the iced tea.

Set out plates, forks, napkins, beverage glasses, and serving utensils. If serving outdoors, wait until later before arranging these items on the table.

2 hours before: Arrange table if serving outdoors. Have in mind where each food item will go on table.

1 hour before: If desired, carefully tuck a few salad greens under the oranges in the *Moroccan Orange Salad.* Place salad greens, cheese, cucumber, and dressing for *Mideastern Green Salad* in containers. Slice mushrooms and add to the *Artichoke-Mushroom Salad*; toss lightly and turn salad into a lettuce-lined bowl. Garnish salad with pimiento. Return all salads to the refrigerator until serving time.

Tabouleh Bread

    1 **16-ounce loaf frozen white bread dough**
    ¾ **cup bulgur**
    ⅓ **cup tomato sauce**
    1 **medium tomato, peeled, seeded, and chopped**
    ⅓ **cup snipped parsley**
    2 **tablespoons lemon juice**
    1½ **teaspoons fresh mint leaves, finely chopped, *or* ½ teaspoon dried mint leaves, crushed**
    2 **teaspoons butter *or* margarine**

■■■ Thaw bread dough. In a bowl combine bulgur and 1½ cups *warm water;* let stand 1 hour. Drain, pressing out excess water. Combine the drained bulgur, the tomato sauce, chopped tomato, parsley, lemon juice, and mint; set aside. On a floured surface roll thawed bread dough into a 20x10-inch rectangle. (If dough is too elastic to roll, cover and let rest for 5 to 10 minutes.) Spread bulgur mixture over dough to 1 inch from edges. Roll up dough, jelly-roll style, from long edge. Moisten and seal edge and ends. Starting from one end of roll, coil roll loosely (snail fashion), seam side down, in a greased 9x1½-inch round baking pan. Cover; let rise in a warm place till nearly double (45 to 60 minutes).

■■■ Bake in a 375° oven for 35 to 40 minutes or till done, covering with foil the last 15 minutes, if necessary, to prevent overbrowning. Remove from the pan to a wire rack. Spread butter or margarine on top of hot loaf. Cool. Cut into wedges to serve.

■■ Preparation time: 1 hour and 40 minutes
■■ Rising time: 45 to 60 minutes
■■ Cooking time: 35 to 40 minutes

Moroccan Orange Salad

    4 **medium oranges**
    ¼ **cup lemon juice**
    1 **tablespoon sugar**
    ¼ **teaspoon ground cinnamon**
    ½ **cup sliced radishes *or* white radishes**
    ¼ **cup pitted ripe olives, halved lengthwise**

■■■ Cut off the peel and the white membrane of oranges. Slice crosswise into very thin slices (or cut into sections). For marinade, combine lemon juice, sugar, cinnamon, and dash *salt.* Arrange orange slices on a serving dish. Top with radishes and olives; spoon marinade over all. Cover and chill till serving time. Garnish with lettuce, if desired. Serves 8.

■■ Total preparation time: 40 minutes

Mideastern Green Salad

- **⅔ cup olive oil *or* salad oil**
- **⅓ cup lemon juice**
- **2 teaspoons sugar**
- **½ teaspoon dried mint, crushed**
- **⅛ teaspoon freshly ground black pepper**
- **2 cups torn spinach leaves**
- **2 cups lettuce *or* radish leaves**
- **1 bunch (2 cups) watercress**
- **2 cups parsley sprigs**
- **1½ cups feta cheese, crumbled**
- **1 cucumber, seeded and coarsely shredded**

▬▬ For dressing, in a screw-top jar combine first 5 ingredients and ¼ teaspoon *salt*. Cover; shake well. Chill. Serve the dressing, greens, cheese, and cucumber separately. Assemble individual servings, as desired, stirring dressing during serving. Serves 8.

▬▬ Total preparation time: 25 minutes

Artichoke-Mushroom Salad

- **2 9-ounce packages frozen artichoke hearts**
- **⅔ cup mayonnaise *or* salad dressing**
- **2 tablespoons dry white wine**
- **2 tablespoons capers, chopped**
- **1 tablespoon Dijon-style mustard**
- **1 teaspoon dried tarragon, crushed**
- **2 cups sliced fresh mushrooms**
  Romaine leaves *or* Belgian endive

▬▬ Cook artichokes according to package directions; drain. (Halve any large pieces lengthwise.) Stir together mayonnaise, wine, capers, mustard, and tarragon. Pour dressing over warm artichokes; stir to coat. Cover; chill for 2 to 24 hours. To serve, lightly toss mushrooms with mixture. Turn into a lettuce-lined serving bowl. Trim with pimiento, if desired. Serves 8.

▬▬ Preparation time: 20 minutes
▬▬ Chilling time: at least 2 hours

Main Course

Highlighting this intriguing progressive dinner is the delicious main course, *Indonesian Sâté* (sah-TAY) and *Turmeric Rice.* Sâté, an exotic-sounding main dish, is simply the Southeast Asian version of grilled kabobs. If the weather moves the party indoors, broil the kabobs under the conventional broiler or cook them on a range-top grill. The side dish, *Turmeric Rice,* makes a good flavor accompaniment to the spicy kabobs.

If you "sign up" for this course decide what serving setup works the best for you. For one outdoor serving option, the host couple pictured above set up table and chairs on their deck. They grilled the kabobs table-side over a large hibachi and passed the skewered meat with the bowls of rice and sauce. Another outdoor serving option is to set up two or three small, low tables with pillows for seating, place a hibachi in the center of each table, and let the guests grill their own kabobs.

Add some Southeast Asian ambience to the party by covering the table with a colorful printed fabric. Brass candlesticks and serving pieces also enhance the main course setting. If you don't own any decorative brass pieces, stoneware makes an attractive alternative.

If you're the hosts for the second course you'll have to leave from the salad course before the other couples do. You'll need to get home to start the charcoal briquettes. (Be sure to arrange them in the hibachis before going to the salad course.) When you get home, all you'll need to do is light them. While the charcoal burns, start cooking the rice. This way the rice and kabobs finish cooking at the same time.

■■■ MAIN COURSE TIMETABLE ■■■

The day before: Cut up the meat for *Indonesian Sâté* and marinate in the spicy mixture. Prepare the iced tea to serve with the entrée.

2 hours before: Set the table with plates, napkins, flatware, glassware, and centerpiece. Prepare the *Peanut Sauce* and have the ingredients measured for the rice. Arrange charcoal in hibachis, but don't start.

Before leaving for salad course: Drain off the marinade from the meat and thread meat chunks on long skewers. Cover and chill until you return.

After returning from salad course: Immediately light the charcoal. While charcoal burns, start cooking *Turmeric Rice*. When coals are ready, grill kabobs. Then, serve kabobs with the sauce and rice. Serve a red wine, such as a cabernet sauvignon, and iced tea.

— If fresh coconuts are unavailable for the unsweetened coconut milk used in *Indonesian Sâté with Peanut Sauce*, look for canned coconut milk at an Oriental food market.

Or, add ¾ cup shredded or flaked coconut to 1½ cups boiling water; let mixture stand 5 minutes. Process in a blender container or a food processor for 1 minute. Strain. Makes about 1 cup coconut milk.

Turmeric Rice

- **½ cup sliced green onion (about 4 onions)**
- **2 tablespoons butter *or* margarine**
- **1½ cups long grain rice**
- **1 tablespoon instant beef bouillon granules**
- **1 tablespoon lemon juice**
- **¼ teaspoon ground turmeric**
- **½ cup light raisins**

■■■ In a large saucepan cook green onion in butter or margarine till tender but not brown. Add rice; cook and stir over low heat till rice is golden. Add bouillon granules, lemon juice, turmeric, and 3 cups *water*; heat to boiling. Reduce heat; cover and simmer for 15 minutes. Remove from heat and stir in raisins. Let stand, covered, for 10 minutes. Garnish with a parsley sprig, if desired. Makes 8 servings.

■■■ Total preparation time: 40 minutes

Indonesian Sâté with Peanut Sauce

- **1 pound boneless beef round steak *or* sirloin steak, cut into 1-inch cubes**
- **1 pound boneless lamb, cut into 1-inch cubes**
- **1 pound chicken breasts, skinned, boned, and cut into 1-inch pieces**
- **1 cup unsweetened coconut milk (2 coconuts)**
- **1 small onion, grated**
- **1½ teaspoons dry mustard**
- **1½ teaspoons ground coriander**
- **½ teaspoon ground turmeric**
- **1 clove garlic, minced**
- **¼ teaspoon ground cumin**
  Peanut Sauce

■■■ Place meat and chicken in shallow nonmetal bowl. Stir together next 7 ingredients and ½ teaspoon *salt*. Pour over meat and chicken; toss to coat. Cover; marinate for 6 to 24 hours in refrigerator. Drain, reserving marinade. On 8 long skewers alternate meat cubes with chicken pieces. Grill over *medium-hot* coals about 20 minutes for medium-done meat and well-done chicken; baste frequently with reserved marinade and turn kabobs for even cooking. (*Or*, place kabobs on rack of unheated broiler pan. Broil 3 to 4 inches from heat 20 minutes or till done, turning once.) If desired, add cherry tomato to each kabob before serving. Serve with Peanut Sauce. Serves 8.

Peanut Sauce: Cook 2 tablespoons sliced *green onion* and 1 small clove *garlic*, minced, in 2 teaspoons hot *cooking oil* till onion is tender. Stir in ½ cup *chicken broth or beef broth*, ¼ cup *peanut butter*, 1 tablespoon *soy sauce*, ½ teaspoon finely shredded *lemon peel*, 1 tablespoon *lemon juice*, 1 teaspoon *chili powder*, ½ teaspoon *brown sugar*, and ¼ teaspoon *ground ginger*. Simmer, uncovered, about 10 minutes, stirring frequently. Remove from heat; cool. Serve warm or at room temperature for dipping.

■■■ Preparation time: 1 hour
■■■ Marinating time: at least 6 hours
■■■ Cooking time: 20 minutes

Dessert Course

The last stop for the traveling entourage is for coffee and dessert. The glamorous dessert table, set out under the stars, is a great way to end an evening of dining. Not only do guests have a choice of impressive desserts, but they also can sample a variety of freshly brewed coffees.

Dessert choices range from Italian wafer-thin butter cookies to Greek tarts and a Hungarian-style yeast cake. Offer a selection of coffees such as espresso, Turkish coffee, cappuccino, and spiced coffee. They're available in the specialty sections of supermarkets and in gourmet food shops. Serve the brews in small coffee or demitasse cups and embellish each serving with whipped cream.

Set out the food and beverages on a table covered with a lace cloth and use your finest china and silver serving pieces. If you don't have a lace tablecloth, yet want a lacy-look, buy some inexpensive lace fabric for the table covering. Illuminate the yard with lanterns or tiny white Christmas lights.

Gugelhupf

    1 package active dry yeast
    ¼ cup warm water (110° to 115°)
    ¼ cup butter *or* margarine
    ½ cup sugar
    1 teaspoon salt
    2 eggs
    ½ cup milk
    2 teaspoons finely shredded lemon peel
 2½ cup all-purpose flour
    ⅔ cup raisins
    2 tablespoons fine dry bread crumbs
      Blanched whole almonds
      Apricot Sauce

▬▬ Soften yeast in warm water. In a small mixer bowl beat together butter or margarine, sugar, and salt. Add eggs; beat well. Add softened yeast, milk, and lemon peel; mix well. Add *1½ cups* of the flour; beat at low speed of electric mixer for ½ minute then beat 2 minutes at high speed, scraping the bowl constantly. Using a spoon, stir in remaining flour. Stir in raisins. Turn mixture into a greased bowl. Cover bowl; let dough rise till double (about 2 hours).

▬▬ Generously butter a 7- or 8-cup fluted tube pan. Sprinkle with bread crumbs, shaking to coat pan evenly. Arrange almonds in bottom of mold. Stir down batter; carefully spoon it into prepared mold. Let dough rise in a warm place till nearly double (about 1 hour). Bake in a 350° oven about 30 minutes or till golden. Cool 10 minutes; remove from mold to wire rack. Cool. Serve with Apricot Sauce. Makes 1 cake.

Apricot Sauce: In a saucepan combine ½ cup *sugar* and 4 teaspoons *cornstarch*. Stir in one 12-ounce can *apricot nectar*. Cook and stir over medium heat till mixture is thickened and bubbly; cook and stir 2 minutes more. Stir in 2 tablespoons *butter or margarine* till melted. Add 1 tablespoon *lemon juice*. Cover surface with waxed paper. Cool. Cover sauce and chill in refrigerator till serving time. Makes 1¾ cups sauce.

▬▬ Preparation time: 45 minutes
▬▬ Rising time: 3 hours
▬▬ Cooking time: 30 minutes

Baklava Tarts

- ¾ cup sugar
- ½ cup water
- ½ teaspoon finely shredded orange peel
- 4 inches stick cinnamon
- 2 whole cloves
- 6 sheets frozen phyllo dough, thawed
- 1¾ cups finely chopped walnuts
- 1 cup finely chopped pecans
- ⅓ cup sugar
- 1½ teaspoons ground cinnamon
- ⅓ cup butter *or* margarine, melted
- 3 tablespoons brandy
- ½ teaspoon vanilla

For syrup, in a saucepan combine the ¾ cup sugar, water, orange peel, stick cinnamon, and cloves. Bring to boiling; reduce heat. Simmer, uncovered, for 15 minutes. Remove from heat; cool.

Trim each phyllo sheet, if necessary, to form a 16x12-inch rectangle. Cover phyllo with a slightly damp towel. Combine walnuts, pecans, the ⅓ cup sugar, and ground cinnamon; set aside.

Place one rectangle of the phyllo dough on a flat surface; brush with some of the melted butter or margarine. Top with a second rectangle of phyllo and brush again with butter. Repeat with the remaining phyllo and butter. With a long, sharp knife cut stacked phyllo lengthwise and crosswise to make twelve 4-inch squares. Place squares in buttered muffin pans, pressing gently in center to form muffin shape. Spoon about ¼ *cup* of the nut mixture into each cup. Bake in a 325° oven about 30 minutes or till phyllo is golden.

Discard cinnamon and cloves from cooled syrup. Stir in brandy and vanilla. Gradually pour cooled syrup over hot pastries (about 1 tablespoon per cup). Cool pastries in pan. Carefully remove pastries to shallow container. Store, covered, in a cool place till serving time. To serve, top each pastry with a whole pecan, walnut, or almond, if desired. Makes 12 tarts.

Preparation time: 50 minutes
Cooking time: 30 minutes

DESSERT COURSE TIMETABLE

The fourth couple helps out the dessert course hosts by doing some of the baking. They prepare the *Gugelhupf,* an exquisite yeast cake. It needs to be baked the day of the party and wrapped in foil or placed in a cake carrier for carrying to the party. The acompanying *Apricot Sauce* is made by the dessert-course host couple.

The day before: Prepare *Apricot Sauce;* cover and chill. Bake *Pizzelles;* cool, then store in tightly covered containers. (*Pizzelles* are good keepers and can be made weeks ahead and stored in a sealed container in the refrigerator or freezer.) Prepare and bake the *Baklava Tarts.* Store in a single layer in a shallow pan or plastic storage container, covered, in refrigerator.

Before leaving for salad course: Set table with empty serving plates, centerpiece, flatware, cups, saucers, and plates. Have coffees ready to brew.

After returning from main course: Start brewing the coffees; place food on serving plates. Whip cream to serve with coffees. When the coffees are ready, invite your guests to help themselves.

Pizzelles

- 3½ cups all-purpose flour
- 2 tablespoons baking powder
- 3 eggs
- 1 cup sugar
- ½ cup butter *or* margarine, melted and cooled
- 1 teaspoon vanilla

Stir together the flour and baking powder. Beat eggs till foamy; stir in sugar. Add the cooled melted butter or margarine and vanilla. Stir in flour mixture; mix well. Chill about 3 hours. Using about *2 tablespoons* dough for each cookie, shape into balls. Heat seasoned pizzelle iron on top of range over medium-high heat. Place one ball of dough on iron. Squeeze lid to close; bake over medium-high heat about 1 to 2 minutes on each side or till golden. (Or, use an electric pizzelle iron according to manufacturer's directions.) Cool wafers on a wire rack. Makes 24 cookies.

To make the decorative wafer-like cookies, *Pizzelles* (peh-ZEL-ees), you'll need an Italian pizzelle iron, either the hand-held type (to use on the range top) or the electric type. Look for one of the irons at a kitchen equipment shop or an import store. Some businesses will rent the irons to you.

Preparation time: 1¾ hours
Chilling time: 3 hours

FAMILY CHRISTMAS DINNER

Roast Turkey with Veal-Walnut Dressing

Cranberry-Carrot Relish

Pinwheel-Cloverleaf Rolls with Butter

Nutmeg Squash ★ Broccoli-Turnip Toss

Marbled Cream Pie ★ Sugarplum Candies

This Christmas menu features some traditional holiday foods with a new look. Once your family tastes this delectable dinner, the recipes will soon become old favorites. Serving Christmas dinner at your home with all the trimmings can be fun, if you make it a shared family feast.

Enlist your relatives to help you prepare the holiday foods. That way no one works too hard, and everyone can enjoy the special time together. You'll find our timetables divide the food preparation among three families. If the menu or the timetables don't fit the needs of your family, then simply adjust them.

▰ HOST FAMILY'S TIMETABLE ▰

Roast Turkey with Veal-Walnut Dressing
Nutmeg Squash · Beverages

If you purchase a frozen turkey for your Christmas dinner, you can thaw the bird a couple of ways. For thawing suggestions, refer to the column at far left on page 80. Another possibility is to thaw your frozen turkey using a microwave oven. To do this, follow the manufacturer's directions that accompany your microwave oven.

2 to 3 days ahead: Start thawing turkey, if frozen, in the refrigerator. Plan the table and room decorations. Make sure holiday tablecloths are ready.

6 to 8 hours ahead: Prepare stuffing and turkey. Start roasting turkey so it will be done at the appropriate serving time. Prepare the *Nutmeg Squash* and chill. Poach apple slices or prepare green onion or parsley trim; cover and chill. Assemble serving utensils and dinnerware. Next, set the table.

30 minutes ahead: Remove turkey from oven and let it stand 15 minutes before carving. Meanwhile, make the gravy and reheat the squash over medium heat for 5 to 8 minutes or until heated through; remember to stir occasionally. Fill wine or milk glasses and start the coffee. Carve turkey; arrange on serving platter and add garnishes. Spoon squash into serving bowl. Place food on table after everyone is seated.

▰ SECOND FAMILY'S TIMETABLE ▰

Pinwheel-Cloverleaf Rolls · Butter · Sugarplum Candies

If you need to travel any distance to your Christmas dinner, make the *Sugarplum Candies* and *Pinwheel-Cloverleaf Rolls*. They're good make-ahead foods and will travel well if you pack them in a cool place.

Several days before: Prepare and bake the *Pinwheel-Cloverleaf Rolls*. Wrap the rolls tightly in foil; seal, label, and freeze.

Also make the *Sugarplum Candies* two or three days ahead of the Christmas dinner. They're so simple an older child could make them. Cover and chill the candies for storage.

Morning of dinner: Thaw frozen rolls in the foil.

15 minutes before: Arrange *Sugarplum Candies* on a serving plate. After the turkey is removed from the oven, reduce oven temperature to 300° and reheat the rolls, wrapped in foil, about 15 minutes. Arrange rolls in basket. Place rolls and butter on the table.

████ THIRD FAMILY'S TIMETABLE ████

Cranberry-Carrot Relish · Broccoli-Turnip Toss · Marbled Cream Pie

The family bringing the pie also brings a carton of whipping cream or a can of pressurized whipped topping for garnishing the pie. Just before you serve the dessert course, add the pastry trim cutouts on top of the whipped cream garnish.

The day before: Make and bake the *Marbled Cream Pie* and pastry trims; chill the pie. Next, prepare the *Broccoli-Turnip Toss.* The marinated turnip and the tomato mixture chill in one covered container and the broccoli in another. Wash and chill the romaine. Fix *Cranberry-Carrot Relish;* chill in covered bowl.

15 minutes before: Arrange broccoli and turnip mixture on serving plate and spoon relish into serving bowl; place on table. Whip cream and pipe it atop the chilled pie; return pie to the refrigerator.

Pinwheel-Cloverleaf Rolls

1¾ **to 2 cups all-purpose flour**
1 **package active dry yeast**
1 **cup milk**
2 **tablespoons cooking oil**
2 **tablespoons honey**
1 **teaspoon salt**
1 **egg**
1 **cup whole wheat flour**
1 **8-ounce package Neufchâtel cheese, softened**
1 **teaspoon milk**
½ **teaspoon dried parsley flakes**
¼ **teaspoon onion powder**
1 **egg yolk**
1 **tablespoon milk**

████ In a large mixer bowl combine *1½* cups of the all-purpose flour and the yeast. In a saucepan heat together the 1 cup milk, the cooking oil, honey, and salt just till warm (115° to 120°). Add to flour mixture in mixer bowl. Add egg. Beat on low speed of electric mixer for ½ minute, scraping sides of bowl constantly. Beat 3 minutes on high speed.

████ Using a spoon, stir in whole wheat flour and as much of the remaining all-purpose flour as you can. Turn out onto a lightly floured surface. Knead in enough of the remaining flour to make a moderately stiff dough that is smooth and elastic (8 to 10 minutes total). Shape into a ball. Place in a lightly greased bowl; turn once to grease surface. Cover and let rise in a warm place till double (about 1 hour). Punch down; divide dough in half. Cover; let rest 10 minutes.

████ Meanwhile, beat together the softened Neufchâtel cheese, the 1 teaspoon milk, the parsley flakes, and onion powder. On a lightly floured surface roll each half of dough into a 12-inch square. Spread each with *half* of the cheese mixture. Roll up. Seal edges. Using heavy-duty thread, cut each rolled portion into twenty-four ½-inch slices. (Place thread under rolled dough where you want to make the cut; pull thread up around sides. Crisscross thread across top of roll, pulling quickly as though tying a knot.)

████ To make each roll, place two slices of dough side by side on a greased baking sheet; top with a third slice of dough. Repeat with remaining dough to make 16 rolls total. Cover; let rise till nearly double (about 30 minutes). Combine egg yolk and the 1 tablespoon milk; brush over rolls. Bake in a 375° oven for 12 to 15 minutes. (To freeze the baked rolls, cool the rolls thoroughly. Wrap in moisture-vaporproof material. Seal, label, and freeze.) Makes 16 rolls.

████ Preparation time: 1 hour
████ Rising time: 1¾ hours
████ Cooking time: 12 to 15 minutes

Cranberry-Carrot Relish

- 2 **large carrots, diced**
- 2 **oranges**
- 2 **cups cranberries**
- ½ **cup chopped onion**
- ¼ **cup raisins**
- ¾ **cup sugar**
- ¾ **cup white vinegar**
- ¼ **teaspoon ground cinnamon**
- ¼ **teaspoon ground ginger**
- ¼ **teaspoon ground allspice**
- ⅛ **teaspoon ground red pepper**

■■■ Cook carrots, covered, in a small amount of boiling water for 5 minutes; drain. Finely shred 2 teaspoons of orange peel. Peel and section oranges, reserving juice. In a saucepan combine carrots, orange sections, reserved orange peel and juice, cranberries, onion, and raisins. Stir in sugar, vinegar, and spices. Bring to boiling; reduce heat. Simmer, uncovered, 10 minutes or till desired consistency. Cover and chill for 6 to 24 hours. Makes 3 cups relish.

■■■ Preparation time: 20 minutes
■■■ Cooking time: 15 minutes
■■■ Chilling time: at least 6 hours

Nutmeg Squash

- 3½ **to 4 pounds winter squash (butternut, acorn, *or* hubbard), cut into large pieces**
- 2 **tablespoons butter *or* margarine**
- 2 **tablespoons brown sugar**
- ½ **teaspoon salt**
- ½ **teaspoon ground nutmeg**
  Brown sugar (optional)
  Poached apple wedges and kumquat leaves (optional)

■■■ Place squash pieces in a large saucepan or Dutch oven. Cook squash in a small amount of boiling salted water, covered, for 20 to 25 minutes or till tender. Drain the squash.

■■■ Scoop pulp from rind of the squash. Mash the pulp. (If squash's consistency seems too thin, place in a saucepan. Cook, uncovered, till desired consistency.) Stir in the butter or margarine, the 2 tablespoons brown sugar, salt, and nutmeg. Heat through. Transfer mixture to a serving bowl. Sprinkle with additional brown sugar, if desired. Garnish the squash with poached apple wedges and a few kumquat leaves, if desired. Makes 8 servings.

■■■ Preparation time: 15 minutes
■■■ Cooking time: 25 to 30 minutes

Nutmeg Squash can be made hours ahead, or even the day before, and then chilled. Reheat the mixture in a saucepan over medium heat 5 to 8 minutes, stirring occasionally.

For the poached apple garnish, simmer ½ cup sugar and ½ cup water in a small saucepan for 5 minutes. Add the unpeeled apple wedges; cook about 3 to 5 minutes or till apples are just tender. Drain.

In the photograph on pages 30 and 31 fluted mushroom garnishes trim the turkey platter. This simple garnish adds flair and appeal to the roasted turkey. And, it's an easy and fun garnish to prepare. All you need is a small, sharp paring knife and several whole mushrooms.

First, hold the knife at an angle and begin at the tip of a fresh mushroom cap. Carve a strip out of the cap in the form of an inverted V. Next, turn the mushroom and continue cutting out inverted V strips in a spiral fashion. Cut out 6 to 8 inverted V strips. Make as many of these little edible garnishes as you need to fill the platter.

*Use the 1 tablespoon butter or margarine only when preparing *Roast Turkey with Veal-Walnut Dressing* with the ground veal; omit the butter when using ground beef or pork.

Roast Turkey with Veal-Walnut Dressing

- 1 6¼- *or* 6¾-ounce package quick-cooking long-grain-and-wild-rice mix
- ½ pound ground veal, lean ground beef, *or* lean ground pork
- 8 ounces chopped fresh mushrooms
- ½ cup chopped green onions with tops
- 1 clove garlic, minced
- 1 tablespoon butter *or* margarine*
- 1 cup coarsely broken walnuts
- 1 beaten egg
- 1 tablespoon Worcestershire sauce
- ¼ teaspoon pepper
- 1 12- to 14-pound turkey *or* two 4- to 5-pound roasting hens
  Cooking oil, butter, *or* margarine
  Pan Gravy

▬ Prepare the rice mix according to package directions. Cook ground meat, mushrooms, onion, and garlic in the 1 tablespoon butter or margarine* (see column at left, below) till meat is browned and vegetables are tender. Drain off any excess fat. Stir in walnuts. Mix egg, Worcestershire sauce, and pepper. Combine the rice, meat mixture, and egg mixture.

▬ Rinse bird; pat dry with paper toweling. Season cavity with salt, if desired. Spoon some stuffing loosely into neck cavity; pull neck skin over stuffing and fasten securely with skewer to back of bird. Spoon more stuffing loosely into body cavity. Put any remaining stuffing into a casserole and bake, covered, the last 40 minutes of roasting. If bird has a band of skin across tail, tuck drumsticks under band; if band is not present, tie legs to tail. Twist wing tips under back.

▬ Place bird, breast side up, on rack in roasting pan. Brush skin with oil. Insert meat thermometer in center of inside thigh muscle, making sure bulb does not touch bone. Cover *loosely* with foil.

▬ Roast in a 325° oven till meat thermometer registers 180° to 185° and drumstick moves easily in socket. Allow 4½ to 5 hours for turkey and 2 to 2½ for roasting hens. (Cut the band of skin or string between legs about ⅔ of the way through roasting so thighs cook evenly.) Uncover bird during last 45 minutes of roasting. When bird is done, remove from oven and cover loosely with foil to keep warm. Let stand 15 minutes before carving (see page 81 for instructions). If desired, garnish platter with fluted mushrooms (see column at far left), green onion brushes (see column at far right, page 75), and parsley. Pass Pan Gravy.

Pan Gravy: After removing roast poultry from pan, leave crusty bits in pan and pour drippings into large measuring cup. Skim off and reserve fat from pan drippings. Return ¼ *cup* of the fat to roasting pan; discard any remaining fat. Stir in ¼ cup *all-purpose flour*. Cook and stir over medium heat till bubbly. Remove pan from heat. Add enough *water or chicken broth* to drippings in measuring cup to equal 2 cups total. Add all at once to flour mixture in pan. Cook and stir till thickened and bubbly; cook and stir 1 to 2 minutes more. Season to taste. Makes 2 cups gravy.

▬ Preparation time: 40 minutes
▬ Cooking time: see recipe

Sugarplum Candies

- ½ of a 5-ounce jar Neufchâtel cheese spread with pineapple (¼ cup)
- 1¾ cups sifted powdered sugar
- ⅛ teaspoon ground cinnamon
  Pitted dried *or* glacéed dates, prunes, figs, *or* apricot halves, *or* walnut halves
  Sugar

▬ Stir together cheese, powdered sugar, and cinnamon. Halve each fruit horizontally. With a fancy tip on a decorating bag or a knife, pipe or spread cheese mixture on one-half of fruit; top with other half. Roll in sugar. For nuts, spread cheese mixture on one walnut half; top with another nut half. Place in small candy cups. Store, covered, in refrigerator. Makes about 60.

▬ Total preparation time: 1 hour

Broccoli-Turnip Toss

1½ **pounds fresh broccoli, cut into
    spears and halved lengthwise**
 4 **cups peeled, cubed turnips** *or* **parsnips
    (about 2 pounds)**
 1 **cup cherry tomatoes, halved**
⅓ **cup salad oil**
⅓ **cup tarragon vinegar**
¼ **cup sliced green onion**
 2 **teaspoons sugar**
 1 **teaspoon sesame oil (optional)**
¼ **teaspoon salt**
   Few dashes bottled hot pepper sauce
   Romaine leaves

■ Steam the broccoli spears, covered, over boiling water about 10 minutes or till tender; drain thoroughly. Meanwhile, cook the turnips or parsnips, covered, in a small amount of boiling salted water 5 to 7 minutes; drain. Combine the turnips or parsnips with the cherry tomato halves.

■ For the marinade, mix the salad oil; tarragon vinegar; sliced green onion; sugar; sesame oil, if desired; salt; and bottled hot pepper sauce. Toss the marinade with the turnips or parsnips and tomatoes. Cover and chill the turnip-tomato mixture and broccoli spears separately in the refrigerator for 6 to 24 hours.

■ To serve, line a tray or bowl with the romaine leaves. Arrange the chilled broccoli spears atop the romaine. With a slotted spoon remove turnip-tomato mixture from the marinade. Place atop the broccoli spears. Drizzle some of the marinade over the vegetables. Makes 8 servings.

■ Preparation time: 30 minutes
■ Cooking time: 10 minutes
■ Chilling time: at least 6 hours

Marbled Cream Pie

1½ **cups all-purpose flour**
¼ **cup sugar**
   Dash salt
¼ **cup shortening**
 2 **beaten eggs**
¾ **cup sugar**
⅓ **cup all-purpose flour**
 3 **cups milk**
 1 **teaspoon finely shredded lemon peel**
 3 **slightly beaten eggs**
 1 **teaspoon vanilla**
 2 **squares (2 ounces) unsweetened
    chocolate, chopped**
   Whipped cream

■ For the crust and pastry cutouts, in a bowl combine the 1½ cups flour, the ¼ cup sugar, and salt. Cut in shortening to fine crumbs. Stir in the 2 eggs. Divide dough in half; form into two balls. Roll one ball on a lightly floured surface into a 12-inch circle. Line a 9-inch pie plate with pastry; crimp edges high. Lightly prick shell; line with foil and fill with dry beans to prevent crust from puffing. Bake in a 450° oven for 5 minutes. Remove beans and foil; continue baking 5 to 7 minutes longer or till golden. Roll remaining pastry to ⅛-inch thickness. Cut out star shapes with a cookie cutter. Bake in a 400° oven for 8 minutes. Cool.

■ Meanwhile, for the filling, combine the ¾ cup sugar and ⅓ cup flour. Stir in milk and lemon peel. Cook and stir till thickened and bubbly. Gradually stir about *1 cup* of the hot mixture into the 3 eggs. Return egg mixture to saucepan. Cook and stir 2 minutes more. Remove from heat. Measure *2 cups* filling; stir in vanilla. Set vanilla filling aside.

■ To remaining hot filling in saucepan, add chocolate; stir till melted. Pour vanilla filling into baked crust. Carefully spoon chocolate filling atop; gently swirl through fillings to marble. Cover and chill for 6 to 24 hours. To serve, pipe ring of whipped cream atop pie. Top with star cutouts. Chill. Makes 8 servings.

■ Preparation time: 1¼ hours
■ Chilling time: at least 6 hours

Prepare the marinated vegetable salad, *Broccoli-Turnip Toss*, with turnips or parsnips. Both vegetables are most plentiful in the fall and winter months.

Sometimes it's hard to remember the difference between turnips and parsnips. Turnips are bulbous and usually have a purple-collared white skin. Parsnips, on the other hand, look like white carrots. Both vegetables need to have the outer skin removed before you cook them in boiling salted water.

The sesame oil—if used—will add a distinctive flavor to your salad.

ORIENTAL DINNER

APPETIZER SPARERIBS   CHINESE BEER OR SAKE

HOT & SOUR SOUP

SEAFOOD YAKI   HOT TEA

CHINESE ORANGE BEEF   BUTTERED PEA PODS
COOKED BEAN THREADS OR HOT COOKED RICE

CHILLED PINEAPPLE QUARTERS   CHILLED PLUM WINE

Does the idea of throwing an elaborate Oriental dinner throw you? Then plan a co-op party. Get a group of friends together and let them help with the party planning, work, and cost. You'll find that cooperation makes a gathering fun for everyone.

Assign one part of the Oriental dinner menu to each couple. At the party, join forces to put the meal together. This lets you pull off a great party that you might be unable to do on your own. Since this dinner party has several courses, plan to spend an evening of leisurely dining with your guests.

Table setting: Oriental lacquer-ware place settings set a dramatic mood for this dinner party. If you don't own any Oriental-looking dishes, no problem: Just use your best dinnerware. All you need is six dinner plates, six soup bowls, and 12 dessert plates. (Use six for the soup bowl underliner and six for the dessert.) You'll also need a teapot and cups, serving dishes, and glasses for the beverages.

Create an Oriental mood for your party. Decorate the dining room with tall vases holding stems of quince or cherry blossoms. They—as well as orchid blossoms—will add a colorful touch. Green plants or bonsai plants make handsome table centerpieces.

Start off the sit-down portion of the meal by serving the soup in bowls set on underliner plates placed on the dinner plates. For dramatic-looking place settings, use bamboo trays and striking napkins. (If you like, make your own dinner napkins. Buy a piece of fabric with an Oriental-looking print, cut it into 18-inch squares, and hem.) Place a few fresh blossoms and a votive candle wrapped in small leaves tied with twine on each tray. Chopsticks help lend an Oriental touch. Diners can use them to eat the tofu and vegetables in the soup, as well as foods from the main course.

HOSTS' TIMETABLE

Hot and Sour Soup · Seafood Yaki · Beverages

The day before: Prepare the soup; cover and chill.

6 to 8 hours before: Set table and arrange flowers around the room. Chill beer and wine. Thaw seafood, if frozen; shell and clean shrimp and cut up fish. Prepare marinade and *Hot Mustard Sauce* for *Seafood Yaki;* chill seafood, marinade, and sauce. Arrange briquettes in a hibachi or grill.

30 minutes before: Start briquettes. Add seafood to the marinade; marinate 15 minutes. Pour soup into a saucepan. Thread marinated seafood on skewers; place on a tray and chill until ready to cook over the coals. Divide the hot sauce among six individual bowls. Preheat oven for the *Appetizer Spareribs*.

At serving time: At end of appetizer course, start reheating soup. Serve in bowls. For the next course, while other participants clear the table, refill beverage glasses and bring in dishes of the hot sauce. Then, start grilling *Seafood Yaki*. Prepare tea (see directions, page 290). Serve kabobs with sake or hot tea.

The host couple arranges for any serving and cooking equipment needed by the other couples. Be sure to do this several days before the dinner party.

The host couple also provides all of the beverages for the party. Serve cold Chinese beer or hot Japanese sake with the ribs, sake or hot tea with the seafood kabobs, and plum wine with the pineapple dessert.

SECOND COUPLE'S TIMETABLE

Chinese Orange Beef · Bean Threads or Rice · Pea Pods

6 to 8 hours before: Prepare and cook the orange peel for the *Chinese Orange Beef;* drain, cover, and chill. Cut the meat into strips and prepare the marinade for the beef; cover and chill. Section the oranges into a bowl, saving the juice also; cover and chill. Wash and string pea pods if using fresh vegetables. Prepare the orange and onion garnishes.

30 minutes before: Add meat strips to marinade about 30 minutes before serving the main course. If serving rice, start cooking it. As guests finish kabobs, prepare bean threads, if not serving rice, and cook the pea pods. While bean threads and pea pods cook, prepare *Chinese Orange Beef.* Arrange the food in serving dishes; add the garnishes.

Items for second couple to carry to the party are: cooked orange peel, orange sections and juice, beef strips, marinade, bean threads or ingredients for rice, cornstarch, oil, pea pods, and butter.

Remember to cook pea pods briefly—about 2 minutes—in boiling salted water. Drain, season, and add butter.

THIRD COUPLE'S TIMETABLE

Appetizer Spareribs · Chilled Pineapple Quarters

The day before: Prepare the *Appetizer Spareribs*; cook, cover, and store in the refrigerator.

6 to 8 hours before: Clean leaf lettuce for the rib garnish; chill. Prepare carrot curls for garnish; place in ice water and chill. Cut up the pineapple; cover and chill the pineapple quarters on a tray. Chill the extra pineapple pieces and strawberries separately.

At the party: Immediately place the ribs in an oven or microwave oven to reheat. Place the fruit in the refrigerator until dessert time. Check the rib reheating times in the column at far right on page 45. When ribs are hot, place on a serving platter and garnish with carrot curls, if desired. Serve ribs with Chinese beer or sake.

At dessert time, garnish the pineapple quarters with the extra pineapple chunks, fresh strawberries, and fresh mint sprigs. Serve with chilled plum wine.

Here's a checklist of items the third couple should take to party: the already-made *Appetizer Spareribs* in a shallow pan, lettuce and carrot curl garnishes, pineapple quarters on a tray, the extra pineapple chunks, and fresh strawberries and mint for the dessert trim.

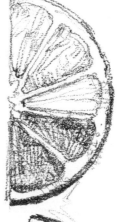

Add this colorful garnish to the *Chinese Orange Beef* platter. To make the orange half-slices for a garnish, slice an unpeeled orange starting at stem end. Make slices ¼ to ½ inch thick. Cut each slice in half.

Cut between the fruit and the peel, loosening only about ¾ of the peel from the fruit slice. Leave the peel attached at one side of slice.

Turn back the loosened orange peel and arrange it across the face of the orange half-slice.

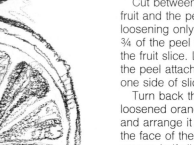

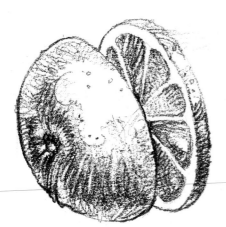

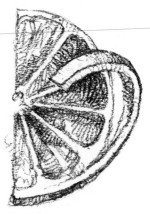

Chinese Orange Beef

- 3 small oranges
- ½ cup water
- 2 tablespoons sugar
- 1½ pounds boneless beef tenderloin *or* sirloin, cut 1 inch thick
- ¼ cup thinly sliced green onion
- ¼ cup soy sauce
- 2 cloves garlic, minced
- 1 tablespoon sesame oil
- 2 teaspoons grated gingerroot *or* ½ teaspoon ground ginger
- ½ teaspoon crushed red pepper
- 2 teaspoons cornstarch
- 2 tablespoons cooking oil *or* peanut oil
  Cooked Bean Threads *or* Hot Cooked Rice (see recipe, page 44)

▬▬ Remove peel from *1* of the oranges; scrape off white membrane. Cut peel into very fine strips (½ cup). In a small saucepan combine strips, water, and sugar. Bring to boiling; reduce heat. Simmer, covered, 15 to 20 minutes or till orange peel is tender. Remove from heat; cool in liquid. Drain well. Cover; chill.

▬▬ Partially freeze meat. Thinly slice across the grain into paper-thin bite-size strips. For the marinade, combine green onion, soy sauce, garlic, sesame oil, gingerroot, and red pepper. Add meat to marinade in bowl. Marinate for 30 minutes at room temperature.

▬▬ Peel remaining 2 oranges. To section the 3 oranges, use a very sharp or serrated knife. Working over a bowl remove the sections by cutting to the center of the fruit between one section and the membrane. Then turn knife and slide knife down the other side of section next to membrane. Remove seeds. Allow orange sections and juice to fall into the bowl.

▬▬ Drain meat well, reserving marinade. Stir cornstarch into the reserved marinade. Preheat a wok or large skillet over high heat; add oil. Add *half* of the beef to hot wok or skillet; stir-fry 2 to 3 minutes or till brown. Remove beef. Stir-fry remaining beef 2 to 3 minutes. Return all meat to wok or skillet. Stir the reserved marinade and stir into beef. Cook and stir till

thickened and bubbly. Stir in the drained, cooked orange peel and the orange sections and their juice; cover and cook 1 minute.

▬▬ To serve, place the Cooked Bean Threads or Hot Cooked Rice on a heated serving platter with the beef mixture. If desired, garnish the serving platter with orange half-slices (see illustrations on opposite page) and green onion brushes (see column at far right, page 75). Makes 6 servings.

Cooked Bean Threads: Cut or break 3 ounces bean threads (cellophane noodles) into 4-inch lengths. Cook bean threads in boiling water for 5 minutes or till tender. Drain well and keep hot.

▬▬ Preparation time: 40 minutes
▬▬ Marinating time: 30 minutes
▬▬ Cooking time: 10 minutes

Do most of the work for *Chinese Orange Beef* ahead of time. It helps make preparing the food at the party quick and easy.

For example, you cook and chill the orange peel in advance. The marinade for the meat can be prepared early and chilled in the refrigerator. And, the oranges can be sectioned, covered, and chilled. Even the beef can be cut into strips ahead of time.

The Japanese word "yaki" means broiled, and that's how these seafood kabobs are cooked. You can broil them under the range's broiler or cook them outside over charcoal on a barbecue grill.

To select fresh pineapples for the dessert, look for ones that are plump, slightly soft to the touch, fresh looking, and heavy for their size. The crown leaves should be deep green in color. Avoid pineapples that are old looking and that have dry, brown leaves, traces of mold, or an unpleasant odor.

The shell color, thumping, or the ease with which leaves can be pulled out of the crown are not reliable indications of ripeness or quality.

Seafood Yaki

- 1 **pound fresh** *or* **frozen shrimp, shelled and cleaned (about 24 medium shrimp)**
- 1 **pound fresh** *or* **frozen red snapper fillets, skinned**
- ½ **pound fresh** *or* **frozen scallops**
- ⅓ **cup soy sauce**
- ¼ **cup sake** *or* **dry sherry**
- ¼ **cup water**
- 1 **teaspoon sugar**
- 1 **teaspoon grated gingerroot** *or* **¼ teaspoon ground ginger**
- 2 **medium green peppers, cut into 1½-inch squares**
  Hot Mustard Sauce

■■■ Thaw shrimp, red snapper, and scallops, if frozen. Shell shrimp. Cut down back of each shrimp, using a knife point to remove and scrape out the vein. Cut red snapper into 2-inch pieces or 3-inch strips.

■■■ For the marinade, in a bowl combine soy sauce, sake or dry sherry, water, sugar, and gingerroot. Add shrimp, red snapper, and scallops to the marinade. Marinate for 15 minutes. Drain, reserving marinade.

■■■ On twelve 9- or 10-inch skewers alternately thread shrimp, scallops, and red snapper loosely with green peppers. Grill over *medium* coals for 8 to 10 minutes, turning once; brush often with reserved marinade. (*Or,* place on the rack of an unheated broiler pan. Broil 4 inches from heat about 8 to 10 minutes, turning once; brush often with reserved marinade.) Pass the Hot Mustard Sauce. Makes 6 servings.

Hot Mustard Sauce: In a bowl combine ⅓ cup *rice vinegar or white vinegar,* 1 tablespoon prepared Chinese *hot-style mustard,* 1 tablespoon *sugar,* ½ teaspoon *soy sauce,* and ¼ teaspoon *salt.* Serve in individual sauce dishes or small bowls for dipping seafood. Makes about ½ cup sauce.

■■■ Preparation time: 1 hour
■■■ Marinating time: 15 minutes
■■■ Cooking time: 8 to 10 minutes

Hot Cooked Rice

- 2 **cups cold water**
- 1 **cup long grain rice**
- 1 **tablespoon butter** *or* **margarine**
- 1 **teaspoon salt**

■■■ In a saucepan combine the cold water, rice, butter or margarine, and salt. Cover the saucepan with a tight-fitting lid. Bring to boiling; reduce heat. Cook 15 minutes; *do not lift cover.* Remove from heat. Let stand, covered, for 10 minutes. Makes 6 servings.

■■■ Total preparation time: 30 minutes

Chilled Pineapple Quarters

- 2 **fresh medium pineapples**
  Fresh whole strawberries (optional)
  Fresh mint (optional)

■■■ Thoroughly rinse pineapple; pat dry. If desired, twist off the crown. Cut each pineapple into quarters lengthwise. Cut out the hard center core. Starting from one end, cut the fruit from the peel, leaving pineapple in its shell (a serrated grapefruit knife works well for this). Slice fruit from each pineapple quarter crosswise and then lengthwise into bite-size pieces.

■■■ Cover 6 of the pineapple quarters with plastic wrap; set on a tray or in a shallow pan. Store in the refrigerator and chill for 6 to 24 hours. Remove pineapple chunks from the 2 remaining quarters. Cover and chill in the refrigerator.

■■■ Just before serving, set the 6 quarters on chilled individual serving plates. Garnish the quarters with the extra pineapple chunks. If desired, garnish with fresh strawberries and fresh mint. Makes 6 servings.

■■■ Preparation time: 40 minutes
■■■ Chilling time: at least 6 hours

Hot and Sour Soup

1 **whole medium chicken breast, skinned, halved lengthwise, and boned**
1 **tablespoon soy sauce**
1 **tablespoon dry sherry** *or* **sake**
4 **cups water**
2 **tablespoons instant chicken bouillon granules**
½ **cup water chestnuts, drained and thinly sliced**
½ **cup bamboo shoots, halved lengthwise**
2 **tablespoons rice vinegar** *or* **white vinegar**
½ **teaspoon pepper**
8 **ounces (about 1½ cups) fresh bean curd (tofu)**
2 **tablespoons thinly sliced green onion**

▬ Finely chop the chicken. In a bowl combine chicken, soy sauce, and dry sherry or sake. Set aside.

▬ In a large saucepan bring water and bouillon granules to boiling. Stir in the chicken mixture, water chestnuts, bamboo shoots, vinegar, and pepper. Simmer, covered, 5 minutes. Slice the fresh bean curd into 1½x¼-inch strips. Add to the soup.

▬ Simmer the soup, covered, 3 minutes longer. Remove the soup from the heat. Stir in thinly sliced green onion. (If desired, make soup ahead, cover, and chill; reheat over high heat about 5 minutes before serving.) Makes 6 servings.

▬ Preparation time: 30 minutes
▬ Cooking time: 8 minutes

Appetizer Spareribs

2 **pounds meaty pork spareribs, sawed in half across the bones**
1 **tablespoon sugar**
1 **tablespoon curry powder** *or* **five spice powder**
½ **cup tomato sauce**
¼ **cup packed brown sugar**
¼ **cup finely chopped onion**
2 **tablespoons soy sauce**
2 **teaspoons grated gingerroot** *or* ½ **teaspoon ground ginger**
¾ **teaspoon dry mustard**
1 **clove garlic, minced**

▬ Cut the meat into 2-rib portions. Rinse and pat dry with paper toweling. Combine sugar and curry or five spice powder. Thoroughly rub the ribs with mixture. Cover and let stand for 1 hour at room temperature or 4 to 6 hours in refrigerator.

▬ Place ribs, meaty side down, in a foil-lined large shallow roasting pan. Bake, uncovered, in a 450° oven for 30 minutes. Drain off fat. Turn meaty side up. Reduce heat to 350° and bake 15 minutes more.

▬ Meanwhile, prepare sauce. In a small saucepan combine tomato sauce, brown sugar, onion, soy sauce, gingerroot or ground ginger, mustard, and garlic. Cook, uncovered, stirring occasionally about 5 minutes or till onion is tender. Drain fat from ribs. Spoon sauce atop ribs. Bake 15 minutes more. (Ribs can be prepared ahead of time, chilled, and reheated; see column at right for instructions.) If desired, serve ribs on a lettuce-lined platter and garnish with carrot curls. Makes 6 servings.

▬ Preparation time: 15 minutes
▬ Chilling time: 4 to 6 hours
▬ Cooking time: 1 hour

Ask your butcher to saw the pork ribs in half across the bones for *Appetizer Spareribs.* This will make the ribs easier to handle as appetizers.

You can prepare the ribs ahead of time. Cook the ribs, then cover them and store in the refrigerator. About 30 minutes before serving, place ribs in a shallow pan. Cover loosely and reheat in a 350° oven for 20 to 25 minutes or till heated through.

Or, reheat half the ribs at a time, uncovered, in a microwave oven on high power for 2½ to 3 minutes, turning the dish once.

DINNER PARTIES

Dinner parties have long been the most popular and glorified of entertaining endeavors. A perfectly prepared dinner can range from an elaborate formal party using your finest dinnerware, to a relaxed casual meal, to just about anything in between.

In this chapter we include marvelous-tasting recipes that appeal to all tastes, humble or luxurious, simple or complex. The dinner-party recipe section starts off with impossible-to-turn-down appetizers. These delicious first-course recipes introduce the meal, set the scene, and whet the appetite. To help you plan fascinating menus, our main-dish section holds diverse and interesting entrées. The side dishes, fresh salads, innovative vegetable dishes, and perfect pasta are superb. And our dessert specialties will make it difficult for you to choose from among the inviting pies, cakes, ice creams, pastries, and fruit desserts.

So browse through this chapter to plan your menu. Then enjoy your dinner party, all of it—selecting the menu, preparing the food, savoring the delicious recipes, and, most of all, relishing that warm feeling experienced after a delightful evening of fine food and good friends.

Marinated Scallops over Papaya

- ¾ **pound fresh** *or* **frozen scallops**
- 1 **cup water**
- 1 **tablespoon lemon juice** *or* **lime juice**
- ½ **teaspoon salt**
- 1 **bay leaf**
- ⅓ **cup lemon juice** *or* **lime juice**
- ¼ **cup salad oil**
- 2 **tablespoons water**
- 1 **tablespoon snipped chives**
- ½ **teaspoon salt**
- ¼ **teaspoon dried dillweed**
- ⅛ **teaspoon bottled hot pepper sauce**
- 2 **fresh medium papayas** *or* **avocados**

▬▬ Thaw scallops, if frozen. Cut any large scallops in half. In a saucepan combine the 1 cup water, the 1 tablespoon lemon juice or lime juice, ½ teaspoon salt, and bay leaf. Bring to boiling; add the scallops and return to boiling. Reduce heat and simmer, uncovered, about 1 minute or till scallops are opaque. Drain scallops; discard bay leaf.

▬▬ For marinade, in a mixing bowl combine the ⅓ cup lemon juice or lime juice, the salad oil, the 2 tablespoons water, snipped chives, ½ teaspoon salt, the dried dillweed, and hot pepper sauce. Add the cooked scallops; toss to coat. Cover and marinate in the refrigerator for 6 hours, stirring occasionally.

▬▬ To serve, cut the papayas or avocados in half lengthwise; remove seeds and peel. Slice the fruit crosswise; arrange slices on 8 lettuce-lined salad plates. Drain scallops, reserving the marinade. Spoon the scallops over the papaya or avocado slices. If desired, drizzle some of the reserved marinade over each serving. Makes 8 servings.

▬▬ Advance preparation time: 15 minutes
▬▬ Marinating time: at least 6 hours
▬▬ Final preparation time: 20 minutes

Tuna Louis Cocktail

¼ **cup whipping cream**
1 **cup mayonnaise *or* salad dressing**
¼ **cup finely chopped green pepper**
¼ **cup chili sauce**
2 **tablespoons thinly sliced green onion**
1 **teaspoon lemon juice**
⅛ **teaspoon salt**
1 **6½-ounce can tuna (water pack)**
2 **medium oranges**
2 **small apples**
1 **cup thinly sliced celery**
 Bibb lettuce leaves

▬ For the dressing, in a bowl beat the whipping cream till soft peaks form. Fold in the mayonnaise or salad dressing, finely chopped green pepper, chili sauce, sliced green onion, lemon juice, and salt. Cover and chill in the refrigerator for 1 hour or till serving time. Chill the tuna for 1 hour or till serving time.

▬ Remove tuna from refrigerator; drain and break into large chunks. Peel and section oranges. Core and chop apples. Arrange the tuna chunks, orange sections, apple pieces, and sliced celery in 8 lettuce-lined cocktail cups or glasses. Pour some of the dressing over each serving. Makes 8 servings.

Crab Louis Cocktail: Prepare the Tuna Louis Cocktail as above, *except* for the tuna substitute 1 pound *crab legs*, cooked, chilled, and shelled, *or* one 6-ounce can *crab meat,* drained, cartilage removed, and cut into pieces. Continue as directed.

▬ Preparation time: 35 minutes
▬ Chilling time: at least 1 hour

Shrimp Cocktail

1 **pound fresh *or* frozen shelled shrimp**
 Desired sauce
 Lettuce leaves
 Lemon wedges
 Cherry tomatoes

▬ Cook fresh or frozen shrimp in boiling salted water for 1 to 3 minutes or till pink. Drain and chill in the refrigerator for 2 hours or till serving time. Prepare desired sauce (see below). Arrange chilled shrimp in 6 to 8 lettuce-lined cocktail cups or glasses. Spoon about *1 tablespoon* of sauce atop *each* serving. Garnish with lemon and tomatoes. Makes 6 to 8 servings.

Cocktail Sauce: In a small bowl stir together ¾ cup *chili sauce,* 2 tablespoons *lemon juice,* 1 tablespoon *prepared horseradish,* 2 teaspoons *Worcestershire sauce,* ½ teaspoon finely chopped *onion,* and a few dashes *bottled hot pepper sauce.* Cover and chill till serving time. Makes about 1 cup.

Spinach Sauce: In a blender container combine ⅓ cup *mayonnaise or salad dressing;* ⅓ cup *dairy sour cream;* ¼ cup snipped *parsley;* ¼ cup frozen chopped *spinach,* thawed and well drained; 1 tablespoon *lemon juice;* ¼ teaspoon dried *tarragon,* crushed; and ⅛ teaspoon *garlic salt.* Cover; blend till smooth. Cover; chill till serving time. Makes 1 cup.

Lemon-Mustard Sauce: In a small bowl combine ½ cup *plain yogurt,* ½ cup *dairy sour cream,* 1 tablespoon *Dijon-style mustard,* ¼ teaspoon finely shredded *lemon peel,* 1 tablespoon *lemon juice,* and ¼ teaspoon *salt.* Cover the sauce and chill till serving time. Makes about 1 cup.

Tartar Sauce: Combine 1 cup *mayonnaise or salad dressing,* ¼ cup finely chopped *dill pickle,* 1 tablespoon snipped *parsley,* 1 tablespoon finely chopped *onion,* 1 tablespoon *chopped pimiento,* and 1 teaspoon *lemon juice.* Cover and chill till serving time. Makes about 1¼ cups.

▬ Total preparation time: 35 minutes
▬ Chilling time: at least 2 hours

A good first-course choice is a seafood, fruit, or vegetable appetizer with a sauce or a dressing.
 Because these cocktails require the use of a fork, you should serve them at the dining table. Place each cocktail in a dish on a liner plate before your guests are seated. Then, remove both the liners and the cocktail dishes before serving the next course.

"Escargot" (es-car-GO), a French word, simply refers to edible land snails. Connoisseurs of these tiny morsels serve them with special snail dishes, snail forks, and snail tongs like those pictured on the opposite page. You may find them unnecessary for your dinner party, however. A good accompaniment to snails is a fruity white wine such as a Chardonnay.

Canned snails and snail shells, packaged separately, are available in the specialty food sections of many supermarkets.

You don't have to own special snail equipment to enjoy *Escargot*—you can improvise. Bake the snails in individual quiche dishes, as shown at left. To remove the snails from their shells, use a cocktail fork and a kitchen fork.

Marinated Vegetables

2 medium carrots, cut into sticks
2 cups cauliflower flowerets
1 medium cucumber *or* zucchini, halved
     and thinly sliced
1 small onion, halved lengthwise, sliced,
     and separated into strips
¼ cup salad oil
¼ cup white wine vinegar
¼ cup water
1 teaspoon sugar
½ teaspoon dried dillweed

■ In a medium saucepan cook carrots, covered, in a small amount of boiling salted water for 5 minutes. Add cauliflower and cook, covered, for 3 minutes more; drain. Rinse with cold water; drain well. In a mixing bowl combine cooked carrots and cauliflower, cucumber or zucchini, and onion.

■ For marinade, in a screw-top jar combine oil, vinegar, water, sugar, dillweed, ¼ teaspoon *salt,* and ⅛ teaspoon *pepper.* Cover and shake well; pour over vegetables. Toss gently to coat. Cover; marinate in the refrigerator for 6 hours, stirring occasionally.

■ To serve, use a slotted spoon and arrange the vegetables on 8 to 10 lettuce-lined salad plates, if desired. Makes 8 to 10 servings.

■ Preparation time: 30 minutes
■ Marinating time: at least 6 hours

Escargot

2 7½-ounce cans snails (36 snails)
   Lemon Butter, Garlic Butter, *or* Herb Butter
36 snail shells
   French bread, sliced diagonally and cut
     into 1-inch-wide sticks

■ Drain and rinse snails. Prepare Lemon Butter, Garlic Butter, or Herb Butter. Spoon about ½ teaspoon of the desired butter into *each* snail shell. Add a snail and about ½ *teaspoon* more of desired butter.

■ Place 6 filled shells, open end up, on each of 6 snail dishes. (*Or,* place 6 filled snail shells, open end up, into individual quiche pans as in the upper left photograph.) Bake in a 450° oven for 5 to 7 minutes or till the butter is bubbly. Serve the snails immediately.

■ To eat, grasp a snail shell with a snail holder or fork and remove the snail from the shell with a special snail fork or cocktail fork. Dip the French bread into the hot butter in the shell. Makes 6 servings.

Lemon Butter: In a small bowl combine ½ cup softened *butter or margarine,* 3 tablespoons *lemon juice,* 1 tablespoon thinly sliced *green onion,* 1 tablespoon finely snipped *parsley,* and ⅛ teaspoon *salt.*

Garlic Butter: Prepare the Lemon Butter as above, *except* use 2 cloves *garlic,* minced, for lemon juice.

Herb Butter: Prepare the Lemon Butter as above, *except* substitute ½ teaspoon dried *thyme,* crushed, and ½ teaspoon dried *marjoram,* crushed, for the lemon juice.

■ Preparation time: 30 minutes
■ Cooking time: 5 to 7 minutes

Escargot with Garlic Butter

This refreshing dinner
is perfect for the end
of a hot summer's
day. You can make
the first-course soup
and the cheesecake
the evening before
you entertain to avoid
cooking during the
heat of the day.

★ see recipe, page 167

Chilled Avocado Soup

¼ cup chopped onion
1 small clove garlic, minced
1 tablespoon butter *or* margarine
1 tablespoon all-purpose flour
¼ teaspoon salt
¼ teaspoon dried dillweed
2 cups chicken broth
2 medium avocados, seeded, peeled, and cut into chunks
1 cup light cream *or* milk
2 tablespoons dry sherry
½ cup dairy sour cream
1 medium tomato, peeled, seeded, and coarsely chopped

■■■ In a medium saucepan cook onion and garlic in hot butter or margarine till onion is tender but not brown. Stir in the flour, salt, and dillweed. Add the chicken broth all at once; cook and stir till the mixture is slightly thickened and bubbly. Cook and stir for 1 minute more. Cool slightly.

■■■ Place *half* of the broth mixture into a blender container or food processor bowl. Add *half* of the avocado chunks. Cover and blend or process till the mixture is smooth. Pour the smooth mixture into a mixing bowl. Repeat with the remaining broth mixture and avocado chunks. Stir the light cream or milk and dry sherry into avocado mixture. Cover the surface with clear plastic wrap and chill in the refrigerator for 3 hours or till cold.

■■■ To serve, ladle the chilled soup into 8 individual soup bowls. Garnish each serving with *1 tablespoon* of the sour cream and *some* of the chopped tomato. Makes 8 servings.

■■■ Preparation time: 30 minutes
■■■ Chilling time: at least 3 hours

Vichyssoise*

2 large leeks, thinly sliced (1 cup)
¼ cup butter *or* margarine
1½ pounds potatoes, peeled and thinly sliced
2 cups chicken broth
⅛ teaspoon ground nutmeg
1 cup milk
1 cup light cream
½ cup whipping cream

■■■ Cook leeks in hot butter till tender. Add potatoes, broth, and nutmeg. Cook, covered, for 30 minutes. Cool slightly. Place *half* of mixture into a blender container or food processor bowl. Cover; blend or process till smooth. Pour into a bowl. Repeat. Stir in milk, light cream, whipping cream, 2 teaspoons *salt*, and a dash *white pepper*. Cover and chill for 3 hours. Garnish with green onion, if desired. Serves 6.

■■■ Total preparation time: about 4 hours
★ *pictured on the cover*

Sherried Tomato Soup

1 medium onion, chopped (½ cup)
1 medium carrot, coarsely shredded (½ cup)
2 tablespoons butter *or* margarine
¼ cup all-purpose flour
Dash ground nutmeg
1 32-ounce can (4 cups) tomato juice
2 cups beef broth
⅓ cup dry sherry
1 tablespoon honey
2 tablespoons snipped parsley

■■■ In a saucepan cook onion and carrot in hot butter till tender. Stir in flour, nutmeg, and 1 teaspoon *salt*. Add juice and broth. Cook and stir till bubbly. Stir in sherry and honey. Cover; simmer for 5 minutes or till vegetables are tender. Stir in parsley. Serves 6.

■■■ Total preparation time: 30 minutes

Consommé

4¾ pounds beef soup bones *or* 2½ pounds
    chicken necks, wings, and backs
3 medium onions, quartered
1½ cups celery leaves
6 sprigs parsley
4 whole black peppercorns
2 *or* 3 bay leaves
1 *or* 2 cloves garlic, halved
1 tablespoon dried basil, crushed, *or*
    2 teaspoons dried thyme, crushed
10 cups cold water
Choose 2 or 3 of the following:
1½ cups potato peelings
1½ cups carrot peelings
1½ cups turnip leaves *or* peelings
1½ cups parsnip leaves *or* peelings
4 *or* 5 outer cabbage leaves
¾ cup sliced green onion tops
¾ cup sliced leek tops

▬ For stock, in a 10-quart stockpot or Dutch oven place the beef bones or chicken pieces. Add the onion quarters, celery leaves, parsley, peppercorns, bay leaves, garlic, basil or thyme, and 1 tablespoon *salt.* Add the cold water. Choose 2 or 3 of the vegetable peelings, leaves, or tops; add to the stockpot or Dutch oven. Bring the mixture to boiling. Reduce heat; cover and simmer over low heat for 3 hours.

▬ Remove the soup bones or chicken pieces from stock with a slotted spoon. When cool enough to handle, remove meat and discard bones, reserving meat for another use. Strain the stock through a sieve lined with 1 or 2 layers of cheesecloth; discard vegetables and seasonings.

▬ For consommé, clarify the stock following the directions in column at far right. Skim off fat with a metal spoon, or chill consommé and lift off solidified fat. To serve, heat the consommé through. Ladle into individual soup bowls. Makes 12 servings.

Mushroom Consommé: Prepare Consommé as above, *except* before serving, stir in 1 cup thinly sliced fresh *mushrooms.* Heat through. Sprinkle each serving with snipped *parsley,* if desired.

Tofu Consommé: Prepare Consommé as at left, *except* before serving, stir in 8 ounces fresh *tofu (bean curd),* cut into ½-inch cubes. Heat through. Sprinkle each serving with a few pieces of thinly sliced *green onion,* if desired.

Shrimp Consommé: Prepare Consommé as at left, *except* before serving, stir in two 4½-ounce cans *shrimp,* drained and rinsed. Heat through. Sprinkle each serving with snipped *chives,* if desired.

▬ Preparation time: 25 minutes
▬ Cooking time: 3 hours

Shrimp-Vegetable Bisque

1 pound zucchini, sliced (3½ cups)
2 medium carrots, sliced (1 cup)
½ cup chopped celery
½ cup sliced green onion
½ cup butter *or* margarine
1 tablespoon all-purpose flour
1¾ cups milk
2 cups water
1 10¾-ounce can condensed cream of
    mushroom soup
½ cup dairy sour cream
½ cup dry white wine
2 teaspoons instant chicken bouillon
    granules
1 4½-ounce can tiny shrimp, drained

▬ In a covered Dutch oven cook zucchini, carrots, celery, and green onion in hot butter or margarine about 20 minutes or till tender. Stir in flour; add milk all at once. Cook and stir till thickened and bubbly. Cook and stir for 1 minute more. Pour into a blender container; cover and blend till smooth. In the same pan combine water, soup, sour cream, wine, and bouillon granules. Stir in blended mixture and shrimp. Heat through, but *do not boil.* Makes 8 servings.

▬ Total preparation time: 45 minutes

Consommé is a clear rich soup made by boiling down meat or poultry stock until its volume is reduced by about half. Season the broth used to make consommé lightly because the reducing process intensifies the seasonings.

To make the consommé you must clarify the stock. Clarifying removes solid flecks too small for even a cheesecloth to strain out. These flecks will muddy a soup's appearance.

To clarify any broth, stir together ¼ cup *cold water,* 1 *egg white,* and 1 *eggshell,* crushed. Add to the strained stock and bring to boiling. Remove the stock from the heat and let stand for 5 minutes. Strain the stock again through a sieve lined with cheesecloth.

Canapés are small savory appetizers with an edible base, traditionally a thin piece of bread. Most party givers serve these ornate open-faced sandwiches as finger food.

For before-party ease, prepare your canapés several hours ahead, then store them covered in the refrigerator. To serve your make-ahead canapés, broil or bake them just before serving.

For canapés that look as great as they taste, add the visual variety of different shapes. Follow the bread-cutting diagrams at right.

Curried Chicken Canapés

- 10 **slices firm-textured white, whole wheat, _or_ rye bread**
- ¼ **cup mayonnaise _or_ salad dressing**
- ¼ **cup dairy sour cream**
- 3 **tablespoons finely chopped chutney**
- ½ **teaspoon curry powder**
- 1 **cup chopped cooked chicken**
  Snipped parsley _or_ chopped pimiento (optional)

 Remove crusts from bread. In a bowl combine mayonnaise or salad dressing, sour cream, chutney, and curry powder. Stir in chicken. Spread about _2½ tablespoons_ of the chicken mixture on _each_ slice of bread. Cut bread slices into desired shapes (see illustrations below). Garnish with snipped parsley or chopped pimiento, if desired. Makes 40 servings.

▬ Total preparation time: 40 minutes

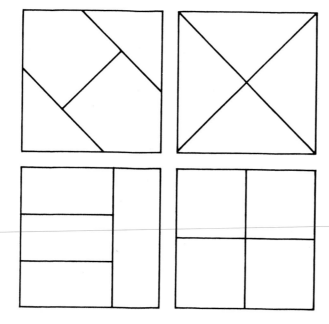

Canapé Bread Shapes

Salmon Canapés

- 6 **slices firm-textured white bread, toasted, and 6 slices firm-textured rye bread, toasted, _or_ 48 melba toast rounds**
- 1 **7¾-ounce can salmon, drained, flaked, and skin and bones removed**
- ⅓ **cup mayonnaise _or_ salad dressing**
- 2 **tablespoons finely chopped pitted ripe olives**
- 1 **tablespoon snipped parsley**
- 1½ **teaspoons prepared mustard**
- 1 **teaspoon finely chopped onion**
- ½ **teaspoon Worcestershire sauce**
- ½ **cup shredded mozzarella cheese (2 ounces)**
  Pitted ripe olives, sliced (optional)

▬ Remove the crusts from the bread slices. (_Or_, use the melba toast rounds.)

▬ In a medium mixing bowl combine salmon, mayonnaise or salad dressing, the 2 tablespoons chopped ripe olives, the parsley, mustard, onion, and Worcestershire sauce. For the canapés, spread about _4 teaspoons_ of the salmon mixture on _each_ slice of bread. Cut bread slices into desired shapes (see illustrations at left). Or, spread some mixture on each melba toast round.

▬ To serve, place canapés on a shallow baking sheet or an oven-proof serving platter; sprinkle with the shredded cheese. Broil canapés 3 to 4 inches from heat for 2 minutes or till the cheese is melted. Garnish with the additional ripe olive slices, if desired. Serve immediately. Makes 48 servings.

Tuna Canapés: Prepare Salmon Canapés as above, _except_ substitute one 6½-ounce can _tuna,_ drained and flaked, for the salmon. Continue as directed.

▬ Preparation time: 40 minutes
▬ Cooking time: 2 minutes

Seafood Pâté

Seafood Pâté

    8 ounces fresh *or* frozen fish fillets, *or*
        one 6½-ounce can tuna (water pack),
        drained and flaked, *or* one 7¾-ounce can
        salmon, drained, flaked, and skin
        and bones removed
    1 teaspoon unflavored gelatin
    ¼ cup cold water
    1 4½-ounce can shrimp, drained and rinsed
    1 8-ounce package Neufchâtel cheese,
        softened
    ½ cup finely chopped celery
    ⅓ cup plain yogurt
    2 tablespoons dry sherry
    ½ teaspoon fines herbes
        Lettuce leaves
        Watercress *or* parsley sprigs (optional)
        Toasted pita bread *or* flour tortilla triangles
        Vegetable dippers

■■■ Place fresh or frozen fish fillets in a greased skillet; add boiling water to cover. Simmer, covered, for 5 to 10 minutes or till fish flakes easily when tested with a fork; drain and flake.

■■■ In a saucepan soften the gelatin in the cold water; let stand for 5 minutes. Cook and stir over low heat till the gelatin is dissolved. Reserve some of the shrimp for garnish, if desired; chop remaining shrimp. In a mixing bowl combine the fish, tuna, or salmon; chopped shrimp; cheese; celery; yogurt; sherry; fines herbes; and gelatin mixture. Beat mixture till combined. Turn into a lightly oiled 3-cup mold. Cover and chill in refrigerator for 6 hours or till firm.

■■■ Unmold the pâté onto a lettuce-lined plate. If desired, trim with watercress or parsley sprigs, and the reserved shrimp. Serve with pita or tortilla triangles, and vegetable dippers. Makes 2⅔ cups.

■■■ Preparation time: 30 minutes
■■■ Chilling time: at least 6 hours

When a recipe calls for vegetable dippers, offer your guests an interesting variety.

Steam carrot sticks or baby carrots, kohlrabi sticks, asparagus spears, brussels sprouts, and cauliflower or broccoli flowerets until they are crisp-tender. For even crunchier dippers, simply serve them raw. Serve these dippers fresh: mushrooms, cherry tomatoes, radishes, and celery sticks.

To eat *Artichokes Continental*, pull off one of the artichoke leaves. Then, dip its base into the yogurt mixture in the center. Draw the leaf through your teeth, eating only the tender flesh.

Once you have pulled off all the leaves, you will find a deliciously delightful prize—the artichoke heart.

Artichokes Continental*

6 **small artichokes**
Lemon juice
1 **cup dairy sour cream**
½ **cup plain yogurt**
1 **2-ounce jar red caviar**

■ Trim artichokes (see top photograph below); brush with lemon juice. Place in 1 inch boiling salted water. Cover and simmer for 20 to 30 minutes or till a leaf pulls out easily. Invert to drain. Spread tops apart; pull out center leaves. Scoop out chokes (see bottom photograph below); chill. Combine sour cream and yogurt. Reserve *1 tablespoon* caviar; stir the remaining caviar into yogurt mixture; spoon into centers. Garnish with reserved caviar. Makes 6 servings.

■ Preparation time: 1 hour
■ Chilling time: at least 2 hours
  * *pictured on page 12*

With a sharp knife, remove the bottom stems so the artichokes sit flat. Remove the loose outer leaves. Cut off 1 inch from the tops. Snip off the sharp leaf tips with kitchen shears. Brush lemon juice on the cut edges to keep them from turning brown.

When the cooked artichokes are cool enough to handle, spread the tops apart with your fingers and pull out the center leaves. Scoop out the fuzzy chokes with a spoon, as shown. Discard the chokes and thoroughly chill the artichokes.

Chicken Ravigote

1 **egg**
⅓ **cup mayonnaise** *or* **salad dressing**
1 **tablespoon finely snipped parsley**
1 **tablespoon capers, drained and finely chopped**
1 **tablespoon chopped pimiento**
½ **teaspoon dry mustard**
½ **teaspoon prepared horseradish**
½ **teaspoon lemon juice**
1 **cup cubed cooked chicken** *or* **turkey**
Bibb lettuce leaves

■ To hard-cook the egg, place the egg in a saucepan; cover with cold water. Bring to boiling; reduce heat to just below simmering. Cover and cook for 15 minutes. Run cold water over the egg till cool. Remove the shell and chop the egg.

■ Meanwhile, in a mixing bowl combine mayonnaise or salad dressing, snipped parsley, *2 teaspoons* of the capers, the chopped pimiento, dry mustard, horseradish, and the lemon juice. Add the chopped hard-cooked egg and the chicken or turkey; toss gently to combine. Cover and chill the mixture in the refrigerator for 2 hours or till cold.

■ Before serving, arrange the chilled mixture in 4 lettuce-lined cocktail cups or glasses. Garnish with the remaining capers. Makes 4 servings.

Ham Ravigote: Make Chicken Ravigote as above, *except* substitute 1 cup cubed *fully cooked ham* for the chicken or turkey. Continue as directed.

■ Total preparation time: 30 minutes
■ Chilling time: at least 2 hours

Hot Tomato Especial

- 1 12-ounce can vegetable juice cocktail
- 1 cup beef broth
- 2 thin slices onion
- 4 whole cloves
  Dash bottled hot pepper sauce
- ⅓ cup dry white wine
- 4 lemon slices (optional)

■ In a saucepan combine vegetable juice cocktail, beef broth, onion slices, cloves, and hot pepper sauce. Bring to boiling; reduce heat. Cover and simmer for 20 minutes. Strain the hot mixture, discarding solids. Stir the white wine into the hot mixture. Pour into 4 mugs. Float a lemon slice in each of the mugs, if desired. Makes 4 (6 ounce) servings.

■ Total preparation time: 30 minutes

Lime-Tomato Sipper

- 1 teaspoon instant chicken bouillon granules
- 1 cup boiling water
- 3 cups tomato juice
- 2 tablespoons lime juice
- 1 teaspoon sugar
- 1 teaspoon Worcestershire sauce
- ¼ teaspoon celery salt
- ¼ teaspoon dried basil, crushed
- 8 stalks celery with leaves

■ Dissolve bouillon granules in boiling water. In a pitcher combine bouillon, tomato juice, lime juice, sugar, Worcestershire sauce, celery salt, and basil. Cover and chill for 2 hours or till cold.

■ To serve, pour chilled tomato mixture into 8 glasses. Garnish each serving with a stalk of celery. Makes 8 (4-ounce) servings.

■ Total preparation time: 15 minutes
■ Chilling time: at least 2 hours

Berries in Champagne

- 1 quart fresh *or* frozen strawberries *or* red raspberries
- ¼ cup sugar
- 1 750-milliliter bottle champagne, chilled
  Mint sprigs (optional)

■ Thaw strawberries or raspberries, if frozen. In a medium mixing bowl crush *1 cup* of the fresh or the thawed berries. Place the remaining berries in a large mixing bowl; halve any large strawberries. Add sugar to the crushed berries; stir till dissolved. Pour the sweetened berry mixture over the berries in the large mixing bowl. Stir gently to combine. Cover and chill in the refrigerator till serving time.

■ To serve, spoon the berry mixture into 8 chilled goblets. Pour some of the chilled champagne into each. Garnish each serving with fresh mint, if desired. Makes 8 (6-ounce) servings.

■ Total preparation time: 15 minutes

Fruit Shrub

- 1½ cups cranberry juice cocktail *and* 1½ cups apple juice, chilled, *or* 3 cups cranberry-apple drink, chilled
- 1 cup pineapple juice, chilled
- 2 tablespoons lemon juice
  Pineapple, lemon, *or* orange sherbet
  Mint sprigs (optional)

■ In a pitcher combine the cranberry juice cocktail and apple juice or use the cranberry-apple drink. Stir in the pineapple juice and lemon juice. Pour the juice mixture into 8 chilled juice glasses. Top each serving with a small scoop of sherbet. If desired, garnish each serving with a mint sprig. Makes 8 (4-ounce) servings.

■ Total preparation time: 10 minutes

ROASTING BEEF AND VEAL

Roast meat at a constant 325° oven temperature unless otherwise indicated.

Beef or Veal Cut	Approximate Weight	Internal Temperature when Removed from Oven	Approximate Cooking Time (total time)
Beef Rib Roast	4 to 6 lbs.	140° (rare) 160° (medium) 170° (well done)	2 to 2½ hrs. 2½ to 3¼ hrs. 2¾ to 4 hrs.
Rib Roast	6 to 8 lbs.	140° (rare) 160° (medium) 170° (well done)	2½ to 3 hrs. 3 to 3½ hrs. 3½ to 4¼ hrs.
Boneless Rib Roast	5 to 7 lbs.	140° (rare) 160° (medium) 170° (well done)	2¾ to 3¾ hrs. 3¼ to 4¼ hrs. 4 to 5½ hrs.
Boneless Round Rump Roast	4 to 6 lbs.	150° to 170°	2 to 2½ hrs.
Round Tip Roast	3½ to 4 lbs.	140° to 170°	2¼ to 2½ hrs.
Rib Eye Roast (Roast at 350°)	4 to 6 lbs.	140° (rare) 160° (medium) 170° (well done)	1¼ to 1¾ hrs. 1½ to 2 hrs. 1¾ to 2¼ hrs.
Tenderloin Roast (Roast at 425°)	4 to 6 lbs.	140° (rare)	¾ to 1 hr.
Veal Leg Round Roast	5 to 8 lbs.	170° (well done)	2¾ to 3¼ hrs.
Loin Roast	4 to 6 lbs.	170° (well done)	2¼ to 3 hrs.
Boneless Shoulder Roast	4 to 6 lbs.	170° (well done)	3 to 4 hrs.

To roast meat: Season beef and veal roasts by sprinkling with a little salt and pepper. Place the meat, fat side up, on a rack in a shallow roasting pan. Insert a meat thermometer. *Do not add water or other liquid, and do not cover the roasting pan.*

Except as noted in the chart above, roast the meat in a 325° oven until the meat thermometer registers the desired internal temperature.

For easy carving, let the meat stand about 15 minutes. During this standing time, the internal temperature will rise about 5° F.

Use roasting times in chart above only as a guide to the total cooking time for your cut of meat, because individual cuts vary in size, shape, and tenderness.

Rib Roast Elegant

- 1 **4-pound beef rib roast**
- 20 **fresh large mushrooms**
- ½ **cup dairy sour cream**
- 2 **tablespoons prepared horseradish**
- 2 **tablespoons Dijon-style mustard**
  Snipped chives (optional)

■ Place the beef rib roast, fat side up, on a rack in a 15½x10½x2-inch roasting pan. Sprinkle meat with salt and pepper. Insert a meat thermometer into thickest portion of meat, away from fat or bone.

■ Roast in a 325° oven for 2 to 2½ hours for rare or till thermometer registers 140°; 2½ to 3 hours for medium or till thermometer registers 160°; 2¾ to 3¼ hours for well done or till thermometer registers 170°.

■ Meanwhile, thoroughly clean the fresh mushrooms. Remove the stems and reserve for another use. Place the mushroom caps, hollow side up, into a 12x7½x2-inch baking dish.

■ In a small mixing bowl combine the dairy sour cream, prepared horseradish, and Dijon-style mustard. Spoon the sour cream mixture into the mushroom caps. Sprinkle with snipped chives, if desired. Bake the filled mushroom caps, uncovered, in a 325° oven for 15 minutes or till heated through. Serve with the rib roast. Makes 10 servings.

■ Total preparation time: 2¼ to 3½ hours

Bavarian Roast

- 1 **4- to 5-pound boneless beef round rump roast**
- 1 **8-ounce can stewed tomatoes**
- 1 **medium onion, chopped (½ cup)**
- 1 **medium carrot, shredded (½ cup)**
- ½ **cup beer**
- ½ **teaspoon salt**
- ½ **teaspoon caraway seed**
  Dash pepper
- 1 **8-ounce carton dairy sour cream**
- 2 **tablespoons all-purpose flour**
  Parsley sprigs (optional)

■ Sprinkle beef with salt and pepper. Place meat, fat side up, on a rack in a shallow roasting pan. Insert a meat thermometer into thickest part of meat. Roast, uncovered, in a 325° oven 2 hours for medium rare or till thermometer registers 150°, or 2¼ to 2½ hours for well done or till thermometer registers 170°. Transfer meat to a heated serving platter, reserving 2 tablespoons of the drippings. Let meat stand 15 minutes.

■ Meanwhile, prepare the sauce. For sauce, in a saucepan combine tomatoes, onion, carrot, beer, salt, caraway seed, and pepper. Bring to boiling; reduce heat. Simmer, covered, for 15 minutes or till vegetables are tender. Combine sour cream and flour; gradually stir in the reserved drippings. Stir about ½ cup of the cooked vegetable mixture into sour cream mixture; return all to saucepan. Cook and stir till thickened and bubbly. Cook and stir for 1 minute more. Slice meat; serve sauce over slices. Garnish with parsley, if desired. Makes 10 to 12 servings.

■ Total preparation time: 2½ to 3 hours

In *Rib Roast Elegant* large mushroom caps filled with a rich, zesty sour cream sauce accompany the roasted beef.

If you'd prefer, use dairy sour cream dip (chive or horseradish) rather than the sour cream sauce to fill mushroom caps.

Filet Lyonnaise

1 **5-pound beef tenderloin**
1 **cup butter *or* margarine, softened**
2 **cloves garlic, minced**
3 **beaten eggs**
8 **ounces fresh spinach, finely chopped**
   (6 cups)
¾ **cup soft bread crumbs (1 slice)**
   Large whole fresh mushrooms
1 **10½-ounce can condensed beef broth**
   Tiny new potatoes, quartered
   Butter *or* margarine
3 **medium onions, cut into very thin wedges**
½ **cup dry sherry**
   Lemon leaves (optional)

■ Trim fat from tenderloin. Make a double butterfly cut (see photograph at right). Pound with a meat mallet to a 10x8-inch rectangle. In a small mixing bowl combine the 1 cup softened butter or margarine and the garlic; spread over meat.

■ In a mixing bowl combine eggs, spinach, and bread crumbs; spoon atop butter mixture on meat. Roll up jelly-roll style, beginning from a long side. Place the meat roll, seam side down, on a rack in a shallow roasting pan. Sprinkle salt on meat. Insert a meat thermometer. Roast, uncovered, in a 400° oven for 50 minutes or till thermometer registers 140° for rare or to desired doneness.

■ Meanwhile, flute mushrooms, if desired. With a small paring knife or a lemon zester held at an angle, begin at the center of each mushroom cap and carve a strip out of the cap in the form of an inverted V. Turn mushroom and continue cutting strips in a circular fashion, making desired number of cuts in each mushroom cap. Set aside.

■ In a small saucepan bring beef broth to boiling; reduce heat. Simmer, uncovered, for 12 to 15 minutes or till volume is reduced to ⅔ cup. Meanwhile, cook the potatoes in boiling salted water for 10 minutes; drain. Cook the whole mushrooms in a small amount of hot butter or margarine for 4 to 6 minutes. Keep potatoes and mushrooms warm. Remove meat from pan, reserving the pan drippings; keep warm.

■ In a large skillet cook onions in the reserved drippings till tender but not brown. Stir in the reduced beef broth and the sherry; heat through. Remove onions with a slotted spoon.

■ Meanwhile, if desired, arrange lemon leaves on a heated serving platter. Slice the meat crosswise into 1-inch-thick slices. Arrange meat, slices overlapping, around one side of the platter. Place the potatoes, mushrooms, and onions onto the other side of the platter. Drizzle the broth-sherry mixture over all. Makes 14 to 16 servings.

■ Total preparation time: 1½ hours

For a double butterfly cut, make a single lengthwise cut down center of the meat, cutting to within ½ inch of the other side. Make two more cuts, one on each side of the first cut, cutting through the thickest portions of meat to within ½ inch of the other side, as shown.

Filet Lyonnaise

MENU
SUMMER FEAST

Crudités

Filet Lyonnaise

Steamed Beets

Whole Wheat Rolls
with Butter

Mandarin Cream
Cones ★

Red Wine

This outstanding menu is especially suited for a summertime dinner party for a large number of guests.

You'll find that crudités (crew-DEE-tays)—sliced raw vegetables—are a pleasing appetizer. They also go perfectly with your favorite dip.

Make the brandy snap cookies for *Mandarin Cream Cones* the day before. About an hour before guests arrive, finish the cones and chill them in the refrigerator.

For *Filet Lyonnaise*, you can also use two 2½-pound beef tenderloins rather than one 5-pound beef tenderloin. The cooking time is the same for both.

★ *see recipe, page 168*

Beef and Scallop Stir-Fry offers an excellent opportunity for you to show off your wok skills. If you don't own a wok, no problem—just use a large skillet.

Serve this delicious stir-fry atop *Deep-Fried Rice Sticks* or, if you prefer, hot cooked rice. The noodle-like rice sticks, readily available in Oriental grocery stores, take only a few seconds to prepare. To fascinate your guests, invite them into the kitchen to watch the rice sticks puff up and rise to the surface of the hot cooking oil.

Beef and Scallop Stir-Fry

- **8 ounces fresh *or* frozen scallops**
- **1 pound boneless beef sirloin steak *or* top round steak**
- **⅓ cup dry sherry**
- **3 tablespoons water**
- **3 tablespoons soy sauce**
- **2 tablespoons thinly sliced green onion**
- **1 tablespoon sesame oil *or* cooking oil**
- **1 teaspoon grated gingerroot**
- **¼ teaspoon crushed red pepper**
- **1 star anise *or* ¼ teaspoon aniseed**
- **1 clove garlic, minced**
- **1 tablespoon cornstarch**
- **3 medium carrots, bias-sliced into 1-inch pieces**
- **2 cups broccoli cut into 1-inch pieces**
- **2 tablespoons cooking oil**
- **1 8-ounce can bamboo shoots, drained Deep-Fried Rice Sticks *or* hot cooked rice**

■ Thaw scallops, if frozen. Halve any large scallops; chill. Partially freeze the beef; cut on the bias into bite-size strips.

■ For marinade, combine the sherry, water, soy sauce, green onion, the 1 tablespoon sesame oil or cooking oil, gingerroot, red pepper, star anise or aniseed, and minced garlic. Add the beef strips to the marinade; cover and marinate in the refrigerator for 1 hour, stirring occasionally. Drain the meat, reserving marinade. Discard the star anise, if used. Stir the cornstarch into the reserved marinade; set aside.

■ Meanwhile, in a medium saucepan cook the carrots, covered, in a small amount of boiling salted water for 5 minutes. Add the broccoli and cook, covered, for 2 minutes more. Drain well.

■ Preheat a wok or large skillet over high heat; add the 2 tablespoons cooking oil. Stir-fry the carrots and broccoli in the hot cooking oil about 2 minutes or till crisp-tender; remove. Add more oil, if necessary. Add the scallops; stir-fry for 3 to 4 minutes; remove. Stir-fry the beef, half at a time, for 2 to 3 minutes or till brown. Return all beef to wok. Add bamboo shoots.

■ Stir cornstarch mixture; stir into beef mixture. Cook and stir till thickened and bubbly. Return vegetables and scallops to wok; cover and cook for 2 minutes more. Serve with Deep-Fried Rice Sticks or with hot cooked rice. Makes 4 to 6 servings.

Deep-Fried Rice Sticks: Fry 2 ounces unsoaked *rice sticks*, a few at a time, in deep hot *cooking oil* (375°) about 5 seconds or just till sticks puff and rise to top. Remove with a slotted spoon or wire strainer; drain on paper toweling. Keep warm in oven.

■ Marinating time: 1 hour
■ Preparation time: 35 minutes

Steak with Wine Sauce

- **4 beef top loin steaks, cut 1 inch thick**
- **2 tablespoons butter *or* margarine**
- **½ cup dry red, rosé, *or* white wine**
- **¼ cup chopped onion**
- **½ teaspoon dried thyme, crushed *or* dried tarragon, crushed**
- **1 tablespoon snipped parsley**
- **Dash salt**
- **Dash pepper**
- **1 cup cherry tomatoes, halved**

■ In a large skillet cook steaks in hot butter or margarine over medium heat to desired doneness, turning once. Allow 9 to 10 minutes total cooking time for rare or 11 to 12 minutes for medium. Sprinkle with salt and pepper. Transfer the steaks to a heated serving platter; keep warm.

■ For sauce, in the same skillet combine the wine, onion, and thyme or tarragon. Bring to boiling. Cook, uncovered, for 3 to 4 minutes or till the volume is reduced by half. Remove from heat; stir in the parsley, salt, and pepper. Stir in the halved cherry tomatoes. Serve sauce over steaks. Makes 4 servings.

■ Total preparation time: 20 minutes

Pepper Steak

1 pound beef sirloin steak *or* round steak
2 cloves garlic, minced
2 tablespoons butter *or* margarine
2 medium green peppers, cut into ¾-inch pieces
2 cups sliced fresh mushrooms
½ cup chopped onion
¾ cup beef broth
2 tablespoons all-purpose flour
1 teaspoon Worcestershire sauce
½ teaspoon dried oregano, crushed
¼ teaspoon salt
⅛ teaspoon pepper
⅛ teaspoon bottled hot pepper sauce
   Hot cooked rice

■ Partially freeze the beef; cut on the bias into bite-size strips. In a large skillet cook the beef and garlic in hot butter or margarine for 2 to 3 minutes or till almost done. Add the green pepper pieces, sliced mushrooms, and chopped onion; cook for 3 to 4 minutes or till the onion is crisp-tender.

■ Combine the beef broth, flour, Worcestershire sauce, oregano, salt, pepper, and bottled hot pepper sauce. Stir the broth mixture into the beef mixture. Cook and stir till mixture is thickened and bubbly. Cook and stir for 1 minute more. Serve over hot cooked rice. Makes 4 servings.

■ Total preparation time: 40 minutes

Special Filet of Beef

8 beef tenderloin steaks, cut ¾ inch thick
2 cups sliced fresh mushrooms
2 tablespoons sliced green onion
1 small clove garlic, minced
2 tablespoons butter *or* margarine
4 teaspoons cornstarch
¾ cup cold water
¼ cup dry red wine
2 tablespoons capers
2 tablespoons snipped parsley
1 teaspoon instant beef bouillon granules
   Dash pepper

■ Place the steaks on the rack of an unheated broiler pan. Broil 3 inches from heat to desired doneness, turning steaks once with tongs. Allow 10 to 12 minutes total broiling time for medium. Season the steaks with salt and pepper.

■ Meanwhile, prepare the sauce. In a medium saucepan cook the sliced mushrooms, green onion, and garlic in hot butter or margarine over medium heat for 4 to 5 minutes or till tender. Stir in the cornstarch. Add the cold water, red wine, capers, snipped parsley, beef bouillon granules, and pepper. Cook and stir till the mixture is thickened and bubbly. Cook and stir for 2 minutes more. Serve the sauce over steaks. Makes 8 servings.

■ Total preparation time: 25 minutes

Take a cue from Mediterranean cooks and use capers to enhance your sauces. Pickled buds of the caper bush add a distinctive flavor to meats, poultry, and fish.

When you use capers, spoon out those you need from the brine. To keep the remaining capers from drying out, store them in the jar with the brine. After you've used all the capers, add the leftover brine to soups and sauces.

"En croûte," a French term, refers to food that is covered with pastry and then baked. *Beef Rolls en Croûte* features a delicate covering of paper-thin phyllo dough sheets.

This recipe is great for making ahead. Prepare the *Beef Rolls en Croûte* up to the point of securing the beef rolls with string. Then, chill the rolls until you're ready to roll them in the phyllo dough.

Beef Rolls en Croûte

1½	pounds beef top round steak, cut ½ inch thick
½	pound ground pork
4	ounces braunschweiger
½	cup chopped green onion
2	tablespoons milk
1	clove garlic, minced
¼	teaspoon dry mustard
1	large carrot, cut into 2-inch julienne strips
2	tablespoons cooking oil
1	cup water
¼	cup chopped green onion
2	teaspoons instant beef bouillon granules
1	teaspoon Worcestershire sauce
¼	teaspoon dried thyme, crushed
¼	teaspoon dried marjoram, crushed
¼	teaspoon pepper
12	sheets frozen phyllo dough, thawed (8 ounces)
6	tablespoons butter *or* margarine, melted
½	cup dairy sour cream
2	tablespoons all-purpose flour
2	tablespoons snipped parsley
½	teaspoon paprika
	Tomato rose (optional)
	Watercress (optional)

■ Trim fat from steak. Cut steak into 6 equal-sized pieces. Using a meat mallet, pound each piece to a ¼-inch-thick rectangle. In a mixing bowl combine ground pork, braunschweiger, the ½ cup chopped green onion, milk, garlic, and mustard. Spread *one-sixth* of the pork mixture over *each* piece of meat. Arrange the carrot strips crosswise atop meat. Starting from a short side, roll up jelly-roll style, as shown. Secure the meat roll-ups with string, as shown.

■ In a large skillet brown meat roll-ups on all sides in hot oil. Drain off fat. Combine water, the ¼ cup chopped green onion, bouillon granules, Worcestershire sauce, thyme, marjoram, and pepper. Pour over meat. Bring to boiling; reduce heat. Cover and simmer for 30 minutes. Remove meat, reserving juices in skillet. Pat meat dry with paper toweling. Remove string.

■ Using *6* phyllo dough sheets, *half* the butter, and *half* the meat roll-ups, stack phyllo sheets, brushing each sheet generously with butter. (Keep remaining sheets covered with a damp towel.) Cut phyllo stack crosswise into thirds, as shown. Position one meat roll-up at one end of each phyllo strip. Carefully lift short ends of phyllo over meat, pressing against meat. Roll up, folding in sides, as shown. Press ends to seal. Using a knife, make 3 diagonal cuts in the top layers of each roll, as shown. Repeat with remaining phyllo, butter, and meat roll-ups. Place rolls, seam side down, in a shallow baking pan. Brush with butter. Bake in a 400° oven for 15 to 18 minutes or till done.

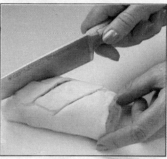

Serve *Beef Rolls en Croûte* for a very elegant dinner party. Show off the phyllo-encased beef rolls by placing them on, rather than under, the rich sour cream sauce. You can pass the remaining sauce to let your guests help themselves. To make the food presentation even more stylish, garnish your platter with a beautiful tomato rose and sprigs of fresh watercress.

■ Meanwhile, for sauce, strain the reserved skillet juices; skim fat. Measure juices; add water, if necessary, to equal 1 cup liquid. Combine sour cream, flour, parsley, and paprika. Stir in the reserved liquid. Add sour cream mixture to skillet. Cook and stir till thickened and bubbly. Cook and stir for 1 minute more. To serve, spoon some of the sauce onto a heated serving platter; arrange the beef rolls atop. Garnish with a tomato rose and watercress, if desired. Pass the remaining sauce. Makes 6 servings.

■ Preparation time: 1¾ hours
■ Cooking time: 15 to 18 minutes

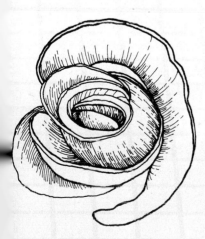

Cut the base from a ripe tomato, but do not sever. Using a sawing motion, continue cutting a narrow strip of tomato in spiral fashion, tapering the end into a point to remove. Curl strip onto the base in the shape of a rose.

Toasted almonds add a distinctive nutty flavor to *Deviled Beef with Almonds*.

To toast the almonds, spread them in a shallow baking pan and bake in a 350° oven for 6 to 7 minutes, stirring twice. Or, you can toast them in a skillet over low heat. Watch them closely since they can go from toasted to overbrown in a short time.

Saucy Steak in Bulgur Ring

- 1 **pound beef top round steak**
- 1 **cup bulgur wheat**
- 3 **tablespoons butter** *or* **margarine**
- 2¼ **cups beef broth**
- 1 **cup chopped celery**
- ¼ **cup long grain rice**
- 2 **large onions, chopped (2 cups)**
- 2 **medium green peppers, cut into**
     ¾-inch pieces
- 2 **cloves garlic, minced**
- 2 **tablespoons butter** *or* **margarine**
- 2 **teaspoons curry powder**
- 1 **teaspoon paprika**
- ½ **teaspoon ground ginger**
- ¼ **teaspoon ground red pepper**
- 2 **tablespoons butter** *or* **margarine**
- ½ **cup plain yogurt**
- ½ **cup dairy sour cream**
- 2 **tablespoons all-purpose flour**
- ¼ **cup snipped parsley**

▬ Partially freeze the meat. Thinly slice into bite-size strips. In a skillet or large saucepan cook the bulgur in the 3 tablespoons hot butter or margarine till lightly toasted, stirring frequently. Add beef broth, celery, and ¼ teaspoon *salt*. Bring to boiling. Stir in the uncooked rice. Reduce heat. Cover and simmer about 20 minutes or till bulgur and rice are tender.

▬ Meanwhile, in a large skillet cook the onion, green pepper, and garlic in 2 tablespoons hot butter or margarine till onion is tender but not brown. Stir in the curry powder, paprika, ginger, red pepper, and ¼ teaspoon *salt;* remove from skillet.

▬ Brown meat, half at a time, in 2 tablespoons hot butter or margarine. Drain off fat. Return all meat and the onion mixture to skillet. Add ½ cup *water*. Cover; simmer about 15 minutes or till meat is tender, stirring frequently. (If mixture becomes too thick, add 1 more tablespoon water.) Combine the yogurt, sour cream, and flour; stir into beef mixture. Cook and stir till thickened and bubbly. Cook and stir for 1 minute more.

▬ To serve, press the bulgur mixture into a 4-cup ring mold. Unmold on a heated serving platter. Fill the center with some of the beef mixture; pass remaining. Sprinkle parsley atop. Serve immediately. Serves 6.

▬ Total preparation time: 1 hour

Deviled Beef with Almonds

- 2 **pounds beef stew meat, cut into**
     1-inch pieces
- 2 **tablespoons cooking oil**
- 2 **medium onions, chopped (1 cup)**
- 1½ **cups water**
- 1 **tablespoon dry mustard**
- 1 **tablespoon Worcestershire sauce**
- ½ **teaspoon salt**
- ½ **teaspoon ground cumin**
- ⅛ **teaspoon pepper**
- 2 **tablespoons cold water**
- 1 **tablespoon cornstarch**
- ½ **cup whole blanched almonds, toasted**
     Parsley *or* **carrot curls (optional)**
     Hot cooked noodles *or* **rice**

▬ In a large saucepan brown meat, half at a time, in hot cooking oil. Add chopped onions; cook till onions are tender but not brown. Drain off fat. Stir in the 1½ cups water, dry mustard, Worcestershire sauce, salt, cumin, and pepper. Cover and cook over low heat for 1¼ to 1½ hours or till meat is tender.

▬ Combine the 2 tablespoons cold water and cornstarch; add to meat mixture. Cook and stir till thickened and bubbly. Cook and stir for 2 minutes more. Add almonds; heat through. Spoon mixture onto a heated serving platter. If desired, garnish with parsley or carrot curls (see column at far left, page 92). Serve with noodles or rice. Makes 8 servings.

▬ Preparation time: 15 minutes
▬ Cooking time: 1¼ to 1½ hours

Mexican Short Ribs

3 pounds beef chuck short ribs, cut into
    2½-inch lengths
2 tablespoons cooking oil
1 medium onion, chopped (½ cup)
2 cloves garlic, minced
1 teaspoon chili powder
1 8-ounce can tomato sauce
¼ cup water
¼ cup rum *or* sherry
2 tablespoons sliced pimiento-stuffed olives
2 bay leaves
½ teaspoon salt
½ teaspoon dried marjoram, crushed
½ teaspoon dried thyme, crushed
½ teaspoon paprika
1 egg
2 tablespoons cold water
4 teaspoons cornstarch

▬ In a Dutch oven brown ribs on all sides in hot oil; remove from Dutch oven. Add the chopped onion, garlic, and chili powder to Dutch oven; cook till onion is tender but not brown. Stir in the tomato sauce, the ¼ cup water, rum or sherry, olives, bay leaves, salt, marjoram, thyme, and paprika. Return ribs to Dutch oven; turn to coat. Cover and bake in a 350° oven for 1½ hours. Uncover and bake for 20 minutes more.

▬ Meanwhile, to hard-cook the egg, place egg in a saucepan; cover with cold water. Bring to boiling; reduce heat to just below simmering. Cover and cook for 15 minutes. Run cold water over egg till cool. Remove shell; chop egg.

▬ Transfer ribs to a heated serving platter, reserving pan juices. Keep ribs warm. Remove bay leaves from pan juices; skim fat. Measure juices; add water, if necessary, to equal 1½ cups liquid. Return to Dutch oven. Combine the 2 tablespoons cold water and cornstarch; stir into juices. Cook and stir till thickened and bubbly. Cook and stir for 2 minutes more. Spoon atop ribs. Garnish with chopped egg. Serves 6.

▬ Preparation time: 25 minutes
▬ Cooking time: 2 hours

Saucy Liver and Onions with Noodles

½ pound fresh pork sausage links, cut into
    1-inch pieces
½ pound beef liver, cut into strips
2 large onions, cut into thin wedges (3 cups)
2 cloves garlic, minced
2 tablespoons butter *or* margarine
½ cup water
1 teaspoon instant chicken bouillon granules
⅛ teaspoon pepper
½ cup shredded Monterey Jack cheese
    (3 ounces)
¼ cup snipped parsley
4 ounces medium noodles (3 cups)
    Shredded Monterey Jack cheese (optional)

▬ In a large skillet cook sausage pieces over medium heat for 8 to 10 minutes or till almost done. Drain well, reserving 1 tablespoon of the pan drippings. Push the sausage to one side of skillet. Add the liver; cook over medium heat for 4 to 5 minutes or till liver and sausage are done. Remove liver and sausage from skillet; drain well.

▬ In the same skillet cook onion wedges and garlic in hot butter or margarine, covered, over low heat about 15 minutes or till very tender, stirring occasionally. Uncover and cook over medium heat for 5 to 10 minutes more or till onion wedges are golden brown, stirring frequently. Combine the water, bouillon granules, and pepper; add to skillet. Cook, uncovered, over low heat, for 5 minutes, stirring frequently. Stir in the sausage and liver; heat through. Stir in the ½ cup shredded Monterey Jack cheese and parsley.

▬ Meanwhile, cook noodles according to package directions; drain. To serve, toss the meat mixture with the hot noodles till well coated. Serve immediately. Pass additional shredded Monterey Jack cheese, if desired. Makes 4 servings.

▬ Total preparation time: 1 hour

"Phyllo" is a Greek word meaning "leaf." Greeks use this special dough to make baklava, their famous layered nut pastry. To find phyllo (also spelled filo), check your local supermarket's freezer display case.

These delicate, paper-thin sheets of dough require special handling. While preparing *Beef in Phyllo*, keep a damp cloth over the sheets of phyllo until you're ready to use them. This will prevent the phyllo from drying out and cracking.

Beef in Phyllo

- **1 pound ground beef**
- **2 medium onions, chopped (1 cup)**
- **½ cup chopped green pepper**
- **½ cup chopped celery**
- **2 cloves garlic, minced**
- **¼ cup grated Parmesan cheese**
- **¼ cup snipped parsley**
- **½ teaspoon ground cinnamon**
- **¼ teaspoon salt**
- **¼ teaspoon ground nutmeg**
- **1 beaten egg**
- **10 to 12 sheets frozen phyllo dough, thawed (8 ounces)**
- **½ cup butter *or* margarine, melted**
- **3 tablespoons butter *or* margarine**
- **3 tablespoons all-purpose flour**
- **¼ teaspoon salt**
- **Dash pepper**
- **1¼ cups light cream**
- **⅓ cup dry white wine**
- **⅓ cup grated Parmesan cheese**
- **Lemon slices (optional)**

■ For filling, in a large skillet cook the ground beef, chopped onion, green pepper, celery, and garlic till meat is brown and vegetables are tender. Remove from heat. Drain off fat. Stir in the ¼ cup Parmesan cheese, the snipped parsley, cinnamon, ¼ teaspoon salt, and nutmeg. Stir in the beaten egg; set aside.

■ Using *5 or 6* phyllo dough sheets and *¼ cup* of the melted butter or margarine, stack phyllo sheets, brushing each sheet generously with butter. (Keep the remaining phyllo sheets covered with a damp towel.) Spread *half* of the beef filling over phyllo stack to within 1 inch of edges. Fold edges of one short side and long sides over filling. Roll up jelly-roll style, starting with folded short side (see photograph at right). Press ends to seal. Place the roll, seam side down, into a lightly greased shallow baking pan. Brush with

melted butter or margarine. Using a knife, make several diagonal cuts in the top phyllo layers of roll (see photograph below). Repeat with remaining phyllo, melted butter, and meat filling. Bake in a 350° oven about 40 minutes or till done.

■ Meanwhile, for sauce, melt the 3 tablespoons butter or margarine. Stir in the flour, ¼ teaspoon salt, and pepper. Add the cream all at once. Cook and stir till thickened and bubbly. Cook and stir for 1 minute more. Stir in the wine. Add the ⅓ cup Parmesan cheese, stirring till melted.

■ Place the beef rolls on a heated serving platter. Spoon the sauce atop. Garnish with thin lemon slices, if desired. Slice rolls to serve. Makes 6 to 8 servings.

■ Preparation time: 45 minutes
■ Cooking time: 40 minutes

Spread half of the beef filling over one phyllo stack to within 1 inch of edges. Fold edges of one short side and long sides over filling. Roll up jelly-roll style, starting with the folded short side, as shown. Seal, transfer to pan, brush with butter, and score top, as shown.

Stuffed Breast of Veal

3 slices bacon
½ pound ground beef
1 medium onion, chopped (½ cup)
1 cup soft bread crumbs (1⅓ slices)
1 6-ounce can sliced mushrooms, drained
⅓ cup dairy sour cream
1 beaten egg
¼ cup snipped parsley
1 teaspoon dried dillweed
½ teaspoon dried tarragon, crushed
½ teaspoon dried basil, crushed
1 3- to 4-pound veal breast, boned, *or*
one 4- to 5-pound veal leg round roast,
boned, rolled, and tied
3 tablespoons cooking oil
1 tablespoon cornstarch
¼ cup dairy sour cream
¾ cup beef broth

■ For stuffing, in a skillet cook bacon till crisp; drain and crumble. In the same skillet cook beef and onion till meat is brown and onion is tender. Remove from heat. Drain off fat. Stir in bacon, bread crumbs, *half* of the mushrooms, the ⅓ cup sour cream, the egg, parsley, dillweed, tarragon, basil, ½ teaspoon *salt*, and a dash *pepper*. With wide end of veal facing you, cut a deep slit in long side. If using a round roast, untie and separate meat pieces. Spoon stuffing into pocket or between meat pieces. Close with skewers; secure with string. In a Dutch oven brown veal in hot cooking oil; transfer to a roasting pan. Cover; roast in a 325° oven for 2 to 2½ hours for breast, or 2¾ to 3½ hours for round roast, basting occasionally.

■ Transfer veal to a platter, reserving drippings; remove skewers and untie. Cover; keep warm. For gravy, strain drippings. Return to Dutch oven. Stir cornstarch into sour cream; gradually stir in the cold broth. Add broth mixture and remaining mushrooms to drippings. Cook and stir till thickened and bubbly. Cook and stir for 2 minutes more. To serve, slice meat. Pass gravy. Makes 10 to 12 servings.

■ Preparation time: 40 minutes
■ Cooking time: 2 to 3½ hours

Paprika Schnitzel

1½ pounds veal leg round steak *or* sirloin
steak, cut ½ to ¾ inch thick
2 beaten eggs
2 tablespoons milk
⅓ cup all-purpose flour
1 cup fine dry bread crumbs
4 to 6 tablespoons butter *or* margarine
¾ cup chicken broth
½ cup dairy sour cream
1 tablespoon all-purpose flour
1 tablespoon paprika
Lemon slices *or* wedges (optional)
Parsley sprigs (optional)

■ Remove bones from veal, if necessary. Cut veal into 6 pieces and score on both sides; pound with a meat mallet to ⅛-inch thickness. Sprinkle with salt and pepper. Combine eggs and milk. Coat veal with the ⅓ cup flour; shake gently to remove excess flour. With tongs, dip veal into the egg mixture, allowing excess to drip off. Coat with bread crumbs, pressing lightly to adhere; let stand for 15 minutes or till the bread crumb coating is dried.

■ In a large skillet cook veal, half at a time, in *2 tablespoons* of the hot butter or margarine for 2 minutes on medium heat or till light brown. Turn and cook for 1 to 2 minutes more, adding more butter, if necessary. Transfer to a heated serving platter and keep warm.

■ For sauce, pour chicken broth into skillet. Combine sour cream, the 1 tablespoon flour, and paprika; stir into chicken broth. Cook and stir till thickened and bubbly. Cook and stir for 1 minute more. Garnish veal with lemon slices or wedges and parsley, if desired. Pass the sauce with veal. Makes 6 servings.

■ Total preparation time: 40 minutes

If you plan to use a veal breast for *Stuffed Breast of Veal*, you'll probably need to special-order it from your butcher. Call the meat department three or four days ahead to ensure having a veal breast on the day of your party. Or, for the breast substitute a veal leg round roast, which would work just as well in this recipe.

Ossobuco

- **4 to 4½ pounds veal shanks, cut into 6 serving-size pieces**
- **3 tablespoons cooking oil**
- **2 medium onions, chopped (1 cup)**
- **½ cup chopped celery**
- **½ cup chopped carrot**
- **1 large clove garlic, minced**
- **1 16-ounce can tomatoes, cut up**
- **½ cup water**
- **¼ cup snipped parsley**
- **¼ cup dry white wine**
- **1 bay leaf**
- **1 teaspoon instant beef bouillon granules**
- **1 teaspoon dried basil, crushed**
- **½ teaspoon salt**
- **½ teaspoon dried thyme, crushed**
- **Dash pepper**
- **Milanese-Style Risotto *or* hot cooked rice**
- **Gremolata**
- **¼ cup cold water**
- **2 tablespoons all-purpose flour**

■ In a large heavy skillet or Dutch oven slowly brown the veal shanks in hot cooking oil. Remove the meat from pan. Add the chopped onion, celery, carrot, and garlic to pan; cook, uncovered, till the onion and celery are tender. Drain off fat. Return the meat to pan. Add the *undrained* tomatoes, the ½ cup water, snipped parsley, wine, bay leaf, bouillon granules, basil, salt, thyme, and pepper. Bring to boiling; reduce heat. Cover and simmer about 1 hour or till the meat is tender. Meanwhile, prepare Milanese-Style Risotto or rice and Gremolata.

■ Remove the meat from pan, reserving cooking liquid. Arrange the meat on one end of a heated serving platter; cover and keep warm. For sauce, combine the ¼ cup cold water and flour; add to cooking liquid.

*Ossobuco and
Milanese-Style Risotto*

Cook and stir till thickened and bubbly. Cook and stir for 1 minute more. To serve, spoon Milanese-Style Risotto or hot cooked rice on remaining portion of platter. Pour some of the sauce over meat. Pass the remaining sauce. Sprinkle Gremolata atop meat. Makes 6 servings.

Gremolata: In a small mixing bowl combine 2 tablespoons snipped *parsley;* 1 clove *garlic,* minced; and 1 teaspoon finely shredded *lemon peel.*

■ Total preparation time: 1½ hours

Milanese-Style Risotto

- **¼ cup chopped onion**
- **¼ cup finely chopped prosciutto *or* fully cooked ham**
- **2 tablespoons butter *or* margarine**
- **2 cups water**
- **1 cup short, medium, *or* long grain rice**
- **2 teaspoons instant beef bouillon granules**
- **⅛ teaspoon thread saffron, crushed**
- **Dash pepper**
- **⅓ cup grated Parmesan *or* Romano cheese**

■ In a medium saucepan cook the chopped onion and prosciutto or ham in hot butter or margarine till onion is tender but not brown.

■ Add the water, rice, beef bouillon granules, crushed saffron, and pepper. Cover with a tight-fitting lid. Bring to boiling; reduce heat. Continue cooking for 15 minutes; do not lift cover. Remove from heat. Let stand, covered, for 5 to 8 minutes. The rice should be tender but still slightly firm and the mixture should be creamy. (If necessary, stir in enough water to make of creamy consistency.) Stir in Parmesan or Romano cheese. Serve with Ossobuco. Makes 6 servings.

■ Total preparation time: 35 minutes

**MENU
DINNER ITALIANO**

Antipasto Tray

Ossobuco

Steamed Asparagus Spears

Milanese-Style Risotto

Italian Bread with Parsley Butter

Spumoni Ice Cream

Red Wine

The star of this company-special menu is *Ossobuco* (OH-soh-BOO-koh), a classic Italian dish featuring veal shanks. "Ossobuco" means "hollow bone." Many people consider the marrow the best part of the bone.

Follow Italian tradition by serving *Ossobuco* with saffron-flavored *Milanese-Style Risotto* (ruh-SOT-o). Italians use arborio wide-grain rice when making risotto, but short, medium, or long grain rice substitute well. The rice should be tender but still slightly firm, and the mixture should be creamy.

ROASTING PORK

Roast meat at a constant 325° oven temperature.

Pork Cut	Approximate Weight	Internal Temperature when Removed from Oven	Approximate Cooking Time (total time)
Shoulder Arm Picnic	5 to 8 lbs.	170°	3 to 4 hrs.
Smoked Shoulder Picnic Whole			
cook-before-eating	5 to 8 lbs.	170°	3 to 4½ hrs.
fully cooked	5 to 8 lbs.	140°	2½ to 3¼ hrs.
Shoulder Arm Roast	3 to 5 lbs.	170°	2 to 3 hrs.
Shoulder Blade Boston Roast	4 to 6 lbs.	170°	3 to 4 hrs.
Boneless Shoulder Blade Boston Roast	3 to 5 lbs.	170°	2 to 3 hrs.
Smoked Shoulder Roll	2 to 3 lbs.	170°	1¼ to 1¾ hrs.
Loin Blade Roast	3 to 4 lbs.	170°	2¼ to 2¾ hrs.
Loin Center Loin Roast	3 to 5 lbs.	170°	1¾ to 2½ hrs.
Loin Center Rib Roast	3 to 5 lbs.	170°	1¾ to 2½ hrs.
Rib Crown Roast	4 to 6 lbs.	170°	2¾ to 3½ hrs.
Boneless Loin Top Loin Roast (double)	3 to 5 lbs.	170°	2 to 3 hrs.
Boneless Loin Top Loin Roast	2 to 4 lbs.	170°	1¼ to 2 hrs.
Loin Sirloin Roast	3 to 5 lbs.	170°	2¼ to 3¼ hrs.
Tenderloin	1 lb.	170°	¾ to 1 hr.
Leg (fresh ham)	12 to 16 lbs.	170°	5 to 6 hrs.
Leg (fresh ham), half	5 to 8 lbs.	170°	3¼ to 4¾ hrs.

To roast pork: Season the roast by sprinkling with salt and pepper. Place the meat, fat side up, on a rack in a shallow roasting pan.

Insert a meat thermometer, placing it so its bulb rests in the center of the thickest portion of the meat, and does not rest in fat or touch a bone.

Do not add water or other liquid, and do not cover the roasting pan. Roast the meat in a 325° oven until the meat thermometer registers the specified internal temperature (see chart above).

For easy carving, let the meat stand about 15 minutes after removing from the oven. Before carving rolled and tied roasts, first remove the string.

Use the roasting times in the chart above as a guide to total cooking time.

Pork Steaks with Dill Sauce

    4   pork shoulder steaks, cut ¾ inch thick
          (2½ to 3 pounds)
    2   tablespoons cooking oil
    ½   cup chopped onion
    ½   cup sliced fresh mushrooms
    1   clove garlic, minced
    ½   cup dry white wine
    2   teaspoons Worcestershire sauce
    1   teaspoon dried dillweed
    1   teaspoon instant chicken bouillon granules
    1   cup dairy sour cream
    2   tablespoons all-purpose flour
        Hot cooked noodles
        Fresh dill or parsley (optional)

■■ In a large skillet brown steaks slowly on both sides in hot cooking oil. Remove steaks from skillet; set aside. Drain, reserving 1 tablespoon drippings in the skillet. Add onion, mushrooms, and garlic; cook till vegetables are tender but not brown.

■■ Remove the skillet from heat; stir in the white wine, Worcestershire sauce, dillweed, and chicken bouillon granules; add pork steaks. Return skillet to heat; cover and simmer over low heat about 40 minutes or till pork is well done.

■■ Remove steaks; keep warm. Skim fat from pan juices. Measure the pan juices and vegetables; add water, if necessary, to equal 1 cup liquid. For dill sauce, combine sour cream and flour. Stir into the pan juices and vegetable mixture in the skillet. Cook and stir till thickened and bubbly. Cook and stir for 1 minute more. Season to taste with salt and pepper.

■■ Place hot cooked noodles on a heated serving platter; arrange pork steaks on noodles. Spoon some of the dill sauce over top; pass remaining. Garnish with fresh dill or parsley, if desired. Makes 4 servings.

■■ Preparation time: 30 minutes
■■ Cooking time: 40 minutes

Grilled Pork Chops with Pineapple-Kumquat Sauce

    4   pork loin chops, cut 1 inch thick
          (1¾ to 2 pounds)
    1   8-ounce can pineapple slices (juice pack)
    ¼   cup slivered almonds
    2   tablespoons butter or margarine
    2   tablespoons brown sugar
    1   tablespoon wine vinegar
    2   teaspoons cornstarch
    ⅓   cup preserved kumquats, drained, sliced,
          and seeded
    2   kiwi, quartered (optional)

■■ Sprinkle the pork chops lightly with salt, place on a grill. Grill chops over *medium* coals for 10 to 12 minutes or till brown on one side.

■■ Meanwhile, for sauce, drain pineapple slices, reserving the juice. Measure juice; add water, if necessary, to equal ½ cup liquid. Set aside. Cut the pineapple slices into ½-inch pieces. In a medium saucepan cook the pineapple and slivered almonds in hot butter or margarine over medium heat for 4 to 5 minutes, stirring constantly. Combine the reserved juice mixture, brown sugar, wine vinegar, and cornstarch; stir into mixture in saucepan. Stir in the kumquats. Cook and stir till thickened and bubbly. Cook and stir for 2 minutes more. Keep warm.

■■ Turn the pork chops; grill for 10 to 12 minutes more or till well done. Spoon some of the sauce over the chops during the last 5 minutes.

■■ Place the chops on a heated serving platter. Pass the remaining sauce. Garnish with kiwi quarters, if desired. Makes 4 servings.

■■ Total preparation time: 25 minutes

If a recipe calls for medium coals, how do you know when the coals are the right temperature? Here's a technique that works every time.

Hold your hand palm-side down just above the hot coals at the height the food will cook. Begin counting "one thousand one, one thousand two," etc. If you need to withdraw your hand after four counts, the coals have reached medium heat.

If you've never tied
pork ribs together,
give it a try. But if
you're sure you're
not adept enough,
have your butcher tie
the ribs for you when
you special-order the
meat.

For a refreshing
finale to a grand
dinner, serve sorbet
(the French word for
sherbet) in chilled
dessert dishes.
Garnish each dish
with a piece of fresh
fruit and mint leaves.

★ *see recipe, page 48*

Rice-Stuffed Rib Crown

4   **pounds pork loin back ribs
      (16 to 20 ribs)**
1   **medium onion, chopped (½ cup)**
½   **medium green pepper, chopped (¼ cup)**
2   **cloves garlic, minced**
2   **tablespoons butter *or* margarine**
1   **16-ounce can tomatoes, cut up**
1   **cup water**
2   **bay leaves**
½   **teaspoon dried thyme, crushed**
½   **teaspoon dried basil, crushed**
¼   **teaspoon salt**
⅛   **teaspoon ground red pepper**
1   **cup long grain rice**
¼   **cup light corn syrup**
1   **teaspoon soy sauce**
      Onion Mums (optional)
      Cherry Tomato Roses (optional)
      Whole bay leaves (optional)

▬ Using kitchen cord or string tie the 2 or 3 slabs of back ribs together, rib side outward, forming a circle and leaving a center 5 inches in diameter (the center is for a rice stuffing that goes in later). Place rib crown in a shallow roasting pan. Roast, uncovered, in a 450° oven for 20 minutes.

▬ Meanwhile, prepare the rice stuffing. In a saucepan cook the onion, green pepper, and garlic in hot butter or margarine till tender but not brown. Stir in the *undrained* tomatoes, water, the 2 bay leaves, the thyme, basil, salt, and red pepper. Stir in uncooked rice. Bring mixture to boiling; reduce heat. Cover and simmer for 15 to 20 minutes or till rice is done and liquid is absorbed.

▬ Remove meat from the oven and drain off fat. Reduce the oven temperature to 350°. Spoon the rice stuffing into center of rib crown. Cover the rice loosely with foil to prevent drying out. Stir together the corn syrup and soy sauce. Brush meat with the corn syrup mixture. Roast in a 350° oven about 1¼ hours more or till meat is done. Brush the rib crown again with corn syrup mixture just before serving. If desired, make Onion Mums and Cherry Tomato Roses for garnish; set aside.

▬ Place the rib crown on a heated serving platter. Garnish with Onion Mums, Cherry Tomato Roses, and whole bay leaves, if desired. To serve, spoon the rice stuffing from the center. Next, cut the cord or string and remove. Use a fork to steady the ribs; cut between the ribs to serve. Makes 4 servings.

Onion Mums: For each "flower," cut off top of a small onion and peel off the outer skin; leave root end intact. Using a sharp, thin-bladed knife, cut onion into quarters from top to about ¼ inch from the root end. Cut each quarter in half again to about ¼ inch from root end. Repeat the cutting, making many small wedge-shaped pieces. Be sure you don't cut through root end. To tint onion flowers orange, use 4 parts yellow food coloring to 1 part red food coloring; add food coloring to ice water. Add the cut onion to ice water; cover and chill in the refrigerator. After soaking onion for a few hours, gently pull back some of the sections, forming flower petals. Let onion soak in water till desired color is obtained.

Cherry Tomato Roses: To make each "rose," score an X on the blossom end of each cherry tomato. Using a sharp knife carefully peel back the skin partway down the side of the tomato to make 4 petals.

▬ Total preparation time: 2 hours

Rice-Stuffed Rib Crown

In a blender container or a food processor bowl combine the drained shrimp, water chestnuts, green onion, egg, and soy sauce. Cover; blend or process to a puree. Set shrimp puree aside.

Slice the pork tenderloin into twelve 1-inch-thick pieces. Place the pieces on the rack of an unheated broiler pan. Broil 3 to 4 inches from heat for 5 minutes. Turn and broil 6 to 7 minutes more or till meat is done. Cool slightly.

To wrap, place one of the meat pieces on an egg roll skin. Spread some of the shrimp puree atop the meat. Fold the egg roll skin, envelope style, over meat, moistening and sealing the seams well. (*Or*, moisten outside edges of the egg roll skin; bring corners of egg roll skin together and press firmly atop meat to seal, pressing skin together firmly atop meat.) Repeat wrapping with the remaining egg roll skins, meat pieces, and shrimp puree.

In a saucepan or deep-fat fryer, heat shortening or oil to 365°. Fry bundles, 2 at a time, in the hot fat for 2 to 3 minutes or till golden brown. Remove from fat with a slotted spoon; drain well on paper toweling. Keep fried bundles hot in a warm oven. Serve with Sweet-Sour Sauce. Makes 6 servings.

Sweet-Sour Sauce: In a small saucepan combine ½ cup unsweetened *pineapple juice* and 1 tablespoon *cornstarch*. Stir in 3 tablespoons *water*, 2 tablespoons *plum jelly*, 1 tablespoon *vinegar*, and 1 tablespoon *soy sauce*. Cook and stir till thickened and bubbly. Cook and stir 2 minutes more.

Preparation time: 20 minutes
Cooking time: 25 minutes

Plan *Egg Rolls Wellington* (pictured above), an Oriental version of the classic beef main dish, for your next dinner party. Serve this impressive pork and shrimp entrée with *Sweet-Sour Sauce* and accompany with julienne vegetables.

Egg Rolls Wellington

1	**4½-ounce can shrimp, rinsed and well drained**
⅓	**cup water chestnuts, drained**
1	**green onion, cut up**
1	**egg**
1	**tablespoon soy sauce**
1	**pound pork tenderloin**
12	**egg roll skins**
	Shortening *or* cooking oil for deep-fat frying
	Sweet-Sour Sauce

Southern-Style Barbecued Ribs

4 pounds pork loin country-style ribs
1 medium onion, chopped (½ cup)
½ cup light molasses
½ cup catsup
2 teaspoons finely shredded orange peel
⅓ cup orange juice
2 tablespoons cooking oil
1 tablespoon vinegar
1 tablespoon bottled steak sauce
½ teaspoon prepared mustard
½ teaspoon Worcestershire sauce
¼ teaspoon garlic powder
¼ teaspoon salt
¼ teaspoon pepper
¼ teaspoon bottled hot pepper sauce
⅛ teaspoon ground cloves

■ In a large saucepan or Dutch oven add enough water to the ribs to cover. Bring the mixture to boiling; reduce heat. Cover; simmer the ribs for 45 to 60 minutes or till tender. Remove from the heat; thoroughly drain the ribs.

■ Meanwhile, prepare the sauce. To make sauce, in a small saucepan combine the chopped onion, molasses, catsup, orange peel and juice, cooking oil, vinegar, steak sauce, prepared mustard, Worcestershire sauce, garlic powder, salt, pepper, hot pepper sauce, and cloves. Bring the mixture to boiling; reduce heat. Boil sauce gently, uncovered, for 15 to 20 minutes or till the sauce is reduced to 1½ cups; stir once or twice.

■ Grill the ribs over *slow* coals. (Hold hand, palm-side down, about 4 inches above the hot coals. Count "one thousand one, one thousand two," etc. If you need to withdraw your hand after five or six counts, the coals are slow.) Grill the ribs about 45 minutes, turning every 15 minutes and brushing with the sauce till the ribs are well coated. Arrange the ribs on a heated serving platter. Pass the remaining sauce. Makes 6 servings.

■ Total preparation time: 2 hours

Chinese Mandarin Ribs

6 pounds pork loin back ribs *or* meaty spareribs, cut into serving-size pieces
1 cup soy sauce
½ cup cooking oil
1 clove garlic, minced
1 tablespoon dry mustard
2 teaspoons ground ginger
½ cup orange marmalade
Green onion brushes (optional)

■ Place a large plastic bag in a large bowl. Add the ribs. For the marinade, combine soy sauce, cooking oil, garlic, dry mustard, and ginger. Pour marinade over the ribs; close bag tightly. Place in the refrigerator. Marinate for 6 hours, turning bag several times to distribute the seasonings. Drain ribs; reserve *1 cup* of the marinade.

■ Place the ribs, meaty side down, in a deep roasting pan. Roast, uncovered, in a 450° oven for 30 minutes. Drain off fat. Turn ribs meaty side up. Reduce oven temperature to 350°. Roast ribs, covered, for 1 to 1½ hours or till tender.

■ Meanwhile, prepare the glaze. To make the glaze, in a small saucepan stir together the reserved marinade and orange marmalade. Heat thoroughly, stirring occasionally.

■ Uncover the ribs the last 10 minutes of roasting. Brush ribs with the glaze. Just before serving, brush ribs with additional glaze. To serve, arrange ribs on a heated serving platter. Garnish with green onion brushes, if desired (see directions at right). Pass any remaining glaze. Makes 6 servings.

■ Preparation time: 20 minutes
■ Marinating time: at least 6 hours
■ Cooking time: 2 hours

Impress your dinner guests by tempting them with food that's as appealing to the eye as it is to the palate. Do this by adding an attractive garnish that contrasts in color and texture with the entrée. Remember, however, always use garnishes simply and sparingly; they should never overpower the food.

Add a dash of excitement when you present a rib platter by garnishing it with green onion brushes. To make the brushes, slice off the roots and most of the top portion from the ends of green onions. Make slashes at both ends to produce a fringe. Place the green onions in ice water, and the ends will curl back to resemble brushes.

This year, volunteer to serve Easter dinner at your house. It's easy—when you have a menu that takes advantage of make-ahead recipes. Make the dessert and rolls the day before.

Early on Easter Sunday set the table with your best dinnerware. A fresh spring flower arrangement adds a festive touch for a centerpiece.

Just before your guests arrive, put on the ham and prepare the vegetables.

see recipe, page 164

Ham Lasagna

- 1 10-ounce package frozen cut broccoli
- ¼ cup butter *or* margarine
- ¼ cup all-purpose flour
- ¼ teaspoon ground nutmeg
- ¼ teaspoon pepper
- 2¼ cups milk
- ¾ cup grated Romano *or* Parmesan cheese
- 8 ounces lasagna noodles
- 2 tablespoons cooking oil
- 3 cups cubed fully cooked ham
- 12 ounces thinly sliced mozzarella *or* Monterey Jack cheese
- 2 4-ounce cans sliced mushrooms, drained Paprika

■ Thaw broccoli. In a saucepan cook broccoli in a small amount of boiling water for 4 minutes or till crisp-tender. Drain well. Pat broccoli dry on paper toweling.

■ To make sauce, in a heavy saucepan melt butter or margarine. Stir in the flour, nutmeg, and pepper. Add the milk all at once. Cook and stir till thickened and bubbly. Cook and stir 1 minute more. Add the Romano or Parmesan cheese; cook and stir till melted.

■ In a large saucepan cook noodles till tender in boiling salted water with cooking oil added to water. Drain; rinse noodles.

■ Layer *one-third* of noodles in a greased 13x9x2-inch baking dish. Arrange broccoli on top of noodles. Add *half* of ham, *half* of cheese, and *one-third* of sauce. Make another layer of noodles. Arrange mushrooms atop noodles. Add remaining ham, remaining cheese, and another *one-third* of the sauce. Make another layer of noodles; cover with remaining sauce.

■ Bake, uncovered, in a 375° oven for 25 to 30 minutes or till heated through. (*Or,* assemble in advance and chill; bake 45 minutes or till hot.) Sprinkle with paprika. Let stand 10 minutes. Serves 10.

■ Preparation time: 1 hour
■ Cooking time: 30 minutes
■ Standing time: 10 minutes

Raspberry-Wine Glazed Ham

- 1 4- to 5-pound fully cooked boneless ham
- ¼ cup dry white wine
- 2 tablespoons lemon juice
- 2 teaspoons cornstarch
- ⅓ cup seedless red raspberry jam
- 1 tablespoon butter *or* margarine Watercress (optional)

■ Trim fat from ham. If desired, score the ham using a sharp knife to make shallow cuts diagonally across the ham in a diamond pattern. (For a cutting guide, use a strip of paper.) Make the cuts in the ham only about ¼ inch deep.

■ Place ham on a rack in a shallow baking pan. Insert a meat thermometer, placing it so its bulb rests in center of the thickest portion of the meat and does not rest in fat. *Do not add water or other liquid, and do not cover baking pan.* Bake ham in a 325° oven for 1½ to 1¾ hours or till meat thermometer registers 140°.

■ Meanwhile, prepare the glaze. To make glaze, in a small saucepan stir white wine and lemon juice into the cornstarch. Add about *half* of the raspberry jam. Cook and stir till thickened and bubbly. Cook and stir 2 minutes more. Stir in the remaining jam. Add the butter or margarine. Heat and stir the mixture till butter or margarine is melted.

■ To glaze the ham, spoon fat from baking pan 20 to 30 minutes before the end of baking time. Brush ham with the glaze. Continue baking and basting with the glaze till the thermometer registers 140°. Spoon any of the remaining glaze over ham. Garnish with watercress, if desired. Makes 12 servings.

■ Total preparation time: 2 hours

Ham and Artichoke-Stuffed Crepes

Basic Crepes
2 **eggs**
¼ **cup butter** *or* **margarine**
¼ **cup all-purpose flour**
2 **cups light cream** *or* **milk**
¼ **teaspoon finely shredded lemon peel**
¼ **cup dry white wine**
1 **14-ounce can artichoke hearts, drained**
1½ **cups diced fully cooked ham**
½ **cup sliced fresh mushrooms**
¼ **cup rusk crumbs (about 2 rusks)** *or* **fine dry bread crumbs**
¼ **cup snipped parsley**
Paprika

◼ Prepare Basic Crepes (see the recipe at right). Set aside. (For the directions on freezing crepes ahead, see the information at far right.)

◼ To hard-cook eggs, place eggs in a saucepan; cover with cold water. Bring to boiling; reduce heat to just below simmering. Cover and cook for 15 minutes. Run cold water over eggs till cool. Remove shells; slice the eggs. Set the eggs aside.

◼ Meanwhile, prepare the wine sauce. To make the sauce, in a medium saucepan melt the butter or margarine. Stir in flour. Add light cream or milk all at once; add lemon peel. Cook and stir over medium heat till thickened and bubbly. Cook and stir 1 to 2 minutes more. Stir in wine. Set the sauce aside.

◼ For the filling, chop drained artichokes; combine with ham, sliced mushrooms, crumbs, and snipped parsley. Stir in *½ cup* of the wine sauce. Cover the remaining sauce; set aside.

◼ To fill the crepes, spoon about *2 to 3 tablespoons* of the filling along center of unbrowned side of *each* crepe. Fold two opposite edges so they overlap atop filling. Fold remaining edges toward center to form a square packet (see photograph at right).

◼ Place the crepes, seam side down, in a greased 13x9x2-inch baking dish. Cover the baking dish with foil. Bake in a 375° oven for 20 minutes or till heated through. Cook and stir the remaining wine sauce over low heat till heated through. Remove the crepes from the oven. Spoon the hot sauce over the crepes. To garnish, arrange the slices of hard-cooked egg down the center of crepes lengthwise. Sprinkle the egg slices with a little paprika. Makes 6 servings.

Basic Crepes: In a small mixing bowl combine 1½ cups *milk,* 1 cup all-purpose *flour,* 2 *eggs,* 1 tablespoon *cooking oil,* and ¼ teaspoon *salt.* Beat with a rotary beater till combined. Heat a lightly greased 6-inch skillet. Remove from heat. Spoon in about *2 tablespoons* of the crepe batter; lift and tilt skillet to spread the batter. Return skillet to heat; brown on one side only. (*Or,* cook on an inverted crepe pan.) Invert the pan over paper toweling; remove crepe. Repeat to make 16 to 18 crepes, greasing skillet occasionally.

◼ Preparation time: 1½ hours
◼ Cooking time: 20 minutes

Spoon the filling into center of the crepe. Next, fold the two opposite edges so they overlap atop the filling. Then, fold the remaining edges toward the center to form a square packet, as shown. Place the crepes seam side down for baking and serving.

No rule says you must make crepes the same day you plan to use them. In fact, you can make them a day, a week, or up to four months ahead and store them in your freezer.

Just make a stack, alternating each crepe with 2 layers of waxed paper. Then, overwrap the stack in a moisture-vaporproof bag and freeze.

Let the crepes thaw at room temperature about 1 hour before using.

To roast lamb: Season the lamb roast by sprinkling with salt and pepper. Place meat, fat side up, on a rack in a shallow roasting pan.

Insert a meat thermometer into the roast so the thermometer's bulb rests in the center of the thickest portion of meat. It should not rest in fat, touch bone, nor rest on the bottom of the roasting pan.

Do not add water or other liquid; do not cover the roasting pan. Roast the meat in a 325° oven till the meat thermometer registers the desired internal temperature.

For easy carving, let the meat stand about l5 minutes. Remove and discard the string from rolled and tied roasts.

Use the roasting times in the chart at right as a guide to the total cooking time for the cut of meat you are preparing.

■ROASTING LAMB■

Roast meat at a constant 325° oven temperature.

Lamb Cut	Approximate Weight	Internal Temperature on Removal from Oven	Approximate Cooking Time (total time)
Leg, whole	5 to 9 lbs.	140° (rare) 160° (medium) 170° to 180° (well done)	2 to 3 hrs. 2½ to 3¾ hrs. 3 to 4½ hrs.
Leg, half	3 to 4 lbs.	160° (medium)	1½ to 1¾ hrs.
Square Cut Shoulder	4 to 6 lbs.	160° (medium)	2 to 2½ hrs.
Boneless Shoulder	3 to 5 lbs.	160° (medium)	2 to 3 hrs.
Crown Roast	3 to 4 lbs.	140° (rare) 160° (medium) 170° to 180° (well done)	1¾ to 2 hrs. 2 to 2¼ hrs. 2¼ to 2¾ hrs.

Italian Lamb Stew

1½	**pounds boneless lamb, cut into ½-inch pieces**
1	**tablespoon cooking oil**
1	**small onion, thinly sliced and separated into rings**
1	**clove garlic, minced**
6	**cups beef broth**
1	**tablespoon lemon juice**
2	**teaspoons dried oregano, crushed**
1	**teaspoon dried basil, crushed**
½	**teaspoon salt**
	Dash pepper
2	**medium tomatoes, cut into wedges**
1	**large green *or* red sweet pepper, cut into 1-inch pieces**
1	**small zucchini, thinly sliced**
¼	**cup snipped parsley**

■ In a large saucepan or Dutch oven brown the lamb, half at a time, in hot cooking oil. Remove meat and set aside, reserving drippings in pan. Cook onion and garlic in reserved drippings till tender but not brown. Drain off fat. Return all meat to pan; add beef broth, lemon juice, oregano, basil, salt, and pepper. Bring the mixture to boiling; reduce heat. Cover and simmer for 45 minutes.

■ Stir in the tomatoes, green or red sweet pepper, sliced zucchini, and snipped parsley. Simmer the mixture, uncovered, about 15 minutes more or till lamb and vegetables are tender. Makes 6 servings.

■ Preparation time: 30 minutes
■ Cooking time: 1 hour

Lamb Chops Supreme

6 **lamb leg sirloin chops, cut 1 inch thick**
12 **slices bacon**
6 **chicken livers, halved**
2 **tablespoons Dijon-style mustard**
¼ **teaspoon dried tarragon, crushed**
¼ **teaspoon dried rosemary, crushed**

■■ Cut a pocket in each chop; set aside. Partially cook bacon; set aside. Cook livers in bacon drippings over medium heat for 5 minutes; set aside.

■■ Combine mustard, tarragon, and rosemary; spread *1 teaspoon* in the pocket of *each* chop. Place *2 liver halves* into *each* chop. Wrap *2 slices* of bacon around the outside of *each* chop; fasten with wooden picks. Place chops on rack of unheated broiler pan. Broil 4 to 5 inches from heat for 6 to 7 minutes. Turn; broil for 5 to 6 minutes more or till done. Serves 6.

■ Preparation time: 20 minutes
■ Cooking time: 15 minutes

Sweet-Sour Lamb Chops

¾ **cup catsup**
¼ **cup packed brown sugar**
¼ **cup vinegar**
½ **teaspoon chili powder**
2 **tablespoons orange liqueur**
12 **lamb loin chops, cut 1 inch thick**

■■ For sauce, combine catsup, brown sugar, vinegar, and chili powder. Bring to boiling; reduce heat. Simmer, uncovered, for 15 minutes. Stir in liqueur.

■■ Meanwhile, place lamb chops on rack of unheated broiler pan. Broil 4 to 5 inches from heat for 6 to 7 minutes. Turn chops; broil 5 to 6 minutes more, brushing often with sauce. Pass sauce. Serves 6.

■ Total preparation time: 25 minutes

Lamb Chops with Orange-Papaya Sauce

1 **cup water**
¾ **cup dry white wine**
1 **teaspoon finely shredded lemon peel**
3 **tablespoons lemon juice**
3 **cloves garlic, halved**
1 **teaspoon ground ginger**
6 **lamb leg sirloin chops**
   or **loin chops, cut 1 inch thick**
   Orange-Papaya Sauce

■■ For marinade, combine the water, wine, lemon peel, lemon juice, garlic, and ground ginger. Place lamb chops in a large plastic bag set in a deep bowl. Pour the marinade over the chops; close bag tightly. Marinate in the refrigerator for 6 hours, turning bag several times to coat lamb evenly with the marinade. Drain chops; discard the marinade.

■■ Place lamb chops on grill. Grill over *medium* coals for 10 to 12 minutes. (Hold hand, palm-side down, just above coals. Count "one thousand one, one thousand two," etc. If you need to withdraw your hand after four counts, the coals are medium.) Meanwhile, prepare Orange-Papaya Sauce. Turn the lamb chops and grill for 10 to 12 minutes more or till done, brushing frequently with some of the Orange-Papaya Sauce. Pass the remaining sauce. Makes 6 servings.

Orange-Papaya Sauce: In a small saucepan combine 2 tablespoons *brown sugar,* 1 tablespoon *cornstarch,* ½ teaspoon *salt,* and ½ teaspoon ground *ginger.* Stir in 1½ teaspoons finely shredded *orange peel,* 1 cup *orange juice,* and 1 tablespoon snipped fresh *mint leaves or* 1 teaspoon dried *mint flakes.* Cook and stir till thickened and bubbly. Cook and stir for 2 minutes more. Stir in 1 *papaya,* peeled, seeded, and cut up; 1 *orange,* peeled, sectioned, and cut up; and 2 tablespoons *butter or margarine.* Heat through; keep warm over low heat or on grill.

■ Preparation time: 10 minutes
■ Marinating time: 6 to 24 hours
■ Cooking time: 20 to 24 minutes

For a change of pace, broil—rather than grill—*Lamb Chops with Orange-Papaya Sauce.* Just follow these easy instructions.

Place the chops on the rack of an unheated broiler pan. Broil 3 inches from heat for 10 to 12 minutes for medium or for 14 to 16 minutes for well done, turning once.

Brush the lamb chops frequently with *Orange-Papaya Sauce* during the last 2 to 3 minutes of cooking. Pass the remaining sauce.

When you are ready to prepare a turkey, you can use either of two methods to thaw the bird. One way is to put the turkey in the refrigerator. Leave the original wrap on the frozen bird and place the bird on a tray. Thaw in the refrigerator, allowing 3 to 4 days for turkey to thaw (about 24 hours for each 5 pounds).

The other method of thawing is in cold water. Place the frozen turkey in its original wrap in a sink filled with cold water. Change the water every 30 minutes. Allow about 30 minutes thawing time for each pound of turkey.

ROASTING DOMESTIC BIRDS

Poultry	Ready-to-Cook Weight	Oven Temperature	Guide to Roasting Time	Special Instructions
Chicken	1½ to 2 lbs.	400°	1 to 1¼ hrs.	Brush the dry areas of skin occasionally with pan drippings. Cover chicken loosely with foil.
	2½ to 3 lbs.	375°	1¼ to 1½ hrs.	
	3½ to 4 lbs.	375°	1¾ to 2 hrs.	
	4½ to 5 lbs.	375°	2¼ to 2½ hrs.	
Capon	4 to 7 lbs.	375°	2 to 3 hrs.	Brush the dry areas with pan drippings. Roast as above.
Cornish Game Hen	1 to 1½ lbs.	375°	1½ hrs.	Cover loosely with foil and roast for ½ hour. Uncover and roast about 1 hour or till done. If desired, baste occasionally during the last hour of roasting.
Stuffed Whole Turkey	8 to 12 lbs.	325°	3½ to 4½ hrs.	Cover the bird loosely with foil. Press lightly at the end of drumsticks and neck; leave an air space between bird and foil. Baste bird occasionally, if desired. Uncover the last 30 minutes of roasting.
	12 to 16 lbs.	325°	4 to 5 hrs.	
	16 to 20 lbs.	325°	4½ to 5½ hrs.	
	20 to 24 lbs.	325°	5 to 6½ hrs.	
Foil-Wrapped Turkey	8 to 10 lbs.	450°	1¼ to 1¾ hrs.	Wrap the turkey, breast side up, in a piece of greased, heavy foil. Place the bird in a roasting pan without a rack. Roast in a 450° oven. Open the foil the last 20 minutes of roasting to brown the turkey.
	10 to 12 lbs.	450°	1¾ to 2¼ hrs.	
	12 to 16 lbs.	450°	2¼ to 3 hrs.	
	16 to 20 lbs.	450°	3 to 3½ hrs.	
	20 to 24 lbs.	450°	3½ to 4½ hrs.	
Domestic Duckling	3 to 5 lbs.	375°	1½ to 2¼ hrs.	Prick skin well all over. During roasting, spoon off fat. Do not rub the bird with oil.
Domestic Goose	7 to 9 lbs.	350°	2½ to 3 hrs.	Prick skin well all over. During roasting, spoon off fat. Do not rub the bird with oil.
	9 to 11 lbs.	350°	3 to 3½ hrs.	
	11 to 13 lbs.	350°	3½ to 4 hrs.	
Guinea Hen	1½ to 2 lbs.	375°	¾ to 1 hr.	Place uncooked sliced bacon over breast. Roast, loosely covered with foil. Uncover hen the last 20 minutes of roasting.
	2 to 2½ lbs.	375°	1 to 1½ hrs.	

Preparation for roasting: Remove the giblets and neck piece from body and neck cavities. Rinse bird; pat dry with paper toweling. Rub cavities with salt, if desired. *Do not stuff bird until just before cooking.*

To stuff a bird, loosely spoon some stuffing into neck cavity; pull neck skin over stuffing and fasten skin securely to the back with a skewer. Loosely spoon stuffing into body cavity. If the turkey has a band of skin across the tail, tuck the drumsticks under band; if band of skin is not present, tie legs securely to tail. Twist wing tips under back.

For an unstuffed bird, place quartered onions and celery sticks into the body cavity of the bird, if desired. Prepare and roast the bird. Discard the vegetables after roasting, if desired.

Roasting directions: Place the bird, breast side up, on a rack in a shallow roasting pan. Brush skin of bird, *except* duckling and goose, with cooking oil. If a meat thermometer is used, insert it into the center of the inside thigh muscle, making sure the bulb does not touch a bone.

Roast in an uncovered pan (unless specified otherwise) according to the chart at left. When the bird is two-thirds done, cut the band of skin or string between legs so thighs will cook evenly. Continue roasting until done. Remove bird from oven; cover loosely with foil to keep warm. Let stand 15 minutes before carving.

Test for doneness: The meat thermometer inserted in the thigh should register 180° to 185° and the thickest part of the drumstick should feel very soft when pressed between fingers. The drumstick also should move up and down and twist easily in the socket. Remember, roasting times can be only approximate because birds differ in size, shape, or variety.

To roast turkey in a covered roasting pan: Rinse the turkey and pat dry. Stuff, if desired. Prepare for roasting as directed above. Place turkey, breast side up, on a rack in a roasting pan. Brush the skin with cooking oil or melted butter. Insert a meat thermometer into the center of the inside thigh muscle, making sure the bulb does not touch bone. Do not add water. Cover the roasting pan with a lid having the vent open. Roast the bird in a 325° oven allowing about 20 to 25 minutes per pound. Remove the cover; drain and reserve pan juices. Increase oven temperature to 475°.

Continue roasting about 20 minutes more or till turkey is browned. When bird is done, the meat thermometer should register 180° to 185° and the drumstick should twist easily in the socket.

To roast turkey in a commercial cooking bag: Rinse turkey and pat dry. Stuff, if desired; prepare for roasting as directed at left. Place 1 tablespoon *all-purpose flour* in the commercial cooking bag; shake to coat interior. Place bag in a large roasting pan. Brush turkey with cooking oil or melted butter. Place turkey inside bag, breast side up. Close bag loosely with a twist tie. Make six ½-inch slits in the top of the bag to allow for escape of steam. Roast according to manufacturer's directions. About 15 minutes before the end of the roasting time, cut the bag open. Insert a meat thermometer into the center of the inside thigh muscle of turkey, making sure bulb does not touch bone. When the turkey is done, the meat thermometer should register 180° to 185° and the drumstick should twist easily in the socket.

Carving: Remove the bird from the oven and let stand for 15 minutes before carving; cover to keep the bird warm. Place bird, breast side up, onto a carving board. Grasp the leg with your fingers; pull leg away from the body of the bird. Cut through the meat between thigh and body. With the tip of the knife, disjoint the thigh bone from the backbone. Holding the leg vertically, with large end down, slice meat parallel to the bone and under some tendons, turning leg for even slices. Or, first separate the thigh and drumstick. Slice thigh meat by cutting slices parallel to the bone.

Before carving the white meat, make a deep horizontal cut into the breast close to the wing. Note that the wing tips have been twisted under the back before roasting so that carving can be done without removing wings. Cut thin slices from the top of the breast down to the horizontal cut. Final smaller slices can follow the curve of the breastbone. Turn the bird and repeat each step to carve the other side of the bird.

Select squab (young
farm-bred pigeons)
for the main course,
or, if you like,
substitute Cornish
game hens for the
squab. While the
entrée cooks,
arrange the first-
course salads using
a slice of red
cabbage for the
base. Arrange leaves
of both kinds of
endive atop the
cabbage slice.

★ see recipe, page 157

Squab Calvados

3 large apples, peeled, cored, and
   chopped (about 3 cups)
2 tablespoons butter or margarine
½ cup snipped dried figs
3 tablespoons Calvados, apple brandy,
   or brandy
1 teaspoon lemon juice
⅛ teaspoon ground nutmeg
⅓ cup apple jelly
4 12- to 16-ounce ready-to-cook squab
   or four 1¼-pound Cornish game hens
Butter or margarine, melted
Deep-Fried Rice Sticks
Cooking oil for deep-fat frying

■■■ In a skillet cook apples in the 2 tablespoons hot
butter for 2 minutes. Remove from heat. Stir in figs, *2
tablespoons* of the Calvados or brandy, lemon juice,
and nutmeg. For glaze, melt jelly. Remove from heat;
stir in the remaining Calvados or brandy.

■■■ Season cavities of squab or Cornish hens with
salt and pepper. Lightly stuff birds with fruit mixture.
Tie legs together with string. Place birds, breast side
up, on rack in a shallow roasting pan. Brush skin with
a little melted butter; cover loosely with foil. Roast
squab in a 375° oven for 30 minutes. Uncover; roast
about 30 minutes more or till birds are tender. (Roast
Cornish hens, covered, in a 375° oven for 30 minutes.
Uncover; roast about 1 hour more.) Brush birds with
some of the glaze the last 15 minutes of roasting.

■■■ Arrange birds on a serving platter. Brush with
the remaining glaze. Top with Deep-Fried Rice Sticks.
If desired, garnish with curly endive, dried figs, and
kumquats. Makes 4 servings.

Deep-Fried Rice Sticks: Fry 2 ounces unsoaked
rice sticks, a few at a time, in deep hot cooking oil
(375°) about 5 seconds or just till sticks puff and rise
to top. Remove with a slotted spoon or wire strainer;
drain on paper toweling. Keep warm in the oven.

■■■ Preparation time: 30 minutes
■■■ Cooking time: 1 hour (squab); 1½ hours (hens)

This hearty main dish with its unusual-sounding, fun-to-say name—*Cock-a-Leekie Soup*—is a Scottish soup made with chicken broth, cooked chicken, and leeks.

Build a casual dinner party around the soup by adding a crisp salad and a variety of breads, rolls, and crackers. Top off the dinner with a chilled fresh fruit dessert.

Cock-a-Leekie Soup*

- 1   2½- to 3-pound broiler-fryer chicken, cut up
- 4   cups water
- 1   cup finely chopped carrot
- 1   cup finely chopped celery
- ½   cup finely chopped onion
- 2   sprigs parsley
- 2   teaspoons salt
- ¼   teaspoon white pepper *or* pepper
- 1   bay leaf
- 1½   cups thinly sliced leeks (½ pound)
- 1   small potato, peeled and chopped (½ cup)
- ½   cup quick-cooking barley
- 2   cups light cream
    Sliced leeks (optional)

■ In a large kettle or Dutch oven combine the cut-up chicken and water. Add carrot, celery, onion, parsley, salt, pepper, and bay leaf. Bring to boiling; reduce heat. Cover and simmer for 25 to 30 minutes or till chicken is tender.

■ Remove chicken pieces, bay leaf, and parsley from the broth. Discard bay leaf and parsley. Let chicken and broth cool. When chicken is cool enough to handle, remove meat, discarding skin and bones. Chop meat and set aside. Skim off fat from the broth. Add the 1½ cups leeks, chopped potato, and barley to the broth. Bring mixture to boiling; reduce heat. Cover and simmer 15 to 20 minutes.

■ Stir in the light cream and reserved chopped chicken. Heat soup through. To serve, ladle soup into individual soup bowls and top with additional sliced leeks, if desired. Makes 6 servings.

■ Preparation time: 55 minutes
■ Cooling time: at least 30 minutes
■ Cooking time: 30 minutes
* *pictured on page 13*

Oyster-Potato Stuffed Turkey

- 6   medium potatoes, peeled
- ½   pound bulk pork sausage
- 2   cups chopped celery
- 1   cup shredded carrot
- ½   cup chopped onion
- 1   8-ounce can oysters *or*
    1 pint shucked oysters
- 3   cups crumbled corn bread
- 1½   teaspoons poultry seasoning
- ½   teaspoon salt
- ⅛   teaspoon pepper
- 1   16- to 20-pound turkey
    Cooking oil

■ Coarsely shred the peeled potatoes. Place shredded potatoes in a large bowl of cold water; set the potatoes aside.

■ In Dutch oven cook sausage till done. Drain sausage, reserving drippings in Dutch oven; set sausage aside. Drain potatoes well; add to drippings along with celery, carrot, and onion. Cover and cook vegetables over medium heat 8 to 10 minutes or till tender, stirring occasionally.

■ Drain oysters, reserving ½ cup liquid (add water if necessary). Cut up the oysters. In a large bowl combine oysters, sausage, vegetables, crumbled corn bread, poultry seasoning, salt, and pepper. Add oyster liquid, tossing gently to moisten. *(Do not stuff the turkey until just before roasting.)*

■ Sprinkle the cavity of turkey with salt. Follow the preparation and roasting directions on pages 80 and 81, using the oyster-potato mixture for stuffing and brushing turkey with cooking oil. Roast turkey till done according to the tests for doneness on page 81 and carve the bird following the suggestions on page 81. Makes 16 to 20 servings.

■ Preparation time: 1½ hours
■ Cooking time: 5½ to 7 hours

Cheese-Filled Chicken Breasts

 3 whole large chicken breasts
 1 3-ounce package cream cheese, softened
 2 tablespoons finely chopped ripe olives
 ⅛ teaspoon thread saffron, crushed
 6 large fresh mushroom caps
 1 egg
 1 tablespoon water
 ½ cup seasoned fine dry bread crumbs
 2 tablespoons snipped parsley
 3 tablespoons all-purpose flour

■ Remove skin from chicken breasts; discard. Split chicken breasts in half lengthwise. To remove bones from chicken breasts: Hold chicken breast half, bone side down. Starting from the breastbone side of the breast, cut meat away from the bone using a thin sharp knife (see top photograph at right). Cut as close to the bone as possible.

■ Place each piece of chicken between two pieces of clear plastic wrap. With a meat mallet pound chicken breast halves to ¼-inch thickness; remove plastic wrap. Sprinkle with salt.

■ In a bowl stir together the softened cream cheese, finely chopped ripe olives, and saffron. Spread the cheese mixture on one side of each breast half. Center one mushroom cap atop each breast half. Fold in edges of chicken envelope-style (see bottom photograph at right).

■ Mix egg and water. Combine the dry bread crumbs and snipped parsley. Dip chicken rolls in flour; then dip them in the egg-water mixture. Roll in crumb-parsley mixture on all sides. Place in a 10x6x2-inch baking dish. Bake in a 350° oven for 45 to 50 minutes or till done. Drain on paper toweling. Cool. Cover and chill in the refrigerator for 2 hours or till serving time. Makes 6 servings.

■ Preparation time: 45 minutes
■ Cooking time: 50 minutes
■ Chilling time: at least 2 hours

To remove bones from chicken, place each chicken breast half, bone side down, on a work surface. Start from the breastbone side and cut the meat away from the bone, as shown, cutting as close to the bone as possible.

Spread some of the cheese mixture on one side of each boned chicken breast. Then, place a fresh mushroom cap atop each. Fold in the edges of the chicken breast half envelope-style, as shown.

Tetrazzini-Style Chicken

 1 7-ounce package spaghetti, broken up
 1 10¾-ounce can condensed cream
   of chicken soup
 ⅓ cup grated Parmesan cheese
 3 tablespoons dry sherry
 1 teaspoon dried parsley flakes
 2 5-ounce cans chunk-style chicken
 1 4-ounce can sliced mushrooms, drained

■ Cook spaghetti in a large amount of boiling water about 10 minutes or till tender. Meanwhile, in a large saucepan combine soup, *half* of the cheese, the sherry, parsley, and ½ cup *water*. Bring to boiling. Stir in chicken and mushrooms. Drain spaghetti; add to saucepan. Cook and stir till hot. Turn into serving dish; sprinkle with remaining cheese. Makes 4 servings.

■ Total preparation time: 25 minutes

When the entertaining budget needs stretching but you still want to feature an elegant main dish, try this menu. The entrée is a delectable take off on the classic Italian dish made with precious veal.

To simplify the menu, prepare the soup several hours in advance, then chill it. The tart also should be made early enough to cool to room temperature. If making homemade pasta, you can chill the dough for up to 3 days before cutting and cooking it.

★ see the index for page number

Chicken Marsala*

3 large carrots, cut into julienne strips
3 stalks celery, bias-sliced into 1-inch pieces
2 cups fresh or frozen brussels sprouts (halve any large ones)
3 whole medium chicken breasts, skinned, halved lengthwise, and boned
2 cups sliced fresh mushrooms
¼ cup sliced green onion
4 tablespoons butter or margarine
1 cup chicken broth
⅓ cup Marsala or dry sherry

■■■ Place carrots, celery, and brussels sprouts in steamer basket over boiling water. Cover and steam for 10 minutes or till just tender. Keep warm.

■■■ Place each chicken breast half between two pieces of clear plastic wrap. Pound with the flat side of a meat mallet to ¼-inch thickness. Remove plastic. Halve each piece of chicken lengthwise.

■■■ In a large skillet cook the mushrooms and green onion in 2 tablespoons of the hot butter or margarine till just tender. Remove from the skillet.

■■■ In a large skillet cook half the chicken in the remaining hot butter or margarine over medium-high heat about 2 minutes on each side. Remove from skillet. Repeat with the remaining chicken. (Add more butter or margarine, if necessary.) For sauce, to the skillet drippings add chicken broth and Marsala or dry sherry. Bring to boiling; simmer, uncovered, till liquid is reduced to half. Return chicken and the mushroom mixture to the skillet. Heat through.

■■■ Arrange steamed vegetables and chicken on serving platter. Spoon mushroom mixture and sauce atop chicken. Serve immediately. Makes 6 servings.

■■■ Total preparation time: 45 minutes
* pictured on the cover

Herbed Chicken Stir-Fry

2 tablespoons all-purpose flour
2 teaspoons instant chicken bouillon granules
1 teaspoon seasoned salt
½ teaspoon dried basil, crushed
¼ teaspoon dried oregano, crushed
¾ cup cold water
1 small onion, chopped (¼ cup)
1 clove garlic, minced
2 tablespoons cooking oil
2 whole medium chicken breasts, skinned, halved lengthwise, boned, and cubed
3 medium zucchini, thinly sliced
3 tomatoes, cut into eighths
Chow mein noodles (optional)

■■■ In a small bowl combine the flour, bouillon granules, seasoned salt, basil, and oregano. Stir in the cold water till combined; set aside.

■■■ In a large skillet or wok stir-fry the onion and garlic in hot oil till tender. Remove onion and garlic from the skillet; set aside.

■■■ Stir-fry the chicken in a skillet or wok, half at a time, for 3 to 4 minutes. (Add more oil, if necessary.) Remove chicken from the skillet; set aside. Add zucchini; stir-fry 5 minutes. Add bouillon mixture and tomatoes; cook and stir till mixture is bubbly. Add the chicken and onion-garlic mixture to the skillet. Cover and cook 1 minute more. Serve with chow mein noodles, if desired. Makes 4 servings.

■■■ Total preparation time: 40 minutes

Chicken Marsala

When preparing *Barbecued Poultry with Bacon and Rice Stuffing* for four servings, use the stuffing ingredients, as indicated in the recipe, with any of the following poultry selections: one 3- to 4-pound whole roasting chicken; one 4- to 5-pound domestic duck or wild goose; two 2-pound wild ducks or pheasants; four 1- to 1½-pound Cornish game hens; eight 4- to 6-ounce quail.

Barbecued Poultry with Bacon and Rice Stuffing

   Hickory chips (about 6 cups)
 2 slices bacon
 ½ cup chopped carrot
 ½ cup chopped celery
 ¼ cup thinly sliced green onion
 1 cup chicken broth
 ½ cup long grain rice
 1 tablespoon soy sauce
 1 teaspoon poultry seasoning
   Choice of poultry (see selections listed at left)
   Cooking oil, melted butter *or* margarine, *or* bacon slices
   Endive (optional)

■ About 1 hour before cooking time, soak the hickory chips in enough water to cover.

■ To prepare the stuffing, cook bacon in a saucepan till crisp. Drain, reserving drippings in saucepan. Crumble bacon; set aside. Cook carrot, celery, and onion in reserved drippings about 5 minutes. Add chicken broth, *uncooked* rice, soy sauce, and poultry seasoning. Bring to boiling; reduce heat. Cover and cook over low heat for 20 to 25 minutes or till liquid is absorbed. Stir in crumbled bacon; set aside.

■ To prepare the poultry, rinse in cold running water and pat dry with paper toweling. Season the body cavity with a little salt, if desired. *(Do not stuff the bird till just before cooking.)*

■ To stuff the bird, spoon some stuffing loosely into neck cavity; skewer neck skin to back. Lightly spoon remaining stuffing into body cavity. (Bake any additional stuffing in a casserole, covered, in a 375° oven for 20 to 30 minutes.) Tuck drumsticks under band of skin across tail or tie legs to tail. Twist wing tips under back.

■ In a covered grill, arrange *medium-hot* coals around a heavy foil drip pan. Drain hickory chips. Sprinkle coals with some of the dampened chips.

■ Place poultry, breast side up, on grill over foil pan. Except for domestic duck, brush the skin with cooking oil or melted butter or margarine, or lay uncooked bacon slices over breast. Prick the skin of domestic duck well all over to allow fat to escape. (During grilling, remove fat from drip pan.) Insert meat thermometer. Lower the grill hood.

■ Grill poultry till meat thermometer registers 185° and drumstick moves easily in socket. Brush the dry areas of skin occasionally with cooking oil or melted butter or margarine. Grill *quail* 15 to 18 minutes; *wild duck or Cornish game hens* 1 to 1½ hours; *pheasant* 1¼ to 1¾ hours; *chicken* 1½ to 2 hours; *domestic duck or wild goose* 2 to 2½ hours. Sprinkle hickory chips over coals every 20 to 30 minutes. Add more coals as needed. Garnish with endive, if desired. Makes 4 servings.

■ Preparation time: 1 hour
■ Cooking time: see recipe

Minty-Orange Chicken

 2 2½- to 3-pound broiler-fryer chickens, cut up
 ½ cup orange marmalade
 3 tablespoons butter *or* margarine
 2 tablespoons honey
 1 teaspoon dried mint leaves, crushed
 ¼ teaspoon salt

■ Place chicken pieces, bone side down, over *medium-hot* coals. Grill about 25 minutes. Meanwhile, to make sauce, in a saucepan combine marmalade, butter or margarine, honey, mint, and salt. Heat and stir till hot. Turn chicken bone side up; grill 15 to 20 minutes more or till tender. Brush chicken often with sauce the last 10 minutes of cooking. Serves 8 to 10.

■ Total preparation time: 50 minutes

Chicken Italiano

1 lime
¼ cup cooking oil
1 0.6-ounce package Italian salad
  dressing mix
1 2½- to 3-pound broiler-fryer
  chicken, cut up

▬ Finely shred the peel and squeeze juice from the lime. For marinade, combine lime peel and juice, oil, salad dressing mix, and 2 tablespoons *water*. Place chicken in shallow dish; pour marinade over. Marinate in the refrigerator for 3 hours.

▬ Remove chicken, reserving the marinade. Place chicken, bone side down, over *medium-hot* coals. Grill about 25 minutes. Turn chicken bone side up; grill 15 to 20 minutes more or till tender, brushing chicken frequently with marinade the last 15 minutes of cooking. Makes 4 to 6 servings.

▬ Preparation time: 10 minutes
▬ Marinating time: at least 3 hours
▬ Cooking time: 45 minutes

Skewered Chicken

3 whole medium chicken breasts, skinned,
  halved lengthwise, and boned
¼ cup soy sauce
3 tablespoons dry white wine
2 tablespoons lemon juice
2 tablespoons cooking oil
¾ teaspoon fines herbes, crushed
½ teaspoon grated gingerroot
1 clove garlic, minced
¼ teaspoon onion powder
  Dash pepper

▬ Cut chicken into strips, 1¼ inches wide and ¼ inch thick. Thread strips of chicken loosely onto 6 to 8 skewers. Place the filled skewers in two layers in a 12x7½x2-inch baking dish. Combine remaining ingredients. Pour over chicken. Cover and chill in the refrigerator for 3 hours. Drain. Grill chicken over *hot* coals 3 to 4 minutes per side. Makes 6 to 8 servings.

▬ Preparation time: 25 minutes
▬ Marinating time: at least 3 hours
▬ Cooking time: 8 minutes

Basted Chicken-on-a-Spit

2 2½- to 3-pound broiler-fryer chickens
  Barbecue Sauce *or* Herb Sauce

▬ Season cavity of each chicken with a little salt and pepper. Skewer neck skin to back of chickens. Mount one chicken on a spit rod. Secure with holding forks. Repeat with second chicken; secure with forks. Test for balance (see text at right).

▬ In a grill with a rotisserie place *medium-hot* coals around drip pan. Attach the spit; position drip pan under meat. Turn on the motor, lower grill hood. Grill chickens for 1½ to 1¾ hours or till leg joints move easily. Baste occasionally during last 20 to 30 minutes with desired basting sauce. Serves 8 to 10.

Barbecue Sauce: In a small saucepan combine ½ cup *catsup*, 2 tablespoons *water*, 1 tablespoon *brown sugar*, 1 tablespoon *lemon juice*, 1 tablespoon *prepared mustard*, 1 teaspoon *chili powder*, and ½ teaspoon *onion salt*. Cook and stir till boiling; reduce heat and simmer 5 minutes. Makes ⅔ cup sauce.

Herb Sauce: In a saucepan combine ¼ cup *butter or margarine;* 1 teaspoon *water;* ½ teaspoon *minced dried onion;* ½ teaspoon dried *oregano,* crushed; ¼ teaspoon dried *thyme,* crushed; ¼ teaspoon dried *rosemary,* crushed; and ⅛ teaspoon *garlic salt.* Heat and stir till butter melts. Makes ¼ cup sauce.

▬ Preparation time: 15 minutes
▬ Cooking time: 1¾ hours

When preparing *Basted Chicken-on-a-Spit,* test the chicken for balance on a rotisserie spit by holding one end of the rod in the palm of each hand, then turn gently. If the chicken flops or turns unevenly, readjust the holding forks or rod as necessary.

Cornish Hens à l'Orange

Cut up and chill the canned hearts of palm and refrigerate the salad dressing ahead of time. Then, when it comes time to arrange the first-course salads, all your ingredients will be chilled. If you'd like, add some pimiento to the salad for color.

Use stemmed sherbets for the dessert. Sprinkle a few toasted sliced almonds atop the chocolate-sauced pears for a garnish.

Lime Chicken

½ teaspoon finely shredded lime peel
½ cup lime juice
3 tablespoons cooking oil
2 teaspoons dried tarragon, crushed
½ teaspoon salt
¼ teaspoon pepper
⅛ teaspoon onion powder
1 2½- to 3-pound broiler-fryer chicken, halved lengthwise *or* quartered

■■■ In a small mixing bowl combine the finely shredded lime peel, the lime juice, cooking oil, tarragon, salt, pepper, and onion powder. Set aside.

■■■ Rinse chicken; pat dry with paper toweling. Break wing, hip, and drumstick joints of chicken so bird will remain flat during broiling. Twist the wing tips under the back. Brush the chicken generously with the lime mixture. Place chicken, skin side down, on rack of unheated broiler pan. Broil chicken 5 to 6 inches from heat for 20 minutes, brushing occasionally with the lime mixture. Turn chicken, skin side up, and broil for 15 to 20 minutes more or till chicken is tender, brushing occasionally with the lime mixture. Makes 4 servings.

■■■ Preparation time: 10 minutes
■■■ Cooking time: 40 minutes

Chicken with Apple Glaze

1 2½- to 3-pound broiler-fryer chicken,
    halved lengthwise *or* quartered
1 teaspoon cornstarch
¼ teaspoon ground cinnamon
⅛ teaspoon ground ginger
⅛ teaspoon ground nutmeg
½ cup apple juice
2 tablespoons butter *or* margarine

▬ Rinse chicken; pat dry with paper toweling. Break wing, hip, and drumstick joints of chicken so bird will remain flat during broiling. Twist the wing tips under the back. Place chicken, skin side down, on rack of unheated broiler pan. Broil chicken 5 to 6 inches from heat for 20 minutes.

▬ Meanwhile, prepare the apple glaze. In a small saucepan combine cornstarch, ground cinnamon, ground ginger, and ground nutmeg. Stir in the apple juice. Add butter or margarine. Cook and stir till the mixture is thickened and bubbly. Cook and stir for 2 minutes more; keep warm.

▬ Turn the chicken, skin side up, and broil for 10 minutes more. Brush with the apple glaze. Broil about 10 minutes more or till chicken is done, brushing occasionally with glaze. Arrange the chicken on a heated serving platter. Pass any remaining glaze with chicken. Makes 4 servings.

▬ Preparation time: 10 minutes
▬ Cooking time: 40 minutes

Cornish Hens à l'Orange

3 1- to 1½-pound Cornish game hens,
    halved lengthwise
    Melted butter *or* margarine *or* cooking oil
1 5- to 6-ounce package regular long grain
    and wild rice mix
1 4-ounce can chopped mushrooms, drained
¼ cup thin pieces of orange peel cut into
    julienne strips
3 tablespoons brown sugar
2 tablespoons cornstarch
⅔ cup water
½ cup orange juice
½ teaspoon instant chicken bouillon granules
¼ teaspoon salt
1 tablespoon brandy

▬ Rinse hens; pat dry with paper toweling. Break wing, hip, and drumstick joints of hens so birds will remain flat during broiling. Twist the wing tips under backs. Brush game hens with melted butter or oil; sprinkle with salt and pepper.

▬ Place hens, skin side down, on rack of unheated broiler pan. Broil hens 5 to 6 inches from heat about 15 minutes or till light brown, brushing occasionally with butter or oil. Turn hens, skin side up, and broil for 15 to 20 minutes more or till tender, brushing occasionally with butter or oil.

▬ Meanwhile, in a saucepan cook the rice according to package directions. Stir in mushrooms. In another saucepan simmer orange peel strips, covered, in a small amount of water for 15 minutes; drain well. In a small saucepan combine brown sugar and cornstarch. Stir in water, orange juice, bouillon granules, and salt. Cook and stir till thickened and bubbly. Cook and stir for 2 minutes more. Remove from heat. Stir in orange peel strips and brandy.

▬ To serve, spoon rice onto 6 serving plates. Arrange hen halves atop rice; spoon some sauce atop. Pass remaining sauce. Garnish with kumquat flowers and celery leaves, if desired. Makes 6 servings.

▬ Total preparation time: 1 hour

To prepare the orange peel for the sauce in *Cornish Hens à l'Orange,* cut the peel from an orange using a vegetable peeler. Then, slice the peel into julienne strips

For a kumquat flower garnish, make several lengthwise cuts from the top of the kumquat almost to the bottom, or stem end, of the kumquat, cutting to but not through the fruit. Gently pull back the sections of peel, taking care not to tear the peel.

Broil the Cornish game hens 5 to 6 inches from the heat. If your broiler compartment does not allow enough distance, remove the rack and place the game hens directly in the broiler pan.

To prepare carrot curls for garnishing *Tuna-Vegetable Bake*, make thin lengthwise strips of carrot, using a vegetable peeler. Roll carrot strips up and secure with a wooden pick. Place in ice water for several hours to curl. Just before garnishing, remove the wooden picks.

Tuna-Vegetable Bake

- 12 slices whole wheat *or* white bread, cut into 1-inch cubes (8½ cups)
- 1 cup shredded carrot
- 1 cup finely chopped celery
- ½ cup finely chopped green onion
- ¼ cup butter *or* margarine
- 1 cup milk
- 3 beaten eggs
- 1 10¾-ounce can condensed cream of celery soup
- ½ cup shredded American cheese (2 ounces)
- 1 4-ounce can mushroom stems and pieces, drained
- 2 tablespoons chopped pimiento
- 2 6½-ounce cans tuna, drained and flaked
  Carrot curls (optional)

■ Place the bread cubes in a large shallow baking pan. Bake in a 300° oven for 20 minutes or till toasted, stirring once. Set aside.

■ Meanwhile, in a small covered saucepan cook the shredded carrot, celery, and green onion in hot butter or margarine till tender. Remove from heat and stir in the milk.

■ In a large mixing bowl combine bread cubes and vegetable mixture; toss gently to mix. Press the mixture into six greased 10-ounce au gratin dishes, forming crusts with high sides. Bake, uncovered, in a 350° oven for 10 minutes.

■ Meanwhile, in a mixing bowl combine the beaten eggs, condensed soup, cheese, mushrooms, and pimiento; fold in tuna. Divide the tuna mixture among the crusts. Bake, uncovered, in a 350° oven for 35 to 40 minutes or till a knife inserted near the center of the tuna mixture comes out clean. Garnish with carrot curls, if desired. Makes 6 servings.

■ Preparation time: 50 minutes
■ Cooking time: 35 to 40 minutes

Saucy Salmon in Patty Shells

- 1 10-ounce package (6) frozen patty shells
- 1 10¾-ounce can condensed cream of shrimp soup
- ½ cup milk
- ½ teaspoon dried dillweed
- 1 2½-ounce jar sliced mushrooms, drained
- ⅓ cup dairy sour cream
- 1 15½-ounce can salmon, drained and skin and bones removed

■ Prepare patty shells according to package directions. Meanwhile, in a saucepan combine the condensed soup, milk, and dillweed. Stir in mushrooms; heat through, stirring occasionally. Stir in sour cream; heat through but *do not boil*. Fold in the salmon; heat through. Spoon into patty shells. Serves 6.

■ Total preparation time: 35 minutes

Curried Tuna

- 2 tablespoons butter *or* margarine
- 2 tablespoons all-purpose flour
- 2 to 3 teaspoons curry powder
- ¼ teaspoon salt
  Dash pepper
- 1½ cups milk
- 1 medium apple, chopped
- ½ cup raisins
- ½ cup coarsely chopped cashews *or* peanuts
- 1 6½-ounce can tuna, drained and flaked
  Hot cooked rice

■ In a saucepan melt butter or margarine. Stir in flour, curry powder, salt, and pepper. Add milk all at once. Cook and stir till thickened and bubbly. Cook and stir for 1 minute more. Stir in the chopped apple, raisins, and nuts; fold in the tuna. Heat through. Serve over hot cooked rice. Makes 4 servings.

■ Total preparation time: 25 minutes

Freeze-Ahead Salmon Bake

3 ounces medium noodles
1 11-ounce can condensed cheddar
cheese soup
½ cup dairy sour cream
½ cup milk
½ cup thinly sliced celery
1 4-ounce can green chili peppers, rinsed,
seeded, and chopped
1 tablespoon minced dried onion
1 15½-ounce can salmon, drained and skin
and bones removed
¾ cup coarsely broken tortilla chips

■■■ In a large saucepan cook the noodles in a large amount of boiling salted water for 7 to 8 minutes or till just tender. Drain well and set aside.

■■■ Meanwhile, in a large mixing bowl combine the condensed soup, sour cream, and milk. Stir in the celery, chili peppers, and dried onion. Add the cooked noodles; toss gently. Fold in the salmon. Turn the mixture into a 10x6x2-inch baking dish. Seal, label, and freeze for at least 8 hours.

■■■ Before serving, bake the frozen casserole, covered, in a 375° oven for 1 hour. Stir the casserole. Top with tortilla chips. Bake, uncovered, about 20 minutes more or till heated through. Makes 4 to 6 servings.

■■■ Advance preparation time: 25 minutes
■■■ Freezing time: at least 8 hours
■■■ Final preparation time: 1 hour and 20 minutes

Asparagus and Salmon Loaf

16 ounces fresh asparagus spears *or*
one 10-ounce package frozen asparagus
spears
3 tablespoons butter *or* margarine
3 tablespoons all-purpose flour
½ teaspoon dried dillweed
⅛ teaspoon salt
1 cup chicken broth
1 15½-ounce can salmon, drained, flaked,
and skin and bones removed
1½ cups cooked rice
3 slightly beaten eggs
1 tablespoon shredded onion
Celery leaves (optional)
Cherry tomatoes (optional)

■■■ Cut fresh asparagus tip ends into 4-inch lengths. (Reserve any remaining asparagus stems for another use.) Cook the asparagus tips, covered, in a small amount of boiling salted water for 5 to 8 minutes or till partially cooked. (*Or,* cook frozen asparagus according to package directions just till partially cooked.) Drain well and set aside.

■■■ Meanwhile, in a saucepan melt the butter or margarine; stir in the flour, dillweed, and salt. Add the chicken broth all at once; cook and stir till thickened and bubbly. Cook and stir for 1 minute more. Fold in the salmon, cooked rice, beaten eggs, and onion.

■■■ Arrange the partially cooked asparagus tips crosswise in the bottom of a greased 8x4x2-inch loaf pan; press the salmon mixture over top.

■■■ Bake, uncovered, in a 350° oven for 50 to 55 minutes or till a knife inserted near the center comes out clean. Let stand for 10 minutes. Unmold the salmon loaf onto a heated serving platter. (*Or,* cover and chill in the refrigerator to serve cold.) Garnish the platter with celery leaves and cherry tomatoes, if desired. Slice to serve. Makes 6 servings.

■■■ Preparation time: 25 minutes
■■■ Cooking time: 50 to 55 minutes
■■■ Standing time: 10 minutes

■■■ MENU ■■■
PATIO DINNER

Asparagus and
Salmon Loaf

Waldorf Salad

Make-Ahead
Cornmeal Batter
Rolls★ with
Butter

Angel Food Cake with
Strawberries

Iced Tea

When the temperature soars, plan a cool and refreshing meal for your guests. You can make the salmon loaf ahead and chill it. And why not bake the cake in advance too? Stir up the rolls the day before and bake them just before serving.

Use fresh, sliced strawberries to top the wedges of airy angel food cake.
★ *see recipe, page 133*

In Egypt this popular dish is known as "sayyadiah," which means *Fish with Rice*. This tasty international specialty is a versatile recipe. Depending on what's available, you can prepare it with fish fillets, steaks, or dressed fish. And, you can toast either slivered almonds or pine nuts to sprinkle atop the finished fish and rice.

Fish with Rice

1 **pound fresh** *or* **frozen fish fillets** *or* **steaks,** *or* **1 to 1¼ pounds fresh** *or* **frozen dressed ocean perch** *or* **red snapper**
¼ **cup lemon juice**
2 **medium onions, chopped (1 cup)**
2 **cloves garlic, minced**
1 **tablespoon olive oil** *or* **cooking oil**
1 **cup long grain rice**
2 **cups chicken broth**
½ **teaspoon ground cumin**
⅓ **cup slivered almonds** *or* **pine nuts**
2 **tablespoons olive oil** *or* **cooking oil**
¼ **cup all-purpose flour**

■■■ Thaw fish, if frozen. Rinse fish and pat dry with paper toweling. Rub surfaces and cavities with lemon juice. Let stand at room temperature for 1 hour.

■■■ In a large saucepan cook onion and garlic in the 1 tablespoon hot olive oil or cooking oil till onion is tender but not brown. Stir in the uncooked rice; cook and stir constantly over high heat for 5 to 10 minutes or till rice is light brown. Remove from heat; cool slightly. Stir in chicken broth and ground cumin. Bring to boiling; reduce heat. Cover and simmer for 20 to 25 minutes or till the rice is tender.

■■■ Meanwhile, in a large skillet heat almonds or pine nuts in the 2 tablespoons hot olive oil or cooking oil for 2 minutes or till golden, stirring constantly. Remove nuts from skillet, reserving oil; set aside.

■■■ Drain fish. Coat fish with the flour. In the same skillet cook the fish fillets or steaks in the hot cooking oil for 2 to 3 minutes on each side or till fish flakes easily when tested with a fork. (*Or,* cook dressed fish for 5 to 6 minutes on each side.) Add more oil, if necessary.

■■■ Turn the rice onto a heated serving platter. Arrange the fish atop the cooked rice; sprinkle with the almonds or pine nuts. Makes 4 servings.

■■■ Total preparation time: 1¼ hours

Fillet Rolls Deluxe

8 **fresh** *or* **frozen fish fillets (2 pounds)**
2 **tablespoons chopped onion**
1 **tablespoon butter** *or* **margarine**
⅔ **cup water**
⅓ **cup long grain rice**
1 **teaspoon instant chicken bouillon granules**
1 **3-ounce can chopped mushrooms, drained**
¼ **cup snipped parsley**
3 **tablespoons butter** *or* **margarine**
3 **tablespoons all-purpose flour**
¼ **teaspoon salt**
   Dash pepper
1½ **cups milk**
¼ **cup dry white wine**
1 **cup shredded process Swiss cheese (4 ounces)**
   Paprika

■■■ Thaw fish, if frozen. In a saucepan cook onion in the 1 tablespoon hot butter or margarine till tender but not brown. Add water, uncooked rice, and bouillon granules. Bring to boiling; reduce heat. Cover and simmer for 20 minutes or till rice is tender. Stir in the drained mushrooms and parsley.

■■■ Sprinkle the fish fillets with salt; spread some of the rice mixture atop each fillet. Roll up the fillets jelly-roll style; secure with wooden picks. Place the rolls, seam side down, in a 12x7½x2-inch baking dish.

■■■ In a saucepan melt the 3 tablespoons butter or margarine; stir in the flour, the ¼ teaspoon salt, and the pepper. Add milk all at once. Cook and stir till thickened and bubbly. Stir in the wine; pour over fish rolls. Bake, uncovered, in a 400° oven for 25 to 30 minutes or till fish is almost done. Sprinkle with shredded cheese and paprika. Bake, uncovered, for 5 minutes more or till fish flakes easily when tested with a fork. Makes 8 servings.

■■■ Preparation time: 50 minutes
■■■ Cooking time: 30 to 35 minutes

Fish Mousse with Newburg Sauce

1 pound frozen fish fillets
2 beaten eggs
½ cup thinly sliced green onion
½ cup finely chopped celery
½ cup milk
½ teaspoon ground nutmeg
¼ teaspoon salt
  Dash pepper
2 cups soft bread crumbs (2½ slices)
1 tablespoon butter *or* margarine
  Romaine leaves (about 6 large)
¼ cup butter *or* margarine
2 tablespoons all-purpose flour
1½ cups milk
3 beaten egg yolks
3 tablespoons dry white wine
2 tablespoons snipped parsley
2 teaspoons lemon juice
¼ teaspoon salt
  Sliced pimiento (optional)
  Pimiento-stuffed olive, sliced (optional)
  Lemon slices, halved (optional)
  Lettuce leaf (optional)

▬ Place the frozen block of fish in a greased skillet. Add enough water to cover. Bring to boiling; reduce heat. Cover and simmer about 15 minutes or till fish flakes easily when tested with a fork, stirring occasionally to break up. Remove fish from skillet with a slotted spoon; drain and cool.

▬ In a large mixing bowl combine the 2 eggs, green onion, celery, the ½ cup milk, nutmeg, ¼ teaspoon salt, and pepper. Finely flake the fish. Stir fish and bread crumbs into the egg mixture. Generously grease a 4-cup metal mold with the 1 tablespoon butter or margarine. Pour boiling water over romaine leaves; drain and pat dry. Arrange the romaine leaves along the sides of the mold, cutting leaves as necessary to fit. Carefully spoon the fish mixture into mold. Cover with foil. Bake in a 350° oven about 35 minutes or till firm and moist. Let stand for 5 minutes.

▬ Meanwhile, for sauce, in a saucepan melt the ¼ cup butter or margarine. Stir in the flour. Add the 1½ cups milk all at once. Cook and stir till thickened and bubbly. Stir *half* of the hot mixture into the egg yolks; return to saucepan. Cook and stir till bubbly. Cook and stir for 2 minutes more. Remove from heat. Stir in the wine, parsley, lemon juice, and ¼ teaspoon salt.

▬ To serve, carefully unmold mousse onto a heated serving platter. Spoon some of the sauce over mousse. Garnish mousse with pimiento strips and sliced olive, if desired. Place lemon slice halves atop a lettuce leaf by mousse, if desired. Pass any remaining sauce. Makes 6 servings.

▬ Preparation time: 50 minutes
▬ Cooking time: 35 minutes

Romaine-encased *Fish Mousse with Newburg Sauce* is an excellent choice if you are planning to serve a buffet-style dinner.

If you use a fish-shape mold, as we did for the mousse shown at left, you can decorate the unmolded fish with strips of pimiento and an olive slice. Don't limit your imagination to fish-shape molds, however. This mousse will taste terrific no matter what shape it is. Just substitute any decorative oven-proof mold. The lettuce and lemon half-slices are appealing garnish trims regardless of the mold used.

Accompany this elegant mousse with a basket of buttered French bread slices and a tray of crisp relishes, such as radishes and carrot and celery sticks.

The best way to thaw frozen fish, when your recipe calls for it, is in the original wrapping in the refrigerator. A one-pound package of fish takes about 24 hours to thaw.

For faster thawing, place the wrapped package of fish under cold running water. This reduces thawing time to one or two hours for a one-pound package.

Do not thaw fish at room temperature or in warm water. Once thawed, use the fish within a day.

Broiled Fish with Scandinavian Tartar Sauce

2 **pounds fresh** *or* **frozen fish fillets** *or* **steaks**
1 **egg**
¼ **cup mayonnaise** *or* **salad dressing**
¼ **cup plain yogurt**
2 **tablespoons snipped parsley**
1 **tablespoon finely chopped onion**
1 **teaspoon lemon juice**
½ **teaspoon dried basil, crushed**
2 **anchovy fillets, drained**
2 **tablespoons butter** *or* **margarine, melted**

■■■ Thaw fish, if frozen. To hard-cook egg, place egg in saucepan; cover with cold water. Bring to boiling; reduce heat to just below simmering. Cover and cook for 15 minutes. Run cold water over egg till cool. Remove shell; finely chop egg.

■■■ Meanwhile, for sauce, in a small mixing bowl stir together mayonnaise or salad dressing, yogurt, parsley, onion, lemon juice, and basil. Finely chop the anchovy fillets. Fold the chopped anchovies and hard-cooked egg into the mayonnaise mixture. Cover and chill in the refrigerator for 1 hour or till serving time.

■■■ Cut the fish into 6 to 8 serving-size portions. Place fish in a single layer on a greased rack of broiler pan or in a greased baking pan. Tuck under any thin edges. Brush *1 tablespoon* of the melted butter or margarine onto fish. Sprinkle with salt and pepper.

■■■ Broil fish 4 inches from the heat till fish flakes easily when tested with a fork (allow 5 to 6 minutes for each ½ inch of thickness). Brush fish with remaining butter or margarine during cooking. If fish is more than 1 inch thick, turn after half the cooking time.

■■■ Garnish the sauce with additional chopped hard cooked egg, if desired. Serve the chilled sauce with the broiled fish. Makes 6 to 8 servings.

■■■ Preparation time: 30 minutes
■■■ Chilling time: 1 to 2 hours
■■■ Cooking time: 10 minutes

Fish Soufflé Casserole

1 **pound fresh** *or* **frozen fish fillets**
1½ **cups herb-seasoned stuffing mix**
1 **12-ounce package frozen spinach soufflé, thawed**
1 **2½-ounce jar sliced mushrooms, drained**
¼ **cup chopped pimiento**
1 **tablespoon mayonnaise** *or* **salad dressing**
1 **teaspoon Dijon-style mustard**
½ **teaspoon onion salt**
¾ **cup shredded Swiss cheese (3 ounces)**
1 **slightly beaten egg**
½ **cup light cream** *or* **milk**

■■■ Thaw fish, if frozen. Separate into fillets; pat fish dry with paper toweling. Sprinkle *1 cup* of the stuffing mix in a greased 10x6x2-inch baking dish. Layer the spinach soufflé, mushrooms, and pimiento atop the stuffing mix. Arrange the fish fillets atop. In a small mixing bowl combine the mayonnaise or salad dressing, mustard, and onion salt. Spread over the fish and pimiento layer. Sprinkle the shredded cheese atop.

■■■ Combine the beaten egg and light cream or milk; pour over casserole. Sprinkle the remaining stuffing mix atop casserole. Let stand for 10 minutes. Bake, covered, in a 350° oven for 25 minutes. Uncover; bake for 15 to 20 minutes more or till fish flakes easily when tested with a fork. Makes 6 servings.

■■■ Preparation time: 25 minutes
■■■ Standing time: 10 minutes
■■■ Cooking time: 40 to 45 minutes

Fish Mold with Cucumber

  2 **tablespoons butter** *or* **margarine**
  ½ **cup dry white wine**
  1 **pound frozen fish fillets**
  3 **beaten eggs**
  1 **cup light cream**
  ¼ **cup snipped chives**
  ¼ **teaspoon salt**
     Dash pepper
  2 **cups soft bread crumbs (2½ slices)**
  2 **tablespoons butter** *or* **margarine**
  2 **tablespoons all-purpose flour**
  1 **teaspoon instant chicken bouillon granules**
  ¼ **cup light cream**
  ½ **cup dairy sour cream**
  1 **medium cucumber**

■■■ In a skillet combine 2 tablespoons butter and the wine; bring to boiling. Add frozen fish fillets. Cover and simmer about 10 minutes or till fish flakes easily when tested with a fork, stirring occasionally to break up. Drain, reserving ½ cup of the poaching liquid; cool.

■■■ In bowl combine eggs, the 1 cup light cream, chives, salt, and pepper. Finely flake fish. Stir fish and crumbs into egg mixture. Generously grease a 4-cup metal mold; sprinkle with flour. Spoon fish mixture into mold. Cover with foil. Bake in a 350° oven for 40 to 50 minutes or till firm and moist. Let stand for 5 minutes.

■■■ Meanwhile, for sauce, in a small saucepan melt 2 tablespoons butter; stir in *1 tablespoon* of the flour and the bouillon granules. Combine reserved poaching liquid and the ¼ cup light cream; add all at once. Cook and stir till thickened and bubbly. Combine the sour cream and remaining flour; stir into the hot mixture. Cook and stir till thickened and bubbly. Cook and stir for 1 minute more.

■■■ Finely shred *half* of the cucumber; slice remaining. Spread shredded cucumber on a platter. Unmold fish onto shredded cucumber; garnish with sliced cucumber. Serve with sauce. Makes 6 to 8 servings.

■■■ Preparation time: 40 minutes
■■■ Cooking time: 40 to 50 minutes

Sole Mediterranean

  1 **pound fresh** *or* **frozen sole fillets**
  1 **16-ounce can tomatoes, cut up**
  ½ **cup chopped onion**
  ¼ **cup chopped green pepper**
  2 **tablespoons chopped celery**
  ¾ **teaspoon garlic salt**
  ½ **teaspoon dried oregano, crushed**
  1 **small eggplant, cut into ½-inch slices**
  2 **tablespoons cooking oil**
  2 **tablespoons cold water**
  1 **tablespoon cornstarch**
  ½ **cup shredded mozzarella cheese**
     (2 ounces)

■■■ Thaw fish, if frozen. In a medium saucepan combine the *undrained* tomatoes, onion, green pepper, celery, garlic salt, and oregano. Bring to boiling; reduce heat. Simmer, uncovered, for 15 minutes, stirring the mixture occasionally.

■■■ Meanwhile, in a large skillet cook the eggplant slices in hot cooking oil just till light brown, turning once. Drain, if necessary, on paper toweling.

■■■ Arrange the eggplant slices in a 12x7½x2-inch baking dish. Top with the fish fillets. Sprinkle with salt. For sauce, combine the cold water and cornstarch; stir into the tomato mixture in saucepan. Cook and stir till thickened and bubbly. Cook and stir for 2 minutes more. Pour sauce over fish. Cover with foil. Bake in a 350° oven about 30 minutes or till fish flakes easily when tested with a fork. Top with the shredded mozzarella cheese and bake, uncovered, for 2 to 3 minutes more. Makes 4 to 6 servings.

■■■ Preparation time: 30 minutes
■■■ Cooking time: 35 minutes

■■■ MENU ■■■
GREEK-STYLE
DINNER

Greek Salad

Sole Mediterranean

Buttered Carrots

Toasted Pita Bread
Wedges

Baklava

Coffee

To prepare a Greek-style salad for this informal dinner, toss together some escarole and romaine. Add some crumbled feta cheese and pitted ripe olives.
  For the dressing, combine two parts olive oil to one part red wine vinegar; season with salt, pepper, and a little oregano. Drizzle the chilled dressing over the salad just before serving and toss.

■■■

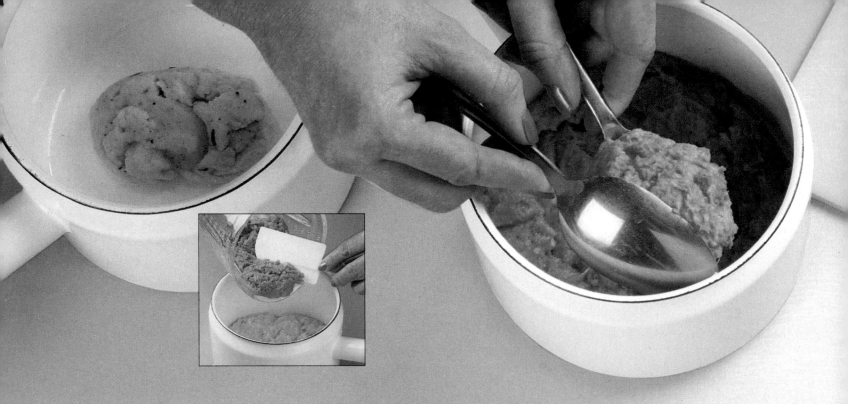

For an elegant, French-inspired meal serve *Salmon Quenelles* (ca-NELL) *with Chive Crème Fraîche* (krem-FRESH).

Quenelles are a light-textured, mousse-like dumpling made with very finely ground fish, veal, or poultry. They are poached in broth.

Select a delightful dry white French or American wine to accompany the entrée. A good match of food and wine is as important as preparing the food properly.

Salmon Quenelles with Chive Crème Fraîche

	Chive Crème Fraîche
8	ounces fresh *or* frozen salmon, pike, *or* cod fillets
¼	cup water
2	tablespoons butter *or* margarine
¼	cup all-purpose flour
¼	teaspoon salt
¼	teaspoon dried tarragon, crushed
	Dash pepper
1	egg
1	egg white
1	tablespoon light cream *or* milk
2	cups hot water
½	teaspoon salt
	Cooked leeks (optional)
	Julienne beets, cooked (optional)
	Julienne carrots, cooked (optional)
	Snipped chives (optional)

■ Prepare the Chive Crème Fraîche. Thaw the salmon, pike, or cod, if frozen. In a saucepan bring the ¼ cup water and the butter or margarine to boiling, stirring till butter melts. Add flour, the ¼ teaspoon salt, the tarragon, and pepper all at once, stirring vigorously till combined. Cook and stir over low heat till mixture forms a ball that does not separate, as shown above. Remove from heat. Cool slightly, about 10 minutes.

■ Using a wooden spoon, beat in the whole egg, then the egg white. Set mixture aside.

■ Pat fish dry with paper toweling; remove skin, if necessary. Chop fish. Process fish, *half* at a time, in a blender container or food processor bowl, stopping frequently to scrape sides of container. Add fish and light cream or milk to flour mixture, as shown; beat till mixed. Cover and chill in the refrigerator for 2 hours.

■ Grease a 12-inch skillet. Use two large spoons to mold *one-fourth* of the fish mixture (about ⅓ cup) into an oval shape, as shown above. Gently place in the skillet, as shown opposite, top. (*Or,* for small quenelles, mold a scant *2 tablespoons* fish mixture into an oval shape.) Repeat with the remaining fish mixture.

Chive Crème Fraîche is another French classic. It's a tangy mixture of whipping cream and cultured buttermilk that thickens as it stands. Fresh chives go into the sauce just before serving, and also are used as a garnish.

■ Combine the 2 cups hot water and the ½ teaspoon salt; gently pour down side of skillet. Bring mixture just to simmering. Cover and simmer gently for 25 minutes for the large quenelles or 10 minutes for the small quenelles or till mixture is set.

■ Using a slotted spoon, remove the quenelles from the skillet; drain on paper toweling. Serve quenelles immediately with cooked leeks, beets, and carrots, if desired. Spoon Chive Crème Fraîche atop; sprinkle with snipped chives, if desired. Makes 4 large or 15 small quenelles.

Chive Crème Fraîche: In a small saucepan heat 1 cup *whipping cream* over low heat till warm (90° to 100°). Pour into a small bowl. Stir in 2 tablespoons *buttermilk*. Cover; let stand at room temperature for 24 to 30 hours or till mixture is thickened. *Do not stir*. Stir 1 teaspoon snipped *chives* into the mixture just before serving. (Mixture may be stored in a covered container in the refrigerator for up to one week.) Makes 1 cup.

■ Advance preparation time: 45 minutes
■ Preparation time: 30 minutes
■ Chilling time: at least 2 hours
■ Cooking time: 25 minutes

When preparing *Lobster Gratiné*, you can use either freshly cooked or canned lobster. One 5-ounce can of lobster yields about 1 cup of cooked lobster meat.

Fish and Shells Romano

 1 **16-ounce package frozen fish fillets**
1½ **cups medium shell macaroni**
 1 **medium onion, chopped (½ cup)**
 2 **tablespoons cooking oil**
 1 **cup tomato juice**
 1 **1½-ounce envelope spaghetti sauce mix**
 1 **16-ounce can zucchini in Italian-style tomato sauce**
 ¼ **cup grated Romano *or* Parmesan cheese**

▗▖ Allow unwrapped frozen fish to stand at room temperature for 20 minutes. Meanwhile, cook macaroni according to package directions; drain. In a large saucepan cook onion in hot oil till tender but not brown. Stir in tomato juice and spaghetti sauce mix.

▗▖ Cut fish into 1-inch cubes. Stir fish and *undrained* zucchini into spaghetti sauce mixture. Bring to boiling. Stir in cooked macaroni. Turn into a 10x6x2-inch baking dish. Top with cheese. Bake in a 350° oven for 25 to 30 minutes or till hot. Serves 6.

▗▖ Preparation time: 30 minutes
▗▖ Cooking time: 25 to 30 minutes

Shark is fast becoming a popular restaurant choice. So, won't your guests be pleased— and surprised—when you serve tangy *Broiled Shark Kabobs* for dinner.
  Shark is a mild-flavored, lean fish with firm, white meat. Another plus for diners: shark meat is free of bones.

Broiled Shark Kabobs

 ⅓ **cup Italian salad dressing**
 ¼ **cup catsup**
 3 **tablespoons lemon juice**
 1 **pound fresh shark fillets, cut into 1-inch cubes**
 3 **medium carrots, cut into 1-inch pieces**
 3 **small zucchini, cut diagonally into 1-inch pieces**

▗▖ For marinade, combine salad dressing, catsup, and lemon juice. Add fish pieces. Cover and marinate at room temperature for 30 minutes. Meanwhile, cook the carrots in a small amount of boiling salted water for 7 minutes. Add zucchini; cook for 3 to 4 minutes more or till crisp-tender.

▗▖ Drain fish, reserving the marinade. On 8 skewers, alternately thread fish with zucchini and carrot pieces. Place on unheated rack of broiler pan. Broil 4 to 5 inches from heat for 10 to 12 minutes, turning often and brushing the reserved marinade onto fish and vegetables. Makes 4 servings.

▗▖ Preparation time: 45 minutes
▗▖ Cooking time: 10 to 12 minutes

Lobster Gratiné

 ¼ **cup sliced fresh mushrooms**
 ¼ **cup sliced green onion**
 2 **tablespoons butter *or* margarine**
 ½ **of a 10-ounce package frozen chopped spinach, thawed**
 ¾ **cup light cream *or* milk**
 2 **beaten eggs**
 2 **tablespoons dry sherry**
 ½ **teaspoon dried tarragon, crushed**
 2 **cups cubed cooked lobster meat**
 ¼ **cup shredded Swiss *or* Gruyère cheese**
 2 **tablespoons grated Parmesan cheese**
 2 **tablespoons fine dry bread crumbs**
 1 **tablespoon butter *or* margarine, melted**

▗▖ In a saucepan cook mushrooms and onion in 2 tablespoons hot butter or margarine for 2 to 3 minutes or till tender. Drain spinach well; stir spinach, cream, eggs, sherry, and tarragon into mushroom mixture. Cook and stir just till mixture thickens slightly but *do not boil*. Gently stir in lobster. Divide the hot spinach mixture among 4 large ramekins or four 1-cup casseroles. For the topping, combine the shredded Swiss or Gruyère cheese, Parmesan cheese, dry bread crumbs, and the 1 tablespoon melted butter or margarine; sprinkle evenly over casseroles. Bake, uncovered, in a 375° oven for 15 to 20 minutes or till cheeses are melted and topping is brown. Serves 4.

▗▖ Preparation time: 25 minutes
▗▖ Cooking time: 15 to 20 minutes

Malay Shrimp Kabobs

- 1 **pound fresh** *or* **frozen large shrimp in shells**
- 2 **tablespoons sliced green onion**
- 1 **small clove garlic, minced**
- 2 **teaspoons cooking oil**
- ¾ **cup chicken broth**
- 3 **tablespoons peanut butter**
- ½ **teaspoon finely shredded lemon peel**
- 1 **tablespoon lemon juice**
- 1 **tablespoon soy sauce**
- 1 **teaspoon chili powder**
- ½ **teaspoon brown sugar**
- ¼ **teaspoon ground ginger**
  Hot cooked rice

▬▬ Thaw shrimp, if frozen. Peel shrimp, leaving last section and tail intact. Devein shrimp. For marinade, in a small saucepan cook the green onion and garlic in hot cooking oil till tender but not brown. Stir in the chicken broth, peanut butter, lemon peel, lemon juice, soy sauce, chili powder, brown sugar, and ginger. Simmer, uncovered, for 10 minutes, stirring frequently. Remove from heat; cool.

▬▬ Marinate the shrimp in peanut butter mixture at room temperature for 1 hour, turning to coat shrimp well. Drain shrimp, reserving marinade. Thread the drained shrimp onto 4 skewers.

▬▬ Grill the shrimp over *hot* coals for 8 to 10 minutes or till done, turning once. Reheat the marinade. Spoon hot cooked rice onto a heated serving platter; arrange the skewers atop. Pass the heated marinade with the shrimp. Makes 4 servings.

▬▬ Preparation time: 30 minutes
▬▬ Marinating time: 1 hour
▬▬ Cooking time: 8 to 10 minutes

Crab and Cheese Crepes

- 1½ **cups milk**
- 1 **cup all-purpose flour**
- 3 **eggs**
- 1 **teaspoon butter** *or* **margarine, melted**
- 1 **9-ounce package frozen artichoke hearts**
- 3 **tablespoons butter** *or* **margarine**
- 3 **tablespoons all-purpose flour**
- ⅛ **teaspoon ground nutmeg**
- 1½ **cups light cream** *or* **milk**
- ¼ **cup dry white wine**
- ½ **cup shredded Swiss cheese (2 ounces)**
- 1 **8-ounce container soft-style cream cheese**
- 2 **7-ounce cans crab meat, drained, flaked, and cartilage removed**

▬▬ For crepes, in a mixing bowl combine the 1½ cups milk, the 1 cup flour, eggs, the 1 teaspoon melted butter, and ¼ teaspoon *salt*. Beat with a rotary beater till combined. Heat a lightly greased 6-inch skillet. Remove from heat. Spoon in 2 tablespoons batter; lift and tilt skillet to spread batter. Return to heat; brown on one side only. (*Or*, cook on an inverted crepe pan.) Invert pan over paper toweling; remove crepe. Repeat to make 18 crepes, greasing skillet occasionally. Set the crepes aside.

▬▬ Cook artichokes according to package directions; drain. Meanwhile, for sauce, in a skillet melt the 3 tablespoons butter; stir in the 3 tablespoons flour, nutmeg, ½ teaspoon *salt,* and dash *pepper*. Add the 1½ cups cream all at once. Cook and stir till thickened and bubbly. Cook and stir for 1 minute more. Stir in the wine. Add Swiss cheese, stirring till melted.

▬▬ To fill the crepes, spread *1 scant tablespoon* of the cream cheese over the unbrowned side of each crepe. Sprinkle each with *1 tablespoon* of the crab; fold into quarters. Arrange 3 folded crepes in each of 6 individual baking dishes. Pour the sauce over crepes. Arrange artichokes around crepes. Bake crepes in a 350° oven for 10 to 15 minutes or till heated through. Makes 6 servings.

▬▬ Preparation time: 1½ hours
▬▬ Cooking time: 10 to 15 minutes

▬▬ MENU ▬▬
CREPE DINNER FOR SIX

Chicken Broth with Sliced Mushrooms

Fresh Spinach Salad with Herb Dressing

Crab and Cheese Crepes

Bananas and Pineapple à la Foster★

Coffee

Serve this meal course by course, dishing up individual portions of the soup, salad, and entrée from the kitchen. For ease in serving the crepes just place the individual baking dishes onto the dinner plates.

At dessert time, use a chafing dish to prepare the sauce at the table, then spoon the sauce over vanilla ice cream. End dinner with freshly brewed coffee.

★ *see recipe, page 169*

To devein shrimp for *Fried Shrimp Hawaiian,* make a shallow slit with a sharp knife along the back of the shrimp. Look for a sandy black vein that appears as a dark line running down the center of the back. If you see one, use the tip of the knife to scrape it out. Discard the vein and rinse the shrimp under cold running water.

Quick Shrimp Creole

- 1 medium onion, chopped (½ cup)
- ½ cup chopped green pepper
- 3 tablespoons butter *or* margarine
- 1 16-ounce can tomatoes, cut up
- 1 15-ounce can tomato sauce
- 1 teaspoon dried thyme, crushed
- ½ teaspoon dried oregano, crushed
- ¼ teaspoon sugar
- ¼ teaspoon garlic salt
  Several dashes bottled hot pepper sauce
- 1½ cups quick-cooking rice
- 2 4½-ounce cans shrimp, drained and rinsed

■■■■ In a large saucepan cook the onion and green pepper in hot butter or margarine till tender but not brown. Stir in the *undrained* tomatoes, tomato sauce, thyme, oregano, sugar, garlic salt, hot pepper sauce, and ¼ teaspoon *pepper.* Bring to boiling; reduce heat. Cover and simmer for 5 minutes. Add rice. Cover and simmer about 15 minutes more or till rice is tender. Stir in shrimp; heat through. Serves 4.

■■■■ Total preparation time: 40 minutes

Fried Shrimp Hawaiian

- 1 pound fresh *or* frozen shrimp in shells
- 1 beaten egg yolk
- ½ cup milk
- ¼ teaspoon salt
- ½ cup all-purpose flour
- ¾ cup crushed saltine crackers
- ⅓ cup chopped macadamia nuts
  Cooking oil for deep-fat frying

■■■■ Thaw shrimp, if frozen. Peel shrimp, leaving last section and tail intact. Devein shrimp (see far left). Butterfly the shrimp by making a slit down back, cutting almost but not all the way through the shrimp.

■■■■ In a mixing bowl combine the egg yolk, milk, and salt. Add the flour; beat with a rotary beater till smooth. Combine the crushed crackers and nuts. Holding shrimp by tail segment, dip into batter, then into nut mixture, coating evenly. Fry, a few at a time, in deep hot oil (375°) for 2 to 3 minutes or till golden. Drain on paper toweling; keep warm in a 325° oven while frying remaining. Makes 4 servings.

■■■■ Preparation time: 40 minutes
■■■■ Cooking time: 20 minutes

Shrimp-Stuffed Zucchini

- 4 medium zucchini (about 1½ pounds)
- ⅓ cup mayonnaise *or* salad dressing
- 1 3-ounce package cream cheese, softened
- ½ cup shredded Swiss cheese (2 ounces)
- 2 tablespoons milk
- ¼ teaspoon dried basil, crushed
- 2 4½-ounce cans shrimp, drained and rinsed
- ¼ cup fine dry bread crumbs
- 2 teaspoons butter *or* margarine, melted
  Paprika

■■■■ Halve zucchini lengthwise. Scoop out pulp, leaving ¼-inch shell. Chop enough pulp to measure 1 cup; set aside. In a covered skillet cook zucchini shells, cut side down, in a small amount of boiling water about 3 minutes or just till tender. Drain. Remove zucchini shells from skillet and turn cut side up. Sprinkle with salt.

■■■■ In a mixing bowl combine mayonnaise or salad dressing, cream cheese, Swiss cheese, milk, and basil. Gently fold in the shrimp and the reserved chopped zucchini pulp; spoon into zucchini shells. Place the filled shells in a shallow baking dish. For topping, combine the bread crumbs and melted butter or margarine; sprinkle atop. Sprinkle with paprika. Bake, uncovered, in a 350° oven about 25 minutes or till heated through. Makes 4 servings.

■■■■ Preparation time: 30 minutes
■■■■ Cooking time: 25 minutes

Oyster Pie

- 2 cups sliced fresh mushrooms
- ¼ cup butter *or* margarine
- 1 pint shucked oysters
- ¾ cup light cream *or* milk
- ¼ cup all-purpose flour
- 1 tablespoon snipped parsley
- ¼ teaspoon celery salt
  Pastry for Single-Crust Pie
  Milk

■ For filling, in a medium saucepan cook mushrooms in hot butter or margarine just till tender. Remove mushrooms from pan; set aside. Add *undrained* oysters to saucepan. Cook over medium heat for 2 to 5 minutes or till edges of oysters curl.

■ Remove oysters with a slotted spoon, reserving liquid in saucepan. Combine the ¾ cup light cream or milk and flour; stir into saucepan. Stir in the parsley and celery salt. Cook and stir till thickened and bubbly. Cook and stir for 1 minute more. Remove from heat. Stir in the mushrooms and oysters. Turn the mixture into a 1½-quart casserole.

■ Prepare Pastry for Single-Crust Pie. On a lightly floured surface roll out pastry to fit top of casserole. Cut slits for escape of steam. Place over the oyster mixture; trim and flute edges. Brush the pastry with additional milk. Bake in a 375° oven for 30 to 35 minutes or till golden. Let stand for 10 minutes before serving. Makes 4 servings.

Pastry for Single-Crust Pie: In a mixing bowl stir together 1 cup *all-purpose flour* and ½ teaspoon *salt*. Cut in ¼ cup *shortening or lard* till pieces are the size of small peas. Using 3 to 4 tablespoons cold *water,* sprinkle 1 tablespoon of the water over part of the mixture; toss with a fork. Push to side of bowl. Repeat with enough of the cold water till all is moistened. Form dough into a ball.

■ Preparation time: 30 minutes
■ Cooking time: 30 to 35 minutes
■ Standing time: 10 minutes

Clam and Ham Pie

- 1 medium onion, chopped (½ cup)
- 1 medium potato, peeled and chopped
- ½ cup chopped carrot
- ½ cup chopped green pepper
- 2 tablespoons butter *or* margarine
- 1 3-ounce package cream cheese, softened
- 1 6½- *or* 7½-ounce can minced clams, drained (½ cup)
- ½ cup diced fully cooked ham
- 3 beaten eggs
- 1½ cups soft bread crumbs (2 slices)
- ½ cup shredded cheddar cheese (2 ounces)
- ½ cup milk
  Pastry for Lattice-Top Pie

■ For filling, in a saucepan cook onion, potato, carrot, and green pepper, covered, in hot butter or margarine about 10 minutes or till crisp-tender. Remove from heat; stir in cream cheese. Add clams and ham. Combine eggs, bread crumbs, cheddar cheese, and milk; fold in the clam mixture.

■ Prepare Pastry for Lattice-Top Pie. On a lightly floured surface roll one ball of pastry into a 14-inch circle. Line a 10-inch quiche dish with pastry; trim to ½ inch beyond edge of dish. Turn the filling into the pastry-lined dish. Roll out the remaining pastry to a 12-inch circle. Cut into ½-inch-wide strips. Weave strips atop filling to make a lattice crust. Press ends of strips into rim of crust. Fold the bottom pastry over the lattice strips; seal and flute. Bake in a 375° oven about 45 minutes or till golden. Let stand for 10 minutes before serving. Makes 6 servings.

Pastry for Lattice-Top Pie: Stir together 2 cups *all-purpose flour* and 1 teaspoon *salt.* Cut in ⅔ cup *shortening or lard* till pieces are the size of small peas. Using 6 to 7 tablespoons cold *water,* sprinkle 1 tablespoon of the water over part of the mixture; toss with a fork. Push to side of bowl. Repeat with enough of the cold water till all is moistened. Form into two balls.

■ Preparation time: 40 minutes
■ Cooking time: 45 minutes
■ Standing time: 10 minutes

The flavor combination of *Clam and Ham Pie* is sure to please you and your guests alike. It's so full of tasty ingredients that it makes a firm pie, and is easy to cut into wedges.

If you like, you can use a whole wheat pastry for a double crust pie instead of the *Pastry for Lattice-Top Pie.* Weave strips of whole wheat pastry atop the filling for a lattice top.

California-Style Broccoli

1½ **pounds broccoli** *or* **two 10-ounce packages frozen cut broccoli**
1 **3-ounce package cream cheese, softened**
½ **cup plain yogurt**
3 **tablespoons milk**
½ **teaspoon garlic salt**
½ **cup sliced pitted ripe olives**
2 **medium tomatoes, cut into wedges**

▬▬ Wash broccoli and remove the leaves and tough parts of stalk. Cut tops into flowerets; slice stems. (*Or,* run hot water over frozen broccoli in a colander till separated.)

▬▬ In a large saucepan cook the broccoli, covered, in a small amount of boiling salted water about 10 minutes or till crisp-tender. Drain well. Cover and chill about 2 hours in the refrigerator or till cold.

▬▬ Meanwhile, make the dressing. In a small mixer bowl beat cream cheese on medium speed of electric mixer till fluffy. Add yogurt, milk, and garlic salt, beating till smooth. Fold in olives. Cover and chill about 2 hours or till serving time.

▬▬ To serve, arrange broccoli and tomato wedges on a serving platter. Spoon the dressing atop broccoli and tomatoes. Makes 8 servings.

▬▬ Preparation time: 25 minutes
▬▬ Chilling time: at least 2 hours

Caraway Corn

1 **16-ounce can whole kernel corn**
¼ **cup sliced green onion**
½ **teaspoon caraway seed**
1 **tablespoon butter** *or* **margarine**

▬▬ In a medium saucepan combine the *undrained* corn, the sliced green onion, and the caraway seed. Bring the mixture to boiling; reduce heat. Simmer, covered, for 5 minutes. Drain. Add the butter or margarine; stir to coat. Turn the corn mixture into a heated serving bowl. Makes 4 servings.

▬▬ Total preparation time: 15 minutes

Broccoli-Corn Scallop

1 **10-ounce package frozen chopped broccoli**
2 **beaten eggs**
1 **cup finely crushed whole wheat crackers**
½ **cup milk**
½ **teaspoon minced dried onion**
1 **17-ounce can cream-style corn**
1 **8-ounce can whole kernel corn, drained**
1 **tablespoon butter** *or* **margarine, melted**

▬▬ Cook the broccoli according to package directions; drain well. Spread broccoli over the bottom of a 10x6x2-inch baking dish. In a mixing bowl combine the eggs, *½ cup* of the crushed crackers, milk, and minced onion. Stir in the cream-style and whole kernel corn. Spread the corn mixture over broccoli.

▬▬ For topping, combine the remaining crushed crackers and the melted butter or margarine; sprinkle atop the corn mixture. Bake, uncovered, in a 350° oven about 35 minutes or till a knife inserted near the center comes out clean. Makes 8 servings.

▬▬ Preparation time: 20 minutes
▬▬ Cooking time: 35 minutes

Crisp Broccoli Stir-Fry is a simple Oriental-style side dish that features fresh broccoli. If you need to, however, you can use frozen broccoli instead.

Substitute one 20-ounce package or two 10-ounce packages frozen cut *broccoli*, thawed. Thoroughly drain the broccoli on several layers of paper toweling. Then, prepare the recipe as directed.

Crisp Broccoli Stir-Fry

1½ **pounds broccoli**
3 **tablespoons cold water**
3 **tablespoons soy sauce**
1½ **teaspoons cornstarch**
1 **teaspoon sugar**
2 **tablespoons cooking oil**
1 **cup celery bias-sliced into ½-inch lengths**
1 **large onion, cut into thin wedges**

■■■ Wash broccoli and remove the leaves and tough parts of stalk. Cut broccoli into 1-inch pieces; set aside. In a covered saucepan cook broccoli in boiling water for 2 minutes; drain. In a small mixing bowl combine the cold water, soy sauce, cornstarch, and sugar; set aside.

■■■ Preheat a wok or large skillet over high heat; add cooking oil. Stir-fry broccoli, celery, and onion for 3 to 5 minutes or till vegetables are crisp-tender. Stir the soy mixture; stir into the vegetables. Cook and stir till thickened and bubbly. Cover and cook for 2 minutes more. Serve immediately. Makes 6 servings.

■■■ Total preparation time: 30 minutes

Tarragon, an aromatic herb, has a hint of licorice flavor. It is a perennial plant with slender, pointed, dark green leaves.

In recipes, tarragon works well in either the fresh or the dried form. Because of tarragon's full flavor, however, you should use it discreetly. To see just how well this herb can blend with vegetables, such as green beans and tomatoes, be sure to try *Green Beans Tarragon.*

Green Beans Tarragon

- 1 **16-ounce package frozen French-style green beans**
- 1 **small onion, chopped (¼ cup)**
- 2 **tablespoons butter *or* margarine**
- 2 **medium tomatoes, peeled, seeded, and chopped**
- 1 **tablespoon snipped parsley**
- ½ **teaspoon dried tarragon, crushed**

▬▬ Cook the green beans according to package directions; drain well. Meanwhile, in a large saucepan cook the chopped onion in hot butter or margarine till tender but not brown. Stir in the green beans, chopped tomatoes, snipped parsley, tarragon, ⅛ teaspoon *salt*, and dash *pepper*. Cover and cook for 1 to 2 minutes or till heated through. Serves 6 to 8.

▬▬ Total preparation time: 20 minutes

Green Beans Viennese

- 1 **16-ounce package frozen cut green beans**
- 1 **small onion, chopped (¼ cup)**
- 1 **tablespoon butter *or* margarine**
- 1 **tablespoon all-purpose flour**
- ¼ **teaspoon dried dillweed**
- ½ **cup chicken broth**
- ½ **cup dairy sour cream**

▬▬ Cook the green beans according to package directions; drain well. In a large saucepan cook the chopped onion in hot butter or margarine till tender but not brown. Stir in the flour, dillweed, ¼ teaspoon *salt*, and dash *pepper*. Add the chicken broth all at once. Cook and stir till thickened and bubbly. Cook and stir for 1 minute more. Remove from heat. Stir in the sour cream. Add the green beans to sour cream mixture. Heat through but *do not boil.* Turn the mixture into a heated serving bowl. Makes 8 servings.

▬▬ Total preparation time: 20 minutes

Saucy Brussels Sprouts

- 2 **8-ounce packages frozen brussels sprouts**
- 2 **tablespoons chopped onion**
- ¼ **cup butter *or* margarine**
- ½ **cup dairy sour cream**
- 2 **tablespoons all-purpose flour**
- ½ **of a 6-ounce link cheese food with jalapeño peppers**
- ½ **teaspoon Worcestershire sauce**
- ¾ **cup soft bread crumbs (1 slice)**
- 1 **tablespoon butter *or* margarine, melted Paprika**

▬▬ In a large saucepan cook the brussels sprouts according to package directions. Drain, reserving liquid. Measure the reserved liquid; add water, if necessary to equal ½ cup. Set aside.

▬▬ In the same pan cook onion in the ¼ cup hot butter or margarine till tender but not brown. Stir together the sour cream and flour; add to saucepan along with the reserved vegetable liquid. Cook and stir till thickened and bubbly. Add the cheese food and Worcestershire sauce, stirring till the cheese food is melted. Add the brussels sprouts; stir to coat. Turn the mixture into an ungreased 1-quart casserole.

▬▬ Combine bread crumbs and the melted butter or margarine; sprinkle atop brussels sprouts. Sprinkle paprika atop. Bake in a 350° oven for 10 to 15 minutes or till heated through. Makes 6 to 8 servings.

▬▬ Preparation time: 20 minutes
▬▬ Cooking time: 10 to 15 minutes

Asparagus with Orange Sauce

- 1 **pound asparagus** *or* **one 10-ounce package frozen asparagus spears**
- ⅓ **cup butter** *or* **margarine**
- 1 **tablespoon frozen orange juice concentrate**
- 1 **tablespoon water**
- 2 **egg yolks**

■ Break off woody bases of asparagus at point where spears snap easily. Wash and scrape off scales. In a skillet or saucepan cook, covered, in a small amount of boiling salted water for 5 to 10 minutes or till tender. (*Or,* cook frozen asparagus according to package directions.) Drain and keep warm.

■ For sauce, in a small saucepan combine butter or margarine, orange juice concentrate, and water; bring to boiling. Meanwhile, place the egg yolks in a blender container. Cover and blend till smooth. With blender running on high speed, slowly add the hot butter mixture through the hole in lid. Blend about 30 seconds or till fluffy. Serve the sauce immediately over the asparagus. Makes 4 servings.

■ Total preparation time: 20 minutes

Asparagus en Papillote

- ¼ **cup slivered almonds**
- ¼ **cup butter** *or* **margarine**
- 1½ **pounds asparagus, cut into ¾-inch pieces,** *or* **two 8-ounce packages frozen cut asparagus**
- 1 **cup sliced fresh mushrooms**
- ½ **teaspoon dried tarragon, crushed Parchment** *or* **brown wrapping paper**

■ In a small skillet cook the almonds in hot butter or margarine over low heat for 5 to 7 minutes or till the almonds are golden brown, stirring constantly.

Spoon about *½ cup* of the asparagus mixture onto half of *each* 8-inch square of parchment paper. For each, fold the other half of the paper over the asparagus mixture. Fold the edges to seal, as shown.

■ If using frozen asparagus, run hot water over asparagus in a colander till separated. Pat dry with paper toweling. In a mixing bowl combine the fresh or thawed asparagus, mushrooms, and tarragon. Add the almond-butter mixture; toss gently to coat.

■ Cut the parchment or brown wrapping paper into six 8-inch squares. Spoon about *½ cup* of the asparagus mixture onto one half of *each* square. Fold the other half of the paper over the asparagus mixture to form rectangular packets. Fold the edges to seal (see photograph above)

■ Place the packets on a baking sheet. Bake in a 350° oven for 20 to 25 minutes or till asparagus is tender. To serve, cut an X across the top of each packet. Makes 6 servings.

■ Preparation time: 30 minutes
■ Cooking time: 20 to 25 minutes

En papillote (ahn pa-pee-YOTE) is a French method of baking and serving food in a wrapping of parchment paper.

If you have no parchment paper, brown wrapping paper will work just as well.

When serving *Asparagus en Papillote,* let your guests cut into their own packets so they can savor the delicious aroma.

Swedish Parsnip Soufflé

Swedish Parsnip Soufflé

    2 large carrots, finely shredded
         (1 cup)
    2 pounds parsnips, peeled and sliced
         (4½ to 5 cups)
    ¼ cup butter or margarine
    1 teaspoon sugar
    1 teaspoon salt
    ½ teaspoon ground nutmeg
    1 cup milk
    4 egg yolks
    4 egg whites
    1 tablespoon snipped parsley (optional)

▬▬ Cook carrots, covered, in a small amount of boiling salted water about 5 minutes or till tender; drain and set aside. Cook the parsnips, covered, in a small amount of boiling salted water for 15 to 20 minutes or till tender; drain. Add the butter or margarine, sugar, salt, and nutmeg to drained parsnips; mash. Stir in the cooked carrots and the milk.

▬▬ In a medium mixer bowl beat the egg yolks on high speed of electric mixer about 5 minutes or till thick and lemon colored. Stir *1 cup* of the parsnip mixture into the beaten egg yolk mixture; return all to parsnip mixture.

▬▬ Using clean beaters, beat the egg whites till stiff peaks form (tips stand straight). Gradually pour the parsnip-yolk mixture over beaten egg whites, folding to combine. Turn into an ungreased 2½-quart soufflé dish. Bake in a 350° oven for 50 to 55 minutes or till a knife inserted near the center comes out clean. Sprinkle with snipped parsley, if desired. Serve immediately. Makes 8 servings.

▬▬ Preparation time: 50 minutes
▬▬ Cooking time: 50 to 55 minutes

Apricot-Sweet Potato Bake

    2 pounds sweet potatoes (5 or 6 medium)
    1 cup dried apricots, chopped
    ¼ cup butter or margarine, cut up
    2 eggs
    2 teaspoons finely shredded orange peel

▬▬ In a large saucepan cook the sweet potatoes, covered, in enough boiling salted water to cover for 30 to 40 minutes or till tender. Drain and peel. Meanwhile, cook the apricots, covered, in boiling water for 10 minutes. Drain.

▬▬ In a large mixer bowl combine the sweet potatoes, apricots, and butter; beat till fluffy. Add the eggs, orange peel, and ¾ teaspoon *salt;* beat till combined. Turn into an ungreased 1½-quart casserole. Bake, covered, in a 325° oven for 1 hour. Serves 10.

▬▬ Preparation time: 1 hour
▬▬ Cooking time: 1 hour

Spiced Sweet Potato Bake

    2 pounds sweet potatoes, cooked,
         drained, and peeled (5 or 6 medium)
    ¼ cup butter or margarine
    ¼ cup packed brown sugar
    ½ teaspoon ground cinnamon
    ⅓ cup light cream or milk
    8 marshmallows, halved

▬▬ Mash sweet potatoes. Stir in butter, brown sugar, cinnamon, and ½ teaspoon *salt.* Add cream or milk; beat till fluffy. Turn into a 10x6x2-inch baking dish or a shallow 1½-quart casserole. Bake in a 350° oven for 20 to 25 minutes or till heated through. Top with marshmallows; broil for 1 to 2 minutes or till marshmallows are light brown. Makes 8 servings.

▬▬ Preparation time: 50 minutes
▬▬ Cooking time: about 30 minutes

**MENU
VALENTINE'S DAY
EXTRAVAGANZA**

Cheese and Crackers

Dill Vinaigrette
Salad★

Broiled Sirloin Steaks

Swedish Parsnip
Soufflé

Sponge Cake with
Chocolate Sauce

White Wine Spritzer

You'll want to serve *Swedish Parsnip Soufflé* immediately after you remove it from the oven. Before your guests arrive, simplify last-minute preparation by preparing the carrots and parsnips, and separating the eggs. About an hour before serving, beat the egg yolks and egg whites and bake the soufflé.
★ *see recipe, page 119*

Polynesian Vegetable Combo

- 1 **medium onion, cut into wedges**
- 2 **tablespoons butter *or* margarine**
- 1 **8-ounce can pineapple tidbits (juice pack)**
- 4 **medium carrots, sliced diagonally (2 cups)**
- 1 **medium green pepper, cut into 1-inch squares**
- 3 **tablespoons soy sauce**
- 2 **tablespoons water**
- 2 **teaspoons cornstarch**
- 1 **8-ounce can sliced water chestnuts, drained**

■■■ In a large saucepan cook the onion wedges in hot butter or margarine for 5 minutes; set aside. Drain pineapple tidbits, reserving liquid; set tidbits aside. Add the reserved pineapple liquid and carrots to onion. Bring to boiling; reduce heat. Cover and simmer for 15 minutes. Add green pepper; cover and simmer about 5 minutes more or till tender.

■■■ Combine soy sauce, water, and cornstarch; stir into vegetable mixture. Cook and stir till thickened and bubbly. Cook and stir for 2 minutes more. Add pineapple and water chestnuts; heat through. Serves 6.

■■ Total preparation time: 45 minutes

Bean Sprout Stir-Fry

- 1 **cup frozen French-style green beans**
- 1 **medium carrot, cut into julienne strips (½ cup)**
- 2 **tablespoons butter *or* margarine**
- ¼ **cup sliced green onion**
- 1 **tablespoon sesame seed**
- 3 **cups fresh bean sprouts**
- ½ **cup sliced fresh mushrooms**

■■■ In a small saucepan cook the green beans and carrot strips in a small amount of boiling water for 3 to 5 minutes or till crisp-tender; drain well.

■■■ Preheat a wok or large skillet over high heat; add butter or margarine. Stir-fry green onion and sesame seed in hot butter or margarine about 2 minutes or till onion is tender and sesame seed is light brown. Add the well-drained bean-carrot mixture, the bean sprouts, and mushrooms. Stir-fry for 1 to 2 minutes or till mushrooms are tender and mixture is heated through. Serve immediately. Makes 6 servings.

■■ Total preparation time: 15 minutes

Mustard-Braised Celery

- 1 **bunch celery**
- 2 **tablespoons cooking oil**
- ⅔ **cup chicken broth**
- ¼ **cup cold water**
- 1 **teaspoon cornstarch**
- 2 **tablespoons chopped pimiento**
- 1 **teaspoon dry mustard**
- ¼ **teaspoon salt**
- ½ **cup sliced water chestnuts, drained**

■■■ Separate celery stalks and trim leaves and ends, reserving leaves for garnish, if desired. Cut the celery into 2-inch-long julienne strips.

■■■ Preheat a wok or large skillet over high heat; add cooking oil. Stir-fry celery in hot cooking oil for 2 minutes. Add broth. Reduce heat; cook, covered, about 10 minutes or till crisp-tender. Remove celery from wok. Measure the broth; add water, if necessary, to equal ½ cup liquid. Return broth mixture to wok.

■■■ Combine the cold water and cornstarch; stir into the broth mixture in wok. Add pimiento, mustard, and salt. Cook and stir till thickened and bubbly. Add celery and water chestnuts, stirring to coat vegetables. Cover and cook for 2 minutes more or till heated through. Garnish with celery leaves, if desired. Serve immediately. Makes 6 to 8 servings.

■■ Total preparation time: 35 minutes

Cheese-Sauced Vegetables

   Desired vegetable
2 **tablespoons butter *or* margarine**
2 **tablespoons all-purpose flour**
¾ **teaspoon dried marjoram, crushed, *or* dried basil, crushed**
¼ **teaspoon salt**
   Dash pepper
1¼ **cups milk**
1 **cup shredded Swiss, Gruyère, *or* Monterey Jack cheese (4 ounces)**
½ **cup sliced fresh mushrooms**
2 **tablespoons toasted, sliced almonds *or* 2 slices bacon, crisp-cooked, drained, and crumbled (optional)**

■ Prepare and cook desired vegetable (asparagus, green or wax beans, broccoli, brussels sprouts, cauliflower, or celery) according to the directions given below and to the right. Drain well.

■ Meanwhile, prepare the cheese sauce. In a small saucepan melt butter or margarine. Stir in the flour, marjoram or basil, salt, and pepper. Add milk all at once. Cook and stir over medium heat till thickened and bubbly. Cook and stir for 1 minute more. Reduce heat; add the shredded cheese and sliced mushrooms, stirring till cheese is melted.

■ Drain the desired vegetable. To serve, place in a serving bowl and pour the hot cheese sauce atop. Garnish with the toasted, sliced almonds or bacon pieces, if desired. Makes 4 to 6 servings.

Asparagus: Break off the woody bases of 1 pound fresh *asparagus* at the point where the spears snap easily. Wash; scrape off the scales. Cut the spears diagonally into 2-inch pieces. In a saucepan cook, covered, in a small amount of boiling salted water for 8 to 10 minutes or till crisp-tender. (*Or,* use two 8-ounce packages frozen *cut asparagus.* Cook according to package directions.)

Beans, Green *or* Wax: Wash and remove ends and strings, if present, of 1 pound fresh *green or wax beans.* Cut into 1-inch pieces. (*Or,* slice diagonally end-to-end for French-style beans.) In a saucepan cook, covered, in a small amount of boiling salted water for 20 to 30 minutes for green or wax beans, or 10 to 12 minutes for French-style beans or till crisp-tender. (*Or,* use two 9-ounce packages frozen *cut or French-style green beans.* Cook the beans according to package directions.)

Broccoli: Wash and remove the outer leaves and tough parts of stalks of 1½ pounds fresh *broccoli.* Cut off the flowerets; set aside. Cut the remaining spears into 1-inch pieces. In a saucepan cook broccoli pieces, covered, in a small amount of boiling salted water for 5 minutes. Add the broccoli flowerets; cook about 5 minutes more or till crisp-tender. (*Or,* use two 10-ounce packages frozen *cut broccoli.* Cook according to package directions.)

Brussels Sprouts: Trim the stems from 2 pints fresh *brussels sprouts.* Remove and discard any wilted leaves. Wash the brussels sprouts. Cut any large sprouts in half lengthwise. In a saucepan cook sprouts, covered, in a small amount of boiling salted water for 10 to 15 minutes or till crisp-tender. (*Or,* use two 10-ounce packages frozen *brussels sprouts.* Cook according to package directions.)

Cauliflower: Wash 1 head fresh *cauliflower.* Remove leaves and woody stem. Break into flowerets. In a saucepan cook, covered, in a small amount of boiling salted water for 10 to 15 minutes or just till tender. (*Or,* use two 10-ounce packages frozen *cauliflower.* Cook according to package directions.)

Celery: Separate stalks and trim leaves from 1 bunch *celery.* Bias-slice into ¾-inch pieces. Cook, covered, in a small amount of boiling salted water for 10 to 15 minutes or till tender.

■ Preparation time: 15 minutes
■ Cooking time: 10 to 30 minutes

Cheese-Sauced Vegetables gives you the choice of six different fresh or frozen vegetables.

If you use fresh vegetables, prepare them according to the directions at left. Or, if you'd like, steam the vegetables instead of cooking them in boiling water.

To steam, place the vegetables in a steamer basket over boiling water. The basket should not touch the boiling water. Cover and reduce the heat. Steam till the vegetables are tender. Steaming will take 3 to 5 minutes longer than cooking in water (see the timings at left).

If you use frozen vegetables, steam them according to package directions.

Carrots Véronique

3 **cups coarsely shredded carrots
(6 to 8 medium)**
½ **cup water**
½ **teaspoon salt**
1 **cup seedless green grapes, halved**
2 **tablespoons butter** *or* **margarine**

▬ In a medium saucepan combine the shredded carrots, water, and salt. Bring to boiling; reduce heat. Cover and simmer for 8 to 10 minutes or till carrots are nearly tender. Drain; return carrots to saucepan. Add the grape halves and butter or margarine; toss to mix. Heat through. Makes 6 servings.

▬ Total preparation time: 25 minutes

Stuffed Potatoes Florentine

6 **large baking potatoes**
1 **10-ounce package frozen chopped spinach**
3 **slices bacon**
Dairy sour cream
1 **cup shredded Monterey Jack cheese
(4 ounces)**
½ **teaspoon salt**
Dash pepper

▬ Scrub the baking potatoes thoroughly with a brush; remove any sprouts. Prick potatoes with a fork. Bake in a 425° oven for 45 to 60 minutes or till done.

▬ Meanwhile, cook the spinach according to package directions. Drain; squeeze out excess liquid. In a skillet cook the bacon till crisp; remove and drain on paper toweling. Crumble and set aside.

▬ Cut a lengthwise slice from the top of each potato; discard skin from slice. Reserving shells, scoop out the inside of each potato and add to the potato portions from top slices; mash. Stir in enough sour cream (about ½ cup) to make of stiff consistency. Stir in the spinach, cheese, salt, and pepper.

▬ Spoon the potato-spinach mixture into the reserved potato shells. Place potatoes into a shallow baking pan. Return to the 425° oven; bake for 20 to 25 minutes or till light brown. Sprinkle the bacon pieces atop potatoes. Makes 6 servings.

▬ Preparation time: 20 minutes
▬ Cooking time: about 1½ hours

Vegetable Potpourri

2 **medium carrots, sliced (1 cup)**
1 **medium onion, cut into thin wedges
(½ cup)**
⅓ **cup water**
1 **0.75-ounce envelope Italian salad
dressing mix**
1 **medium eggplant, peeled and cut into
¾-inch cubes (5 cups)**
2 **medium zucchini, cut into ⅜-inch slices
(2¼ cups)**
1 **medium green pepper, seeded and cut
into 1-inch squares (½ cup)**
2 **medium tomatoes, peeled, seeded, and
cut into ½-inch pieces (1 cup)**
Grated Parmesan cheese

▬ In a large skillet combine the carrot slices, onion wedges, and the water; sprinkle the Italian salad dressing mix over all. Bring to boiling; reduce heat. Simmer, covered, for 5 minutes. Stir in the eggplant, zucchini, and green pepper. Simmer, covered, for 5 to 8 minutes more or till the vegetables are nearly tender, stirring occasionally.

▬ Stir in the tomatoes. Uncover and simmer for 2 to 3 minutes more or till tomatoes are heated through. Turn into a heated serving bowl. Sprinkle generously with Parmesan cheese. Makes 6 servings.

▬ Total preparation time: 30 minutes

Carrot Mousse Tart

4 large carrots, very thinly sliced
1 tablespoon butter *or* margarine, melted
3 cups shredded carrots (6 to 8 medium)
1 medium potato, peeled and cubed
2 eggs
¼ cup dairy sour cream
1 teaspoon finely shredded orange peel
¼ teaspoon salt
⅛ teaspoon ground white pepper
⅛ teaspoon ground turmeric (optional)

■■■ In a saucepan cook the thinly sliced carrots in a small amount of boiling salted water for 3 to 4 minutes or till crisp-tender; drain.

■■■ Brush a 9x1½-inch round flan pan or baking pan with the melted butter or margarine. Beginning in the center of the pan and working toward the outer edges, arrange the drained carrot slices in circles, petal fashion, slightly overlapping the slices to cover the bottom and overlapping and pressing them onto the sides of the pan (see photograph, upper right). Set aside. Cover and chill, if desired.

■■■ For filling, cook the shredded carrots and potato in a small amount of boiling salted water about 15 minutes or just till tender; drain well.

■■■ In a blender container or food processor bowl combine eggs, sour cream, orange peel, salt, pepper, and turmeric, if desired. Add *half* of the cooked shredded carrots and potato. Cover and blend or process till nearly smooth. Add the remaining carrots and potato; cover and continue blending till smooth. Cover and chill in the refrigerator, if desired.

Carrot Mousse Tart

■■■ Stir the filling; turn into the carrot-lined pan. Smooth the top with a spatula. If the tart is unchilled, bake uncovered, in a 350° oven for 30 to 35 minutes or till a knife inserted near the center comes out clean. (*Or,* if the tart is chilled, bake about 45 minutes or till set.) Let stand for 5 minutes.

■■■ Using a knife or spatula, carefully loosen the carrot slices from the sides of the pan. Place a serving platter atop the tart in the pan; invert and carefully lift the pan off. (If necessary, replace any carrot slices remaining in the pan.) Serve warm. To serve, cut into wedges. Makes 8 servings.

■■■ Preparation time: 1 hour
■■■ Cooking time: 30 to 35 minutes
■■■ Standing time: 5 minutes

■■■■ **MENU** ■■■■
**SILVER
ANNIVERSARY
DINNER**

Raw-Vegetable Platter
with Dip

Glazed Ham

Carrot Mousse Tart

Dinner Rolls

Praline Ice Cream ★

Coffee or Tea

Carrot Mousse Tart is a beautiful highlight to this menu. To simplify preparation, make the mousse-like filling ahead, and arrange the carrot slices in the pan. Chill them separately in the refrigerator. About an hour before dinner, finish the tart.

For dessert, prepare Praline Ice Cream 5 to 6 hours ahead to allow it plenty of time to ripen and develop flavor.

★ *see recipe, page 162*

Bulgur wheat is one of the main cereal grains of the Middle East. If it's unavailable in your local supermarket, try a health food store. If you still have trouble, you'll find it helpful to know that bulgur wheat and cracked wheat cereal are interchangeable.

Zucchini Parmesan

- 1 **medium onion, sliced into thin wedges**
- 2 **tablespoons butter** *or* **margarine**
- 3 **medium zucchini, sliced ¼ inch thick**
- ½ **cup sliced fresh mushrooms**
- ¼ **cup dry white wine** *or* **chicken broth**
- ½ **teaspoon garlic salt**
- 2 **tablespoons grated Parmesan cheese**

■■ In a medium skillet cook the onion wedges in hot butter or margarine about 5 minutes or till tender but not brown. Add the zucchini slices, mushroom slices, white wine or chicken broth, and garlic salt. Bring to boiling; reduce heat. Cover and simmer about 10 minutes or till zucchini is tender; drain. Sprinkle with Parmesan cheese. Makes 6 servings.

■■ Total preparation time: 25 minutes

Zucchini-Bulgur Stir-Fry

- 4 **cups water**
- 2 **tablespoons instant beef bouillon granules**
- 2 **cups bulgur wheat**
- 2 **tablespoons cold water**
- 2 **tablespoons soy sauce**
- 2 **teaspoons cornstarch**
- 1 **tablespoon cooking oil**
- 3 **cups thinly sliced carrots**
- 1 **clove garlic, minced**
- 1½ **teaspoons grated gingerroot**
- 2 **small zucchini, sliced**
- ¼ **cup sliced green onion**
- 1 **cup peanuts**
- ½ **teaspoon finely shredded lemon peel**

■■ In a saucepan bring the 4 cups water to boiling. Add the beef bouillon granules; stir till dissolved. Remove saucepan from the heat. Stir in the bulgur wheat and let stand for 1 hour; drain. Set the bulgur mixture aside. Combine the 2 tablespoons cold water, soy sauce, and cornstarch. Set aside.

■■ Preheat a wok or large skillet over high heat; add cooking oil. Stir-fry carrots, garlic, and gingerroot for 8 minutes. Add zucchini and green onion. Stir-fry about 2 minutes more or till crisp-tender. Stir soy mixture; stir into vegetables. Cook and stir till thickened and bubbly. Cook and stir for 2 minutes more. Add bulgur, peanuts, and lemon peel to wok. Stir gently till heated through. Makes 6 to 8 servings.

■■ Preparation time: 5 minutes
■■ Standing time: 1 hour
■■ Cooking time: 20 minutes

Stuffed Artichoke Hearts

- 1 **14-ounce can artichoke hearts, drained and rinsed**
- 1 **cup chopped fresh mushrooms**
- 2 **tablespoons sliced green onion**
- 1 **tablespoon butter** *or* **margarine**
- 1 **tablespoon all-purpose flour**
  Dash ground nutmeg
- ½ **cup milk**
- ¼ **cup shredded Swiss cheese (1 ounce)**
- ¼ **cup crushed rich round crackers**
- 1½ **teaspoons butter** *or* **margarine, melted**
  Dash paprika

■■ Arrange artichoke hearts in a greased 9-inch pie plate; set aside. In a medium saucepan cook mushrooms and green onion in the 1 tablespoon hot butter or margarine till most of the liquid is evaporated. Stir in the flour and nutmeg; add the milk all at once. Cook and stir till thickened and bubbly. Cook and stir for 1 minute more. Add the cheese, stirring till melted.

■■ Spoon the mushroom mixture over artichoke hearts. Combine crackers, the 1½ teaspoons butter, and paprika; sprinkle atop. Bake in a 350° oven about 15 minutes or till heated through. Makes 4 servings.

■■ Preparation time: 20 minutes
■■ Cooking time: 15 minutes

Dilly Pea and Potato Casserole

- 1   **10-ounce package frozen peas**
- 1   **10¾-ounce can condensed cream of chicken soup**
- ½   **cup milk**
- ¼   **cup mayonnaise** *or* **salad dressing**
- 1   **teaspoon dried dillweed**
- 1   **12-ounce package frozen shredded hash brown potatoes, thawed**
- 1   **8¼-ounce can sliced carrots, drained**
- ½   **cup shredded American cheese (2 ounces)**

■■■ Run hot water over frozen peas in a colander till separated; set aside. In a small mixing bowl stir together condensed soup, milk, mayonnaise or salad dressing, and dried dillweed; set aside.

■■■ Arrange *half* of the hash brown potatoes in a 10x6x2-inch baking dish. Top with *half* of the peas, then all of the sliced carrots. Spread *half* of the soup mixture atop. Repeat with the remaining hash brown potatoes, peas, and soup mixture. Bake, covered, in a 350° oven for 30 minutes. Sprinkle the shredded cheese atop and bake, uncovered, for 5 minutes more. Makes 8 to 10 servings.

■■■ Preparation time: 20 minutes
■■■ Cooking time: 35 minutes

Swiss Creamed Peas

- 3   **10-ounce packages frozen peas (6 cups)**
- 2   **cups sliced green onions**
- 3   **tablespoons butter** *or* **margarine**
- 2   **tablespoons all-purpose flour**
- 2   **cups light cream**
- 1   **teaspoon finely shredded lemon peel**
- 1½ **cups shredded** *process* **Swiss cheese (6 ounces)**

■■■ In a large saucepan cook the frozen peas according to package directions. Drain well; set aside.

■■■ Meanwhile, prepare the cheese sauce. For sauce, in a medium saucepan cook the green onions in hot butter or margarine till tender but not brown. Stir in flour and ½ teaspoon *salt*. Add the cream and lemon peel all at once. Cook and stir till thickened and bubbly. Cook and stir for 1 minute more. Add the Swiss cheese, stirring till melted *(do not boil)*.

■■■ Return the drained peas to the saucepan. Add the cheese sauce; stir to coat. To serve, spoon into individual sauce dishes. Makes 12 servings.

■■■ Total preparation time: 20 minutes

Succotash with Chili Peppers

- 1   **10-ounce package frozen baby lima beans**
- 1   **10-ounce package frozen whole kernel corn**
- ½   **cup dairy sour cream**
- 1   **tablespoon all-purpose flour**
- ¼   **cup milk**
- 1   **4-ounce can green chili peppers, rinsed, seeded, and chopped**
      Several dashes bottled hot pepper sauce

■■■ In a large saucepan cook the lima beans and corn according to package directions for the beans; drain. Return beans and corn to saucepan. Set aside.

■■■ Combine sour cream and flour; stir in milk, green chili peppers, and hot pepper sauce. Stir sour cream mixture into beans and corn. Cook and stir till thickened and bubbly. Cook and stir for 1 minute more. Turn into a serving bowl. Makes 8 servings.

■■■ Total preparation time: 20 minutes

■■MENU■■
MAY DAY
CELEBRATION

Appetizer Meatballs

Tossed Green Salad

Barbecued Chicken

Swiss Creamed Peas

Dill Braid ★
Butter or Margarine

Strawberry Shortcake

White Wine

Why not celebrate May Day with a special dinner party? The simplicity of this delicious menu will delight you almost as much as the bloom of spring's first flowers.
  Swiss Creamed Peas is a large side dish that makes 12 servings. If you're planning a small dinner party, you may want to cut the recipe in half for 6 servings.
★ *see recipe, page 129*

Green Pea and Corn Salad

1 **16-ounce package frozen peas**
1 **16-ounce can white whole kernel
   corn, drained**
1 **8-ounce can sliced water chestnuts,
   drained**
¼ **cup thinly sliced green onion**
½ **cup mayonnaise *or* salad dressing**
3 **tablespoons milk**
1 **tablespoon lemon juice**
3 **tablespoons grated Parmesan cheese**
½ **cup toasted, slivered almonds
   Lettuce leaves
   Chopped pimiento (optional)**

■■ Run hot water over the frozen peas in a colander till separated. In a large mixing bowl stir together the peas, whole kernel corn, sliced water chestnuts, and thinly sliced green onion.

■■ For dressing, stir together the mayonnaise or salad dressing, milk, and lemon juice. Stir in the grated Parmesan cheese. Pour the salad dressing over the vegetable mixture; toss gently to coat. Cover and chill in the refrigerator about 2 hours or till cold.

■■ Before serving, stir the slivered almonds into the salad. Turn into a lettuce-lined salad bowl. Garnish with pimiento, if desired. Makes 6 to 8 servings.

■■ Preparation time: 15 minutes
■■ Chilling time: at least 2 hours

For *Carrot-Zucchini Salad* (pictured above), you can use purchased oil-and-vinegar salad dressing. Or, for a personal touch to your salad, make this dressing yourself.

In a screw-top jar combine 1 cup *salad oil,* ⅔ cup *vinegar,* 1 to 2 teaspoons *sugar,* and ½ to 1 teaspoon dried *oregano,* crushed. Cover tightly and shake well to mix. Chill till serving time. Shake again before serving. Makes about 1½ cups dressing.

Carrot-Zucchini Salad

4 **lettuce leaves**
1¼ **cups shredded unpeeled zucchini**
1¼ **cups shredded carrots**
¼ **cup alfalfa sprouts**
2 **to 3 tablespoons oil-and-vinegar salad
   dressing
   Carrot flowers (optional)**

■■ Line *each* of four salad plates with *one* lettuce leaf. Layer *some* of the shredded zucchini and *some* of the shredded carrots on *each* salad plate. Place *1 tablespoon* of the alfalfa sprouts atop *each* serving. Pass the oil-and-vinegar salad dressing to drizzle over the salads. If desired, garnish each salad with a ''carrot flower'' made with a paper-thin slice of carrot (see photograph, above). Makes 4 servings.

■■ Total preparation time: 15 minutes

Toasted Barley-Bean Salad

- ½ cup quick-cooking barley
- 1 tablespoon butter *or* margarine
- 1½ cups water
- 1 teaspoon instant chicken bouillon granules
- 1 15-ounce can garbanzo beans, drained
- 1 8-ounce can cut Italian green beans, drained
- 1 8-ounce can red kidney beans, drained
- 1 small onion, thinly sliced and separated into rings
- ½ cup chopped celery
- 2 tablespoons snipped parsley
- ¼ cup salad oil
- ¼ cup vinegar
- ½ teaspoon dry mustard

■ In a large skillet cook the barley in hot butter or margarine over low heat till barley is golden, stirring frequently. Add water and bouillon granules. Cook, covered, for 10 to 12 minutes or till tender. Drain.

■ Meanwhile, in a large mixing bowl combine the garbanzo beans, Italian green beans, kidney beans, onion rings, chopped celery, and snipped parsley. Stir in the drained barley.

■ For dressing, in a screw-top jar combine the salad oil, vinegar, and dry mustard. Cover and shake well to mix. Pour the dressing over the bean mixture. Cover and chill in the refrigerator about 2 hours or till cold. Makes 8 to 10 servings.

■ Preparation time: 40 minutes
■ Chilling time: at least 2 hours

Spinach-Mushroom Salad

- 3 eggs
- ½ cup dairy sour cream
- ½ of a 3-ounce package cream cheese, softened
- 2 tablespoons crumbled blue cheese
- 1 tablespoon dry sherry
- ½ teaspoon grated onion
- ⅛ teaspoon salt
- ⅛ teaspoon paprika
- 6 cups torn fresh spinach
- 1½ cups sliced fresh mushrooms
- 1½ cups cherry tomatoes, halved

■ To hard-cook the eggs, place eggs in a saucepan; cover with cold water. Bring to boiling; reduce heat to just below simmering. Cover and cook for 15 minutes. Run cold water over the eggs till cool. Remove shells; slice the eggs.

■ For salad dressing, in a blender container or food processor bowl combine the sour cream, cream cheese, crumbled blue cheese, sherry, onion, salt, and paprika. Cover and blend or process till smooth. Cover and chill the dressing in the refrigerator about 2 hours or till cold.

■ In a large salad bowl combine the spinach, mushrooms, tomato halves, and sliced eggs. Cover and chill in the refrigerator about 2 hours or till cold. To serve, pour the salad dressing over the spinach mixture. Toss gently to coat. Makes 8 servings.

■ Preparation time: 25 minutes
■ Chilling time: at least 2 hours

Torn fresh spinach is attractive and delicious in *Spinach-Mushroom Salad*. When selecting spinach, look for large, fresh-looking leaves, and avoid spinach that's wilted or yellowed. Store unwashed spinach, loosely covered, in the vegetable crisper of the refrigerator. For best flavor, serve the spinach within a few days of buying it.

Before using spinach, rinse the leaves in a pan of lukewarm water. Remove and discard the stems. Then pat the leaves dry with paper toweling.

Rutabaga-Sweet Potato Salad features an interesting combination of thin julienne strips of rutabaga, sweet potato, and zucchini.

To make julienne strips, first cut a thin slice off one side of the vegetable, if necessary, to make it lie flat on the cutting surface. Placing the flat side down, cut into thin lengthwise slices. Then, cut each slice into narrow strips about ⅛ to ¼ inch thick.

Ripe Olive Salad

    1 egg
    1 cup mayonnaise *or* salad dressing
    ½ cup chopped pitted ripe olives
    ⅓ cup chili sauce
    ¼ teaspoon celery salt
    ¼ teaspoon garlic salt
    ¼ teaspoon dried basil, crushed
    ¼ teaspoon Worcestershire sauce
    6 lettuce wedges

■ To hard-cook the egg, place egg in a saucepan; cover with cold water. Bring to boiling; reduce heat to just below simmering. Cover; cook 15 minutes. Run cold water over egg till cool. Remove shell; chop egg.

■ In a small mixing bowl combine the chopped egg, mayonnaise or salad dressing, chopped olives, chili sauce, celery salt, garlic salt, basil, and Worcestershire sauce. Cover and chill about 2 hours or till cold. Serve atop lettuce wedges. Makes 6 servings.

■ Preparation time: 30 minutes
■ Chilling time: at least 2 hours

Rutabaga-Sweet Potato Salad

    1 medium rutabaga, peeled and cut into
       julienne strips (4 cups)
    1 medium sweet potato, peeled and cut into
       julienne strips (1½ cups)
    ½ cup mayonnaise *or* salad dressing
    1 tablespoon finely chopped green onion
    1 tablespoon vinegar
    ½ teaspoon salt
    ¼ teaspoon dried dillweed
    1 medium zucchini, cut into julienne strips
    ¼ cup thinly sliced radishes
       Lettuce leaves (optional)

■ Cook the rutabaga and sweet potato, covered, in a small amount of boiling salted water for 10 to 15 minutes or till crisp-tender. Drain well.

■ For dressing, combine mayonnaise or salad dressing, green onion, vinegar, salt, and dillweed; set aside. In a mixing bowl combine rutabaga, sweet potato, zucchini, and radish. Pour dressing atop; toss gently. Cover; chill about 2 hours or till cold. Serve in a lettuce-lined salad bowl, if desired. Makes 8 servings.

■ Preparation time: 45 minutes
■ Chilling time: at least 2 hours

Oriental Potato Salad

    4 medium potatoes (1¼ pounds)
    2 cups fresh pea pods *or* one 6-ounce
       package frozen pea pods
    ½ cup thinly sliced carrot
    ¼ cup thinly sliced green onion
    ⅓ cup mayonnaise *or* salad dressing
    ⅓ cup dairy sour cream
    2 tablespoons white wine vinegar
    ½ teaspoon salt
    ½ teaspoon dry mustard
    ¼ teaspoon pepper
    ½ cup peanuts

■ Scrub potatoes. Cook, covered, in boiling salted water for 25 to 40 minutes or till tender. If using frozen pea pods, run hot water over pea pods in a colander till separated. Cut pea pods into 1-inch pieces. Cook carrot slices, covered, in a small amount of boiling salted water for 5 minutes. Add pea pods. Cook about 3 minutes more or till crisp-tender; drain. Peel and cube potatoes; stir potatoes and green onion into carrot mixture. Cover and chill about 2 hours or till cold.

■ For dressing, combine mayonnaise or salad dressing, sour cream, vinegar, salt, dry mustard, and pepper. Cover; chill till serving time. Before serving, combine the vegetable mixture, the dressing, and peanuts; toss gently to coat. Makes 8 servings.

■ Preparation time: 50 minutes
■ Chilling time: at least 2 hours

Dill Vinaigrette Salad*

    2 tablespoons Dill Vinegar
    ¼ cup salad oil
    1 tablespoon thinly sliced shallots
         or green onion
    1 teaspoon sugar
    ¼ teaspoon dry mustard
    ¼ teaspoon paprika
    3 medium carrots
    2 cups pea pods or one 6-ounce
         package frozen pea pods
    1 cup sliced fresh mushrooms
    2 avocados, seeded, peeled, and sliced
       Bibb lettuce

■■■ Prepare Dill Vinegar; let stand 2 weeks. For salad dressing, in a screw-top jar combine the Dill Vinegar, salad oil, shallots or green onion, sugar, dry mustard, paprika, 1 tablespoon *water,* and ⅛ teaspoon *salt.* Cover and shake well to mix. Chill till serving time.

■■■ Cut the carrots into thin lengthwise strips, using a vegetable peeler. (*Or,* crinkle-cut the carrots lengthwise into 1½-inch sticks.) Cook the fresh pea pods in a small amount of boiling salted water for 5 minutes; add the carrots and cook about 5 minutes more or till crisp-tender. (*Or,* cook the frozen pea pods and the carrots for 5 minutes.) Drain and chill.

■■■ To serve, arrange the vegetables and avocado slices on 6 chilled lettuce-lined salad plates. Pass the salad dressing. Makes 6 servings.

Dill Vinegar: In a cruet or screw-top jar combine 1 cup *white vinegar,* 1 whole *clove,* 1 small clove *garlic,* and 2 teaspoons *dillseed.* Cover the vinegar and let stand for 24 hours. After 24 hours remove the garlic from vinegar; discard. Let the vinegar stand for 2 more weeks. At the end of 2 weeks strain and bottle the vinegar in a translucent jar. Makes 1 cup.

■■■ Advance preparation time: 15 minutes
■■■ Standing time: 2 weeks
■■■ Final preparation time: 30 minutes
  * pictured on page 13

Gazpacho Aspic

    1 envelope unflavored gelatin
    ⅓ cup beef broth
    1½ cups vegetable juice cocktail
    2 teaspoons lemon juice
    1 teaspoon Worcestershire sauce
       Several dashes bottled hot pepper sauce
    ⅓ cup chopped tomato
    ⅓ cup chopped green pepper
    ⅓ cup chopped cucumber

■■■ In a saucepan soften gelatin in beef broth; let stand for 5 minutes. Cook and stir over low heat till gelatin is dissolved. Remove from heat. Stir in juice cocktail, lemon juice, Worcestershire, and hot pepper sauce. Chill to the consistency of unbeaten egg whites (partially set). Fold in tomato, green pepper, and cucumber. Pour into a 3-cup mold. Cover and chill about 6 hours or till firm. Unmold. Makes 4 servings.

■■■ Preparation time: 1¼ hours
■■■ Chilling time: at least 6 hours

Creamy Vegetable Mold

    1 12-ounce can vegetable juice cocktail
    1 3-ounce package lemon-flavored gelatin
    ½ cup plain yogurt
    ½ cup thinly sliced celery
    ½ cup shredded carrot
    ⅓ cup finely chopped cucumber
    ¼ cup snipped parsley

■■■ In a saucepan bring juice cocktail to boiling; add gelatin, stirring till dissolved. Remove from heat. Stir in the yogurt. Chill to the consistency of unbeaten egg whites (partially set). Fold in celery, carrot, cucumber, and parsley. Pour into six ½-cup molds. Cover; chill about 6 hours or till firm. Unmold. Makes 6 servings.

■■■ Preparation time: 1¼ hours
■■■ Chilling time: at least 6 hours

Dill Vinegar is the key ingredient in *Dill Vinaigrette Salad.* You'll need to allow 2 weeks for the vinegar to develop its characteristic flavor.

If you don't want to (or just can't!) wait that long to make this tasty salad, substitute 2 tablespoons *white wine vinegar* and ⅛ teaspoon dried *dillweed* for *Dill Vinegar.*

When planning the food for your party menu, consider *Creamy Vegetable Mold.* It's a make-ahead salad that needs several hours to chill. Preparing as much food ahead as possible helps the party preparations go a lot smoother.

For always-interesting salads, vary your toppings. This is almost easier done than said when you start with our versatile *Salad Dressing Base*. As is, the base recipe makes a fine dressing; but its real wonder is that you can use it as the beginning for any of seven jazzy variations.

For your vegetable salads, try *Thousand Island Salad Dressing, Buttermilk Salad Dressing, Creamy Garlic Salad Dressing*, or *Creamy Vegetable Salad Dressing.*

Use *Citrus-Peanut Salad Dressing, Honey-Lime Salad Dressing,* and *Blue Cheese Salad Dressing* to show off your fruit salads.

You can make the base ahead and store it in your refrigerator (it keeps for several weeks).

Salad Dressing Base

½ of a 3-ounce package lemon-flavored gelatin (3 tablespoons)
½ cup boiling water
2 cups mayonnaise *or* salad dressing
1 5⅓-ounce can (⅔ cup) evaporated milk
¼ cup vinegar
2 teaspoons prepared mustard
1 teaspoon salt

Dissolve the lemon-flavored gelatin in the boiling water. In a mixing bowl combine the mayonnaise or salad dressing, evaporated milk, vinegar, mustard, and salt; stir in the dissolved gelatin mixture. Cover tightly and chill in the refrigerator for 2 hours or till cold. Makes about 3 cups salad dressing base.

Thousand Island Salad Dressing: In a mixing bowl combine 1 cup *Salad Dressing Base*, ¼ cup *chili sauce,* 2 tablespoons finely chopped *green pepper,* 1 tablespoon finely chopped *pimiento*, and 1 teaspoon *paprika.* Beat till smooth. Cover and chill till serving time. Makes 1¼ cups dressing.

Blue Cheese Salad Dressing: In a mixing bowl combine 1 cup *Salad Dressing Base,* ¼ cup crumbled *blue cheese,* 2 tablespoons *milk,* and several drops *bottled hot pepper sauce.* Beat till smooth. Cover and chill till serving time. To serve, top with additional crumbled *blue cheese,* if desired. Makes 1¼ cups dressing.

Buttermilk Salad Dressing: In a mixing bowl combine 1 cup *Salad Dressing Base*, ¼ cup *buttermilk*, and ½ teaspoon dried *dillweed.* Beat till smooth. Cover and chill till serving time. Makes 1¼ cups dressing.

Creamy Garlic Salad Dressing: In a mixing bowl combine 1 cup *Salad Dressing Base*, ¼ cup finely shredded *cheddar cheese*, 3 tablespoons *milk*, and ⅛ teaspoon *garlic powder*. Beat till smooth. Cover and chill in the refrigerator till serving time. Makes about 1¼ cups dressing.

Creamy Vegetable Salad Dressing: In a medium mixing bowl combine 1 cup *Salad Dressing Base,* ½ cup finely chopped *cucumber,* 2 tablespoons finely chopped *green pepper,* 2 tablespoons *milk,* and 1 tablespoon snipped *parsley.* Beat till smooth. Cover and chill till serving time. Makes 1½ cups dressing.

Citrus-Peanut Salad Dressing: In a mixing bowl combine 1 cup *Salad Dressing Base*, ¼ cup *peanut butter*, ½ teaspoon finely shredded *orange peel,* and 2 tablespoons *orange juice.* Beat till smooth. Cover and chill till serving time. Makes 1½ cups dressing.

Honey-Lime Salad Dressing: In a mixing bowl combine 1 cup *Salad Dressing Base,* ¼ cup *honey,* ½ teaspoon finely shredded *lime peel*, 2 tablespoons *lime juice,* and 1 teaspoon *celery seed*. Beat till smooth. Cover and chill till serving time. Makes 1¼ cups dressing.

Preparation time: 25 minutes
Chilling time: at least 2 hours

Spicy Pickled Peaches

1 29-ounce can peach halves
Whole cloves
½ cup sugar
½ cup vinegar
3 inches stick cinnamon, broken

Drain peaches, reserving the syrup. Stud *each* peach half with *3 or 4* whole cloves. In a saucepan combine the reserved syrup, the sugar, vinegar, and cinnamon. Add the peach halves. Bring to boiling; reduce heat. Simmer, uncovered, for 3 to 4 minutes. Remove from heat and cool slightly. Cover and chill in the refrigerator for 2 hours or till serving time. Before serving, drain the peach halves and remove the stick cinnamon. Serve with meat, fish, or poultry.

Preparation time: 20 minutes
Chilling time: at least 2 hours

Poinsettia Mold

Poinsettia Mold

2 envelopes unflavored gelatin
2½ cups unsweetened white grape juice
2 tablespoons lemon juice
1 medium apple, cored
1 cup halved seedless green grapes
1 11-ounce can mandarin orange sections, drained
Lettuce leaves

▬ In a saucepan soften gelatin in 1 cup cold *water*; let stand for 5 minutes. Add grape juice and lemon juice; cook and stir over low heat till gelatin is dissolved. Slice *half* of the apple; chop the remaining. Arrange apple slices in the bottom of a 6½- or 7-cup mold. Pour in *¾ cup* of the gelatin mixture. Chill till almost firm. Chill remaining gelatin mixture to the consistency of unbeaten egg whites (partially set). Fold in chopped apple and remaining fruit; gently pour over almost-firm layer in mold. Chill for 6 hours or till firm. Unmold the salad onto a lettuce-lined platter. Garnish with frosted grapes, if desired (see column at far right). Makes 10 servings.

▬ Preparation time: about 1½ hours
▬ Chilling time: at least 6 hours

Blueberry-Peach Salad

1 6-ounce package orange-flavored gelatin
⅓ cup sugar
1 teaspoon finely shredded orange peel
2¼ cups orange juice
2 cups buttermilk
1 8-ounce can crushed pineapple, drained
1 cup chopped, peeled peaches
1 cup fresh *or* frozen unsweetened blueberries
1 cup dairy sour cream

▬ Combine gelatin and sugar; stir in peel and *2 cups* of the orange juice. Cook and stir till gelatin is dissolved; cool. Stir in buttermilk. Chill till partially set. Fold in fruit; turn into a 6½-cup mold. Chill for 6 hours or till firm. Combine sour cream and remaining orange juice; chill. Unmold salad onto lettuce-lined platter, if desired. Pass sour cream mixture. Serves 10.

▬ Preparation time: about 2 hours
▬ Chilling time: at least 6 hours

Quick Banana Mold

1 3-ounce package strawberry-flavored gelatin
2 cups ice cubes
1 teaspoon lemon juice
½ cup banana *or* strawberry yogurt
1 small banana, sliced
1 stalk celery, finely chopped (½ cup)

▬ Dissolve gelatin in ½ cup *boiling water*. Add ice cubes and lemon juice. Stir constantly for 2 to 3 minutes or till mixture thickens slightly; remove any remaining ice cubes. Stir in yogurt till smooth. Fold in the banana slices and celery. Turn into four ½-cup molds; chill for 1 hour or till firm. Makes 4 servings.

▬ Preparation time: 15 minutes
▬ Chilling time: at least 1 hour

Add a festive sparkle to many of your dishes simply by garnishing them with frosted grapes. Even our *Poinsettia Mold*, a fruit salad with a cheerful personality on its own, assumes a gayer outlook when adorned with the tiny clusters of grapes (see photograph at left).

To frost grapes, cut a bunch of *grapes* into small clusters (about 3 to 5 grapes each). Combine one slightly beaten *egg white* with about 2 teaspoons *water*. Brush the grape clusters with the egg white mixture. Then sprinkle the grapes with *sugar*.

Next, place the frosted grapes on a wire rack over waxed paper. Allow the grapes to dry for several hours.

Gelatin salads only seem tricky to unmold; really they're not—if you know these helpful techniques.

With the tip of a paring knife, loosen the edge of the gelatin from the mold. Dip the mold just to the rim in warm water for a few seconds, then remove it.

Tilt the mold slightly to ease the gelatin away from one side and let air in. Then tilt and rotate the mold so air can loosen the gelatin all the way around.

Center an upside-down serving platter over the mold. Holding tightly, invert the plate and mold; shake gently.

Lift off the mold, being careful not to tear the gelatin. If the salad does not slide out easily, repeat the process.

Apricot-Pecan Salad

2½ cups apricot nectar
 1 6-ounce package apricot-flavored gelatin
1½ cups dry white wine
 1 16-ounce can peeled apricot halves, drained and coarsely chopped
 ½ cup sliced celery
 ½ cup chopped pecans

■■■ In a saucepan bring the apricot nectar to boiling. Dissolve the gelatin in nectar. Stir in white wine. Chill to the consistency of unbeaten egg whites (partially set). Fold in the apricots, celery, and pecans. Pour into a 5½- or 6-cup mold. Chill for 6 hours or till firm. Unmold onto a platter. Garnish with curly endive, if desired. Makes 8 servings.

■■■ Preparation time: about 1¼ hours
■■■ Chilling time: at least 6 hours

Cranberry-Orange Slaw

 1 cup cranberries, chopped
 ⅓ cup sugar
 3 cups shredded cabbage
 1 11-ounce can mandarin orange sections, drained
 ⅓ cup plain yogurt
 1 teaspoon finely shredded orange peel
 2 tablespoons orange juice

■■■ Combine cranberries and sugar; stir to dissolve sugar. Cover and chill for 30 minutes. Combine cabbage and orange sections; cover and chill.

■■■ Before serving, stir together the cranberry mixture, plain yogurt, orange peel, and orange juice. Pour the cranberry mixture over the cabbage mixture; toss gently to mix. Makes 6 servings.

■■■ Preparation time: 25 minutes
■■■ Chilling time: 30 minutes

Cheese-Topped Fruit Salad with Currant Dressing

 1 3-ounce package cream cheese, softened
 ¾ cup crumbled Roquefort, Gorgonzola, Stilton, feta, or blue cheese (3 ounces)
    Milk
 2 tablespoons finely chopped celery
 ¼ cup salad oil
 3 tablespoons red wine vinegar
 2 tablespoons dried currants or raisins
 2 teaspoons honey
 6 large lettuce leaves
 3 large apples, pears, or avocados
    Lemon juice

■■■ In a small mixing bowl combine the cream cheese and Roquefort, Gorgonzola, Stilton, feta, or blue cheese. Stir in enough milk (1 to 2 teaspoons), if necessary, to make a fluffy consistency. Stir in the chopped celery. Cover and chill cheese mixture in the refrigerator till serving time.

■■■ For dressing, in a screw-top jar combine the salad oil, red wine vinegar, currants or raisins, and honey. Cover and shake well to mix. Chill in the refrigerator till serving time.

■■■ To serve the salad, line 6 individual salad plates with a large lettuce leaf. Core the apples or pears, or seed and peel avocados. Slice the fruit; dip into lemon juice to prevent the cut edges from browning. Arrange the slices of fruit in a circle atop lettuce. Mound *some* of the cheese mixture in the center of *each* plate. Shake dressing; spoon over the fruit. Serve immediately. Makes 6 servings.

■■■ Total preparation time: 30 minutes

California Fruit Salad

- 1 fresh large papaya
- 1 avocado, seeded, peeled, and thinly sliced
  Lime *or* lemon juice
- 4 cups torn iceberg lettuce
- 2 cups torn Bibb lettuce *or* escarole
- 2 medium oranges, chilled and sectioned
- 1 cup seeded, halved red grapes
- ¾ cup salad oil
- ⅓ cup tarragon vinegar
- ¼ cup sugar
- 1 tablespoon lime juice
- 2 teaspoons finely chopped onion
- ½ teaspoon salt
- ½ teaspoon dry mustard
- ¼ teaspoon paprika

■■■ Peel the papaya. Cut in half lengthwise; seed and reserve 2 tablespoons of the papaya seeds. Slice the papaya lengthwise and quarter. Dip the papaya pieces and the avocado slices into lime or lemon juice to prevent the cut edges from browning.

■■■ In a large salad bowl combine the iceberg lettuce and Bibb lettuce or escarole. Arrange the papaya pieces, avocado slices, orange sections, and red grape halves in circles atop the lettuce. Cover and chill in the refrigerator till serving time.

■■■ For dressing, in a blender container or food processor bowl combine the salad oil, tarragon vinegar, sugar, the 1 tablespoon lime juice, chopped onion, salt, dry mustard, and paprika. Cover and blend or process till smooth. Add the reserved papaya seeds and blend or process till the mixture is thickened and papaya seeds resemble coarsely ground pepper. Cover and chill in the refrigerator till serving time.

■■■ Before serving, shake the chilled dressing well; pour over the salad. Toss gently to coat the fruit and vegetables. Makes 6 to 8 servings.

■■■ Total preparation time: 50 minutes

Curried Fruit Salad

- 2 17-ounce cans fruits for salad
- 1 11-ounce can mandarin orange sections
- 1 medium apple, chopped
- ¼ cup raisins
- 2 teaspoons finely chopped onion
- 2 teaspoons lemon juice
- 1½ teaspoons curry powder
- ¼ teaspoon ground cinnamon
  Lettuce leaves
- ⅓ cup mayonnaise *or* salad dressing
- ⅓ cup dairy sour cream
- ¼ cup finely chopped peanuts

■■■ Drain *one can* fruits for salad; drain orange sections. Combine drained and *undrained* fruits for salad, orange sections, apple, raisins, onion, lemon juice, curry, and cinnamon. Cover and chill for 3 hours.

■■■ Drain fruit mixture, reserving 2 tablespoons syrup. Spoon onto 8 lettuce lined salad plates. Combine reserved syrup, mayonnaise, and sour cream; drizzle over fruit. Sprinkle peanuts atop. Serves 8.

■■■ Preparation time: 20 minutes
■■■ Chilling time: at least 3 hours

Cranberry-Orange Sauce

- 1 12-ounce package (3 cups) cranberries
- 1 cup sugar
- 1 teaspoon finely shredded orange peel
- 1 cup orange juice

■■■ In a saucepan combine cranberries, sugar, orange peel, and juice. Bring to boiling; reduce heat. Simmer, uncovered, for 8 to 10 minutes or till cranberry skins pop, stirring once or twice. Cool. Cover and chill for 2 hours. Makes about 3¼ cups.

■■■ Preparation time: 25 minutes
■■■ Chilling time: at least 2 hours

■■■ MENU ■■■
EAST INDIAN GRILLED DINNER

Curried Fruit Salad

Skewered Chicken ★

Sliced Tomatoes

Pita Bread

Ice Cream

Carbonated Beverage

Spiced Coffee

Don't wait until summer to barbecue. This marinated barbecued chicken takes just minutes to cook on the grill. So you won't have to be outdoors long, even if the weather is a little on the cool side.

And since *Curried Fruit Salad* calls for canned or year-round fruit, you don't need to worry about the seasonal availability of ingredients.

★ *see recipe, page 89*

Garlic-Buttered Spaghetti

    3 **quarts water**
    1 **teaspoon salt**
    1 **tablespoon cooking oil (optional)**
    6 **ounces spaghetti, linguine,** *or* **vermicelli**
    ⅓ **cup sliced green onion**
    1 *or* **2 cloves garlic, minced**
    3 **tablespoons butter** *or* **margarine**
    ¼ **cup finely snipped parsley**
    ¼ **teaspoon salt**
       Dash pepper

■■■ In a large kettle or Dutch oven bring water and salt to a rolling boil. If desired, add cooking oil to help keep the pasta separated. When the water boils, add spaghetti, linguine, or vermicelli a little at a time so the water does not stop boiling. Hold the pasta at one end and dip the other end into the water. As the pasta softens, gently curl it around in the pan till pasta is completely immersed.

■■■ Reduce heat slightly and continue boiling, uncovered, for 9 to 12 minutes or till pasta is tender but still slightly firm. Stir occasionally to prevent sticking. Taste often to test for doneness. Immediately drain pasta in colander; *do not rinse*. Transfer the hot pasta to a heated serving dish.

■■■ Meanwhile, in a small skillet cook green onion and garlic in hot butter or margarine till tender but not brown. Stir in parsley, salt, and pepper.

■■■ Pour the green onion mixture over the pasta. Toss gently till the pasta is well coated. Serve immediately. Makes 6 servings.

Herb-Buttered Spaghetti: Prepare Garlic-Buttered Spaghetti as above, *except* stir in 1 tablespoon *vinegar* and ¾ teaspoon dried *basil, marjoram, or oregano*, crushed, with the parsley, salt, and pepper.

■■■ Total preparation time: 25 minutes

Fettuccine Verde

    3 **quarts water**
    1 **teaspoon salt**
    1 **tablespoon cooking oil (optional)**
    8 **ounces green noodles**
    ¼ **cup butter** *or* **margarine, cut up**
    ¼ **cup dairy sour cream**
    2 **teaspoons dried basil, crushed**
    ⅛ **teaspoon garlic powder**
    ⅛ **teaspoon pepper**
    ¼ **cup grated Parmesan cheese**

■■■ In a large kettle or Dutch oven bring water and salt to a rolling boil. If desired, add the cooking oil to help keep the pasta separated. When the water boils, add the noodles, a little at a time, so the water does not stop boiling.

■■■ Reduce heat slightly and continue boiling, uncovered, for 9 to 12 minutes or till the pasta is tender but still slightly firm. Stir occasionally to prevent sticking. Taste often to test for doneness. Immediately drain pasta in a colander; *do not rinse*. Transfer the hot noodles to a heated serving dish.

■■■ Meanwhile, in a small mixing bowl combine the butter or margarine, dairy sour cream, basil, garlic powder, and pepper.

■■■ Spoon the butter mixture over hot noodles. Toss gently till pasta is well coated. Sprinkle with Parmesan cheese. Serve immediately. Makes 8 servings.

■■■ Total preparation time: 25 minutes

Linguine Hollandaise

6 ounces linguine *or* spaghetti
¼ cup finely chopped onion
1 tablespoon butter *or* margarine
¾ cup milk
1 1-ounce envelope hollandaise sauce mix
Dash pepper
2 tablespoons snipped parsley

■ Cook the linguine or spaghetti according to package directions; drain. Meanwhile, cook the onion in hot butter or margarine till tender but not brown. Stir in milk, hollandaise sauce mix, and pepper. Cook and stir till thickened and bubbly. Cook and stir 1 minute more. Pour over linguine or spaghetti; toss gently to coat. Sprinkle with parsley. Makes 4 servings.

■ Total preparation time: 20 minutes

Savory Couscous

2 cups water
½ cup thinly sliced green onion
2 tablespoons snipped parsley
1 tablespoon instant chicken bouillon granules
¼ teaspoon dried rosemary, crushed, *or* dried thyme, crushed
1½ cups precooked couscous
1 tablespoon butter *or* margarine

■ In a large saucepan combine the water, green onion, parsley, bouillon granules, and rosemary or thyme. Bring to boiling; remove from heat. Add the couscous. Let stand, covered, for 5 minutes. Stir in butter or margarine. Serve immediately. Serves 6.

■ Total preparation time: 15 minutes

Couscous (KOOS-koos), a favorite in North Africa, is steamed semolina or millet. Semolina is a grain milled from durum wheat, a hard wheat also used in making pasta.

Curried Wild Rice

1 4-ounce package (¾ cup) wild rice
½ cup chopped onion
½ cup chopped celery
2 teaspoons curry powder
2 tablespoons butter *or* margarine
2½ cups water
1 medium apple, chopped
1 tablespoon instant chicken bouillon granules
½ cup long grain rice

■ Run cold water over uncooked wild rice in a strainer for 1 minute, lifting rice to rinse well; set aside. In a saucepan cook onion, celery, and curry powder in hot butter till tender. Add wild rice, water, apple, and bouillon granules. Bring to boiling; reduce heat. Cover and simmer 30 minutes. Stir in uncooked long grain rice; turn into a 1½-quart casserole. Cover and bake in a 350° oven for 30 minutes or till done. Serves 10.

■ Total preparation time: 1¼ hours

Millet with Walnuts

½ cup chopped green onion
1 tablespoon cooking oil
1½ cups water
½ cup millet
1 teaspoon instant beef bouillon granules
½ teaspoon dried basil, crushed
¼ teaspoon dried oregano, crushed
1 medium tomato, peeled, seeded, and chopped
¼ cup chopped walnuts
¼ cup grated Parmesan cheese

■ In a saucepan cook green onion in hot oil till tender. Add water, millet, beef bouillon granules, basil, and oregano. Bring to boiling; reduce heat. Simmer, covered, for 25 minutes or till most of the liquid is absorbed. Stir in the tomato, walnuts, and Parmesan cheese. Cook, covered, about 5 minutes more or till all of the liquid is absorbed. Makes 6 servings.

■ Total preparation time: 45 minutes

Millet was one of man's first cereals and still remains a popular diet staple in Asia, India, and Africa. It is a hardy grain that can survive on the most barren of terrains.

You can buy millet in health food stores and usually in large supermarkets.

If your time is tight, you can substitute 4 ounces of packaged medium whole wheat, egg, or regular noodles for the *Homemade Whole Wheat Noodles.*

Cook the purchased noodles according to the package directions. Drain and stir the noodles into the cheese mixture. Bake as directed in *Whole Wheat Noodle Bake.*

Whole Wheat Noodle Bake

Homemade Whole Wheat Noodles
¼ cup chopped onion
¼ cup chopped green *or* red sweet pepper
1 tablespoon butter *or* margarine
1 3-ounce package cream cheese, softened
1 cup cream-style cottage cheese
¼ cup grated Parmesan cheese
¼ cup milk
1 teaspoon prepared mustard
1 teaspoon Worcestershire sauce
¼ teaspoon dried basil, crushed
⅓ cup crushed rich round crackers
1 tablespoon butter *or* margarine, melted

▬ Prepare Homemade Whole Wheat Noodles. Cook noodles in a large amount of boiling salted water for 5 to 10 minutes or till tender; drain.

▬ Cook onion and pepper in 1 tablespoon hot butter or margarine till tender but not brown. Remove from the heat. Add cream cheese, stirring till melted. Stir in cottage cheese, Parmesan cheese, milk, mustard, Worcestershire sauce, and basil. Add cooked noodles to cheese mixture; toss gently to coat. Turn the mixture into a 10x6x2-inch baking dish.

▬ For topping, combine crushed crackers and the 1 tablespoon melted butter or margarine. Sprinkle topping onto noodle mixture. Bake in a 350° oven about 20 minutes or till heated through. Serves 6.

Homemade Whole Wheat Noodles: Stir together ½ cup *whole wheat flour,* ¼ cup *all-purpose flour,* and ½ teaspoon *salt;* make a well in center. Combine 1 beaten *egg* and 2 tablespoons *milk;* stir into flour mixture. Stir in enough *all-purpose flour* (3 to 4 tablespoons) to make a stiff dough. Turn out onto a lightly floured surface; knead dough, as shown, till smooth and elastic (8 to 10 minutes).

▬ Roll dough into a 16x12-inch rectangle. (If dough becomes too elastic during rolling, cover and let rest 15 minutes.) Let stand, uncovered, for 20 minutes. Starting at short side, roll dough loosely, as shown; cut into ¼-inch-thick slices, as shown. Unroll; cut strips into desired lengths. Spread out or hang to dry, as shown, for 2 hours. Makes about 4 ounces.

▬ Advance preparation time: 45 minutes
▬ Standing time: about 2¼ hours
▬ Preparation time: 20 minutes
▬ Cooking time: 20 minutes

To dry *Homemade Whole Wheat Noodles*, spread the noodles on a pasta drying rack or hang them on a nonmetal coat hanger.

For a splash of color, garnish *Whole Wheat Noodle Bake* with green or red sweet pepper rings and fresh basil leaves.

If you use fresh basil for the trim, you also may want to substitute 1 teaspoon snipped *fresh basil* for the ¼ teaspoon dried basil in recipe.

Risotto is an Italian rice dish in which the rice simmers, tightly covered, in a seasoned broth until the mixture is creamy and the rice is "al dente" (slightly firm).

You will enjoy the slightly tangy cheese flavor in *Risotto with Fontina Cheese*.

Pepper Rice

2 green peppers, seeded and quartered
1 medium onion, quartered
½ cup parsley
1 small clove garlic
¼ teaspoon salt
3 tablespoons cooking oil
1 cup long grain rice
2 cups chicken broth

▪▪ In a blender container place peppers, onion, parsley, garlic, salt, and ¼ cup *water*; cover and blend till combined. In a 10-inch skillet heat oil; add uncooked rice. Cook and stir for 5 to 10 minutes or till rice is golden. Remove from heat; cool slightly. Stir in pepper mixture and chicken broth; cover tightly. Bring to boiling; reduce heat. Cook about 20 minutes or till rice is done. Makes 6 servings.

▪▪ Preparation time: 25 minutes
▪▪ Cooking time: 20 minutes

Risotto with Fontina Cheese

¼ cup finely chopped onion
2 tablespoons butter *or* margarine
3 cups chicken broth
1 cup short, medium, *or* long grain rice
2 tablespoons snipped parsley
½ cup shredded fontina, provolone, *or* mozzarella cheese (2 ounces)
¼ cup grated Parmesan cheese

▪▪ Cook onion in hot butter or margarine till tender. Stir in broth, uncooked rice, and parsley; cover tightly. Bring to boiling; reduce heat. Cook for 15 minutes (do not lift cover). Remove from heat. Let stand, covered, for 10 minutes. Stir in the cheeses. Makes 6 servings.

▪▪ Preparation time: 10 minutes
▪▪ Cooking time: 15 minutes
▪▪ Standing time: 10 minutes

Minty Orange Rice Ring

1 cup medium *or* long grain rice
1 cup orange juice
1 cup cold water
1 tablespoon butter *or* margarine
1 tablespoon snipped fresh mint *or* 1 teaspoon dried mint, crushed
1 teaspoon instant chicken bouillon granules
½ teaspoon salt

▪▪ In a saucepan combine the uncooked rice, orange juice, water, butter or margarine, mint, instant chicken bouillon granules, and salt; cover tightly. Bring to boiling; reduce heat. Cook for 15 minutes (do not lift cover). Remove from heat. Let stand, covered, for 10 minutes. Press into a buttered 5½-cup ring mold; unmold. Makes 6 servings.

▪▪ Total preparation time: 35 minutes

Brown Rice Ring

2⅔ cups cold water
1 cup regular brown rice
1½ teaspoons instant beef bouillon granules
½ teaspoon dry mustard
½ teaspoon dried sage, crushed
½ cup coarsely chopped pecans
3 tablespoons snipped parsley
Butter *or* margarine
2 tablespoons fine dry bread crumbs

▪▪ In a saucepan combine the water, uncooked brown rice, instant beef bouillon granules, dry mustard, and sage; cover tightly. Bring to boiling; reduce heat. Cook for 40 minutes (do not lift cover). Remove from heat. Let stand, covered, for 10 minutes. Stir in the pecans and parsley. Butter a 3-cup ring mold; sprinkle with bread crumbs. Press the hot rice mixture into the mold; unmold. Makes 6 servings.

▪▪ Total preparation time: about 1 hour

Dill Braid

    1 package active dry yeast
    ¼ cup warm water (110° to 115°)
 2¾ to 3 cups all-purpose flour
    1 cup dairy sour cream
    1 egg
    1 small onion, finely chopped (¼ cup)
    2 tablespoons sugar
    1 tablespoon butter *or* margarine, softened
    1 tablespoon dried dillweed
    1 tablespoon dillseed (optional)
    1 beaten egg yolk
    2 teaspoons water

■ In a mixer bowl soften yeast in the ¼ cup warm water. Add *1 cup* of the flour; sour cream; egg; onion; sugar; butter; dillweed; dillseed, if desired; and 1 teaspoon *salt*. Beat on low speed of electric mixer for ½ minute, scraping sides of bowl constantly. Beat for 3 minutes on high speed. Using a spoon, stir in as much of the remaining flour as you can.

■ Turn out onto a lightly floured surface. Knead in enough of the remaining flour to make a moderately stiff dough that is smooth and elastic (6 to 8 minutes total). Shape into a ball. Place dough into a lightly greased bowl; turn once to grease surface. Cover; let rise in a warm place till double (1¼ to 1½ hours).

■ Punch dough down; divide into three portions. Cover; let rest 10 minutes. On a lightly floured surface roll each portion into an 18-inch-long rope. Place ropes, side by side, on a lightly greased baking sheet. Braid the ropes loosely from the center to ends (see photograph at upper right). Press the rope ends together to seal. Cover and let rise in a warm place till nearly double (about 30 minutes).

■ Combine egg yolk and the 2 teaspoons water; brush atop loaf. Bake in a 350° oven for 35 to 40 minutes or till the loaf sounds hollow when tapped. Cool on wire rack. Makes 1 loaf.

Starting in the middle, braid by bringing left rope *underneath* center rope, as shown; lay it down. Then, bring right rope under new center rope; lay it down. Repeat to end. On the other end, braid by bringing outside ropes alternately *over* center rope to center.

Sunflower Nut Loaves

    1 cup shelled sunflower nuts
    ½ cup blanched almonds
 5½ to 6 cups all-purpose flour
    2 packages active dry yeast
 1½ cups milk
    ½ cup sugar
    ½ cup butter *or* margarine
    2 eggs

■ Place ½ cup sunflower nuts and the almonds in a blender container. Cover; blend till ground. Combine ground nuts, 2 cups flour, and yeast. Heat and stir milk, sugar, butter, and ¾ teaspoon *salt* just till warm (115° to 120°); stir constantly. Add to flour mixture; add eggs. Beat on low speed of electric mixer for ½ minute, scaping bowl. Beat for 3 minutes on high speed. Chop remaining sunflower nuts; stir into mixture. Stir in as much of the flour as you can. On floured surface, knead in enough remaining flour to make moderately stiff dough that is elastic (6 to 8 minutes total). Shape into ball. Place in greased bowl; turn once. Cover; let rise till double (about 1 hour). Punch down; divide in half. Cover; let rest 10 minutes. Shape into two 7-inch round loaves; place on greased baking sheets. Cover; let rise till nearly double (30 to 45 minutes). Brush with water or milk, if desired. Bake in a 325° oven for 35 to 45 minutes. Cool. Makes 2.

Dill Braid calls for two forms of dill—dillweed and dillseed. The feathery, bright green aromatic dill leaves are dried, bottled, and labeled dillweed or dill leaves. The dill plant bears yellow blossoms that form tiny seeds. You can find them in the market as dillseed.

  Dillweed has a subtle piquant flavor. The seeds, on the other hand, have a warm, slightly sharp, and somewhat bitter taste.

■ Preparation time: 45 minutes
■ Rising time: 2¼ hours
■ Cooking time: 35 to 40 minutes

■ Preparation time: 30 minutes
■ Rising time: about 2 hours
■ Cooking time: 35 to 45 minutes

Whether you serve
this dinner alfresco or
in your dining room,
you will have fun
adding your own
creative touches.

Peruse a specialty
cheese shop for
some mild white
cheeses; perhaps
you'll find some
coated with nuts,
herbs, or cracked
pepper. Then, order
a selection of sliced
meats from the
delicatessen. Or, if
you prefer, slice
some leftover roast
pork, beef, chicken,
turkey, or ham.

★ see recipe, page 50

Harvest Grape Loaf

2½ to 3 cups all-purpose flour
 1 package active dry yeast
 ¼ teaspoon ground cardamom
 ¼ teaspoon ground nutmeg
 ¾ cup milk
 ¼ cup sugar
 3 tablespoons butter *or* margarine
 2 tablespoons orange liqueur *or* orange juice
 2 egg whites
 Poppy seed
 Sugar

■■■ In a mixer bowl combine *1¼ cups* of the flour, yeast, cardamom, and nutmeg. Heat milk, sugar, butter or margarine, and 1 teaspoon *salt* till warm (115° to 120°); stir constantly. Add to the flour mixture; add the orange liqueur or orange juice, and 1 of the egg whites. Beat on low speed of electric mixer for ½ minute, scraping bowl. Beat for 3 minutes on high speed. Stir in as much of the remaining flour as you can. On a lightly floured surface, knead in enough remaining flour to make a moderately stiff dough that is smooth and elastic (6 to 8 minutes total). Shape into a ball. Place into a greased bowl; turn once. Cover; let rise in a warm place till double (about 1 hour).

■■■ Punch down; let rest 10 minutes. Remove *one-fourth* of the dough; set aside. Shape remaining dough into thirty 1-inch balls. Arrange on a greased baking sheet in the shape of a bunch of grapes. On a lightly floured surface, roll reserved dough into an 8x4-inch rectangle; cut in half crosswise. Cut each square in half diagonally to form "leaves"; position at wide end of the bunch of "grapes." Cover; let rise in a warm place till nearly double (30 to 40 minutes).

■■■ Using a sharp knife, slash ribs in leaves. Combine remaining egg white and 1 tablespoon *water*; brush onto dough. Sprinkle grapes with poppy seed. Sprinkle leaves with sugar. Bake in a 375° oven for 20 to 25 minutes or till done. Cool. Makes 1 loaf.

■■■ Preparation time: 45 minutes
■■■ Rising time: about 2 hours
■■■ Cooking time: 20 to 25 minutes

Whole Wheat and Potato Bread

¾ cup peeled, finely chopped potato
1½ cups buttermilk
2½ to 3 cups all-purpose flour
2 packages active dry yeast
3 tablespoons sugar
2 tablespoons shortening
2 teaspoons salt
2½ cups whole wheat flour
Cornmeal

■ In a saucepan cook the potato in buttermilk, uncovered, about 15 minutes or till potato is tender; *do not drain*. (The buttermilk will appear curdled.) Mash potato; add enough cold *water* to measure 2½ cups mixture. Cool to 115° to 120°.

■ In a large mixer bowl combine *2 cups* of the all-purpose flour and the yeast. Stir in the warm mashed potato mixture. Add sugar, shortening, and salt. Beat on low speed of electric mixer for ½ minute, scraping sides of bowl constantly. Beat for 3 minutes on high speed. Using a spoon, stir in the whole wheat flour and as much of the remaining all-purpose flour as you can. Turn out onto a lightly floured surface. Knead in enough remaining all-purpose flour to make a moderately stiff dough that is smooth and elastic (6 to 8 minutes total). Shape into a ball. Place into a lightly greased bowl; turn once to grease surface. Cover; let rise in warm place till double (about 45 minutes).

■ Punch dough down; divide in half. Cover; let rest for 10 minutes. Shape into two 6-inch round loaves. Sprinkle a large greased baking sheet with cornmeal. Place loaves on baking sheet. Cover; let rise till nearly double (about 35 minutes).

■ If desired, brush tops with additional buttermilk and sprinkle with cornmeal. Bake in a 375° oven for 30 to 35 minutes or till done; cover with foil the last 15 minutes of baking to prevent overbrowning. Cool the bread on wire racks. Makes 2 loaves.

■ Preparation time: 45 minutes
■ Rising time: about 1½ hours
■ Cooking time: 30 to 35 minutes

Parmesan Dinner Rolls

4½ to 5 cups all-purpose flour
2 packages active dry yeast
1½ teaspoons Italian seasoning
1 cup milk
½ cup water
2 tablespoons sugar
2 tablespoons butter *or* margarine
1 teaspoon garlic salt
2 eggs
½ cup grated Parmesan cheese
2 tablespoons butter *or* margarine, melted
¼ cup grated Parmesan cheese

■ In a large mixer bowl combine *1½ cups* of the all-purpose flour, yeast, and Italian seasoning. In a saucepan heat milk, water, sugar, 2 tablespoons butter or margarine, and garlic salt just till warm (115° to 120°) and butter is almost melted; stir constantly. Add to flour mixture; add eggs. Beat on low speed of electric mixer for ½ minute, scraping sides of bowl constantly. Beat for 3 minutes on high speed. Using a spoon, stir in the ½ cup Parmesan cheese and as much of the remaining all-purpose flour as you can.

■ Turn the dough out onto a lightly floured surface. Knead in enough remaining flour to make a moderately stiff dough that is smooth and elastic (6 to 8 minutes total). Shape into a ball. Place into a greased bowl; turn once to grease surface. Cover and let rise in a warm place till double (about 45 minutes).

■ Punch dough down. Cover and let rest for 10 minutes. Shape into 16 balls. Dip tops into 2 tablespoons melted butter or margarine, then into the ¼ cup grated Parmesan cheese. Place the rolls into two greased 8x1½- or 9x1½-inch round baking pans. Cover and let rise till nearly double (about 15 minutes). Bake in a 375° oven for 20 to 25 minutes or till done. Serve warm. Makes 16 rolls.

■ Preparation time: 30 minutes
■ Rising time: about 1¼ hours
■ Cooking time: 20 to 25 minutes

Brown-and-Serve Whole Wheat Rolls*

3½ **to 4 cups all-purpose flour**
⅓ **cup nonfat dry milk powder**
2 **packages active dry yeast**
¼ **cup packed brown sugar**
2 **tablespoons butter** *or*·**margarine**
2 **cups whole wheat flour**

■ In a large mixer bowl combine *3 cups* of the all-purpose flour, milk powder, and yeast. Heat brown sugar, butter or margarine, 2 cups *water,* and 2 teaspoons *salt* just till warm (115° to 120°); stir constantly. Add to flour mixture. Beat on low speed of electric mixer for ½ minute, scraping sides of bowl. Beat for 3 minutes on high speed. Using a spoon, stir in whole wheat flour and as much of the remaining all-purpose flour as you can. Turn out onto a lightly floured surface. Knead in enough of the remaining all-purpose flour to make a moderately stiff dough that is smooth and elastic (6 to 8 minutes total). Shape into a ball. Place into a lightly greased bowl; turn once. Cover; let rise in a warm place till double (about 1½ hours).

■ Punch dough down. Cover; let rest 10 minutes. Shape into 24 to 36 rolls; place on greased baking sheets. Cover; let rise till nearly double (30 to 45 minutes). Bake in a 325° oven for 12 to 15 minutes; *do not brown.* Remove from baking sheets; cool. Wrap in moisture-vaporproof wrap. Seal, label, and freeze.

■ To serve, thaw frozen wrapped rolls for 15 minutes. Unwrap; place on ungreased baking sheets. Bake in a 400° oven for 8 to 10 minutes or till done. Serve warm. Makes 24 to 36 rolls.

Brown-and-Serve Rye Rolls: Prepare Brown-and-Serve Whole Wheat Rolls as above, *except* substitute 2 cups *rye flour* for the whole wheat flour, and add 1 teaspoon *caraway seed* with rye flour, if desired.

■ Advance preparation time: about 3¾ hours
■ Final preparation time: 23 to 25 minutes
★ *pictured on page 13*

Cornmeal Batter Rolls

1⅓ **cups all-purpose flour**
¾ **cup yellow cornmeal**
1 **package active dry yeast**
1 **teaspoon baking powder**
¾ **cup milk**
⅓ **cup shortening**
3 **tablespoons sugar**
1 **teaspoon salt**
1 **egg**
  Milk
1 **tablespoon poppy seed** *or* **sesame seed**

■ In a large mixer bowl combine ⅔ *cup* of the flour, the cornmeal, yeast, and baking powder. In a saucepan heat the ¾ cup milk, shortening, sugar, and salt just till warm (115° to 120°) and shortening is almost melted; stir constantly. Add to flour mixture; add egg. Beat on low speed of electric mixer for ½ minute, scraping sides of bowl constantly. Beat for 3 minutes on high speed. Using a spoon, stir in the remaining flour. Cover; let rise in a warm place till double (about 1 hour).

■ Stir batter down with a wooden spoon. Grease muffin cups or line with paper bake cups. Spoon the batter into prepared muffin pans, filling half full. Cover; let rise till nearly double (about 30 minutes).

■ Brush tops lightly with milk; sprinkle with poppy seed or sesame seed. Bake in a 375° oven for 14 to 16 minutes or till done. Serve warm. Makes 12 rolls.

Make-Ahead Cornmeal Batter Rolls: Make the Cornmeal Batter Rolls as directed above *except* do not let rise after mixing the ingredients. Cover and chill the batter in the refrigerator for several hours or overnight. About 1¼ hours before serving, remove the batter from the refrigerator; stir down. Spoon the batter into prepared muffin pans, filling half full. Cover; let rise in a warm place till double (about 1 hour). Bake in a 375° oven for 14 to 16 minutes or till done.

■ Preparation time: 20 minutes
■ Rising time: 1½ hours
■ Cooking time: 14 to 16 minutes

Dinner-party guests savor few foods more than they do warm homemade yeast rolls. Yet we know it's difficult fitting the preparation time into your busy party-day schedule. Either of these two delicious recipes should help solve any time-crunch problems you have.

For *Make-Ahead Cornmeal Batter Rolls,* chill the dough before the first rising. On the day of the party, let the rolls rise, then shape, and bake them.

Or, partially bake the *Brown-and-Serve Whole Wheat Rolls.* Next, freeze them until your party. All that remains is to brown the rolls a few minutes before dining.

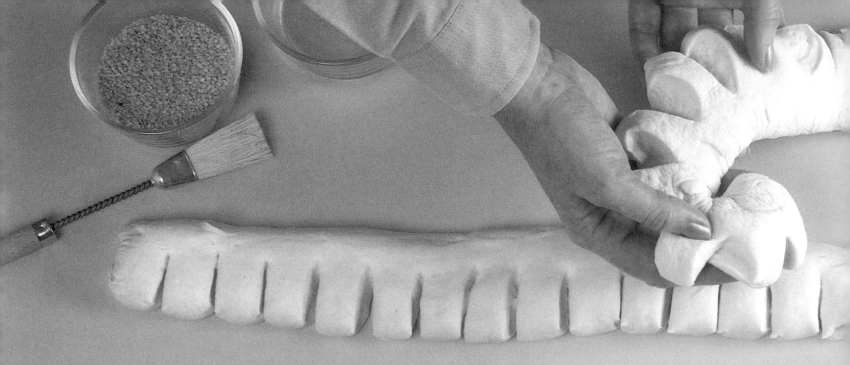

The fermentation rate in *Sicilian Bread Starter*, like that in sourdough starter, depends upon the room temperature: the warmer the room, the faster the fermentation process. Check your starter after 12 to 18 hours to see whether the dough has formed tiny, spongelike bubbles. These indicate it has soured and is ready for use.

You and your guests will enjoy the tangy flavor and interesting texture that this soured "sponge" batter gives to *Sicilian Bread*.

Sicilian Bread

Sicilian Bread Starter
2 packages active dry yeast
2 cups warm water (110° to 115°)
6 to 6½ cups all-purpose flour
4 teaspoons salt
Cornmeal
1 slightly beaten egg white
1 tablespoon water
2 tablespoons sesame seed

■ Prepare Sicilian Bread Starter 24 hours before needed. In a large mixer bowl soften the yeast in the 2 cups warm water. Add *2 cups* of the flour, the salt, and Sicilian Bread Starter. Beat on low speed of electric mixer for ½ minute; scraping bowl constantly. Beat for 3 minutes on high speed. Using a spoon, stir in as much of the remaining flour as you can.

■ On a lightly floured surface knead in enough of the remaining flour to make a stiff dough that is smooth and elastic (8 to 10 minutes total). Shape into a ball. Place into a lightly greased bowl; turn once. Cover; let rise till double (about 1 hour).

■ Punch dough down; divide in half. Cover; let rest for 10 minutes. Roll one portion of dough into a 36-inch-long rope. Using the tip of a sharp knife or kitchen shears, make 1-inch-long cuts at 1-inch intervals along one side of rope beginning at center and working toward one end. Repeat on opposite side of rope, working from center toward other end, as shown.

■ Starting at one end, shape the rope into a loose coil, with cut edge toward the outside. Roll just to the center of rope. Repeat, starting at opposite end of rope and rolling coil in opposite direction, forming a shape loaf, as shown. Place on a greased baking sheet sprinkled with cornmeal. Repeat with remaining dough. Cover; let rise in a warm place till nearly double (about 45 minutes).

■ Combine egg white and the 1 tablespoon water; brush onto loaves. Sprinkle with sesame seed. Place a large baking pan on lower rack of oven and fill with boiling water. Bake bread in a 375° oven for 40 to 45 minutes or till the surface is golden and loaves sound hollow when tapped. Remove from pans. Cool on wire racks. Makes 2 loaves.

Sicilian Bread Starter: Soften 1 package *active dry yeast* in 1 cup warm *water* (110° to 115°). Stir in 2 cups *all-purpose flour* to form a thick batter. Cover with clear plastic wrap; let stand at room temperature for up to 24 hours or till soured. (The dough will be bubbly like a sponge.)

■ Advance preparation time: 10 minutes
■ Standing time: 24 hours
■ Preparation time: 1 hour
■ Rising time: about 2 hours
■ Cooking time: 40 to 45 minutes

Whether you're taking a drive in the country, sunning at the beach, or strolling in the park, you'll find *Sicilian Bread* a great tote-along for an outing. Pick up some cheeses, fruit, and wine and have an outdoor feast.

If one loaf is plenty for your party, bake both but save the second for another occasion. Wrap it tightly in moisture-vaporproof wrap and freeze it for up to 4 months. Thaw the bread for several hours before serving.

You can make *Spinach Pinwheel Crescent* ahead of time and freeze it until you're ready to throw a party.

To make this recipe, first thaw the loaf of frozen bread dough. (This will take about two hours at room temperature. If it's more convenient, let the loaf thaw overnight in the refrigerator.)

Bake the crescent, and then allow it to cool completely on a wire rack. Next, wrap the cooled crescent in heavy foil. Seal, label, and freeze.

To reheat, bake the wrapped crescent in a 350° oven for 15 to 20 minutes or till heated through.

Spinach Pinwheel Crescent

    ¼   cup finely chopped onion
    1   tablespoon butter *or* margarine
    ½   of a 10-ounce package frozen chopped
          spinach, thawed and well-drained
    1   2-ounce can mushroom stems and pieces,
          drained and finely chopped
    ¼   cup grated Parmesan cheese
    1   beaten egg yolk
    ½   teaspoon dried oregano, crushed
    1   16-ounce loaf frozen bread dough, thawed
    1   tablespoon butter *or* margarine, melted
    1   tablespoon grated Parmesan cheese

▬▬ For filling, in a medium saucepan cook the chopped onion in 1 tablespoon hot butter or margarine till tender but not brown. Remove from heat. Stir in the drained spinach, mushrooms, the ¼ cup Parmesan cheese, beaten egg yolk, and oregano.

▬▬ On a lightly floured surface roll the thawed bread dough into a 20x8-inch rectangle. (Since dough is very elastic, it may be necessary to let it rest a few minutes between strokes.) Spread the spinach filling over the rectangle of dough to within 1 inch of edges. Beginning at long edge, roll up, jelly-roll style. Moisten and seal ends and edges. Place, seam side down, on a greased baking sheet. Bend dough to form a crescent. Cover; let rise in a warm place till nearly double (about 40 minutes).

▬▬ Brush the dough with 1 tablespoon melted butter or margarine; sprinkle with the 1 tablespoon Parmesan cheese. Bake in a 350° oven for 25 minutes or till done. Remove from baking sheet. Cool on a wire rack. Makes 1 loaf.

▬▬ Preparation time: 45 minutes
▬▬ Rising time: 40 minutes
▬▬ Cooking time: 25 minutes

Fried Potato Puffs

    1   medium potato, peeled and quartered
    3½ cups all-purpose flour
    1   package active dry yeast
    1¼ cups milk
    ¼   cup sugar
    ¼   cup shortening
    1½ teaspoons salt
    1   egg
          Shortening *or* cooking oil for
            deep-fat frying
          Garlic cloves, halved (optional)

▬▬ In a covered saucepan cook the potato in boiling water for 20 to 25 minutes or till tender. Drain and mash; set aside. In a large mixer bowl combine *2 cups* of the flour and the yeast. In a saucepan heat the milk, sugar, shortening, and salt just till warm (115° to 120°) and shortening is almost melted; stir constantly. Add to flour mixture; add mashed potato and egg. Beat on low speed of electric mixer for ½ minute, scraping sides of bowl constantly. Beat for 3 minutes on high speed. Using a spoon, stir in the remaining flour. Shape into a ball. Place into a lightly greased bowl; turn once to grease surface. Cover; let rise till double (about 1 hour).

▬▬ Punch dough down; divide in half. Cover; let rest for 10 minutes. On a well floured surface roll the dough, *half* at a time, to ¼-inch thickness. Using a 3-inch biscuit cutter or a sharp knife, cut the dough into 3-inch circles or ovals; dip the cutter or knife into flour between cuts. Make two 1½-inch-long parallel slashes off-center in each circle. Pull apart with fingers to widen openings. Reroll trimmings as necessary.

▬▬ Fry the dough circles, a few at a time, in deep, hot shortening or cooking oil (375°) for 1½ to 2 minutes or till puffed and golden brown, turning once during cooking. Remove from fat with a slotted spoon. Drain on paper toweling. If desired, rub garlic over the warm rolls. Serve warm. Makes about 30 rolls.

▬▬ Preparation time: 45 minutes
▬▬ Rising time: 1¼ hours
▬▬ Cooking time: about 30 minutes

Confetti Spoon Bread

2 cups milk
1 cup yellow cornmeal
1 cup milk
¼ cup shredded American cheese (1 ounce)
2 tablespoons butter *or* margarine
1 teaspoon baking powder
1 teaspoon salt
3 beaten egg yolks
½ cup finely shredded zucchini
½ cup finely shredded carrot
¼ cup finely chopped onion
3 egg whites
Butter *or* margarine

■■■ In a saucepan stir the 2 cups milk into cornmeal. Cook, stirring constantly, till the mixture is very thick and pulling away from sides of saucepan. Remove from heat. Stir in the 1 cup milk, shredded American cheese, 2 tablespoons butter or margarine, baking powder, and salt. Stir about *1 cup* of the hot mixture into beaten egg yolks; return all to saucepan. Stir in the zucchini, carrot, and onion.

■■■ In a mixing bowl beat egg whites till stiff peaks form (tips stand straight). Gently fold the egg whites into the vegetable mixture. Turn into a greased 2½-quart casserole. Bake in a 325° oven for 55 to 60 minutes or till knife inserted near the center comes out clean. Serve immediately with butter or margarine. Makes 6 servings.

■■■ Preparation time: 40 minutes
■■■ Cooking time: 55 to 60 minutes

Crunchy Biscuit Ring

4 slices bacon
½ cup finely crushed cornflakes
2 packages (10 each) refrigerated biscuits
¼ cup butter *or* margarine, melted
2 teaspoons prepared mustard

■■■ Cook bacon till crisp. Drain on paper toweling; crumble. Combine bacon and cornflakes; set aside. Cut biscuits into quarters. Combine butter and mustard. Coat biscuit quarters with butter mixture.

■■■ Sprinkle *half* of the cornflake mixture into a greased ovenproof 6½-cup ring mold. Place *half* of the biscuit quarters atop the cornflake layer; sprinkle the remaining cornflake mixture atop. Place remaining biscuit quarters atop cornflake layer. Bake in a 375° oven for 20 to 25 minutes or till done. Unmold and serve warm. Makes 1 loaf.

■■■ Preparation time: 30 minutes
■■■ Cooking time: 20 to 25 minutes

Easy Cheese Loaf

2 cups packaged biscuit mix
2 tablespoons sugar
½ teaspoon fines herbes
½ teaspoon paprika
1 beaten egg
½ cup milk
2 tablespoons cooking oil
1 cup shredded American cheese

■■■ Stir together biscuit mix, sugar, fines herbes, and paprika. Combine egg, milk, and oil. Add to dry ingredients; mix well. Stir in cheese. Turn into a greased 8x4x2-inch loaf pan. Bake in a 375° oven for 30 to 35 minutes or till done. Cool in pan for 10 minutes; remove. Cool on wire rack. Makes 1 loaf.

■■■ Total preparation time: 1 hour

Confetti Spoon Bread is similar to a heavy soufflé. It's a quick bread that's soft enough to dish out with a spoon.
  Serve it at a meal as a side-dish substitute for potatoes or rice.

MENU
BIRTHDAY DINNER

Special Filet of Beef ★

Steamed Brussels
Sprouts

Baked Potato with
Sour Cream

Herb Biscuit Spirals

Birthday Cake

Champagne or
Carbonated Beverage

Make someone's day a little more special with *Special Filet of Beef*. Invite a few friends or family members over to celebrate. If you don't have time to bake and frost a cake from scratch, you can always order a personalized cake from the bakery. Or, surprise your guests with a nontraditional "cake" such as a cheesecake or an ice cream cake.

★ see recipe, page 61

Herb Biscuit Spirals

    2 cups all-purpose flour
    1 tablespoon baking powder
    2 teaspoons sugar
    ½ cup butter *or* margarine
    1 beaten egg
    1 8-ounce carton dairy sour cream
    2 tablespoons milk
    1 tablespoon butter *or* margarine, melted
    2 tablespoons grated Parmesan cheese
    ¼ teaspoon dried dillweed

■ In a large mixing bowl stir together flour, baking powder, and sugar. Cut in the ½ cup butter or margarine till mixture resembles coarse crumbs. Make a well in the center of the dry mixture. In a small mixing bowl combine egg, sour cream, and milk; add all at once to dry mixture. Stir just till dough clings together. Turn dough out onto a lightly floured surface; knead gently for 12 to 15 strokes.

■ Roll or pat dough into a 15x8-inch rectangle. Brush with the 1 tablespoon melted butter or margarine. Combine the Parmesan cheese and dillweed. Sprinkle over dough. Fold dough in half lengthwise to make a 15x4-inch rectangle. Cut into fifteen 1-inch-wide strips. Holding a strip at both ends, twist in opposite directions twice, forming a spiral. Repeat with the remaining strips.

■ Place the twisted dough strips on a lightly greased baking sheet, pressing both ends of strips down. Bake in a 450° oven about 10 minutes or till done. Serve warm. Makes 15 spirals.

■ Preparation time: 30 minutes
■ Cooking time: 10 minutes

Onion Biscuit Rounds

    2 cups packaged biscuit mix
    ⅔ cup light cream
    ⅓ cup finely chopped onion
    2 tablespoons butter *or* margarine
       Sesame seed *or* poppy seed

■ Place biscuit mix in a mixing bowl; add cream. Stir just till dough clings together. Knead gently on a lightly floured surface for 10 to 12 strokes. Roll dough to ¼-inch thickness. Cut with a 2½-inch biscuit cutter, dipping cutter into flour between cuts. Place on an ungreased baking sheet. Press an indentation about 1½ inches in diameter in center of each biscuit. Cook onion in hot butter or margarine till tender. Place *1 teaspoon* of the onion mixture into *each* indentation. Sprinkle biscuit edges with sesame seed or poppy seed. Bake in a 425° oven for 10 to 12 minutes or till done. Serve warm. Makes 10 to 12.

■ Total preparation time: 35 to 40 minutes

Cereal-Whole Wheat Muffins

    2 cups raisin bran cereal
    1 cup whole wheat flour
    ⅓ cup sugar
    1 teaspoon baking powder
    ½ teaspoon baking soda
    1 beaten egg
    1 8-ounce carton lemon yogurt
    2 tablespoons cooking oil
    ½ cup chopped walnuts

■ Stir together cereal, flour, sugar, baking powder, baking soda, and ½ teaspoon *salt*. Combine egg, yogurt, and oil; add to dry ingredients. Stir just till moistened; batter should be lumpy. Fold in walnuts. Grease muffin cups; fill ⅔ full. Bake in a 400° oven for 15 to 20 minutes or till done. Serve warm. Makes 12.

■ Total preparation time: 30 to 35 minutes

Spicy Nut Muffins

  2 **cups all-purpose flour**
  2 **teaspoons baking powder**
  ½ **teaspoon salt**
  ¼ **teaspoon baking soda**
  ¼ **teaspoon ground allspice**
  ¼ **teaspoon ground cinnamon**
  ⅛ **teaspoon ground cloves**
  ⅓ **cup butter *or* margarine, softened**
  ½ **cup packed brown sugar**
  1 **egg**
  ¾ **cup chocolate-flavored milk *or* milk**
  ½ **cup chopped pecans *or* walnuts**
  ⅓ **cup raisins**
  1 **tablespoon sugar**

■ In a mixing bowl stir together the flour, baking powder, salt, baking soda, allspice, cinnamon, and cloves; set aside.

■ In a large mixer bowl beat butter or margarine on medium speed of electric mixer for 30 seconds. Add brown sugar and beat till fluffy. Add the egg; beat for 1 minute. Add dry ingredients and the chocolate-flavored milk or milk alternately to beaten mixture, beating on low speed after each addition till just combined. Stir in the pecans or walnuts and the raisins.

■ Grease muffin cups or line with paper bake cups; fill ⅔ full. Sprinkle with sugar. Bake in a 350° oven for 20 to 25 minutes or till done. Remove from muffin pans; serve warm. Makes 12 muffins.

■ Preparation time: 15 minutes
■ Cooking time: 20 to 25 minutes

Pistachio-Apple Muffins

  1 **cup all-purpose flour**
  1 **teaspoon baking powder**
  ¼ **teaspoon salt**
  ¼ **teaspoon ground nutmeg**
  ½ **cup butter *or* margarine, softened**
  ½ **cup sugar**
  2 **egg yolks**
  2 **tablespoons lemon juice**
  ½ **cup shredded, peeled apple**
  ½ **cup chopped pistachio nuts**
  2 **egg whites**
  2 **tablespoons sugar**
  2 **tablespoons finely chopped pistachio nuts**
  3 **tablespoons butter *or* margarine, melted**

■ In a mixing bowl stir together the flour, baking powder, salt, and nutmeg; set aside.

■ In a large mixing bowl beat the ½ cup butter or margarine on medium speed of electric mixer for 30 seconds. Add the ½ cup sugar and beat till fluffy. Add the egg yolks, one at a time, beating on medium speed for 1 minute after each addition. Add the dry ingredients and lemon juice alternately to beaten mixture, beating on low speed after each addition till just combined. Stir in the shredded apple and the ½ cup chopped pistachio nuts.

■ In a mixing bowl beat egg whites till stiff peaks form (tips stand straight). Fold egg whites into apple mixture. Grease 2-inch muffin cups; fill ⅔ full. Bake in a 375° oven for 15 to 20 minutes or till done. Remove from muffin pans. Place on wire racks.

■ For topping, combine the 2 tablespoons sugar and the 2 tablespoons finely chopped pistachio nuts. Dip the warm muffin tops into the 3 tablespoons melted butter or margarine, then into the nut topping. Serve warm. Makes about 20 muffins.

■ Preparation time: 20 minutes
■ Cooking time: 15 to 20 minutes

Australians named this creamy, airy dessert *Pavlova* in honor of the Russian ballerina, Anna Pavlova, who performed in Australia and New Zealand during the early 1900s.

The meringue border of this dessert is firm, yet the meringue shell under the fresh fruit has a soft, marshmallow-like texture. You can shape the meringue by using either a decorating bag or the back of a spoon.

Pavlova

- **4 egg whites**
- **2 teaspoons vinegar**
- **Dash salt**
- **1 cup sugar**
- **5 cups sliced papaya, kiwi, strawberries, bananas, peaches, *or* pineapple chunks**
- **1 cup whipping cream**
- **¼ cup sugar**
- **1 teaspoon vanilla**
- **Fresh gooseberries (optional)**

▬ Bring egg whites to room temperature. Line a baking sheet or shallow baking pan with foil. Using an 8x1½-inch round baking pan as a guide, draw a circle on the foil. In a mixer bowl combine the egg whites, vinegar, and salt; beat on medium speed of electric mixer till soft peaks form (tips curl over). Gradually add the 1 cup sugar, one tablespoon at a time, beating about 10 minutes more or till mixture forms stiff, glossy peaks and sugar is dissolved.

▬ Spread about *half* of the egg white mixture over the circle to ½-inch thickness. Spoon remaining mixture into a decorating bag fitted with a star tip. Pipe mixture around edge of circle, making sides 2 inches high. (*Or*, spread egg white mixture over circle. Using the back of a spoon, shape into a shell, making the bottom ½ inch thick and sides 2 inches high.) Bake in a 300° oven for 50 minutes. Turn off heat and let dry in oven with the door closed for 2 hours more. *Do not open oven door while drying.*

▬ Drain fruit well. Pat dry with paper toweling, if necessary. Reserve about ¼ *cup* of the fruit for garnish, if desired. In a mixer bowl combine the whipping cream, the ¼ cup sugar, and vanilla; beat on medium speed of electric mixer till soft peaks form. Carefully remove the meringue shell from foil; place on a serving platter. Spoon the fruit into meringue shell. Spread the whipped cream atop. Garnish with the reserved fruit and fresh gooseberries, if desired. To serve, cut into wedges. Serve immediately. Makes 8 servings.

▬ Preparation time: 1¼ hours
▬ Cooking time: 2 hours and 50 minutes

Rhubarb-Peach Cobbler

- **1½ cups all-purpose flour**
- **3 tablespoons sugar**
- **2 teaspoons baking powder**
- **½ teaspoon salt**
- **¼ teaspoon baking soda**
- **¼ cup butter *or* margarine**
- **1 8-ounce carton plain yogurt**
- **1 teaspoon vanilla**
- **1 29-ounce can peach slices**
- **¾ cup sugar**
- **2 tablespoons cornstarch**
- **¾ teaspoon ground cinnamon**
- **⅛ teaspoon salt**
- **3 cups rhubarb cut into ¾-inch pieces**
- **1 teaspoon vanilla**
- **1 tablespoon sugar (optional)**
- **¼ teaspoon ground cinnamon (optional)**
- **Vanilla ice cream *or* light cream**

▬ In a mixing bowl combine the flour, the 3 tablespoons sugar, baking powder, the ½ teaspoon salt, and baking soda. Cut in the butter or margarine till mixture resembles coarse crumbs; set aside. Combine the yogurt and 1 teaspoon vanilla; set aside.

▬ Drain the peach slices, reserving 1⅓ cups syrup. In a large saucepan combine the ¾ cup sugar, cornstarch, the ¾ teaspoon cinnamon, and the ⅛ teaspoon salt. Stir in the reserved peach syrup. Add the rhubarb pieces. Cook and stir till the mixture is thickened and bubbly. Add the drained peaches; heat through. Remove from heat; stir in 1 teaspoon vanilla.

▬ Turn the fruit mixture into a 3-quart casserole. Immediately combine the flour mixture and yogurt mixture; drop from a spoon into mounds atop hot fruit. Combine the 1 tablespoon sugar and the ¼ teaspoon cinnamon; sprinkle atop dough, if desired. Bake in a 400° oven for 30 minutes. Let stand about 1 hour or just till warm. Serve warm with vanilla ice cream or light cream. Makes 8 servings.

▬ Preparation time: 30 minutes
▬ Cooking time: 30 minutes
▬ Cooling time: 1 hour

Pavlova

If you have never tasted fresh chestnuts before, get set for a special treat. They have a delightfully distinctive flavor. And, this soufflé is a wonderful way to sample them.

Chestnut Dessert Soufflé is an elegant way to end the meal. Be sure to serve the soufflé right from the oven before it has a chance to fall. Pass whipped cream to spoon over each puffy serving.

Chocolate-Nut Strudel Braid

- 1 **slightly beaten egg white**
- 1 **cup ground almonds (4 ounces)**
- ½ **of a 4-ounce package German sweet cooking chocolate, grated**
- ¼ **cup sugar**
- 2 **tablespoons milk**
- ¼ **teaspoon almond extract**
- 8 **sheets frozen phyllo dough (18x13-inch rectangles), thawed**
- ⅓ **cup butter *or* margarine, melted**
- ⅓ **cup sugar**
- ¼ **cup water**
- 2 **tablespoons honey**
- ¼ **cup sliced almonds, toasted (optional)**

■ For filling, in a mixing bowl combine the egg white, ground almonds, chocolate, the ¼ cup sugar, milk, and almond extract; set aside. Place a sheet of phyllo dough on a large piece of foil. Brush phyllo with

When preparing *Chocolate-Nut Strudel Braid*, use kitchen scissors to cut into the layered phyllo dough to within ½ inch of the filling, as shown. Make the cuts at 1-inch intervals, forming 1-inch-wide strips.

Fold the strips of phyllo dough over the chocolate-nut filling, alternating the strips from each side, as shown. Tuck the ends of the last strips under the braid to seal in the filling.

melted butter or margarine. Top with a second sheet of phyllo; brush with butter. Repeat layering with remaining phyllo and butter. Spread filling lengthwise down center. Using scissors, cut to within ½ inch of filling at 1-inch intervals (see top photograph at left). Fold strips over filling, alternating strips from each side (see lower photograph at left). Tuck ends under to seal. Transfer braid on foil to a shallow baking pan. Bake in a 350° oven for 35 to 40 minutes or till golden.

■ For syrup, in a saucepan combine the ⅓ cup sugar, the water, and honey. Bring to boiling; reduce heat. Simmer, uncovered, for 3 minutes. Transfer braid from foil to wire rack over a tray. Gradually spoon syrup over braid, allowing it to soak in. Sprinkle sliced almonds atop, if desired. Cool. Serves 12.

■ Preparation time: 45 minutes
■ Cooking time: 35 to 40 minutes

Chestnut Dessert Soufflé

- 8 **ounces fresh chestnuts (about 26)**
- ⅓ **cup sugar**
- 2 **tablespoons milk**
- 1 **tablespoon butter *or* margarine, melted**
- 4 **beaten egg yolks**
- 1 **tablespoon brandy**
- 1 **teaspoon vanilla**
- 4 **egg whites**

■ Cut an X in flat side of each chestnut. Cover nuts with cold water. Simmer, covered, 10 to 15 minutes; drain. When cool enough to handle, peel and mash (should have about 1¼ cups). Stir in sugar, milk, butter, and ⅛ teaspoon *salt*. Beat in egg yolks, brandy, and vanilla. Beat egg whites till stiff peaks form. Fold whites into chestnut mixture. Turn into an ungreased 1-quart soufflé dish. Bake in a 350° oven 40 to 45 minutes. Serve immediately. Serves 4.

■ Preparation time: 1¼ hours
■ Cooking time: 40 to 45 minutes

Peach-Glazed Savarin

2 cups all-purpose flour
1 package active dry yeast
⅔ cup milk
6 tablespoons butter *or* margarine
2 tablespoons sugar
½ teaspoon salt
3 eggs
  Savarin Syrup
  Peach Glaze
1½ cups sliced strawberries, halved grapes,
    or sectioned oranges
  Crème Chantilly (optional)

■ In a large mixer bowl combine *1½ cups* of the flour and the yeast. In saucepan heat milk, butter or margarine, sugar, and salt just till warm (115° to 120°) and butter is almost melted; stir constantly. Add to flour mixture; add eggs. Beat on low speed of electric mixer for ½ minute, scraping bowl. Beat for 3 minutes on high speed. Using a spoon, stir in remaining flour. Cover; let rest 10 minutes. Spoon batter into a well-greased 6-cup savarin mold or ring. Cover; let rise in warm place till nearly double (about 40 minutes).

■ Bake in a 350° oven for 25 to 35 minutes or till done. Cool in pan for 5 minutes; transfer to a wire rack over waxed paper. With a fork, prick top of ring at 1-inch intervals. Prepare Savarin Syrup; gradually drizzle over warm ring till all the syrup is absorbed. Let stand ½ hour. Prepare Peach Glaze; spoon over all. To serve, fill center of ring with desired fruit. If desired, prepare Crème Chantilly to spoon onto slices.

Savarin Syrup: In a saucepan combine 1½ cups *peach nectar* and ½ cup *sugar*. Bring to boiling; remove from heat. Stir in ½ cup *rum*.

Peach Glaze: In a saucepan heat and stir one 12-ounce jar *peach jam* over low heat till melted.

Crème Chantilly: In a mixer bowl combine 1 cup *whipping cream*, 1 tablespoon *powdered sugar*, and 1 teaspoon *vanilla*; beat till soft peaks form.

■ Total preparation time: 2½ hours

Strawberry-Lemon Shortcake

½ cup milk
⅓ cup sugar
1 tablespoon cornstarch
2 beaten egg yolks
¼ teaspoon finely shredded lemon peel
2 tablespoons lemon juice
1 tablespoon butter *or* margarine
1 teaspoon vanilla
1 quart strawberries, sliced
2 tablespoons sugar
  Lemon Shortcake
½ cup whipping cream
  Butter *or* margarine, softened

■ For sauce, in a saucepan combine the milk, the ⅓ cup sugar, cornstarch, and ⅛ teaspoon *salt;* cook and stir till thickened and bubbly. Cook and stir for 2 minutes more. Stir about ½ cup of the hot mixture into egg yolks. Return all to pan; bring to a gentle boil. Cook and stir for 2 minutes more. Remove from heat; stir in lemon peel, lemon juice, the 1 tablespoon butter, and vanilla. Cover with clear plastic wrap; chill.

■ Sprinkle berries with the 2 tablespoons sugar. Prepare Lemon Shortcake; cool in pan for 10 minutes. Meanwhile, beat whipping cream till soft peaks form; fold into chilled sauce. Remove cake from pan; cool on a wire rack 5 minutes. Split horizontally into 2 layers. Spread bottom layer with softened butter. Spoon *half* of the berries and *half* of the sauce atop. Replace top layer. Top with remaining berries; drizzle with sauce. Pass remaining. Serve warm. Serves 8.

Lemon Shortcake: Combine 2 cups *all-purpose flour,* 2 tablespoons *sugar,* 1 tablespoon *baking powder,* ¾ teaspoon finely shredded *lemon peel,* and ½ teaspoon *salt.* Cut in ½ cup *butter or margarine* till mixture resembles coarse crumbs; make a well in the center. Combine 1 beaten *egg* and ⅔ cup *light cream or milk.* Add all at once to dry ingredients; stir just till dough clings together. Spread in a greased 8x1½-inch round baking pan, building up edges slightly. Bake in a 450° oven for 15 to 18 minutes or till done.

■ Total preparation time: 2½ hours

Splitting the tender shortcake into two layers can be a little tricky. To avoid problems, try this technique.

Insert several wooden picks halfway up and around the side of the slightly cooled shortcake layer. Using the picks as a cutting guide, slice the shortcake layer in half horizontally with a sharp, long-bladed knife. Carefully lift off the top. Now, you have two even layers of shortcake.

It's important to use a tube-type baking mold when preparing *Plum Pudding*. This shape enables the pudding to bake evenly.

If you serve this spicy dessert after a holiday dinner, you won't be adding a great number of calories to your meal. One serving of *Plum Pudding* is just 165 calories, and *Vanilla Yogurt Sauce* contains only 12 calories per tablespoon.

Plum Pudding

  1⅔ **cups all-purpose flour**
    1 **teaspoon baking powder**
   ½ **teaspoon baking soda**
   ½ **teaspoon ground cinnamon**
   ½ **teaspoon ground cloves**
   ½ **teaspoon ground nutmeg**
   ¼ **cup butter *or* margarine**
   ⅓ **cup packed brown sugar**
   ½ **teaspoon rum flavoring**
    2 **eggs**
    1 **8-ounce can purple plums (juice pack)**
   ½ **cup raisins**
    1 **tablespoon finely shredded orange peel**
       Vanilla Yogurt Sauce

▬▬ Grease and lightly flour a 6½- or 7-cup tube mold; set aside. Stir together the flour, baking powder, baking soda, cinnamon, cloves, and nutmeg. In a large mixer bowl beat butter or margarine on medium speed of electric mixer for 30 seconds. Add brown sugar and rum flavoring; beat till fluffy. Add eggs, one at a time, beating well on medium speed.

▬▬ Drain plums, reserving ¼ cup juice. Pit and cut up plums. Alternately add dry ingredients and plums and reserved juice to the beaten mixture, beating on low speed after each addition till just combined. Stir in the raisins and finely shredded orange peel.

▬▬ Turn batter into prepared mold. Grease a piece of foil and cover top of mold; seal tightly. Bake in a 300° oven for 1 hour. Uncover and bake about 20 minutes more or till pudding springs back when touched. Cool for 10 minutes. Meanwhile, prepare Vanilla Yogurt Sauce. To serve, unmold pudding onto a serving platter. Garnish with finely shredded orange peel, if desired. Pass the sauce. Makes 12 servings.

Vanilla Yogurt Sauce: Combine 1 cup *vanilla yogurt* and ¼ cup *water;* fold in one 4-ounce container *frozen whipped dessert topping,* thawed.

▬▬ Preparation time: 25 minutes
▬▬ Cooking time: 1 hour and 20 minutes

Banana Meringue Pudding

   3 **cups milk**
   ½ **cup sugar**
   ⅓ **cup cornstarch**
   ¼ **teaspoon salt**
    3 **beaten egg yolks**
    2 **tablespoons butter *or* margarine**
  1½ **teaspoons vanilla**
   18 **vanilla wafers**
    1 **large banana, sliced**
    3 **egg whites**
   ⅓ **cup sugar**

▬▬ For pudding, in a saucepan combine milk, the ½ cup sugar, cornstarch, and salt. Cook and stir over medium heat till the mixture is thickened and bubbly. Cook and stir for 2 minutes more. Gradually stir about *1 cup* of the hot mixture into the beaten egg yolks. Return all to saucepan. Bring to a gentle boil. Cook and stir for 2 minutes more. Remove from heat. Stir in butter or margarine and vanilla. Cover the surface with waxed paper or clear plastic wrap. Cool slightly.

▬▬ In an 8x8x2-inch baking dish layer *half* of the vanilla wafers, *half* of the banana slices, and *half* of the pudding mixture. Repeat the layers.

▬▬ For meringue, in a mixer bowl beat egg whites on medium speed of electric mixer till soft peaks form (tips curl over). Gradually add the ⅓ cup sugar, beating till stiff peaks form (tips stand straight). Spread meringue over pudding, sealing to edges of baking dish. Bake in a 350° oven for 12 to 15 minutes or till the meringue is brown. Cool. Makes 9 servings.

▬▬ Preparation time: 1¼ hours
▬▬ Cooking time: 15 minutes

Double Chocolate Cream Puffs

Chocolate-Mint Fluff
½ cup butter _or_ margarine
1 cup water
1 cup all-purpose flour
3 tablespoons unsweetened cocoa powder
4 teaspoons sugar
Dash salt
4 eggs
Powdered sugar

■ Prepare Chocolate-Mint Fluff; chill. In a saucepan melt butter or margarine. Add the water; bring to boiling. Stir together flour, cocoa powder, sugar, and salt. Add to butter mixture. Stir vigorously. Cook and stir till mixture forms a ball that doesn't separate. Remove from heat; cool slightly, about 5 minutes.

■ Add eggs, one at a time, beating with a wooden spoon after each addition about 1 minute or till smooth. Drop the batter by heaping tablespoonfuls 3 inches apart onto a greased baking sheet, forming 12 mounds. Bake in a 400° oven for 25 to 30 minutes or till puffy. Remove from oven; cool on a wire rack. Split cream puffs, removing any soft dough inside.

■ To serve, fill the puffs with chilled Chocolate-Mint Fluff (see photograph at right). Replace tops. Sprinkle with powdered sugar. Makes 12 servings.

Chocolate-Mint Fluff: In a medium saucepan combine 1 package 4-serving-size _regular chocolate pudding mix_ and 1½ cups _milk_. Add ¼ cup cut-up _cream-filled chocolate-covered peppermint patties_ (4 patties). Cook and stir over medium heat till the mixture is thickened and bubbly and mint patties are melted. Remove from heat. Cover the surface with waxed paper or clear plastic wrap; cool. Prepare one 1¼-ounce envelope _dessert topping mix_ according to package directions. Fold the dessert topping into the cooled pudding mixture. Cover and chill in the refrigerator about 2 hours or till cold.

■ Preparation time: 1½ hours
■ Chilling time: at least 2 hours

After removing any soft dough from inside the cream puffs, spoon in _Chocolate-Mint Fluff_, as shown. Replace the tops and sprinkle with powdered sugar.

Individual Lemon Soufflés

4 slightly beaten egg yolks
¼ cup butter _or_ margarine
½ teaspoon finely shredded lemon peel
¼ cup lemon juice
2 tablespoons sugar
Dash salt
4 egg whites
¼ cup sugar
Powdered sugar

■ In a small saucepan combine egg yolks, butter or margarine, lemon peel, lemon juice, the 2 tablespoons sugar, and salt. Cook and stir over low heat till the mixture is slightly thickened. Remove from heat; stir for 2 minutes more. Set aside.

■ In a large mixer bowl beat egg whites till soft peaks form (tips curl over). Gradually add the ¼ cup sugar, beating till stiff peaks form (tips stand straight). Fold lemon mixture into egg whites. Turn into four ungreased 10-ounce soufflé dishes. Place dishes in a 9x9x2-inch baking pan on oven rack. Pour boiling water into pan around dishes to depth of 1 inch.

■ Bake in a 350° oven for 25 to 30 minutes or till a knife inserted near the centers comes out clean. Sprinkle powdered sugar atop each serving. Serve immediately. Makes 4 servings.

■ Preparation time: 30 minutes
■ Cooking time: 25 to 30 minutes

■■■ **MENU** ■■■
DINNER FOR FOUR

Crab Cocktail

Grilled Pork Chops

Parslied Rice

Steamed Broccoli

Hard Rolls with Butter

Individual Lemon Soufflés

Coffee

For the crab cocktail, arrange chunks of cooked and chilled crab meat or crab claws on individual lettuce-lined salad plates. Accompany it with a small dish of cocktail sauce.

Put the soufflés in the oven when you sit down for the main course. Your dessert can bake as you and your guests dine.

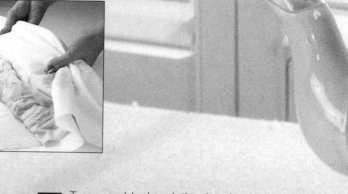

It takes a little practice to perfect the technique for making *Basic Strudel*, but the results are well worth the effort.

You may want to have someone help you stretch the dough. It works well with two people gently stretching the dough from opposite sides. Another tip: Use a lightly floured clean sheet or table cloth to cover the work surface.

Basic Strudel

    3 cups all-purpose flour
    ½ teaspoon salt
    ½ cup butter *or* margarine
    1 beaten egg
    ⅔ cup warm water (110° to 115°)
       Apple-Currant Filling *or*
         Walnut-Raisin Filling
    ¾ cup butter *or* margarine, melted
    1 beaten egg white
       Sugar (optional)

■ In a large mixing bowl stir together flour and salt; cut in the ½ cup butter or margarine till mixture resembles small crumbs. Combine the beaten egg and warm water; add to the flour mixture. Stir till combined. Turn the dough out onto a lightly floured surface; knead for 5 minutes. Divide the dough in half. Cover and let stand at room temperature for 1 hour. Meanwhile, prepare Apple-Currant Filling or Walnut-Raisin Filling; set aside.

■ Cover a large surface (at least 3 by 3 feet) with a floured cloth. On the cloth roll *half* of the dough into a 15-inch square. Brush with *2 tablespoons* of the melted butter or margarine; cover and let the dough rest for 10 minutes.

■ To stretch dough, use back of hands, working underneath dough, as shown. Starting from the middle of the square, gently stretch from one corner to the next till dough is *paper thin,* forming a 40x20-inch rectangle. To avoid tearing, *do not lift too high.* Trim uneven edges with scissors.

■ To assemble, brush the dough with ¼ *cup* of the melted butter or margarine. Beginning 4 inches from one narrow side of dough, spoon *half* of the desired filling in a band about 4 inches wide across the dough. Using the cloth as a guide, gently lift and fold the 4-inch piece of dough over the filling, as shown. Slowly and evenly lift cloth beneath filling, rolling dough into a tight roll, as shown. Seal ends. Place on lightly greased large shallow baking pan; curve slightly to form crescent. Repeat with remaining dough and filling to make 2 crescents.

■ Brush the tops of the strudels with the beaten egg white. Sprinkle with sugar, if desired. Bake in a 350° oven for 35 to 40 minutes or till golden. Remove from pan; cool on wire racks. Makes 2 strudels.

Apple-Currant Filling: In a large mixing bowl combine ⅔ cup *sugar* and 1½ teaspoons ground *cinnamon.* Add 6 cups very thinly sliced peeled *apples* and ½ cup dried *currants;* toss gently to mix.

Walnut-Raisin Filling: In a small skillet melt 2 tablespoons *butter or margarine* over medium heat. Add 1½ cups *soft bread crumbs* (2 slices). Cook, stirring occasionally, till crumbs are golden brown. Remove from heat. Stir in 1½ cups chopped *walnuts;* 1½ cups *raisins;* ¾ cup *sugar;* ¾ cup *apricot jam,* sieved; and ½ cup diced *candied orange peel.*

***

■ Preparation time: 2½ hours
■ Standing time: 1 hour
■ Cooking time: 35 to 40 minutes

Impress guests with flaky *Basic Strudel* filled with either of two delicious choices: raisins and nuts or sliced fresh apples and currants.

Chocolate Genoise Cake

Chocolate Genoise Cake

½ cup unsalted butter
2 squares (2 ounces) semisweet chocolate
6 slightly beaten eggs
1 cup sugar
1 teaspoon vanilla
1 cup all-purpose flour
  Espresso Buttercream

▇ Grease and lightly flour two 9x1½-inch round baking pans. In a saucepan melt butter and chocolate over low heat, stirring often; set aside. In a large mixer bowl combine eggs, sugar, and vanilla. Set bowl over (not touching) 1 to 2 inches of hot (not boiling) water in a large saucepan. Heat over low heat, stirring occasionally, about 10 minutes or till lukewarm (105° to 110°). Remove from heat; remove bowl from saucepan. Beat on high speed of electric mixer about 15 minutes or till nearly tripled in volume. Gently fold in flour, ⅓ cup at a time. Gradually fold in the chocolate mixture. Spread evenly in prepared pans. Bake in a 350° oven for 25 to 30 minutes or till a wooden pick inserted near the center comes out clean. Cool 10 minutes on wire racks. Remove from pans; cool.

▇ Meanwhile, prepare Espresso Buttercream. Fill and frost cake with plain buttercream. Pipe chocolate buttercream around edge of cake. Serves 12 to 16.

Espresso Buttercream: In a mixer bowl beat 6 *egg yolks* with electric mixer till thick and lemon colored; set aside. In a saucepan stir together 1 cup *sugar*, ⅓ cup *water*, and 4 teaspoons *instant espresso coffee powder*; bring to boiling, stirring till dissolved. Cook over medium-high heat, stirring constantly, till mixture reaches the soft-ball stage (236°). Quickly pour the hot mixture in a steady stream over yolks, beating constantly on high speed. Continue beating till mixture is thick and smooth. Cool 15 minutes. Meanwhile, beat 1½ cups *unsalted butter*, softened, till light and fluffy. Beat butter, 1 tablespoon at a time, into cooled yolk mixture. Cover; chill 30 minutes or till stiff enough to spread. Stir ¼ cup *semisweet chocolate pieces*, melted and cooled, into ½ cup of the buttercream.

▇ Total preparation time: 3 hours

Lemon-Apricot Torte

3 eggs
2½ cups all-purpose flour
1 tablespoon baking powder
¾ cup butter *or* margarine
1½ cups sugar
1 tablespoon finely shredded lemon peel
½ teaspoon lemon extract
1 cup milk
  Lemon Butter Frosting
1 12-ounce jar apricot *or* peach preserves

▇ Separate eggs. Grease and lightly flour two 9x1½-inch round baking pans. Stir together flour, baking powder, and ¼ teaspoon *salt*. In a mixer bowl beat butter with electric mixer for 30 seconds. Add sugar, lemon peel, and lemon extract; beat till fluffy. Add yolks, one at a time, beating well. Add dry ingredients and milk alternately to beaten mixture, beating after each. Using clean beaters, beat egg whites till stiff peaks form; fold into batter. Turn into pans. Bake in a 350° oven about 30 minutes or till done. Cool for 10 minutes on wire racks. Remove from pans; cool.

▇ Prepare Lemon Butter Frosting. Heat preserves till melted. Slice cake layers in half horizontally. Place one cake layer on a plate. Spread *one-fourth* of the preserves atop. Top with second cake layer; spread with one-fourth more preserves. Repeat with third layer; top with fourth layer. Frost sides with *some* of the frosting. Spread remaining preserves over top of cake. Using a decorating bag and star tip, pipe remaining frosting in a lattice design on top of cake; pipe a border around top and bottom of cake. Serves 12.

Lemon Butter Frosting: In a mixer bowl beat 6 tablespoons *butter or margarine* till light and fluffy; gradually add 2 cups sifted *powdered sugar*, beating till combined. Beat in 1 *egg yolk*, 1 teaspoon finely shredded *lemon peel*, and ½ teaspoon *lemon extract*. Gradually add another 2 cups sifted *powdered sugar*, beating till smooth. Beat in a few drops *yellow food coloring*, if desired, and enough *milk* (about 2 tablespoons) to make of spreading consistency. Cover.

▇ Total preparation time: 3 hours

Chocolate Genoise (jen-WAHZ) Cake is the perfect choice for a special dinner party. To give the side and top of this handsome cake its spectacular geometric pattern, brush a cake decorator's comb over the buttercream-frosted cake. Most kitchen equipment shops or gourmet stores carry this handy gadget.

Trim the cake with chocolate buttercream made by combining melted chocolate and a small amount of the coffee-flavored buttercream. Use a decorating bag fitted with a special tip to pipe the chocolate buttercream around the top and base of the cake.

What's nice about this menu is that you can prepare most of the food ahead. Start off with the potato salad and relishes. Tuck them in the refrigerator to chill. Next, bake the dessert and prepare the butterscotch sauce before the party starts.

At dinnertime, while the barbecue chef tends to the chicken cooking on the grill, someone else can fix the mushrooms and cook the corn.

Pecan Cake Sundaes with Butterscotch Sauce

1½ **cups all-purpose flour**
½ **teaspoon baking soda**
¼ **teaspoon salt**
½ **cup butter** or **margarine**
1 **cup packed brown sugar**
1 **cup chopped pecans**
⅔ **cup milk**
½ **teaspoon vanilla**
1 **beaten egg**
¾ **cup packed brown sugar**
1 **5⅓-ounce can (⅔ cup) evaporated milk**
¼ **cup light corn syrup**
2 **tablespoons butter** or **margarine**
½ **teaspoon vanilla**
    Vanilla ice cream

■ Grease and lightly flour a 9x9x2-inch baking pan; set aside. Stir together the flour, baking soda, and salt. In medium saucepan melt the ½ cup butter or margarine over medium heat; stir in the 1 cup brown sugar and pecans. Cook and stir till the mixture is bubbly. Remove from heat. Stir in the milk and ½ teaspoon vanilla. Stir in the beaten egg.

■ Add the dry ingredients to the pecan mixture in the saucepan; stir till combined. Turn into prepared pan. Bake in a 350° oven for 25 to 30 minutes or till done. Place cake on a wire rack; cool thoroughly.

■ Meanwhile, for sauce, in a 2-quart saucepan stir together the ¾ cup brown sugar, evaporated milk, light corn syrup, and the 2 tablespoons butter or margarine. Bring the mixture to boiling; cook for 3 to 4 minutes, stirring constantly. Remove from heat. Stir in ½ teaspoon vanilla.

■ To serve, cut the cake into squares. Top with a scoop of vanilla ice cream; spoon some of the sauce over top. Makes 9 to 12 servings.

■ Preparation time: 30 minutes
■ Cooking time: 25 to 30 minutes

Blonde Brownie Torte

1⅔ **cups all-purpose flour**
1 **teaspoon baking powder**
½ **teaspoon salt**
¾ **cup shortening**
1¾ **cups packed brown sugar**
1 **teaspoon vanilla**
4 **eggs**
½ **cup milk**
2 **8-ounce packages cream cheese, softened**
2 **teaspoons vanilla**
⅔ **cup sugar**
⅓ **cup unsweetened cocoa powder**
1½ **cups whipping cream**

■ Grease and lightly flour two 8x1½-inch round baking pans. Stir together flour, baking powder, and salt. In a mixer bowl beat shortening on medium speed of electric mixer for 30 seconds. Add brown sugar and the 1 teaspoon vanilla; beat till fluffy. Add eggs, one at time, beating well. Add dry ingredients and milk alternately to beaten mixture, beating till just combined. Spread batter in prepared pans. Bake in a 350° oven for 25 to 30 minutes or till done. Cool for 10 minutes on wire racks. Remove from pans; cool.

■ Meanwhile, for filling, in a mixer bowl combine the cream cheese and the 2 teaspoons vanilla; beat till fluffy. Gradually add the sugar and cocoa powder, beating on high speed of electric mixer till combined.

■ Slice cake layers in half horizontally. To assemble, place one cake layer on a plate; spread *one-third* of the filling atop. Top with second cake layer; spread with another one-third filling. Repeat with the third cake layer and remaining filling. Place the last cake layer atop. Cover; chill about 2 hours or till cold.

■ Just before serving, beat whipping cream till soft peaks form. Spread over top and sides of cake. Garnish with grated chocolate, if desired. To serve, cut into wedges. Refrigerate to store. Serves 14 to 16.

■ Preparation time: 1½ hours
■ Cooking time: 25 to 30 minutes
■ Chilling time: at least 2 hours

Rhubarb Kuchen à la Mode

- 1 cup all-purpose flour
- 1 tablespoon sugar
- 1½ teaspoons baking powder
- ⅛ teaspoon salt
- 2 tablespoons butter *or* margarine
- 1 beaten egg
- 2 tablespoons milk
- 1 3-ounce package strawberry-flavored gelatin
- ⅓ cup sugar
- 3 tablespoons all-purpose flour
- 1½ pounds rhubarb, sliced (5 cups)
- ⅔ cup sugar
- ⅓ cup all-purpose flour
- 3 tablespoons butter *or* margarine
  Vanilla ice cream

■ For crust, in a mixing bowl stir together the 1 cup flour, the 1 tablespoon sugar, the baking powder, and salt. Cut in the 2 tablespoons butter or margarine till mixture resembles coarse crumbs. Combine the beaten egg and milk; add to flour mixture. Stir till all is moistened. Pat the mixture evenly in the bottom of a 9x9x2-inch baking pan; set aside.

■ Combine strawberry-flavored gelatin, the ⅓ cup sugar, and the 3 tablespoons flour. Stir into rhubarb; turn into the crust-lined pan. For topping, combine the ⅔ cup sugar and the ⅓ cup flour; cut in the 3 tablespoons butter or margarine till mixture resembles coarse crumbs. Sprinkle evenly over rhubarb filling.

■ Bake in a 375° oven about 40 minutes or till rhubarb is tender and topping is light brown. Serve warm or cool. To serve, cut into squares. Top each serving with vanilla ice cream. Makes 9 servings.

■ Preparation time: 40 minutes
■ Cooking time: 40 minutes

Chocolate Truffle Torte

- 1¼ cups all-purpose flour
- ½ teaspoon baking powder
- ½ teaspoon baking soda
- ¼ cup shortening
- 1 cup sugar
- 1 teaspoon vanilla
- 2 egg yolks
- 2 squares (2 ounces) unsweetened chocolate, melted and cooled
- ¾ cup milk
- 2 stiff-beaten egg whites
  Truffle Filling
  Chocolate Glaze

■ Grease and lightly flour two 9x1½-inch round baking pans. Stir together flour, baking powder, baking soda, and ¼ teaspoon *salt*. In a mixer bowl beat shortening with electric mixer for 30 seconds. Add sugar and vanilla; beat till combined. Add egg yolks, one at a time, beating well. Beat in chocolate. Add dry ingredients and milk alternately to beaten mixture, beating till just combined. Fold in stiff-beaten egg whites. Turn batter into prepared pans. Bake in a 350° oven for 15 to 18 minutes or till done. Cool for 10 minutes on wire racks. Remove from pans; cool.

■ Prepare Truffle Filling and Chocolate Glaze. Slice cake layers in half horizontally. Place one layer on a plate; spread *one-third* of the filling atop. Repeat with two more layers. Place the last cake layer atop. Drizzle with glaze. Chill 30 minutes. Serves 12 to 16.

Truffle Filling: Melt ½ cup *semisweet chocolate pieces* over low heat, stirring constantly. Cool to room temperature. Beat 1 cup *whipping cream* till soft peaks form. Fold the chocolate into the whipped cream. Fold in ¼ cup chopped, toasted *almonds*.

Chocolate Glaze: Melt ½ square (½ ounce) *unsweetened chocolate* and 1 tablespoon *butter or margarine*. Stir in ¾ cup sifted *powdered sugar* and ½ teaspoon *vanilla*. Stir in enough *boiling water* (about 1 tablespoon) to make of drizzling consistency.

■ Total preparation time: 3 hours

Lamingtons, a dessert favorite in Australia, make a delightful ending to dinner. Accompany a platter of these tiny, coconut-covered cakes with demitasse cups of strong coffee.

If you don't have self-rising flour for the cake, you can substitute 1¼ cups *all-purpose flour*, 1¼ teaspoons *baking powder*, and ½ teaspoon *salt*.

To frost the *Lamingtons*, place the cake squares, one at a time, onto a slotted spoon or a fork. Hold each cake square over *Cocoa Icing* in the saucepan. Spoon the icing onto the top and sides of each square, as shown.

After coating each cake square with icing, roll the squares in the chopped coconut spread out on waxed paper, as shown. Coat all sides of the cake squares with the coconut. Let dry on a wire rack over waxed paper.

■ Place cake sqaures, one at a time, onto a slotted spoon or a fork. Lift over icing in saucepan; spoon icing onto top and sides of cake square (see top photograph at left). Roll cake squares on all sides in coconut (see lower photograph at left). Let dry on wire rack over waxed paper. Makes 25 cakes.

Cocoa Icing: In a saucepan combine ⅓ cup *butter or margarine*, ⅓ cup *water*, and ¼ cup *unsweetened cocoa powder;* bring to boiling. Remove from heat. Add 3¾ cups sifted *powdered sugar* and ¾ teaspoon *vanilla;* beat till smooth. Add additional *hot water*, if necessary, to make of spooning consistency.

■ Total preparation time: 1¾ hours

Lamingtons

- ¼ cup butter *or* margarine
- ¾ cup sugar
- ¾ teaspoon vanilla
- 1 egg
- 1¼ cups self-rising flour
- ½ cup milk
  Cocoa Icing
- 2½ cups coconut, very finely chopped

■ Grease and lightly flour an 8x8x2-inch baking pan. Beat butter or margarine with electric mixer for 30 seconds. Add sugar and vanilla; beat till combined. Add egg; beat well. Add flour and milk alternately to beaten mixture, beating till just combined (batter will have a curdled appearance). Turn into pan. Bake in a 350° oven for 25 to 30 minutes or till done. Cool 10 minutes on wire rack. Remove from pan; cool. Cut the cooled cake into 1½-inch squares. Prepare Cocoa Icing. Place coconut on waxed paper.

Pudding-Topped Cake

- 1 8¼-ounce can crushed pineapple
- 1 package 1-layer-size yellow cake mix
- 1 3-ounce package cream cheese, softened
- 1½ cups milk
- 1 package 4-serving-size *instant* vanilla pudding mix
- 1 1½-ounce envelope dessert topping mix

■ Grease and lightly flour a 9x9x2-inch baking pan. Drain pineapple, reserving syrup. Prepare cake mix according to package directions, *except* substitute reserved pineapple syrup plus enough water to equal liquid called for in package directions. Turn batter into prepared pan. Bake in a 350° oven about 20 minutes or till done. Cool on a wire rack.

■ Beat cream cheese till fluffy; gradually beat in milk. Add pudding mix; beat for 2 minutes on low speed. Fold in pineapple. Spread atop cake. Prepare topping mix according to package directions; spread atop. Chill about 2 hours or till cold. Serves 9.

■ Preparation time: 1¼ hours
■ Cooking time: 20 minutes
■ Chilling time: at least 2 hours

Upside-Down Date Pudding Cake

1   cup snipped pitted dates
1   cup boiling water
1½ cups all-purpose flour
1   teaspoon baking soda
½   teaspoon baking powder
½   teaspoon salt
1   beaten egg
2   tablespoons butter *or* margarine, melted
½   cup sugar
½   cup packed brown sugar
½   cup chopped walnuts
1½ cups packed brown sugar
1½ cups boiling water
1   tablespoon butter *or* margarine
    Vanilla ice cream

■■■ In a mixing bowl combine snipped dates and the 1 cup boiling water; set aside to cool. Stir together flour, baking soda, baking powder, salt; set aside.

■■■ In a mixing bowl combine the beaten egg and the 2 tablespoons melted butter or margarine; stir in the sugar and the ½ cup brown sugar. Stir in the dry ingredients, walnuts, and date mixture. Turn the batter into a 9x9x2-inch baking pan.

■■■ Combine the 1½ cups brown sugar, 1½ cups boiling water, and 1 tablespoon butter or margarine; pour over date mixture. Bake in a 375° oven for 35 minutes or till done. Cut into squares and serve warm with vanilla ice cream. Makes 9 to 12 servings.

■■■ Preparation time: 40 minutes
■■■ Cooking time: 35 minutes

Mincemeat Cake Roll

1   cup all-purpose flour
1   teaspoon baking powder
½   teaspoon salt
3   eggs
1   cup sugar
1   teaspoon vanilla
½   cup hot water
2   cups prepared mincemeat
    Powdered sugar
1½ cups whipping cream

■■■ Grease and line a 15x10x1-inch jelly-roll pan with waxed paper; set aside. Stir together flour, baking powder, and salt. In a large mixer bowl beat eggs on high speed of electric mixer about 5 minutes or till thick and lemon colored. Gradually add sugar, beating till dissolved. Add vanilla. Add dry ingredients, beating on low speed till just combined. Add hot water; beat till smooth. Stir in ¼ *cup* of the mincemeat.

■■■ Spread the batter evenly in the prepared pan. Bake in a 375° oven for 10 to 12 minutes or till done. Immediately loosen the edges of warm cake from pan; quickly invert over a towel sprinkled with powdered sugar (see column at right). Remove waxed paper. Starting with narrow end, roll up warm cake and towel together. Cool thoroughly on a wire rack.

■■■ Meanwhile, for filling, beat whipping cream till soft peaks form. Combine the remaining mincemeat and *2 cups* of the whipped cream. Carefully unroll the cooled cake; spread with mincemeat mixture. Roll up cake. Spread the remaining whipped cream over top and sides of cake. Makes 10 servings.

■■■ Total preparation time: 1¼ hours

When removing the cake from the pan for *Mincemeat Cake Roll,* use potholders to hold the baking pan. Invert the pan and gently shake it over a kitchen towel sprinkled with powdered sugar. Then, carefully remove the pan so the cake doesn't tear. You'll find that the powdered sugar helps to prevent the warm cake from sticking to the towel.

It's important to roll the cake while it's still warm to keep it from cracking. The towel prevents the rolled cake from sticking together as it cools.

Apple-Cranberry Tart

Apple-Cranberry Tart

Basic Rich Pastry
- 3 *or* 4 medium cooking apples, peeled, cored, and halved
- ½ cup dry white wine
- ¼ cup butter *or* margarine
- ¾ cup sugar
- ⅛ teaspoon ground cinnamon
- 2 teaspoons cornstarch
- ½ teaspoon vanilla
- 1 cup cranberries
- ¼ cup chopped pecans

▬ Bake and cool Basic Rich Pastry. Meanwhile, on round side of each apple half, make 6 to 8 narrow crosswise cuts about ¼ inch wide, cutting partially through the apple (do not make cuts all the way through). In a 10-inch skillet combine wine, butter or margarine, ¼ *cup* of the sugar, the cinnamon, and ¼ cup *water*. Heat to melt butter. Place apple halves in skillet. Cook, covered, 10 to 12 minutes or till apples are tender; turn once to cook evenly. Using a slotted spoon, remove apple halves. Combine cornstarch and 1 tablespoon *cold water;* add to liquid in skillet. Cook and stir till thickened and bubbly. Cook and stir 1 minute more. Remove from heat; stir in vanilla. Cool slightly. Arrange apple halves in bottom of the baked pastry shell; spoon glaze atop and chill.

▬ Meanwhile, for topping, in a small saucepan combine cranberries, remaining ½ cup sugar, and ¼ cup *water*. Bring to boiling, stirring to dissolve sugar. Boil rapidly for 2 minutes or till cranberry skins pop. Remove from heat. Stir in pecans. Cool thoroughly. Spoon the cranberry-nut topping around the apple halves. Chill 2 to 3 hours. Makes 6 to 8 servings.

Basic Rich Pastry: In a mixing bowl combine 1 cup *all-purpose flour* and ¼ teaspoon *salt*. Cut in ¼ cup cold *butter* and 1 tablespoon *shortening* till mixture resembles coarse crumbs. Make a well in the center. Beat together 1 *egg yolk* and 2 tablespoons *cold water*. Add to flour mixture. Using fork, stir till dough forms a ball. Wrap in clear plastic wrap and chill 20 minutes in freezer or 1½ hours in refrigerator before rolling into desired shape. For flan pastry shell, on a lightly floured surface roll dough into a circle 12 or 13 inches in diameter or about 2 inches larger than diameter of pan. Fit dough into a 10- or 11-inch flan pan, pressing bottom and sides gently to remove any air bubbles. Turn overlapping dough edges to inside and press against sides of pan. Prick sides with fork. Line the bottom and sides of pan with heavy-duty foil; fill with *dry beans*. Bake in a 400° oven for 20 minutes. Remove foil and beans. Bake 5 to 10 minutes more or till pastry is golden.

▬ Preparation time: 2⅓ hours
▬ Chilling time: 2 to 3 hours

Strawberry-Coconut Pie

- 1 envelope unflavored gelatin
- 1 cup milk
- 1 pint strawberry ice cream
- 1 package 4-serving-size *instant* coconut cream pudding mix
- 1 cup frozen whole unsweetened strawberries, thawed
- 1 8-ounce carton plain yogurt
- 1 9-inch Baked Pastry Shell (see recipe, page 157), cooled
- ½ cup whipping cream
- 2 tablespoons sugar

▬ In a small saucepan soften gelatin in milk for 5 minutes. Heat and stir over low heat till gelatin dissolves. Remove from heat; add ice cream by spoonfuls, stirring till melted. Stir in coconut cream pudding mix, strawberries, and yogurt. Place in mixer bowl. Beat with electric mixer on low speed for 1 minute. Turn mixture into cooled Baked Pastry Shell.

▬ Beat cream and sugar till soft peaks form (tips curl over). Spread atop pie. If desired, garnish with toasted flaked coconut. Chill about 3 hours or till firm. Let pie stand a few minutes before serving. Serves 8.

▬ Preparation time: 30 minutes
▬ Chilling time: at least 3 hours

MENU
OLD-FASHIONED OVEN MEAL

Sliced Tomatoes on Lettuce with Thousand Island Dressing

Roast Chicken

Butter-Baked Rice

Baked Acorn Squash

Apple-Cranberry Tart

Coffee

All three dishes for this homespun dinner's main course are cooked in the oven. You'll find that oven meals are great when entertaining since the food generally requires little attention.

The dessert, made with apples and cranberries, is the star of this menu. If fresh cranberries are unavailable, use frozen cranberries for the dessert (see information on page 218).

For your table's centerpiece, arrange a bouquet of brightly colored flowers in a favorite container. A dried-flower or silk-flower arrangement also makes an attractive centerpiece.

Put your food processor to use to grind the almonds for *Almond and Plum Tart*. Use the steel blade in the work bowl and process till nuts are very finely chopped. Be careful not to overprocess, or the nuts will start to form a butter.

Almond and Plum Tart*

1¼ **cups all-purpose flour**
2 **teaspoons sugar**
⅓ **cup shortening *or* lard**
3 **to 4 tablespoons cold water**
8 **to 10 plums**
1 **cup finely ground almonds**
   (about 4 ounces)
⅓ **cup sugar**
1 **egg**
½ **teaspoon finely shredded lemon peel**
½ **teaspoon ground cinnamon**
¼ **teaspoon almond extract**
2 **tablespoons butter *or* margarine**
⅓ **cup currant jelly, melted**
   Toasted slivered almonds (optional)

■ In a large bowl stir together the flour, the 2 teaspoons sugar, and ½ teaspoon *salt*. Cut in shortening or lard till pieces are the size of small peas. Sprinkle *1 tablespoon* of the water over part of the mixture; gently toss with a fork. Push to side of bowl; repeat till all is moistened. Form dough into a ball. On a lightly floured surface roll dough into a 12-inch circle. Transfer to a 9-inch quiche dish or pie plate. For quiche dish, trim edges of dough even with rim of pan. For pie plate, fold edges of dough under and flute.

■ Halve and pit plums. In a small mixer bowl combine the ground almonds, the ⅓ cup sugar, egg, lemon peel, cinnamon, and almond extract. Beat on low speed of electric mixer till combined. Spread the almond mixture evenly in pastry shell. Place plum halves, cut side down atop the almond mixture. Dot with butter or margarine.

■ Bake in a 375° oven for 50 minutes or till the crust is brown and juice from plums is nearly evaporated. Cool to room temperature. Brush with melted currant jelly. If desired, sprinkle with toasted sliced almonds. Makes 6 to 8 servings.

■ Preparation time: 40 minutes
■ Cooking time: 50 minutes
■ Cooling time: at least 3 hours
  * *pictured on the cover*

Orange-Rhubarb Pie

1 **cup sugar**
4 **teaspoons quick-cooking tapioca**
¼ **teaspoon ground nutmeg**
4 **cups rhubarb cut into 1-inch pieces**
   (about 1½ pounds rhubarb)
1 **teaspoon finely shredded orange peel**
⅓ **cup orange juice**
   Pastry for Double-Crust Pie
   Milk (optional)
   Sugar (optional)

■ In a large mixing bowl stir together the 1 cup sugar, the quick-cooking tapioca, and nutmeg. Add the rhubarb pieces, finely shredded orange peel, and orange juice; toss gently to coat fruit. Let the fruit mixture stand for 15 minutes.

■ Meanwhile, prepare Pastry for Double-Crust Pie. On lightly floured surface roll one ball of dough from center to edge forming a circle about 12 inches in diameter. Line a 9-inch pie plate with pastry. Trim to ½ inch beyond edge. Turn rhubarb filling into pastry-lined pie plate. Roll out the remaining pastry to form a circle about 12 inches in diameter; cut into ½-inch-wide strips. Weave the strips atop the filling to make a lattice crust; flute edge high. Brush the top of pastry with milk and sprinkle sugar atop, if desired. To prevent overbrowning, cover the edge of pie with foil.

■ Bake pie in a 375° oven for 25 minutes. Remove foil and bake 25 minutes more or till crust is golden. Cool on a wire rack. Makes 8 servings.

Pastry for Double-Crust Pie: In a mixing bowl stir together 2 cups *all-purpose flour* and 1 teaspoon *salt*. Cut in ⅔ cup *shortening* till pieces are the size of small peas. Using a total of 5 to 7 tablespoons *cold water*, sprinkle 1 tablespoon at a time over part of mixture; toss with a fork. Repeat till all is moistened. Form the dough into two balls.

■ Preparation time: 45 minutes
■ Cooking time: 50 minutes

Mocha-Marbled Raisin Pie

¾ cup raisins
¼ cup rum
½ cup sugar
1 envelope unflavored gelatin
1 cup milk
3 squares (3 ounces) semisweet chocolate, cut up
2 slightly beaten egg yolks
1 tablespoon instant coffee crystals
2 egg whites
1 cup whipping cream
¼ cup sifted powdered sugar
1 9-inch Baked Pastry Shell, cooled

■ Soak raisins in rum about 1 hour. Meanwhile, combine ¼ *cup* of the sugar, gelatin, and ⅛ teaspoon *salt*. Stir in milk, chocolate, egg yolks, and coffee crystals. Cook and stir till slightly thickened. Remove from heat; stir in raisin mixture. Chill to consistency of corn syrup; stir occasionally. Remove from refrigerator. Beat egg whites till soft peaks form. Gradually add remaining ¼ cup sugar, beating till stiff peaks form.

■ When gelatin mixture is consistency of unbeaten egg whites (partially set), fold in beaten egg whites. Chill. Beat cream and powdered sugar till soft peaks form. Spoon chocolate mixture and whipped cream alternately into Baked Pastry Shell. Swirl gently to marble. Cover and chill for 6 hours. Serves 8.

Baked Pastry Shell: For a 9-inch piecrust, in a mixing bowl stir together 1¼ cups *all-purpose flour* and ½ teaspoon *salt*. Cut in ⅓ cup *shortening* till pieces are the size of small peas. Using a total of 3 to 4 tablespoons *cold water*, sprinkle 1 tablespoon at a time over part of the mixture; toss with a fork. Repeat till all is moistened. Form into a ball. On lightly floured surface roll out from center to edge, forming circle about 12 inches in diameter. Line a 9-inch pie plate. Trim pastry to ½ inch beyond edge of pie plate. Flute edge. Prick bottom and sides with fork. Bake in a 450° oven for 10 to 12 minutes or till golden. Cool.

■ Preparation time: 2½ hours
■ Chilling time: at least 6 hours

Chocolate Mint Pie

½ cup sugar
1 tablespoon cornstarch
2 cups milk
4 slightly beaten egg yolks
1 teaspoon vanilla
1 16-ounce package semisweet chocolate pieces
1 9-inch Baked Pastry Shell (see recipe at left), cooled
1 envelope unflavored gelatin
¼ cup cold water
3 tablespoons green crème de menthe
4 egg whites
½ cup sugar
Whipped cream (optional)
Shaved chocolate (optional)

■ In a saucepan combine ½ cup sugar and cornstarch. Stir in milk and egg yolks. Cook and stir over medium heat till mixture thickens and coats a metal spoon. Cook and stir 2 minutes more. Remove from heat; stir in vanilla. Stir chocolate into 1¼ *cups* of the thickened mixture till chocolate is melted; pour into the cooled Baked Pastry Shell. Chill in the refrigerator.

■ Meanwhile, soften gelatin in cold water for 5 minutes. Stir into the remaining *hot* thickened mixture till gelatin dissolves. Stir in crème de menthe. Chill to the consistency of corn syrup, stirring occasionally.

■ Remove from refrigerator (gelatin mixture will continue to set). Immediately begin beating egg whites till soft peaks form (tips curl over). Gradually add ½ cup sugar, beating till stiff peaks form (tips stand straight). When gelatin is the consistency of unbeaten egg whites (partially set), fold in stiff-beaten egg whites. Chill till mixture mounds when spooned. Pile mixture over chocolate layer in the pastry shell.

■ Chill in the refrigerator for 6 hours or till set. Garnish with whipped cream and shaved chocolate, if desired. Cover and chill to store. Makes 8 servings.

■ Preparation time: 2 hours
■ Chilling time: at least 6 hours

To make attractive edges on a single- or double-crust pie, try these techniques.
For a fluted edge, press dough with the forefinger (from outside the pie plate) against thumb and forefinger of other hand (placed inside the pie plate). Continue till entire edge is fluted.
For a scalloped pastry edge, hold a round-bowled measuring tablespoon in one hand and press against the thumb and index finger of other hand.

For attractive, flaky piecrusts, bake your pies only in glass, ceramic, or non-shiny metal pie pans. Shiny metal pans reflect the heat and may cause the crust to become soggy.

Cool the baked pie or piecrust on a wire rack so air can circulate around it. This releases steam so that it does not get trapped and make the crust soggy.

Layered Peanut Butter Pie

- 1 cup fine graham cracker crumbs
- ½ cup presweetened cocoa powder
- ⅓ cup finely chopped peanuts
- 6 tablespoons butter *or* margarine, melted
- ½ cup presweetened cocoa powder
- 1 envelope unflavored gelatin
- ⅓ cup milk
- 3 tablespoons light corn syrup
- 1 beaten egg
- 3 tablespoons butter *or* margarine
- ½ teaspoon vanilla
- ⅓ cup sugar
- 1 cup milk
- 2 slightly beaten egg yolks
- ½ cup creamy peanut butter
- 2 egg whites
- ¼ cup sugar
- ½ of a 4-ounce container frozen whipped dessert topping, thawed

■ In a bowl combine graham cracker crumbs, ½ cup cocoa powder, peanuts, and the 6 tablespoons butter or margarine. Press into a 9-inch pie plate. Bake in a 350° oven 10 minutes; set aside.

■ In a saucepan combine ½ cup cocoa powder and *½ envelope* (about 1 teaspoon) of the unflavored gelatin. Add the ⅓ cup milk, corn syrup, beaten egg, and the 3 tablespoons butter. Cook and stir over medium heat just to boiling. Remove from heat; stir in vanilla. Cool 10 minutes. Pour into crust; chill.

■ Combine remaining gelatin and ⅓ cup sugar; stir in 1 cup milk and egg yolks. Cook and stir over medium heat till mixture coats a metal spoon. Remove from heat; stir in peanut butter. Chill to consistency of corn syrup; stir occasionally. Remove from refrigerator. Beat egg whites till soft peaks form (tips curl over); gradually add the ¼ cup sugar, beating till stiff peaks form (tips stand straight). Fold into yolk mixture along with whipped dessert topping. Spoon into crust. Chill for 6 hours or till firm. Makes 8 servings.

■ Preparation time: 1½ hours
■ Chilling time: at least 6 hours

Rum-Walnut Pumpkin Pie

- 1¼ cups all-purpose flour
- ½ teaspoon salt
- ⅓ cup shortening
- 3 to 4 tablespoons cold water
- 1½ cups canned pumpkin
- ¾ cup packed brown sugar
- 1 teaspoon ground cinnamon
- ½ teaspoon salt
- ½ teaspoon ground ginger
- ½ teaspoon ground nutmeg
- 3 eggs
- 1 cup evaporated milk
- 3 tablespoons dark rum
- ¾ cup chopped walnuts
- ½ cup whipping cream
- 2 teaspoons sugar

■ In bowl stir together flour and ½ teaspoon salt. Cut in shortening till pieces are the size of small peas. Sprinkle water, 1 tablespoon at a time, over part of the mixture; toss with fork. Push to side of bowl. Repeat till all is moistened. Form into a ball. On a lightly floured surface roll dough from center to edge, forming a circle about 12 inches in diameter. Line a 9-inch pie plate with pastry. Trim pastry to ½ inch beyond edge. Flute edge high; *do not prick.*

■ In a bowl combine pumpkin, brown sugar, cinnamon, ½ teaspoon salt, ginger, and nutmeg. Lightly beat eggs into mixture with a fork. Stir in evaporated milk and rum; mix well. Stir in nuts. Place pie plate on oven rack; pour pumpkin mixture into shell. To prevent overbrowning, cover edge of pie with foil. Bake in a 375° oven for 25 minutes. Remove foil; bake 20 to 25 minutes more or till a knife inserted near the center comes out clean. Cool on a wire rack.

■ Beat whipping cream and sugar on high speed of electric mixer till soft peaks form. Spoon atop the cooled pie. Cover and chill to store. Makes 8 servings.

■ Preparation time: 30 minutes
■ Cooking time: 45 to 50 minutes
■ Cooling time: 3 hours
■ Final preparation time: 5 minutes

Pumpkin Gelatin Pie

    1 envelope unflavored gelatin
    ½ cup sugar
    ½ teaspoon ground cinnamon
    ½ teaspoon ground nutmeg
    ½ cup milk
    3 slightly beaten egg yolks
    1 16-ounce can pumpkin
    ¼ cup bourbon, brandy, *or* orange juice
    3 egg whites
    ⅓ cup sugar
    1 9-inch Baked Pastry Shell (see recipe,
       page 157), cooled

■ In a saucepan combine gelatin, the ½ cup sugar, cinnamon, nutmeg, and ¼ teaspoon *salt;* stir in milk and egg yolks. Cook and stir over medium heat till mixture thickens and just begins to boil. Cook and stir 2 minutes. Remove from heat. Stir in pumpkin and bourbon, brandy, or orange juice; set aside.

■ In small mixing bowl beat egg whites till soft peaks form (tips curl over). Gradually add the ⅓ cup sugar, beating till stiff peaks form (tips stand straight). Fold beaten egg whites into pumpkin mixture. Pile pumpkin mixture into cooled Baked Pastry Shell. Chill for 6 hours or till firm. Garnish with whipped cream and a little ground nutmeg, if desired. Serves 8.

■ Preparation time: 40 minutes
■ Chilling time: at least 6 hours

Lemon-Sour Cream Tarts

    2 5-ounce cans lemon pudding
    1 8-ounce carton dairy sour cream
    6 graham cracker tart shells
    1 10-ounce package frozen red
       raspberries, thawed
    2 teaspoons cornstarch

■ In a mixing bowl stir together pudding and sour cream; spoon into purchased tart shells. Cover; chill.

■ Drain raspberries, reserving ⅔ cup syrup. Chill the berries. In a small saucepan stir reserved syrup into cornstarch. Cook and stir till thickened and bubbly; cook and stir 2 minutes more. Chill. Top pudding in tart shells with a few raspberries. Spoon about 1 tablespoon raspberry glaze over each. Serves 6.

■ Preparation time: 20 minutes
■ Chilling time: at least 2 hours

Macadamia Chiffon Pie

    ½ cup packed brown sugar
    1 envelope unflavored gelatin
    1 cup milk
    2 slightly beaten egg yolks
    1 teaspoon vanilla
    2 egg whites
    ¼ cup packed brown sugar
    ½ cup chopped macadamia nuts, toasted
    ½ cup whipping cream
    1 9-inch Baked Pastry Shell (see recipe,
       page 157), cooled

■ In a medium saucepan combine the ½ cup brown sugar, the gelatin, and ¼ teaspoon *salt.* Stir in milk and egg yolks. Cook and stir over medium heat till mixture thickens slightly. Remove from heat; stir in vanilla. Chill to the consistency of corn syrup, stirring the mixture occasionally. Remove from refrigerator.

■ Immediately begin beating egg whites till soft peaks form (tips curl over). Gradually add the ¼ cup brown sugar, beating till stiff peaks form (tips stand straight). When gelatin is the consistency of unbeaten egg whites (partially set), fold in stiff-beaten egg whites and ⅓ *cup* of the macadamia nuts. Beat whipping cream till soft peaks form; fold into gelatin mixture. Pile mixture into cooled Baked Pastry Shell. Chill for 6 hours. Garnish with remaining nuts. Serves 8.

■ Preparation time: 1½ hours
■ Chilling time: at least 6 hours

MENU
ISLAND FEAST

Tropical Fruit Cup

Pork Roast

Baked Sweet
Potatoes

Buttered Broccoli
Spears

Macadamia Chiffon
Pie

Iced Tea with Fresh
Fruit Garnish

Stage your luau feast outdoors on the patio. To light an island fever in your guests' hearts (and to light your backyard), stick torches in the lawn and use hurricane lamps as the table's centerpiece. For even more tropical atmosphere, use tablecloths with bold floral prints and place lush greenery and colorful flowers all around. You could even play Hawaiian records for background music.

Be sure to let the frozen *Mocha Sundae Squares* stand only 5 minutes after removing them from the freezer. They soften very quickly.

The *Fudge Sauce* used in this recipe also makes a terrific ice cream topping. We know that ice cream lovers will find it irresistible!

Mocha Sundae Squares

1⅓ **cups finely crushed vanilla wafers**
     (about 30 wafers)
 ¼ **cup finely chopped walnuts**
 ¼ **cup butter *or* margarine, melted .**
 3 **egg whites**
 2 **tablespoons instant coffee crystals**
    Dash salt
 ½ **cup sugar**
 1 **cup whipping cream**
    Fudge Sauce

▪▪ In a small mixing bowl combine the crushed vanilla wafers, chopped walnuts, and melted butter or margarine. Press the mixture into the bottom of an ungreased 9x9x2-inch baking pan. Bake in a 375° oven for 10 minutes. Cool.

▪▪ In a large mixer bowl combine the egg whites, instant coffee crystals, and salt; beat till soft peaks form (tips curl over). Gradually add sugar, beating till stiff peaks form (tips stand straight), about 5 minutes.

▪▪ Beat whipping cream till soft peaks form. Fold the whipped cream into stiff-beaten egg whites. Spread mixture evenly over cooled crust in pan. Freeze for 6 hours or till firm.

▪▪ Prepare Fudge Sauce. Before serving, remove the dessert from the freezer and let stand at room temperature for 5 minutes. Cut the dessert into squares and top with some of the warm Fudge Sauce. Garnish each serving with a walnut half, if desired. Makes 9 servings.

Fudge Sauce: In a small saucepan combine ½ of a 6-ounce package (½ cup) *semisweet chocolate pieces* and ⅓ cup *light corn syrup*. Cook and stir over low heat till chocolate melts. Remove from heat; gradually stir in ⅓ cup *evaporated milk*. Makes 1 cup.

▪▪ Preparation time: 40 minutes
▪▪ Cooling time: 1 hour
▪▪ Freezing time: at least 6 hours
▪▪ Standing time: 5 minutes

Frozen Praline Mousse

 ½ **cup packed brown sugar**
 1 **tablespoon cornstarch**
 ½ **cup cold water**
 2 **teaspoons butter *or* margarine**
 3 **tablespoons chopped pecans**
 2 **tablespoons praline liqueur**
 2 **egg whites**
 ¼ **teaspoon cream of tartar**
 1 **cup whipping cream**

▪▪ For the praline sauce, in a small saucepan stir together brown sugar and cornstarch. Add the water. Cook and stir the mixture over medium-high heat for 4 to 5 minutes or till mixture is thickened and bubbly. Remove from heat.

▪▪ Stir in butter or margarine till melted. Fold in the pecans. Cool praline sauce to room temperature. Chill *half* of the praline sauce in the refrigerator.

▪▪ Stir praline liqueur into the remaining sauce. In a mixer bowl beat the egg whites and cream of tartar till stiff peaks form (tips stand straight). Fold in the praline liqueur mixture. Beat the whipping cream till soft peaks form (tips curl over); fold into egg white mixture. Spoon the mixture into 6 dessert dishes or 6-ounce soufflé dishes. Freeze for 6 hours or till firm.

▪▪ Just before serving, heat the praline sauce. Spoon some of the warm praline sauce over individual servings of the mousse. Makes 6 servings.

▪▪ Advance preparation time: 30 minutes
▪▪ Cooling time: 30 minutes
▪▪ Freezing time: at least 6 hours
▪▪ Final preparation time: 5 minutes

Frozen Praline Mousse

When packing the outer container of an ice cream freezer to freeze homemade ice cream, use the proportion of 6 parts of crushed ice to 1 part of rock salt, by weight.

After freezing the ice cream, you need to make it harder and smoother in texture—a process known as "ripening" the ice cream. First, remove the dasher. Then, cover the can with several layers of waxed paper or foil and plug the opening in the lid with a cork. Replace the lid. Pack additional crushed ice and rock salt into the outer container using 4 parts of ice to 1 part of rock salt, by weight. Next, cover the entire ice cream freezer with a heavy cloth or several layers of newspaper. Finally, let the ice cream ripen about 4 hours. (Don't dig into it any sooner, although we know how hard it is to wait that long!)

Peanutty Ice Cream Roll

- 1 **quart vanilla ice cream**
- 1 **quart strawberry ice cream**
- 1½ **cups peanuts, coarsely chopped**
  Strawberry *or* chocolate-flavored topping

■■■ Line a 15x10x1-inch baking pan with waxed paper or foil; chill. In a chilled bowl stir vanilla ice cream just enough to soften. Spread in prepared pan; cover and freeze about 3 hours or till firm. In a chilled bowl stir strawberry ice cream to soften. Spread over vanilla layer; cover and freeze about 3 hours or till firm. With a metal spatula loosen ice cream from sides of pan. Starting at narrow end, roll up, jelly-roll style, peeling back paper as you roll. Roll in peanuts. Wrap and freeze about 3 hours or till firm. To serve, slice roll crosswise. Pass desired topping. Makes 10 servings.

■■■ Preparation time: 30 minutes
■■■ Freezing time: at least 9 hours

French Lemon Ice Cream

- 1 **package 4-serving-size *instant* lemon pudding mix**
- ¼ **cup sugar-sweetened lemonade mix**
- ¼ **cup sugar**
- ⅛ **teaspoon salt**
- 2 **cups milk**
- 2 **cups light cream**
- 2 **eggs**

■■■ In a large bowl combine the pudding mix, lemonade mix, sugar, and salt. Gradually add the milk, stirring till the lemonade mix is completely dissolved. Add light cream and eggs; beat 1 minute with rotary beater. Freeze in ice cream freezer according to the manufacturer's directions. Ripen. Makes 1½ quarts.

■■■ Preparation time: 15 minutes
■■■ Freezing time: 30 minutes
■■■ Ripening time: at least 4 hours

Praline Ice Cream

- ¾ **cup sugar**
- ¼ **teaspoon cream of tartar**
- ¼ **cup slivered almonds**
- 1 **cup sugar**
- 1 **cup water**
- ½ **teaspoon cream of tartar**
- 6 **eggs**
- 4 **cups whipping cream**
- 2 **cups milk**
- 2 **teaspoons vanilla**

■■■ To make the caramelized sugar, in a large heavy skillet combine the ¾ cup sugar, the ¼ teaspoon cream of tartar, and the slivered almonds. Cook over medium heat, stirring constantly, till the sugar is melted and golden. Pour the mixture onto a greased baking sheet. Cool completely.

■■■ Break the caramelized sugar into small pieces and place *half* of the sugar mixture in a blender container or food processor bowl. Cover and blend or process to the size of coarse crumbs. Remove to a bowl. Repeat with the remaining caramelized sugar.

■■■ To make the ice cream, in a small saucepan combine the 1 cup sugar, water, and the ½ teaspoon cream of tartar. Cook over medium heat without stirring till candy thermometer registers 234°.

■■■ Meanwhile, in a large mixer bowl beat eggs on high speed of electric mixer about 6 minutes or till thick and lemon colored. With mixer running on low speed, gradually beat in the hot sugar syrup. Stir in the whipping cream, milk, and vanilla. Freeze ice cream mixture in a 4- or 5-quart ice cream freezer according to the manufacturer's directions. Before ripening, stir the caramelized sugar into the ice cream mixture. Ripen the ice cream as directed at left. Makes about 2½ quarts.

■■■ Preparation time: 1 hour
■■■ Freezing time: 30 minutes
■■■ Ripening time: at least 4 hours

Easy Tortoni

- 8 *or* 9 soft macaroons, crumbled (1¼ cups)
- ½ cup milk
- ¼ cup sugar
- 2 tablespoons light rum
- 1 1¼-ounce envelope dessert topping mix
- 2 tablespoons chopped maraschino cherries
- 6 maraschino cherries, halved

▮ Reserve *½ cup* of the crumbled macaroons. In a bowl combine remaining macaroons, milk, sugar, and rum; mix well. Set aside. Prepare topping mix according to package directions. Gradually add the macaroon mixture; beat till fluffy and thick. Fold in chopped cherries. Spoon into paper bake cups set in muffin pans. Top with reserved macaroons and a cherry half. Freeze for 3 hours or till firm. Serves 10.

▬ Preparation time: 20 minutes
▬ Freezing time: at least 3 hours

Spumoni Dessert

- 1 3-ounce package (12) ladyfingers, split
- 1 10½-ounce package tiny marshmallows
- 1 cup milk
- 1 cup whipping cream
- ½ cup chopped maraschino cherries
- 1 cup chopped walnuts
- 2 teaspoons vanilla
- ½ teaspoon almond extract
- ¼ cup unsweetened cocoa powder
- ¼ teaspoon rum extract

▮ In a 7-inch springform pan arrange ladyfingers on bottom and side; trim to fit. In a saucepan melt marshmallows in milk over medium-low heat, stirring till smooth. Cool to room temperature. Beat the whipping cream till soft peaks form. Fold the whipped cream into marshmallow mixture. Drain cherries well. To *two-thirds* of mixture fold in cherries, walnuts, vanilla, and almond extract. To the remaining one-third of mixture beat in cocoa and rum extract till combined.

Carefully spoon *half* of cherry mixture into bottom of pan. Top with chocolate mixture, then remaining half of cherry mixture. Freeze for 3 hours or till firm. Before serving, let stand 10 minutes at room temperature. Makes 10 servings.

▬ Preparation time: 50 minutes
▬ Freezing time: at least 3 hours
▬ Standing time: 10 minutes

Cherry Ice Cream

- 1 envelope unflavored gelatin
- 1¼ cups milk
- 1 cup whipping cream
- 2 beaten egg yolks
- ½ cup sugar
- ½ teaspoon vanilla
- ⅛ teaspoon salt
  Dash almond extract
- 2 egg whites
- ¼ cup sugar
- 1½ cups pitted fresh dark sweet cherries, coarsely chopped

▮ In a small saucepan soften gelatin in *¼ cup* of the milk; let stand for 5 minutes. Heat and stir till gelatin is dissolved. Remove from heat. Stir together the remaining milk, the cream, egg yolks, the ½ cup sugar, vanilla, salt, and almond extract. Stir in dissolved gelatin. Pour into an 8x8x2-inch pan. Cover and freeze about 1 hour or till nearly firm.

▮ Beat egg whites till soft peaks form (tips curl over). Gradually add the ¼ cup sugar, beating till stiff peaks form (tips stand straight). Set aside. In a chilled large mixer bowl break frozen mixture into chunks. Beat till fluffy. Fold in egg whites and cherries. Return to pan; freeze till firm. Makes 5 cups.

▬ Preparation time: 2 hours
▬ Freezing time: at least 3 hours

▬▬ **MENU** ▬▬
ITALIAN EVENT

Minestrone

Tossed Salad with
Italian Dressing

Lasagna

Italian Green Beans

Parmesan-Topped
Toasted Bread Slices

Easy Tortoni

Dry Red Wine

Cappuccino-Style
Coffee

Set the dining table with a red-and-white checked cloth and add a candle to the table to lend some atmosphere to this romantic Italian dinner.

Easy Tortoni is simple to serve since it's frozen in individual portions. Remove the paper bake cups before placing on dessert plates.

To make chocolate cups for *Almond Mousse in Chocolate Cups*, spread the melted chocolate in paper bake cups placed in muffin pans. Using a narrow spatula, for each cup spread about 1 tablespoon over bottom and up sides of cup, as shown.

For a chocolate curl garnish, use a bar of milk chocolate, sweet baking chocolate, or semisweet chocolate. Allow the chocolate to come to room temperature, then shave the bar with a vegetable peeler, as shown, into long, thin strips. They will curl as you cut them.

For special impressions, dress up servings of *Cantaloupe-Orange Mousse* with small cantaloupe slices, fresh mint sprigs, and toasted coconut.

Toast the coconut by placing a thin layer of coconut in a shallow baking pan. Bake in a 350° oven for 6 to 7 minutes or till lightly browned, stirring coconut once or twice to prevent overbrowning.

Cantaloupe-Orange Mousse

2 **cups cubed, peeled, and seeded cantaloupe**
½ **cup orange juice**
1 **envelope unflavored gelatin**
1 **4-ounce container frozen whipped dessert topping, thawed**
¼ **cup toasted coconut**

■■■ In blender container or food processor bowl combine cantaloupe and juice. Cover; blend or process till smooth. In saucepan combine melon puree and gelatin; let stand 5 minutes. Stir over low heat till gelatin is dissolved. Chill to consistency of unbeaten egg whites (partially set). Fold in topping. Spoon into 6 dessert dishes. Chill. Top with coconut. Serves 6.

■■■ Preparation time: 1½ hours
■■■ Chilling time: at least 3 hours

Almond Mousse in Chocolate Cups

1½ **cups semisweet chocolate pieces**
¼ **cup packed brown sugar**
1 **envelope unflavored gelatin**
1⅓ **cups milk**
¼ **cup finely chopped almonds, toasted**
⅓ **cup Amaretto**
¾ **cup whipping cream**
Chocolate curls, sliced almonds, *or* whole fresh strawberries (optional)

■■■ In a small saucepan melt chocolate pieces over low heat, stirring constantly. Place 12 paper bake cups in muffin pans. Spoon about *1 tablespoon* of the melted chocolate into *each* paper bake cup. Spread chocolate evenly with a narrow metal spatula over the bottom and up sides of the cups (see top photograph at left). Chill in the refrigerator about 1 hour or till firm.

■■■ Meanwhile, in a saucepan combine brown sugar and unflavored gelatin; stir in milk. Cook, stirring constantly, till the gelatin is dissolved. Remove from heat; stir in finely chopped almonds and the Amaretto.

■■■ Chill gelatin mixture to the consistency of corn syrup, stirring occasionally. Remove from refrigerator (gelatin mixture will continue to set). Beat the whipping cream till soft peaks form. When gelatin is the consistency of unbeaten egg whites (partially set) fold in whipped cream. Chill till the mixture mounds. Spoon into the chilled chocolate cups. Chill about 3 hours or till firm.

■■■ Before serving, garnish each of the servings with chocolate curls (see lower photograph at left), sliced almonds, or whole fresh strawberries, if desired. Makes 12 servings.

■■■ Preparation time: 2 hours
■■■ Chilling time: at least 3 hours

Blueberry Cream Dessert

½ **cup sugar**
1 **envelope unflavored gelatin**
¾ **cup cold water**
1 **8-ounce carton dairy sour cream**
1 **8-ounce carton blueberry yogurt**
½ **teaspoon vanilla**
1¼ **cups graham cracker crumbs**
⅓ **cup butter** *or* **margarine, melted**
¼ **cup sugar**
½ **cup whipping cream**
1 **cup fresh** *or* **frozen blueberries, thawed**

■ In a saucepan mix the ½ cup sugar and unflavored gelatin; stir in the cold water. Heat and stir till gelatin and sugar are dissolved. Combine the sour cream, blueberry yogurt, and vanilla; gradually stir into the gelatin mixture. Chill the yogurt-sour cream mixture to the consistency of unbeaten egg whites (partially set).

■ Meanwhile, in a small bowl combine graham cracker crumbs, melted butter or margarine, and the ¼ cup sugar. Reserve ¼ *cup* of the crumb mixture; press the remaining crumb mixture in the bottom of a 10x6x2-inch baking dish.

■ Beat whipping cream till soft peaks form; fold into yogurt-sour cream mixture. Stir in the blueberries. Turn into graham cracker crust in baking dish. Sprinkle the reserved crumbs atop. Chill for 6 hours or till firm. Cut into squares to serve. Makes 8 servings.

■ Preparation time: 1¼ hours
■ Chilling time: at least 6 hours

Viennese Custard

¾ **cup sugar**
2 **cups milk**
2 **tablespoons sugar**
¼ **teaspoon salt**
1 **tablespoon vanilla**
2 **eggs**
4 **egg yolks**
Whipped cream (optional)

■ To caramelize sugar, in a small heavy saucepan heat the ¾ cup sugar over medium heat, stirring constantly, till melted and golden brown. Immediately pour about *3 tablespoons* of the caramelized syrup into a 3-cup ring mold or six 6-ounce custard cups, tilting the mold or cups to coat the bottom and sides with the caramelized mixture; set aside.

■ Into remaining caramelized syrup stir in milk, the 2 tablespoons sugar, and the salt; heat and stir till sugar is dissolved. Remove from heat; stir in vanilla. Combine eggs and egg yolks, beating slightly to combine. Gradually stir in the milk mixture till combined.

■ Pour into the prepared ring mold or custard cups. Set in a 13x9x2-inch baking pan on oven rack. Pour boiling water around the ring mold or custard cups to a depth of 1 inch. Bake in a 325° oven about 25 minutes for the ring mold (20 to 25 minutes for the custard cups) or till a knife inserted near center comes out clean. Cool on a wire rack. Chill the custard in the refrigerator for 3 hours.

■ To serve, first loosen edges with a spatula or knife; slip point of knife down sides to let air in. Invert the custard onto serving plate. Garnish with whipped cream, if desired. Makes 6 servings.

■ Preparation time: 35 minutes
■ Cooking time: 25 minutes
■ Chilling time: at least 3 hours

Here's how to quick-chill a gelatin mixture to the consistency of unbeaten egg whites (partially set): Place several ice cubes in a large bowl, then add some cold water. Set a smaller bowl containing the gelatin mixture into the ice water, pressing the bowl down to force the ice cubes around the bowl. Stir frequently to check the consistency of the gelatin mixture.

Strawberry Sundae Cheesecake

Strawberry Sundae Cheesecake

1⅔ cups fine graham cracker crumbs
¼ cup finely chopped almonds
½ cup butter *or* margarine, melted
1 6-ounce package strawberry-flavored gelatin
2 cups boiling water
1 pint vanilla ice cream
2 8-ounce packages cream cheese, softened
1 cup whipping cream
Strawberry Sauce
Cream Cheese Frosting

■ In a mixing bowl combine the graham cracker crumbs, chopped almonds, and the melted butter or margarine. Turn crumb mixture into a 9-inch spring-form pan. Press mixture evenly in bottom of pan. Press onto sides to form a firm, even crust to a height of 2 inches. Chill about 1 hour or till firm. (*Or*, bake in a 375° oven for 6 to 9 minutes. Cool on a wire rack.)

■ For the filling, dissolve gelatin in boiling water. Add ice cream by spoonfuls; stir till melted. Chill to the consistency of unbeaten egg whites (partially set).

■ Meanwhile, in a large mixer bowl beat cream cheese till fluffy. Gradually add cream, beating till smooth. Beat in gelatin mixture. Pour mixture into pan. Prepare Strawberry Sauce and Cream Cheese Frosting. Chill cheesecake, sauce, and frosting 6 hours.

■ Before serving, loosen sides of crust from pan. Remove cheesecake from pan. Fill decorating bag with frosting. Using a decorator tube and tip, pipe over top of cheesecake in lattice design. Pipe border around top edge. Spoon sauce into lattice squares. Top with slivered almonds, if desired. Serves 16.

Strawberry Sauce: Thaw and drain one 16-ounce package frozen *sliced strawberries*, reserving syrup. In a small saucepan combine the reserved syrup and 2 teaspoons *cornstarch*. Cook and stir till thickened and bubbly. Cook and stir 2 minutes more. Remove from heat. Stir in berries. Cover and chill.

Cream Cheese Frosting: Combine one 3-ounce package *cream cheese*, ¼ cup *butter or margarine*, and 1 teaspoon *vanilla*; beat till fluffy. Gradually add 1½ cups sifted *powdered sugar*; beat till smooth. Cover and chill.

■ Advance preparation time: 1½ hours
■ Chilling time: at least 6 hours
■ Final preparation time: 30 minutes

Grape Cheesecake

¾ cup fine graham cracker crumbs
½ cup all-purpose flour
½ cup chopped walnuts
¼ cup sugar
½ cup butter *or* margarine, melted
3 8-ounce packages cream cheese, softened
⅔ cup sugar
3 eggs
1½ teaspoons finely shredded orange peel
⅓ cup orange juice
½ cup orange marmalade
⅓ cup white grape juice
3 tablespoons orange liqueur
2 teaspoons cornstarch
2½ cups seedless grapes, halved

■ Combine first 4 ingredients. Add melted butter; mix well. Pat mixture into an ungreased 13x9x2-inch baking pan. Bake in a 350° oven for 8 to 10 minutes. In mixer bowl combine cheese and the ⅔ cup sugar; beat till combined. Add eggs, orange peel, and orange juice; mix well. Pour over baked crust. Bake in a 350° oven about 30 minutes or till set. Cool.

■ For glaze, combine marmalade, grape juice, liqueur, and cornstarch. Cook and stir till bubbly; cook 1 minute more. Cool. Arrange grapes atop cheesecake; top with glaze. Chill 6 hours. Serves 12 to 15.

■ Preparation time: 2 hours
■ Chilling time: at least 6 hours

■■ MENU ■■
DINNER BEFORE THE THEATER

Bibb Lettuce and Artichoke Hearts Salad with Vinegar and Oil Dressing

Roast Prime Rib of Beef

Oven-Browned Potatoes

Buttered Baby Carrots

Whole Wheat Rolls

Strawberry Sundae Cheesecake

Coffee

Order a block of theater tickets for a group of your friends. Then, organize and invite them over for a pre-theater dinner party.

Be sure to serve dinner early so you can have a leisurely meal before curtain time. If time runs short—or if you want to share the evening with friends as long as possible—save dessert and coffee for after the show.

Mandarin Cream Cones are just the right finale to fix when you need a special make-ahead dessert. Prepare the cones and filling, then store them separately. The cones need a tightly covered, airtight container to stay crisp. The cream filling requires covered storage in the refrigerator.

Mandarin Cream Cones

- ½ **cup packed brown sugar**
- 6 **tablespoons butter *or* margarine, melted**
- ¼ **cup light molasses**
- 1 **tablespoon brandy**
- ¾ **cup all-purpose flour**
- ½ **teaspoon ground ginger**
- ½ **teaspoon ground nutmeg**
- ⅛ **teaspoon salt**
- ⅔ **cup sugar**
- ¼ **cup all-purpose flour *or* 2 tablespoons cornstarch**
- ⅛ **teaspoon salt**
- 1⅓ **cups milk**
- 2 **beaten egg yolks**
- 1 **tablespoon orange liqueur**
- 1 **tablespoon butter *or* margarine**
- 1 **teaspoon vanilla**
- 1 **11-ounce can mandarin orange sections, drained and chilled**

■■■ For the cones, in a mixing bowl combine brown sugar, the 6 tablespoons melted butter or margarine, the molasses, and brandy; mix well. Stir together the ¾ cup flour, the ginger, nutmeg, and ⅛ teaspoon salt. Stir in the brown sugar mixture.

■■■ Drop level tablespoons of the batter 6 inches apart on an *ungreased* cookie sheet. (Bake only 3 or 4 cookies at a time.) Bake in a 350° oven for 6 to 7 minutes. Cool 2 minutes on baking sheet; remove with wide spatula. Working quickly, *immediately* roll each cookie to form a cone (see top photograph at right). (For uniform size and shape, use a metal cone for shaping.) If cookies harden before rolling, reheat them in a 350° oven for 30 seconds. Cool the cones thoroughly. Repeat with remaining batter. Store in an airtight container to keep cones crisp.

■■■ For the filling, in a saucepan combine the sugar, the ¼ cup flour or 2 tablespoons cornstarch, and ⅛ teaspoon salt. Stir in milk. Cook and stir over medium heat till mixture is thickened and bubbly. Reduce heat; cook and stir 2 minutes more. Gradually stir *1 cup* of the hot mixture into yolks. Return the yolk mixture to saucepan; bring to gentle boil. Cook and stir 2 minutes more. Remove from heat. Stir in liqueur, the 1 tablespoon butter or margarine, and the vanilla. Cover

When preparing *Mandarin Cream Cones*, allow the cones to cool 2 minutes on a baking sheet before removing them with a wide spatula. Then, immediately roll each cookie to form a cone, as shown.

Fill the cones just before serving. Stand them in a juice glass or small deep bowl and spoon in some of the filling, as shown. For each serving, lay two cones on a dessert plate and garnish with mandarin orange sections.

surface of filling with clear plastic wrap. Cool filling. Chill in refrigerator for 3 hours or till serving time.

■■■ To serve, set a cone in a juice glass or small dish. Spoon some of the filling into each cone (see lower photograph above). Repeat with the remaining cones and filling. Garnish each cone with one or two mandarin orange sections. Serve at once. Makes about 20 cones.

■■■ Advance preparation time: 2 hours
■■■ Chilling time: at least 3 hours
■■■ Final preparation time: 30 minutes

Hawaiian Compote

- 1 papaya (1¼ pounds)
- 1 15¼-ounce can pineapple chunks (juice pack)
- ½ teaspoon grated gingerroot
- 1 large banana

Peel, seed, and cut the papaya into bite-size pieces. Drain pineapple, reserving juice. In a bowl combine pineapple with papaya. Combine reserved juice and gingerroot and bring just to boiling; pour over fruit mixture. Cover and chill 3 hours. Just before serving, slice banana into fruit mixture. Serves 6.

- Preparation time: 20 minutes
- Chilling time: at least 3 hours

Caramel-Chocolate Fondue

- 1 14-ounce can (1¼ cups) Eagle Brand sweetened condensed milk
- 1 12-ounce jar caramel topping
- 1 6-ounce package (1 cup) semisweet chocolate pieces
- ¼ cup brandy or coffee liqueur
  Unpeeled apple slices
  Unpeeled pear slices
- ¼ cup lemon juice
- 1 3½-ounce can (1⅓ cups) flaked coconut
  Chopped almonds
  Chopped walnuts

In a saucepan combine sweetened condensed milk, caramel topping, and chocolate. Stir over low heat till chocolate melts. Stir in brandy or liqueur. Transfer to fondue pot; place over fondue burner. Toss fruit slices with lemon juice; arrange on a platter. Place coconut and nuts in separate bowls. To serve, dip fruit pieces in warm fondue mixture, then dip in coconut or nuts. Makes 3 cups.

- Total preparation time: 30 minutes

Bananas and Pineapple a la Foster

- 4 firm ripe small bananas
- 1 tablespoon lemon juice
- 2 tablespoons butter or margarine
- 3 tablespoons brown sugar
- 1 teaspoon ground cinnamon
- 1 8-ounce can crushed pineapple (juice pack)
  Vanilla ice cream

Bias-slice bananas about ½ inch thick; toss with lemon juice to coat. Set aside. In blazer pan of a chafing dish or a 10-inch skillet melt butter or margarine over medium heat. Add brown sugar and cinnamon; mix well. Add undrained pineapple; bring to boiling. Cook and stir till slightly thickened and bubbly. Stir in bananas; cook 1 minute or just till heated through. Serve over vanilla ice cream. Serves 6.

- Total preparation time: 15 minutes

Cherry Coconut Angels

- 8 cake dessert cups
- 1 8-ounce container soft-style cream cheese
- 3 tablespoons sugar
- 1 tablespoon milk
- ½ teaspoon vanilla
- 1 3½-ounce can (1⅓ cups) flaked coconut
- 1 21-ounce can cherry pie filling, chilled

With a fork remove a small amount of center from each dessert cup. In a small bowl stir together cream cheese, sugar, milk, and vanilla. Frost cups inside and out (but not undersides) with cheese mixture; sprinkle with coconut to cover. Spoon the chilled pie filling into center of each dessert cup. Serves 8.

- Total preparation time: 30 minutes

You can easily vary the recipe for Cherry Coconut Angels. Next time fill the cheese-frosted cake cups with another flavored fruit pie filling. Or, if you're serving a large dinner party, you may want to offer a variety of fruit fillings.

You can make this tasty dessert up to one hour ahead of time. Chill it in the refrigerator until you are ready to serve dessert to your guests.

Divide the meal
preparations with four
other couples. Have
appetizers and wine
or punch at the first
stop. Then, on to the
next home for soup
and breadsticks. For
the main course two
couples could work
together. Dessert and
coffee are then
served at the last
home you visit. Make
the crepes ahead
and chill; then,
prepare the sauce
and heat the crepes
after guests arrive.

★ *see recipe, page 50* .

Red Raspberry Crepes

12 **Dessert Crepes**
1 **8-ounce container soft-style cream cheese**
   or **soft-style cream cheese with**
   strawberries
2 **tablespoons slivered almonds, toasted**
3 **tablespoons sugar**
1 **tablespoon cornstarch**
1 **cup cranberry juice cocktail**
1 **tablespoon butter** *or* **margarine**
1 **pint fresh raspberries** *or* **one 10-ounce**
   package frozen red raspberries, thawed
   and drained
1 **tablespoon orange liqueur**
1 **tablespoon lemon juice**
¼ **cup slivered almonds, toasted**

▬▬ Prepare the Dessert Crepes. Spread cream
cheese over unbrowned side of each crepe, leaving a
¼-inch rim around edge. Sprinkle each crepe with
some of the 2 tablespoons slivered almonds. Fold
each crepe into a triangle by first folding in half, then
folding in half again. Cover crepes; set aside.

▬▬ For the sauce, in a 10-inch skillet combine the
sugar, cornstarch, and dash *salt*. Stir in cranberry
juice cocktail and butter or margarine. Cook and stir
mixture till thickened and bubbly. Cook and stir 2
minutes more. Stir in raspberries, orange liqueur, and
lemon juice. Add the crepes to sauce; heat through.
Sprinkle the ¼ cup toasted almonds atop. Serve
crepes immediately. Makes 6 servings.

Dessert Crepes: In a mixing bowl combine 1 cup *all-
purpose flour*, 2 tablespoons *sugar*, and ⅛ teaspoon
salt. Add 2 beaten *eggs*, 1½ cups *milk*, and ¼ cup
melted *butter or margarine*. Beat with a rotary beater
till combined. Heat a lightly greased 6-inch skillet.
Remove from heat. Spoon in *2 tablespoons* of the
batter; lift and tilt the skillet to spread the batter. Return
to heat; brown on one side (do not turn). Invert the skillet over paper toweling; remove the crepe. Repeat
with remaining batter, greasing skillet as needed.
Makes about 16 crepes.

▬▬ Total preparation time: 1½ hours

Chocolate Waffles with Almond-Custard Sauce

2 **slightly beaten eggs**
1 **cup milk**
2 **tablespoons sugar**
   Dash salt
2 **tablespoons Amaretto**
⅓ **cup dairy sour cream**
⅓ **cup milk**
¼ **cup chocolate-flavored syrup**
2 **tablespoons butter** *or* **margarine,**
   melted
1 **beaten egg yolk**
⅔ **cup all-purpose flour**
½ **teaspoon baking powder**
¼ **teaspoon baking soda**
1 **stiff-beaten egg white**
¼ **cup ground almonds**
¼ **cup sliced almonds**

▬▬ For sauce, in a heavy saucepan stir together the
2 beaten eggs, the 1 cup milk, the sugar, and salt.
Cook and stir over medium heat about 5 minutes or till
mixture thickens and coats a metal spoon. Remove
from heat. Set saucepan in a larger bowl of ice water.
Stir in Amaretto; stir 1 to 2 minutes or till mixture is
cooled. Set aside while preparing waffle batter.

▬▬ For waffle batter, in a medium bowl stir together
the sour cream, the ⅓ cup milk, the chocolate syrup,
melted butter or margarine, and egg yolk. In another
mixing bowl thoroughly stir together the flour, baking
powder, and baking soda; stir into sour cream mixture. Beat till smooth with a rotary beater. Gently fold in
the stiff-beaten egg white.

▬▬ Pour batter onto preheated waffle baker; sprin-
kle some of the ¼ cup ground almonds over batter.
Follow manufacturer's instructions for baking waffles.
To serve the dessert, ladle the sauce over each hot
waffle; top with some of the ¼ cup sliced almonds.
Makes 4 servings.

▬▬ Total preparation time: 30 minutes

Pears a la Blueberries

2   16-ounce cans pear halves
1   8-ounce container soft-style cream cheese
        with pineapple
2   tablespoons sugar
2   teaspoons cornstarch
1½ cups fresh *or* frozen blueberries, thawed
1   teaspoon finely shredded lemon peel

■ Drain pears, reserving ⅔ *cup* of the syrup. Place 12 pear halves, cut side down, on paper toweling to drain. Spread cream cheese on cut surface of 6 pear halves. Top with 6 additional pear halves. Press together, making 6 "whole" pears. Cover and chill 3 hours. (Use any remaining pears as desired.)

■ Meanwhile, make sauce. In saucepan combine sugar and cornstarch; stir in reserved pear syrup. Add ½ *cup* of the blueberries and lemon peel. Cook and stir till mixture is thickened and bubbly. Cook and stir 2 minutes more. Remove from heat; mash blueberries in sauce. Stir in remaining 1 cup blueberries. Cover and chill 3 hours. To serve, stand the pears upright in serving dishes. Spoon sauce over. Serves 6.

■ Preparation time: 45 minutes
■ Chilling time: at least 3 hours

Pears with Chocolate Fluff

1   29-ounce can pear halves, chilled
⅓   cup semisweet chocolate pieces
2   tablespoons light corn syrup
½   teaspoon vanilla
½   of a 4-ounce container frozen whipped
        dessert topping, thawed, *or*
        ½ cup whipping cream, whipped
¼   cup dairy sour cream
¼   cup sliced almonds, toasted

■ Drain pear halves. In a small saucepan combine semisweet chocolate pieces and corn syrup. Heat, stirring constantly, just till chocolate melts; stir in the

vanilla. Cool. In bowl stir together thawed dessert topping or whipped cream and the sour cream; fold in cooled chocolate mixture. Cover and chill for 3 hours. To serve, place pear halves in dessert dishes; top each with some of the chocolate mixture. Sprinkle with almonds. Makes 6 servings.

■ Preparation time: 45 minutes
■ Chilling time: at least 3 hours

Sweet Cheese Dessert Dip

2   5-ounce jars neufchâtel cheese
        spread with pineapple
¼   cup milk
2   tablespoons sugar
2   tablespoons brandy, kirsch, *or*
        orange liqueur
½   teaspoon finely shredded orange peel
1   beaten egg yolk
    Fresh fruit dippers (see suggestions in
        column at right)

■ For dip, in a medium saucepan stir together cheese spread, milk, sugar, brandy, and orange peel. Stir over low heat till mixture is melted. *(Do not boil.)* If necessary, beat with a rotary beater till smooth.

■ Stir some of the hot mixture into the beaten egg yolk; return all to saucepan. Cook and stir till slightly thickened. (If mixture is too thick, add a little more milk and stir till mixture is combined.) Turn into a serving bowl; cover and chill for 3 hours. To serve, place bowl of dip in center of platter. Arrange groups of desired fruit dippers around the dip. Makes 1¼ cups.

■ Preparation time: 15 minutes
■ Chilling time: at least 3 hours

Try any of these fresh fruit suggestions with the *Sweet Cheese Dessert Dip:* cored fresh pears or peaches cut into wedges, banana chunks, seedless green grapes divided into small clusters, fresh strawberries with hulls, dark sweet cherries with stems, cored apples cut into wedges, and fresh or canned pineapple chunks.

Formal Brunch

Raspberry Kir

Ambrosia Orange Cups

Lamb Chop Popover Bake

Marinated Vegetable Salad

Croissants With Butter

Brandy Alexander Soufflés

Carefree entertaining calls for a fuss-free menu. This formal brunch lets you spend less time fussing and more time celebrating. Our party will razzle-dazzle your guests without having you spend days in the kitchen. The key to this sophisticated brunch for six is preplanning.

The setting is as important as the menu when you host a memorable meal for special friends. The sensational setting shown here comes from mixing and matching compatible sets of table appointments.

TIMETABLE

Garnish the food: Part of what makes a party extra special is trimming the food as well as decorating the table. The right food garnishes add the perfect finishing touches to the meal.

For the *Brandy Alexander Soufflés,* make chocolate leaves (see column at far left, page 178) or chocolate curls (see photograph, page 164) and add colorful pomegranate seeds. Another good looking trim is to save a few of the fresh strawberries from the *Ambrosia Orange Cups.* Use them to garnish the soufflés. For a simpler trim, sprinkle the dessert with a little ground nutmeg or cardamom.

Make the *Ambrosia Orange Cups* extravagant by cutting scallops in the orange cups. Then, cut the peel into strips and curl under the ends. If you prefer an old-fashioned look, place the orange cups on a plate lined with a lacy paper doily.

If fresh mint is available, trim the *Raspberry Kir* with a small sprig. Garnish the individual luncheon plates with a fresh parsley sprig as you serve the *Lamb Chop Popover Bake.* Molded butter or butter curls also lend an elegant touch to this formal brunch.

Purchase freshly baked croissants, or, buy frozen croissants and thaw them in time to serve with this midmorning brunch.

The day before: Decide on what you will offer children and guests who prefer something other than the *Raspberry Kir.* Cranberry juice cocktail or white grape juice make tasty, nonalcoholic alternatives.

Put the spinach for the lamb main dish in the refrigerator to thaw overnight. If using chocolate leaves for the dessert garnish, prepare them and keep chilled.

Next, start on the *Brandy Alexander Soufflés.* Chill soufflés with their foil "collars." Prepare the *Marinated Vegetable Salad* and chill the mixture in a covered bowl. Start the *Ambrosia Orange Cups.* Prepare the scalloped orange shells and marinate the chopped oranges; cover and chill both in the refrigerator.

2 hours before: Place a bottle of dry white wine in the refrigerator to chill for *Raspberry Kir.* Set the table. Prepare the berries for the orange cups; chill. Prepare the *Lamb Chop Popover Bake* but do not pour popover batter over chops and spinach until just before baking. Start baking the lamb chop mixture about 40 minutes before you're ready to serve the main course.

Remove the foil collars from the soufflés. Return desserts to the refrigerator. Spoon jam or marmalade into a serving dish and place on table. Make butter curls or molds (see column at far left, page 176); chill.

Wash the lettuce for the salad; drain thoroughly. Arrange the lettuce on a serving platter or in a bowl; cover and chill. Place the rolls in a basket.

30 minutes before: Assemble the fruit mixture and spoon into the orange cups; set on the plates. Place them on the table. Spoon the *Marinated Vegetable Salad* onto the lettuce and chill. Start brewing the coffee or tea so it's ready when needed.

At serving time: Mix the *Raspberry Kir* together and serve it when guests arrive. If guests aren't finished with their drink when brunch is ready, invite them to bring it to the table. When the guests finish the *Ambrosia Orange Cups,* remove their first-course dishes. Serve the *Lamb Chop Popover Bake* and *Marinated Vegetable Salad* next. Pass the croissants and accompaniments. At dessert time, decorate the tops of the *Brandy Alexander Soufflés.*

An exquisite centerpiece sets the pace for pleasant dining. Add an air of casual elegance to your table with a fresh flower arrangement. Or, set a small flowering plant or dried flower bouquet in a silver bowl, glass dish, or small basket. A flowering violet, begonia, or chrysanthemum makes an attractive centerpiece.

If you want fresh cut flowers for a centerpiece, select seasonal flowers from your garden. Or, let a florist know what you need and when you need it.

If you are going to do your own floral centerpiece, reserve an hour or so on the day of the party. Or, if you prefer, arrange the flowers the night before the party. Remember to add fresh water and keep the centerpiece in a cool place.

Fancy butter shapes are stylish, yet simple to make. To use the flexible multicavity mold that lets you prepare several pats of butter at once, spread softened butter into each cavity using a flexible metal spatula. Press to fill all corners. Place the mold in the freezer for at least 5 minutes. Remove butter pats by pressing the back of each cavity, releasing the butter pat onto waxed paper.

For a simpler garnish make butter curls. Dip the butter curler into hot water; pull lightly over a block or stick of firm butter to make curls about ⅛ inch thick. Repeat the hot water dip after making each butter curl.

Chill the butter shapes until served.

Table ambience: Plan some time to add extra touches that will enhance a beautiful meal. Begin by checking over your table coverings and gathering the various serving dishes. The easiest way to set an attractive table is to keep the table decorations simple.

The right table covering is an essential part of your table setting. Choose a covering that pulls the entire meal together. We combined the old and the new for a unique, eclectic spring brunch table setting. Here, formal antique dishes and flatware team with today's casual country-style woven place mats. For another table-setting idea, use an old-fashioned lace covering over a solid cloth. It adds grace and elegance.

A well-dressed table needn't be expensive—if you're resourceful. You may not have a complete set of the most elegant china, but by mixing, matching, and coordinating colors, textures, and patterns, you'll have an endless combination of dinnerware to use in grand style. For mixing and matching china, try starting with a patterned dinnerware—as we did—and accent it with solid colors and subtle patterns.

Sometimes a carefully chosen accessory can add more charm and warmth to your dinner table than elaborate or expensive tableware. To set off your table display, start with simple touches. Plan a special favor for each guest by floating a small rosebud in a small glass dish or votive candleholder. Or, place a long-stemmed fresh carnation or daisy inside the dinner napkin at each place setting. If you're using long-stemmed flowers, add them at the last minute.

In place of—or along with—the flower, add a place card for each guest. Choose formal place cards or whimsical ones. You can find both styles at the stationery counter. You might even consider having someone adept at calligraphy personalize the place cards with the name of each guest.

Personalized dinner napkins with the initials of each of your guests hand-stitched on them, or inexpensive party favors make special take-home gifts when the meal is over. Napkin rings and decoratively folded dinner napkins are other ways to make each place setting look stunning.

When planning a fancy dinner party, remember light and fluffy *Brandy Alexander Soufflés*. For a dramatic presentation, serve the soufflé mixture in wineglasses instead of soufflé dishes.

If you own 8-ounce soufflé dishes instead of the 6-ounce version, you'll find you won't need to use foil collars.

To make chocolate leaves, wash small fresh leaves and dry thoroughly. Melt semisweet chocolate over low heat. With a clean, small paintbrush, brush the melted chocolate on the undersides of the leaves, building up layers of chocolate to make sturdy leaves. Wipe off any melted chocolate that may have run onto the front of the leaves. Place, chocolate side up, on a waxed-paper-lined baking sheet and chill or freeze till hardened. Peel real leaf away from chocolate leaf; avoid touching the chocolate as much as possible to keep it from melting.

Brandy Alexander Soufflés

- 1 envelope unflavored gelatin
- ¼ cup cold water
- 3 egg yolks
- ¼ cup packed brown sugar
- 1 cup light cream
- 1 tablespoon brandy
- 1 tablespoon crème de cacao
- 3 egg whites
- ¼ cup sugar
- ½ cup whipping cream

■ Cut 6 strips of foil to fit around outsides of six 6-ounce soufflé dishes. Butter and sprinkle sugar on one side of each foil strip. Place the foil, buttered side in, around the top of the soufflé dishes so the foil extends 1 inch above dish. Secure with tape or string.

■ Soften gelatin in cold water; let stand 5 minutes. Place over boiling water and stir to dissolve the gelatin; set aside. Meanwhile, beat egg yolks at high speed of electric mixer about 5 minutes or till thick and lemon colored. Gradually beat in brown sugar; then add cream, brandy, and crème de cacao. Gradually beat gelatin mixture into egg yolk mixture. Chill to consistency of corn syrup, stirring occasionally. Immediately beat egg whites till soft peaks form (tips curl over). Gradually add the sugar, beating egg whites till stiff peaks form (tips stand straight).

■ When the gelatin mixture is the consistency of unbeaten egg whites (partially set), fold in the stiff-beaten egg whites.

■ Beat whipping cream till soft peaks form. Fold the whipped cream into egg white-gelatin mixture. Chill till mixture mounds when spooned. Pile the mixture into prepared soufflé dishes. Chill for 4 to 24 hours in the refrigerator. If desired, garnish with chocolate leaves and pomegranate seeds, fresh strawberries, or ground nutmeg. Makes 6 servings.

■ Preparation time: 45 minutes
■ Chilling time: at least 4 hours

Raspberry Kir

- 1 750-milliliter bottle dry white wine, chilled
- ¼ cup raspberry liqueur
- 1 lemon, thinly sliced
  Mint sprigs (optional)

■ In a large pitcher stir together the wine and raspberry liqueur. Place one or two lemon slices in each chilled wineglass. Pour beverage into wineglasses. Garnish each serving with a mint sprig, if desired. Makes 6 (4-ounce) servings.

■ Total preparation time: 5 minutes

Lamb Chop Popover Bake

- 2 10-ounce packages frozen chopped spinach, thawed
- 12 lamb loin chops, cut ½ to ¾ inch thick
- 2 tablespoons cooking oil
- 2 eggs
- 1 cup milk
- 1 tablespoon cooking oil
- 1 cup all-purpose flour
- ¼ teaspoon dried mint, crushed
- ½ teaspoon salt
- ⅛ teaspoon pepper

■ Drain thawed spinach well. Place the spinach in bottom of a 13x9x2-inch baking dish. Trim excess fat from lamb chops. In a skillet brown lamb chops in the 2 tablespoons hot cooking oil; season with salt and pepper. Place chops atop spinach.

■ Beat eggs. Add milk and the 1 tablespoon oil. Stir together the flour, mint, ½ teaspoon salt, and ⅛ teaspoon pepper. Add to egg mixture. Beat till smooth. Pour over lamb chops in baking dish. Bake in a 350° oven about 40 minutes or till done. Serves 6.

■ Preparation time: 30 minutes
■ Cooking time: 40 minutes

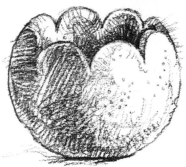

Ambrosia Orange Cups

    6 medium oranges
    1 tablespoon honey
    ¼ teaspoon almond extract
    1 cup blueberries
    1 cup sliced strawberries
    ⅓ cup coconut

■■■ Prepare the orange cups (see column at far right), carefully removing orange sections; set aside. Store the orange cups in a covered container in the refrigerator till serving time.

■■■ Chop enough of the orange sections to make 1 cup; set aside. In a blender container or food processor bowl place the remaining orange sections, the honey, and almond extract. Cover and blend or process till mixture is smooth. Combine the pureed orange mixture and chopped orange. Store in covered container in the refrigerator for 4 to 24 hours.

■■■ Before serving, drain the chopped orange, reserving pureed mixture. Combine the chopped orange, blueberries, strawberries, and coconut. Divide evenly among the orange cups. Drizzle about *1 tablespoon* of the pureed mixture atop fruit mixture in each cup. Makes 6 servings.

■■■ Preparation time: 45 minutes
■■■ Chilling time: at least 4 hours

Marinated Vegetable Salad

    ⅔ cup vinegar
    ⅔ cup olive oil *or* salad oil
    ¼ cup chopped onion
    2 cloves garlic, minced
    1 teaspoon salt
    1 teaspoon sugar
    1 teaspoon dried basil, crushed
    1 teaspoon dried oregano, crushed
    ¼ teaspoon pepper
    1 14-ounce can artichoke hearts, drained
       and halved
    2 medium tomatoes, cut into wedges
    1 cup fresh mushrooms, halved *or* quartered
    1 cup sliced celery
    ¼ cup pitted ripe olives, halved
       Lettuce

■■■ For the marinade, in a saucepan combine the vinegar, oil, chopped onion, garlic, salt, sugar, basil, oregano, and pepper. Bring the mixture to boiling. Reduce heat and simmer, uncovered, 10 minutes.

■■■ In a bowl combine artichoke hearts, tomatoes, mushrooms, celery, and olives. Pour the hot marinade over vegetables; stir to coat. Cover; chill for 4 to 24 hours, stirring occasionally. Drain vegetables; serve in lettuce cups or a lettuce lined bowl. Makes 6 servings.

■■■ Preparation time: 30 minutes
■■■ Marinating time: at least 4 hours

For an imaginative presentation, make orange cups. Begin by slicing off the top portion of each orange, as shown.

Mark the scallops with a sharp knife using a measuring spoon or small cutter for a guide. Cut along the marked line to make the scallops in each orange.

Then, use a grapefruit knife to cut around the inside of each orange to loosen the pulp. Carefully remove the orange sections, leaving shell intact.

Use a citrus zester on the sides of the oranges to cut thin strips of the peel at every other scallop. Do not remove the peel strips but curl them under the orange, as shown.

When the autumn leaves start to fall and the air turns crisp, invite a group of friends to a picnic lunch staged in a park. Keep the table service simple when serving these easy-does-it picnic foods. If you use disposable plastic and paper items, cleanup will be a snap.

Check out the picnic spot a couple of weeks before your party. Prepare a simple how-to-get-there diagram and enclose it with the party invitations. Be at the picnic site before your guests so you can reserve a picnic table. Then, when guests arrive, let them pitch in and help with the remaining meal preparations.

California Cocktail
Chicken & Shrimp Pita Sandwiches
Crunchy Pea Salad
Currant-Glazed Savarin
Fresh Fruit

Autumn Picnic

Packing for the picnic: Organize the packing by starting with a complete list of food and equipment. This way you'll be sure nothing is forgotten. Divide the list into two sections: one listing the cold foods to pack in coolers just before you leave, and the other listing all of the items you can pack ahead.

Put all of the prepared-ahead ingredients in individual plastic bags or tightly closed containers. Then, keep all the smaller items for one recipe together in a larger plastic container. Use an ice chest or cooler to keep all the cold foods cold. Put heavy items and plastic containers on the bottom of the cooler, then top with lots of crushed ice.

In the cooler you'll want to place the vegetable juice cocktail and wine for the *California Cocktail,* the pita sandwich ingredients, the salad, beer, fresh fruit, and a separate bag of ice cubes for the cocktail. Bring chilled apple cider in an insulated beverage server.

For the nonperishable items—the paper and plastic ware, tablecloth, washcloths and towels, serving spoons, cake cutting knife and server, corkscrew, ice tongs, pitcher, and tray—use a picnic basket, a big cardboard box, or paper bags. The box and bags can double as the after-party trash containers. Or, take along large plastic bags for easy cleanup. Don't forget to pack the dessert.

The day before: Prepare the *Currant-Glazed Savarin* including the syrup and glaze. Don't glaze the cake on the plate you're planning to use for serving. Instead transfer the glazed cake from the original plate to a serving plate using two spatulas.

Cook the chicken breasts for the *Chicken and Shrimp Pita Sandwiches*; cut up chicken. Cover and chill in refrigerator. Make extra ice cubes for cooler.

Chill the wine and vegetable juice cocktail for the *California Cocktail*, the beer, and apple cider.

Gather all the items that will go into the picnic basket, cardboard box, or paper bags. When packing the equipment, check off the items from your list as you add them to the picnic basket.

3 hours before: Chop the vegetables for the sandwiches and mix with chicken and shrimp. Mix the dressing for the sandwich filling; add to chicken-shrimp mixture. Chill ingredients for the sandwich filling until ready to pack them into the cooler.

Prepare garnishes for the cocktail and chill. Combine the ingredients for the *Crunchy Pea Salad*. Place in a serving bowl, then cover and chill until you are ready to pack the cooler.

Before leaving for picnic: Pack the cooler with beverages, sandwich makings, salad, fresh fruit, and plenty of ice. Pour the cider into the insulated beverage server. Use ice from your freezer for the cooler or buy ice on the way to the picnic site. Pack the cake in a suitable carrier so it will arrive safely. Don't forget the pumpkins and all the equipment if planning a pumpkin carving contest as picnic entertainment!

At the picnic site: Enlist guests to help arrange the food and picnic supplies. Mix the *California Cocktail* and serve. When ready for lunch, set out the ingredients for the sandwiches and let the guests assemble their own pita sandwiches. Serve the rest of the foods and beverages buffet style.

Enlist your friends to help at the picnic site. Assign two people to spread out the tablecloths. Delegate the cocktail mixing to another person.

Two other guests can help set up the buffet spot while you arrange the foods on the buffet table. In no time the work will be out of the way, and you'll be ready to enjoy the party along with your guests.

Let your guests help with the food preparation by assembling their own *Chicken and Shrimp Pita Sandwiches*. Not only do your friends feel they've shared the work, but it also cuts down on the picnic preparations you have to do.

Place the sandwich ingredients on a picnic table or arrange in large baskets with all the necessary essentials.

When preparing the *Chicken and Shrimp Pita Sandwiches,* one way to save time is to substitute 3 cups diced *or* cubed, cooked, fresh *or* frozen chicken or five 5-ounce cans chunk-style chicken for the chicken breasts.

This way you don't have to cook the chicken breasts in water. Simply drain and cut up the canned chicken before using in the sandwich filling.

Currant-Glazed Savarin

2 cups all-purpose flour
1 package active dry yeast
⅔ cup milk
6 tablespoons butter *or* margarine
2 tablespoons sugar
½ teaspoon salt
3 eggs
1¼ cups water
½ cup packed brown sugar
⅓ cup brandy
1 10-ounce jar currant jelly

■■ In a large mixer bowl combine *1½ cups* of the flour and the yeast. In a saucepan heat milk, butter or margarine, sugar, and salt just till warm (115° to 120°) and butter is almost melted; stir constantly. Add to the flour mixture; add eggs. Beat at low speed of electric mixer for ½ minute, scraping sides of bowl constantly. Beat 3 minutes at high speed. Using a spoon, stir in remaining flour. Spoon dough into a well-greased 6- or 7-cup savarin mold or ring mold. Cover and let rise till nearly double (1 to 1¼ hours). (*Or,* cover; place in oven. Turn oven to 250°; turn off after 1 minute. Open oven door slightly; let dough rise till nearly double, about 40 minutes. Remove from oven.)

■■ Bake the savarin in a 350° oven for 30 to 35 minutes or till done. Cool 5 minutes, then remove from the pan onto a wire rack placed over a tray.

■■ Meanwhile, for syrup in a saucepan combine water and brown sugar. Bring to boiling; boil for 5 minutes. Remove from heat; carefully stir in brandy. Prick cake with tines of long fork. Slowly spoon the syrup over top and sides of cake till all the syrup is absorbed. Let stand at least 30 minutes. Meanwhile, in a saucepan heat the currant jelly slowly till melted. Let cool 10 to 15 minutes to thicken slightly. Spoon over cake. To serve, place cake on a plate and fill center of ring with grapes, if desired. Makes 8 servings.

■■ Preparation time: 30 minutes
■■ Rising time: 1 to 1¼ hours
■■ Cooking time: 30 to 35 minutes
■■ Standing time: at least 30 minutes

Chicken and Shrimp Pita Sandwiches

3 medium chicken breasts
2 cups water
1 4½-ounce can shrimp, drained and rinsed
2 medium tomatoes, chopped
2 medium avocados, seeded, peeled, and chopped
2 tablespoons thinly sliced green onion
2 tablespoons snipped parsley
½ cup dry white wine
¼ cup lemon juice
2 tablespoons cooking oil
1 tablespoon honey
2 teaspoons prepared mustard
1 clove garlic, minced
  Few drops bottled hot pepper sauce
8 large pita bread rounds, halved
2 cups torn spinach
2 cups alfalfa sprouts
  Shredded Swiss cheese

■■ In a skillet or Dutch oven bring the chicken and water to boiling. Reduce heat; cover and simmer about 20 minutes or till chicken is tender. Drain the chicken; cool slightly. Discard the skin and bones; cut meat into ¾-inch cubes. Cover; chill for 2 to 24 hours.

■■ In a bowl combine the chicken cubes, shrimp, chopped tomato, chopped avocado, the green onion, and parsley. For the dressing, in a screw-top jar combine wine, lemon juice, oil, honey, mustard, garlic, and hot pepper sauce; shake well to mix. Pour dressing over chicken-vegetable mixture; toss to mix. Chill till serving time. To serve, fill the pita halves, alternating layers of spinach, alfalfa sprouts, and chicken-vegetable mixture. Top with Swiss cheese. Serve immediately. Makes 8 servings.

■■ Preparation time: 45 minutes
■■ Chilling time: at least 2 hours

California Cocktail

1 **24-ounce can vegetable juice cocktail**
1 **750-milliliter bottle dry white wine**
Ice cubes
Dried dillweed
Green onions, cucumber sticks, *or*
  lemon slices

■■■ Chill the vegetable juice cocktail and the dry white wine till serving time. Before serving, combine the vegetable juice cocktail and white wine. Fill 8 tall glasses with ice cubes. Pour the vegetable juice cocktail-wine mixture over the ice. Sprinkle each serving lightly with dried dillweed. Garnish each glass with a whole green onion, a cucumber stick, or a lemon slice. Makes 8 (6-ounce) servings.

■■■ Total preparation time: 5 minutes

Crunchy Pea Salad

½ **cup dairy sour cream**
2 **tablespoons wine vinegar**
1 **tablespoon milk**
2 **teaspoons sugar**
¾ **teaspoon salt**
⅛ **teaspoon garlic powder**
2 **10-ounce packages frozen peas, thawed**
1 **8-ounce can sliced water chestnuts**
¼ **cup sliced green onion**
3 **tablespoons cooked bacon pieces**
  (3 slices bacon)

■■■ For dressing, in a small bowl combine the sour cream, vinegar, milk, sugar, salt, and garlic powder.

■■■ In a large bowl combine peas, water chestnuts, onion, and bacon pieces. Add the dressing; toss lightly to coat. Cover and chill about 2 hours. Serves 8.

■■■ Preparation time: 25 minutes
■■■ Chilling time: 2 hours

Entertainment for the party: Have a pumpkin-carving contest. Give each guest a pumpkin, sharp knife, and spoon. Tell everyone to carve a unique design on a pumpkin. Then, let the group judge the most creative jack-o'-lantern.

In case of rain: Move the picnic and pumpkin carving indoors. Your guests won't mind sitting on the living-room or family-room floor. For lunch, spread the picnic tablecloths on the floor and bring out some pillows to sit on. Add some background music with your favorite records or tapes. Spread out drop cloths or plastic sheets before starting the pumpkin-carving activity.

The garage can serve as the picnic spot, also—just move a picnic table indoors or set up some card tables and chairs. If the weather permits, leave the garage door open so you get the feeling you're still outdoors.

soup party

spiced beer toddy or soft drinks

assorted crackers   fresh vegetable tray

country-style bean chili

chicken-vegetable burgoo

hot and hearty sausage soup

whole wheat-herb loaves   Italian bread

lemon-berry freezer pies

Invite a group of friends over for a potluck soup party. With this buffet-style menu you can serve up to 24 people. A couple of weeks in advance, send out invitations to six other families or groups of friends. Include one recipe or food suggestion with each invitation. Have extra recipe copies on hand for guests to take home.

Each family prepares a dish at home and brings it with them to your house; all you need to do during the party is reheat the three soups and set out the other foods. Plan some indoor and outdoor activities to occupy everyone until it's time to eat.

TIMETABLE

For serving the meal, set out foods in a logical order to keep them at their optimum serving temperature.

Put dishes and serving utensils out first. Then add foods served at room temperature, such as *Whole Wheat-Herb Loaves,* Italian bread, and crackers.

Next, set out any foods that are served cold—the edible centerpiece, the drinks, and the beer.

The last to add are foods that should be kept hot, such as *Chicken-Vegetable Burgoo, Country-Style Bean Chili,* and *Hot and Hearty Sausage Soup.* If you have space, use a counter-top setup. That way, you can keep soups warm on the range top or in slow cookers.

Keep *Lemon-Berry Freezer Pies* frozen until ready to start serving. Then remove pies from freezer to soften slightly.

The day before: Your family prepares and freezes two recipes of the *Lemon-Berry Freezer Pies,* making four pies. You also buy and chill the soft drinks. Another family prepares *Hot and Hearty Sausage Soup* and chills it in the refrigerator. *Chicken-Vegetable Burgoo* is made by a third family and chilled. Another family cooks and chills the *Country-Style Bean Chili.*

A fifth family, who is responsible for the fresh vegetable tray, prepares and soaks the radish roses, following the directions in column at far left on page 190. A sixth family thaws the frozen dough for the *Whole Wheat-Herb Loaves.* Every family can buy and chill its choice of imported or domestic beer.

6 to 8 hours before: You and your family set up the buffet area and decide upon the seating arrangements. If you don't have enough tables and chairs, ask your friends to bring some to the party. The family in charge of the vegetable tray washes and cleans the fresh vegetables and stores them in the refrigerator. The family responsible for *Whole Wheat-Herb Loaves* prepares and bakes two recipes of the bread, making eight small loaves.

45 minutes before: At the party, the families responsible for *Chicken-Vegetable Burgoo* and *Country-Style Bean Chili* start reheating those soups. One family arranges the vegetable tray so it becomes an edible centerpiece for the buffet area. A seventh family prepares and serves the *Spiced Beer Toddy.*

30 minutes before: The family who brought *Hot and Hearty Sausage Soup* reheats it. You prepare the coffee. Ask some people to help set out the crackers, Italian bread, *Whole Wheat-Herb Loaves,* and butter.

15 minutes before: Add the vegetables to *Chicken-Vegetable Burgoo.* Arrange the cold and hot foods in the buffet area. As guests start to serve themselves, remove *Lemon-Berry Freezer Pies* from the freezer.

After warming up on a glass of *Spiced Beer Toddy,* you may appreciate a cold beer or an iced soft drink with the hot soup course.

For fun, buy a variety of different imported beers, ales, and lagers. Each family can bring a cold six-pack along with their food contribution. Turn to page 308 for more information on beer.

Create an edible centerpiece by arranging relishes in vegetable containers in a wicker basket.

Use pepper shells to hold celery and carrot sticks, green onions, and canned green chili peppers. Hollow out red cabbage to make a bowl for assorted vegetables. Snip an artichoke top and pull back leaves for a pot for mushrooms.

In your centerpiece include other vegetables such as sliced crookneck squash, pea pods, broccoli and cauliflower flowerets, and radish roses.

For radish roses, cut bottoms and tops from radishes. Thinly slice each radish lengthwise on 3 or 4 sides, cutting about ¾ of the way down. Chill in ice water till ready to use.

For a finishing touch, tie green onions to the basket handle using kitchen cord or twine. Use green onion tops for a ribbon.

Buffet-style dining: When entertaining large groups, serving buffet style is an easy way to go. Have all guests help themselves to food from serving containers placed in one or more buffet areas. Arrange the items in a logical sequence in the buffet area and allow some space near each serving dish so guests can set their plates down while serving. Start the buffet line with the dinner plates and soup bowls. Serve the soups first, then the bread and butter, vegetable tray, and choice of beverage.

When planning a buffet-style party, you can set places for your guests with flatware and napkins already on the table. Or, if you don't have enough room to seat everyone at a table, offer them lap trays or tray tables, letting them pick up their flatware and napkins in the buffet area. To accommodate the large number of people for this soup party, you may find yourself using a combination of seating methods.

If you plan to let guests pick up their flatware, wrap each set in a colorful kitchen towel for ease of carrying. The towels serve as napkins. Place the wrapped utensils in a container at the end of the buffet line.

Spiced Beer Toddy

- 8 cups water
- 2 12-ounce cans frozen lemonade concentrate
- ½ cup honey
- 12 inches stick cinnamon, broken
- 2 teaspoons whole allspice
- 2 teaspoons whole cloves
- 4 12-ounce cans beer
- 1 cup gin *or* vodka

■■■ In an 8-quart Dutch oven combine the water, lemonade concentrate, and honey. For spice bag, place cinnamon, allspice, and cloves in cheesecloth and tie; add to lemonade mixture. Bring to boiling; reduce heat. Cover; simmer for 10 minutes. Remove spice bag; discard. Add beer and gin or vodka; heat through. Serve warm. Makes 22 (6-ounce) servings.

■■■ Total preparation time: 20 minutes

Whole Wheat-Herb Loaves

- 2 teaspoons minced dried onion
- 2 teaspoons water
- 2 tablespoons butter *or* margarine, melted
- 1 tablespoon toasted wheat germ
- ½ teaspoon dried rosemary, crushed
- ½ teaspoon dried thyme, crushed
- ⅛ teaspoon garlic powder
- 1 16-ounce loaf frozen whole wheat bread dough, thawed
- 2 teaspoons butter *or* margarine, melted
  Toasted wheat germ

■■■ In a small mixing bowl combine the dried onion and water; let stand for 5 minutes. Stir in the 2 tablespoons melted butter or margarine, the 1 tablespoon wheat germ, rosemary, thyme, and garlic powder.

■■■ On a lightly floured surface divide the thawed dough into 4 portions. Roll each into an 8x4-inch rectangle. Spread *one-quarter* of the onion-butter mixture over *each* dough rectangle. Roll up each rectangle jelly-roll style, beginning from the shortest end. Pinch edges of dough together to seal.

■■■ Place each roll, seam side down, into a greased 4½x2½x1½-inch individual loaf pan. Brush tops with the 2 teaspoons melted butter or margarine; sprinkle with additional wheat germ. Cover; let rise till nearly double (about 45 minutes). Bake in a 350° oven about 25 minutes or till done. Makes 4 loaves to serve 12 (double recipe to serve 24).

■■■ Preparation time: 20 minutes
■■■ Rising time: 45 minutes
■■■ Cooking time: 25 minutes

Before the adults serve themselves, guide young children through the buffet area. They may need help spooning soup, slicing bread, and carrying everything to their dining spot.

For this potluck soup party, all of the soups are 100 percent reheatable. The soup chefs prepare and cook the soups at home, then chill them until party time.

At your house you'll find it easy to reheat the big pots of soup, because each recipe has complete reheating instructions. And, we made sure that reheating the soups involves little or no final preparation so you can clear out of the kitchen to join the party activities.

Country-Style Bean Chili

- 2 medium onions, sliced and separated into rings
- 1 large green pepper, cut into strips and halved crosswise
- 1 tablespoon cooking oil
- 2 15½-ounce cans red kidney beans, drained
- 2 15-ounce cans garbanzo beans, drained
- 2 13¾-ounce cans chicken broth
- 2 12-ounce cans beer
- 1 16-ounce can refried beans
- 1 tablespoon paprika
- 1 tablespoon chili powder
- 1 tablespoon prepared mustard
- 1 tablespoon chopped canned green chili peppers
- ½ teaspoon dried basil, crushed
- ½ teaspoon dried oregano, crushed
  Croutons
- 2 cups shredded sharp cheddar cheese (8 ounces)

■■■ In a Dutch oven or large kettle cook the onion and green pepper in hot cooking oil till tender but not brown. Stir in the red kidney beans, garbanzo beans, chicken broth, beer, refried beans, paprika, chili powder, mustard, chili peppers, basil, and oregano.

■■■ Bring the mixture to boiling; reduce heat. Cover and simmer for 1 hour, stirring occasionally. (Cool and chill the soup at this point, if planning to reheat.) Top each serving with croutons and shredded cheddar cheese. Makes 8 to 10 servings.

■■■ To reheat the chilled soup, place it in a Dutch oven or large kettle; cover and bring to boiling (about 45 minutes), stirring occasionally. Top each serving with croutons and shredded cheese.

■■■ Preparation time: 20 minutes
■■■ Cooking time: 1 hour
■■■ Reheating time: 45 minutes

Chicken-Vegetable Burgoo

- 1 5- to 5½-pound stewing chicken, cut up
- 8 cups water
- 1 medium onion, cut into wedges
- 3 stalks celery, cut up
- 2 bay leaves
- 2 cloves garlic, halved
- 1 teaspoon salt
- ¼ teaspoon pepper
- 3 medium carrots, thinly bias sliced
- 1 medium onion, chopped (½ cup)
- 2 tablespoons instant chicken bouillon granules
- 2 teaspoons dried marjoram, crushed
- 2 cups sliced fresh mushrooms
- 1 small zucchini, thinly sliced
- 1 10-ounce package frozen peas

■■■ In a Dutch oven or large kettle combine the chicken, water, onion wedges, celery, bay leaves, garlic, salt, and pepper. Bring to boiling; reduce heat. Simmer, covered, for 2 hours or till chicken is tender. Remove chicken from broth; set aside. Strain broth, discarding vegetables; skim off fat. Return broth to the Dutch oven or kettle. Add the carrots, chopped onion, bouillon granules, and marjoram. Simmer, covered, for 15 minutes or till carrots are crisp-tender.

■■■ Meanwhile, when the chicken is cool enough to handle, remove and discard skin and bones. Cut chicken into 1-inch pieces; add to broth. (Cool and chill the soup at this point, if planning to reheat.) Add mushrooms, zucchini, and peas. Cover and simmer for 10 to 15 minutes more or till vegetables are tender. Makes 8 to 10 servings

■■■ To reheat the chilled soup, place it in a Dutch oven or large kettle; cover and bring to boiling (about 30 minutes), stirring occasionally. Add the mushrooms, zucchini, and peas; reduce heat. Simmer for 10 to 15 minutes more or till vegetables are tender.

■■■ Preparation time: 1 hour
■■■ Cooking time: 2½ hours
■■■ Reheating time: 40 to 45 minutes

Hot and Hearty Sausage Soup

- 2 pounds Italian sausage links
- 2 cups dry white wine
- 2 cloves garlic, minced
- 1 medium onion, finely chopped (½ cup)
- 5 cups chopped cabbage
- 1 28-ounce can tomatoes, cut up
- 1 cup water
- 1 4-ounce can green chili peppers, rinsed, seeded, and chopped

■ Using the tines of a fork, prick the sausage casing several times. Cut the sausage into 1-inch pieces; place in a large mixing bowl. For the marinade, add the dry white wine and minced garlic to sausage pieces; marinate for 30 minutes.

■ Drain the sausage pieces, reserving the marinade. In a Dutch oven or large kettle cook the sausage and onion till the meat is brown and onion is tender. Drain off fat. Add the reserved marinade. Bring to boiling; reduce heat. Cover and simmer for 20 minutes. Stir in the chopped cabbage, *undrained* tomatoes, water, and green chili peppers. Cover and simmer for 20 minutes more, stirring occasionally. (Cool and chill the soup at this point, if planning to reheat.) Makes 8 to 10 servings.

■ To reheat the chilled soup, place it in a Dutch oven or large kettle; cover and bring to boiling (about 30 minutes), stirring occasionally. If the soup is too thick, add an additional 1 cup *water* and heat through.

■ Preparation time: 20 minutes
■ Marinating time: 30 minutes
■ Cooking time: 40 minutes
■ Reheating time: 30 minutes

Lemon-Berry Freezer Pies

- 2½ cups graham cracker crumbs
- ½ cup sugar
- 1¼ cups butter *or* margarine, melted
- ⅔ cup seedless red raspberry jam
- 3 pints lemon sherbet, softened
- 1 8-ounce container frozen whipped dessert topping, thawed
- 1 8-ounce carton lemon yogurt

■ For crust, combine crumbs and sugar. Stir in melted butter or margarine, toss to combine. Divide between two 9-inch pie plates. Press the mixture onto bottom and up sides to form an even crust. Chill for 1 hour. Dollop *⅓ cup* of the jam into *each* chilled crust. Spread *3 cups* of the sherbet evenly over jam in *each* crust. Combine whipped topping and lemon yogurt; dollop *half* over sherbet layer in *each* pie. Freeze for 4 to 24 hours. Before serving, let pies stand at room temperature about 25 minutes to soften. Makes 2 pies to serve 12 (double recipe to serve 24).

■ Preparation time: 15 minutes
■ Chilling time: at least 1 hour
■ Freezing time: at least 4 hours
■ Standing time: 25 minutes

Tangy *Lemon-Berry Freezer Pies* will snap everyone's taste buds to attention after a cozy, fireside meal of hot soup and bread.

For easier serving and eating, let the pies stand at room temperature about 25 minutes to soften. Or, let them soften in the refrigerator for 45 minutes to an hour before serving.

BRUNCH, LUNCH, AND SUPPER PARTIES

Dinner parties are a great way to entertain, but not the only way. When it comes to friends, anytime and any occasion is right for entertaining. Have guests over for a weekend brunch, lay out a lazy summer lunch, or throw a supper party before an evening on the town. Make the occasion as fancy or as informal as you wish. The only rule that's absolute is to have a great time while you entertain.

Brunch, lunch, and supper parties have lighter meals with fewer courses than dinner parties. But no matter what the party, success depends on great-tasting foods. In this chapter you'll find the recipes to make those foods. The recipes range from the quick-to-fix variety to more elaborate ones that require a bit of time and effort. Each is designed to fit perfectly into the type and style of party you're throwing.

Whether you host a brunch, lunch, or supper party, the main star is the entrée. For surefire success, select a savory main dish from this section. Accompany it with a delightful side dish and an impossible-to-refuse dessert, also from this chapter. The only additional ingredient you'll need is your friends.

Cubed Steak Bake

6 beef cubed steaks
3 tablespoons cooking oil
2 medium onions, sliced
2 10-ounce packages frozen peas, thawed
2 medium tomatoes, seeded and chopped
½ teaspoon dried rosemary, crushed
½ cup shredded American cheese (2 ounces)

■■■ Brown steaks in hot oil. Remove meat, reserving drippings. Cook onions in drippings till tender. Place steaks in a 13x9x2-inch baking dish. Combine peas, tomatoes, rosemary, ½ teaspoon *salt*, and ¼ teaspoon *pepper;* spoon atop meat. Place onions atop. Bake, covered, in a 350° oven for 35 to 45 minutes or till meat is done. Sprinkle cheese atop. Serves 6.

■■■ Total preparation time: 55 to 65 minutes

Sauerkraut Strata

3 slightly beaten eggs
1½ cups milk
2 teaspoons minced dried onion
½ teaspoon caraway seed
2 cups croutons
1 8-ounce can sauerkraut, rinsed, drained, and snipped
1 3-ounce package sliced corned beef, chopped
1 cup shredded Swiss cheese (4 ounces)

■■■ Combine eggs, milk, onion, caraway, and ⅛ teaspoon *pepper.* Stir in croutons, sauerkraut, beef, and *half* of the cheese. Turn into a 10x6x2-inch baking dish. Bake in a 350° oven for 40 minutes. Sprinkle remaining cheese atop; bake about 3 minutes more or till melted. Let stand 5 minutes. Serves 4 to 6.

■■■ Preparation time: 20 minutes
■■■ Cooking time: about 43 minutes
■■■ Standing time: 5 minutes

Beef Pot Roast with Tomato-Wine Gravy

- 1 3- to 3½-pound beef chuck pot roast
- 2 tablespoons cooking oil
- 1 10¾-ounce can condensed tomato soup
- ½ cup dry red wine
- 1 clove garlic, minced
- 1 bay leaf
- ½ teaspoon ground allspice
- ¼ teaspoon salt
- ⅛ teaspoon pepper
- 1 medium onion, sliced
- 1 large stalk celery, sliced
- 1 large carrot, sliced
- 2 tablespoons cornstarch
- 2 tablespoons cold water
  Parsley sprigs

■■■ In a 4-quart Dutch oven brown meat on both sides in hot cooking oil; drain off fat. In a mixing bowl combine condensed tomato soup, red wine, garlic, bay leaf, allspice, salt, and pepper; pour over the meat. Add onion, celery, and carrot. Bring to boiling; reduce heat. Cover and simmer for 1½ to 2 hours or till the meat is tender.

■■■ To serve, transfer the roast and vegetables to a heated serving platter, reserving the cooking liquid. Cover platter and keep meat and vegetables warm. If necessary, skim fat from cooking liquid.

■■■ For gravy, stir cornstarch into cold water; stir into the reserved cooking liquid in the Dutch oven. Cook and stir mixture till thickened and bubbly. Cook and stir for 2 minutes more. Spoon some of the gravy over the roast; pass the remaining gravy. Garnish with parsley sprigs, if desired. Makes 8 servings.

■■■ Preparation time: 30 minutes
■■■ Cooking time: 1½ to 2 hours

Burgundy Burgers

- 2 slices bacon
- 2 slightly beaten eggs
- ¾ cup soft bread crumbs (1 slice)
- ¼ cup thinly sliced green onion
- ¼ cup finely chopped fresh mushrooms
- 2 tablespoons snipped parsley
- 2 tablespoons steak sauce
- 2 tablespoons burgundy *or* dry red wine
- ⅛ teaspoon garlic salt
- ⅛ teaspoon pepper
- 1½ pounds ground beef
  Lettuce leaves
- 8 tomato slices
- 8 slices French bread, cut ½ inch thick, toasted, and buttered
  Dairy sour cream
  Sliced green onion

■■■ In a skillet cook the bacon till crisp; drain on paper toweling. Crumble and set aside. In a mixing bowl combine beaten eggs, bread crumbs, the ¼ cup green onion, mushrooms, parsley, steak sauce, burgundy or dry red wine, garlic salt, and pepper. Stir in the crumbled bacon. Add the ground beef; mix well.

■■■ Shape the meat mixture into eight ½-inch-thick patties. Place patties on a rack of an unheated broiler pan. Broil 3 inches from heat to desired doneness, turning once (allow about 8 minutes total time for rare; about 10 minutes for medium; about 12 minutes for well done). (*Or,* grill patties over *medium-hot* coals for 5 to 6 minutes. Turn and grill about 6 minutes more for medium doneness.)

■■■ Place a lettuce leaf and tomato slice on each piece of French bread. Top with a burger. Add a dollop of sour cream and sprinkle with additional green onion. Makes 8 servings.

■■■ Preparation time: 25 minutes
■■■ Cooking time: 8 to 12 minutes

If you're looking for a delicious but simple main dish to make ahead for a supper menu, try our *Cubed Steak Bake*. You can make this elegant casserole the day before your party.

Prepare the recipe as directed except, before baking, cover and chill it in the refrigerator up to 24 hours.

To serve, remove the dish from the refrigerator. Bake, covered, in a 350° oven about 50 minutes or till heated through. Uncover and sprinkle with shredded cheese.

**MENU
SOMBRERO
SUPPER**

Margarita★ or
Limeade

Deviled Steak
Tostados

Avocado Salsa

Vanilla Ice Cream

To ensure a smashing time at your next party, begin the celebration with a piñata. Piñatas are made of paper, cardboard, or pottery. They may be round or square, or look like an animal or clown. But they must be hollow, so they can be filled with treats.

In Mexico, children wear blindfolds, and hit at their piñata with long sticks. The piñata swings from a string attached to the ceiling or a tree branch until the winner breaks it open and the treats fall to the ground.

You can make your own piñata with a plain paper sack. Decorate it with gift wrap, then stuff it with candies or fun party favors.

★ see recipe, page 304

Stroganoff Bundles

1¼ **pounds ground beef**
1 **medium green pepper, chopped (¾ cup)**
1 **medium onion, chopped (½ cup)**
1 **medium carrot, shredded (½ cup)**
1 **8-ounce carton dairy sour cream**
2 **teaspoons all-purpose flour**
1 **teaspoon Worcestershire sauce**
⅛ **teaspoon garlic salt**
½ **of a 17¼-ounce package (1 sheet) frozen puff pastry, thawed**
1 **7½-ounce can semi-condensed cream of mushroom soup**

■■■ In a skillet cook beef, green pepper, onion, and carrot till meat is brown and onion is tender; drain off fat. Combine *½ cup* of the sour cream, flour, Worcestershire sauce, and garlic salt. Stir into meat mixture.

■■■ Roll puff pastry into an 18x12-inch rectangle. Cut into six 6-inch squares. Spoon about *one-sixth* of the filling into the center of *each* square. Moisten edges of squares. Fold all 4 corners of each square to center. Seal edges by crimping (see photograph below). Place in an ungreased shallow baking pan. Bake in a 375° oven about 25 minutes or till golden. Meanwhile, make the sauce. Combine the soup and remaining sour cream. Heat through over low heat (*do not boil*). Spoon sauce over bundles. Serves 6.

■■ Preparation time: 40 minutes
■■ Cooking time: 25 minutes

Moisten the edges of pastry squares with water. Fold all four corners of each square over the meat filling to center. With the insides of the edges together, seal by crimping with fingers, as shown. Place bundles in an ungreased shallow baking pan.

Deviled Steak Tostados

Avocado Salsa
1 **2-pound beef round steak, cut 1½ inches thick**
¼ **cup water**
3 **tablespoons Dijon-style mustard**
2 **tablespoons cooking oil**
1 **tablespoon soy sauce**
8 **6-inch tortillas**
Shortening

■■■ Prepare the Avocado Salsa. Score meat diagonally on both sides; place in a shallow baking dish. For the marinade, combine the water, mustard, cooking oil, and soy sauce. Brush onto both sides of meat. Marinate at room temperature for 2 hours.

■■■ Rub both sides of tortillas with shortening. Place tortillas on an ungreased baking sheet. Bake in a 400° oven for 10 minutes, turning after 5 minutes.

■■■ Drain meat, reserving the marinade. Grill meat over *medium-hot* coals for 17 to 20 minutes. Turn; grill 17 to 20 minutes more for rare to medium-rare doneness, brushing with reserved marinade the last 10 to 15 minutes. In a saucepan heat the reserved marinade on grill.

■■■ To serve, carve meat across grain into thin slices; arrange on platter. Spoon *half* of the Avocado Salsa into *each* avocado half. Garnish with cilantro or parsley, if desired. Place some meat atop each tortilla; spoon on marinade and top with salsa. Serves 8.

Avocado Salsa: Halve lengthwise and seed 1 large *avocado*. Carefully scoop pulp from each half, leaving firm shells; brush the insides of the shells with *lemon juice* and set aside. Chop pulp; stir in 1 tablespoon *lemon juice*. Stir in 1 small *tomato*, seeded and chopped; 1 *or* 2 canned *green chili peppers*, rinsed, seeded, and chopped; 1 tablespoon sliced *green onion*; and ⅛ teaspoon *salt*. Cover; chill about 2 hours.

■■ Preparation time: 40 minutes
■■ Marinating time: 2 hours
■■ Cooking time: 34 to 40 minutes

*Deviled Steak Tostados
with Avocado Salsa*

You can make *Fancy Wrapped Veal Steak* the day before you entertain and chill it in the refrigerator overnight.

Spread the veal with cheese mixture and wrap in the puff pastry as directed in the recipe. Place the bundles, seam side down, in a shallow baking pan. Cover and chill in the refrigerator up to 24 hours.

About a half hour before serving time, remove the veal bundles from the refrigerator and brush them with the egg mixture. Bake in a 375° oven for 30 to 35 minutes or till the pastry is golden.

Fancy Wrapped Veal Steak

1½ **pounds veal leg round steak *or* beef sirloin steak, cut ¾ inch thick**
2 **tablespoons cooking oil**
¼ **of an 8-ounce container soft-style cream cheese with chives and onion**
1 **teaspoon Dijon-style mustard**
½ **of a 17¼-ounce package (1 sheet) frozen puff pastry, thawed**
1 **beaten egg**
1 **tablespoon water**

▬▬ Cut veal or beef into 6 serving-size pieces; trim fat. In a skillet cook meat on both sides in hot cooking oil for 30 to 45 seconds or just till brown. Remove and drain well on paper toweling. Sprinkle meat with salt and pepper. In a small mixing bowl combine cream cheese and mustard; set aside.

▬▬ On a lightly floured surface roll puff pastry into a 15x12-inch rectangle. Cut into six 6x5-inch rectangles. Spread *1 scant tablespoon* of the cheese mixture atop *each* piece of meat. Place *one* piece of meat, cheese side down, atop *each* rectangle of pastry. Fold pastry to fit around meat (see photograph below). Moisten and seal edges. Place, seam side down, in a shallow baking pan. Combine the beaten egg and water; brush onto pastry. Bake in a 375° oven 25 to 30 minutes or till done. Makes 6 servings.

▬▬ Preparation time: 35 minutes
▬▬ Cooking time: 25 to 30 minutes

Place *one* piece of meat, cheese side down, atop *each* rectangle of pastry. Starting at a short side, fold the ends of the pastry up over the meat, as shown. Moisten and seal the edges. Place, seam side down, in a shallow baking pan.

Veal Brunch Puff

5 **tablespoons butter *or* margarine**
3 **beaten eggs**
½ **cup all-purpose flour**
½ **cup milk**
¼ **teaspoon salt**
1 **pound veal leg round steak, cut ¼ inch thick**
2 **tablespoons butter *or* margarine**
1 **9-ounce package frozen onions in cream sauce**
2 **medium tomatoes, peeled, seeded, and chopped**
½ **cup shredded Swiss cheese (2 ounces)**
1 **tablespoon snipped parsley**

▬▬ For puff, in a 10-inch skillet with an oven-proof handle, melt the 5 tablespoons butter or margarine; tilt to coat bottom. In a mixing bowl combine beaten eggs, flour, milk, and salt; beat with a rotary beater till smooth. Stir in the melted butter from the skillet. Beat till smooth; pour batter into skillet. Bake in a 450° oven for 15 minutes. Reduce oven to 350°; bake for 5 to 10 minutes more or till puffed and light brown.

▬▬ Meanwhile, using a meat mallet, pound veal to ⅛-inch thickness. Cut veal into ¼-inch-wide strips. In another skillet cook veal in the 2 tablespoons butter or margarine, *half* at a time, about 1 minute or till brown. Remove from skillet; drain well on paper toweling.

▬▬ Cook the onions according to package directions, *except* omit the butter. Stir in the veal strips, chopped tomatoes, and shredded Swiss cheese. Cook and stir over low heat till cheese is melted and mixture is heated through. Spoon meat mixture into the puff. Sprinkle with parsley. Serve immediately. Makes 6 servings.

▬▬ Preparation time: 15 minutes
▬▬ Cooking time: 20 to 25 minutes

Sausage-Stuffed Chops

¼ **pound bulk pork sausage**
2 **tablespoons chopped celery**
2 **tablespoons chopped onion**
1½ **cups corn bread stuffing mix**
¾ **cup chopped apple**
⅛ **teaspoon salt**
⅛ **teaspoon dried rosemary, crushed**
   Dash pepper
1 **to 2 tablespoons apple juice or apple cider**
8 **pork loin rib chops, cut 1¼ inches thick**
½ **cup red currant jelly**
½ **cup apple juice or apple cider**
2 **teaspoons cornstarch**
   Apple slices (optional)

▬▬ For stuffing, in a large skillet cook sausage, celery, and onion till sausage is done and vegetables are tender, stirring occasionally. Remove from heat. Drain off fat. Stir in stuffing mix, apple, salt, rosemary, and pepper. Sprinkle with the 1 to 2 tablespoons apple juice or cider to moisten; toss gently.

▬▬ Make a pocket in each chop by cutting from fat side almost to bone. Sprinkle the pockets with salt and pepper. Spoon about ⅓ cup of the stuffing into pocket of *each* chop (see photograph at upper right). If desired, skewer with wooden picks. Place stuffed chops in a shallow baking pan. Bake, covered, in a 350° oven for 45 minutes.

▬▬ Meanwhile, in a small saucepan combine currant jelly, the ½ cup apple juice or cider, and cornstarch. Cook and stir till slightly thickened and bubbly. Cook and stir for 2 minutes more.

▬▬ Drain chops. Spoon some of the jelly mixture over chops. Bake, uncovered, for 30 minutes more or till meat is well done. Remove wooden picks. Heat remaining jelly mixture; serve with chops. Garnish with apple slices, if desired. Makes 8 servings.

▬▬ Preparation time: 30 minutes
▬▬ Cooking time: 1¼ hours

Using a teaspoon, carefully spoon about ⅓ cup of the stuffing into the pocket of *each* chop, as shown. If desired, insert two wooden picks into the chops diagonally to close the pockets. Remove the picks before serving.

Five Spice Pork Roast

1 **4-pound pork shoulder roast**
1½ **teaspoons five spice powder**
2 **tablespoons cooking oil**
¼ **cup chopped onion**
1 **to 2 tablespoons sesame seed**
1 **clove garlic, minced**
1 **cup apple juice or apple cider**
½ **cup dry white wine**
3 **tablespoons soy sauce**
2 **tablespoons cold water**
4 **teaspoons cornstarch**
   Hot cooked rice
   Green onion fans (optional)

▬▬ Rub roast with five spice powder. In a 4-quart Dutch oven brown meat in hot oil. Add onion, sesame seed, and garlic; cook and stir for 2 to 3 minutes or till sesame seed is golden. Add apple juice or cider, wine, and soy sauce. Bring to boiling; reduce heat. Cover; simmer for 2½ to 3 hours or till tender. Transfer meat to a platter, reserving juices; keep warm.

▬▬ Skim fat from juices. Add water, if necessary, to measure 1½ cups liquid. Return to pan. Combine the cold water and cornstarch; stir into juices. Cook and stir till thickened and bubbly. Cook and stir for 2 minutes more. Spoon over meat. Serve with cooked rice. Garnish with green onion fans, if desired. Serves 8.

▬▬ Preparation time: 25 minutes
▬▬ Cooking time: 2½ to 3 hours

You can purchase the commercial five spice powder in Oriental food stores or in many large supermarkets.
   Or, with this simple recipe you can create your own. To make five spice powder, combine 1 teaspoon ground *cinnamon*, 1 teaspoon crushed *aniseed*, ¼ teaspoon crushed *fennel seed*, ¼ teaspoon ground *cloves*, and ¼ teaspoon freshly ground *pepper*.

for 5 minutes. Combine eggs, *undrained* cottage cheese, the peas, milk, and seasoned salt; stir in rice mixture. Turn into an ungreased 9-inch quiche pan or pie plate.

▬ Arrange sausage link halves in a spoke fashion atop rice mixture. Bake, uncovered, in a 325° oven about 45 minutes or till a knife inserted near the center comes out clean. Let stand for 5 minutes. Garnish with a sprig of rosemary, if desired. Makes 4 servings.

▬ Preparation time: 20 minutes
▬ Cooking time: 45 minutes
▬ Standing time: 5 minutes

Breakfast Quiche

- 1 **pound bulk pork sausage**
- 1 **package (8) refrigerated crescent rolls**
- 1 **cup frozen loose-pack hash brown potatoes, thawed**
- 1 **cup shredded cheddar cheese**
- 5 **beaten eggs**
- ¼ **cup milk**
- ½ **teaspoon salt**
- ⅛ **teaspoon pepper**
- 2 **tablespoons grated Parmesan cheese**

▬ Cook sausage till brown; drain off fat. Separate dough into 8 triangles; place in an ungreased 12-inch pizza pan, with points toward center. Press to form a crust; seal. Spoon sausage over crust. Sprinkle with potatoes. Top with cheddar cheese. Combine eggs, milk, salt, and pepper; pour over all. Sprinkle with Parmesan cheese. Bake in a 375° oven for 25 to 30 minutes or till a knife inserted near the center comes out clean. Makes 6 to 8 servings.

▬ Preparation time: 35 minutes
▬ Cooking time: 25 to 30 minutes

If you don't have fresh rosemary to garnish the top of *Cottage Cheese and Rice Bake* (pictured above), add a sprig of fresh parsley or a tomato rose (see the illustration on page 63) for a colorful trim.

Cottage Cheese and Rice Bake

- ½ **cup quick-cooking rice**
- 2 **teaspoons minced dried onion**
- ⅛ **teaspoon dried rosemary, crushed, *or* dried thyme, crushed**
- ⅛ **teaspoon dried basil, crushed**
  Dash ground red pepper
- 2 **beaten eggs**
- 1 **cup cream-style cottage cheese**
- 1 **cup frozen peas**
- ½ **cup milk**
- ¼ **teaspoon seasoned salt**
- 4 **brown-and-serve sausage links, halved lengthwise**

▬ In a saucepan bring ½ cup *water* to boiling. Stir in uncooked rice, the onion, rosemary or thyme, basil, and red pepper. Cover; remove from heat. Let stand

Mexican-Style Strata

- ¾ pound bulk pork sausage
- 15 ½-inch-thick slices French bread
- ¾ cup shredded Monterey Jack cheese
- ¾ cup shredded pepper cheese
- 1½ cups thinly sliced zucchini
- 4 beaten eggs
- 1 cup milk
- 1 8-ounce can tomato sauce
- ⅓ cup green chili salsa
  Butter or margarine

■ Cook sausage till brown; drain off fat. Line a 12x7½x2-inch baking dish with ten of the bread slices, overlapping slightly. Sprinkle the cheeses atop. Layer zucchini slices atop cheese; add sausage. Combine eggs, milk, tomato sauce, chili salsa, and ¼ teaspoon salt; pour over sausage. Butter the remaining bread slices; cut into ½-inch cubes. Place atop casserole. Chill for 1 hour in the refrigerator. Bake in a 325° oven for 40 to 45 minutes or till a knife inserted near the center comes out clean. Let stand for 10 minutes. Makes 8 to 10 servings.

■ Preparation time: 30 minutes
■ Chilling time: 1 hour
■ Cooking time: 40 to 45 minutes
■ Standing time: 10 minutes

Pork Sausage in Cider

  Honeyed Apple Rings
- 8 ounces fresh pork sausage links
- 2 tablespoons chopped onion
- 1½ teaspoons all-purpose flour
- ½ cup apple cider or apple juice
- 1 teaspoon finely snipped parsley

■ Prepare Honeyed Apple Rings. Prick sausage links with a fork. In a covered skillet cook the sausage links in 2 tablespoons water for 5 minutes; drain. Cook sausage links, uncovered, till brown. Drain, reserving 2 tablespoons drippings in the skillet. Set links aside.

■ For sauce, cook onion in reserved drippings till tender. Stir in flour and a dash salt. Add apple cider or apple juice all at once. Cook and stir till thickened and bubbly. Cook and stir for 1 minute more. Stir in parsley. Return sausage links to skillet; cover and heat through. Transfer links to a platter; arrange warm Honeyed Apple Rings around sausage. Spoon some of the sauce atop; pass remaining. Makes 4 servings.

Honeyed Apple Rings: Wash and core 2 medium apples; cut into ½-inch-thick rings. In a saucepan stir together 2 tablespoons honey, 1 tablespoon vinegar, ⅛ teaspoon ground cinnamon, and dash salt. Bring to boiling; reduce heat. Add apple rings. Cover; cook for 10 to 12 minutes or till rings are transparent.

■ Total preparation time: 40 minutes

Savory Bratwurst Sandwich

- 3 slices bacon
- ½ cup chopped onion
- ¼ cup packed brown sugar
- ¼ cup vinegar
- 1 teaspoon salt
- ½ cup cold water
- 2 teaspoons cornstarch
- 4 fully cooked bratwurst, thinly sliced
- ¾ cup chopped green pepper
- ½ cup shredded carrot
- 3 cups shredded cabbage
- 4 pita bread rounds, halved

■ Cook bacon till crisp; drain, reserving 2 tablespoons of drippings. Crumble the bacon; set aside. Cook onion in drippings till tender. Stir in brown sugar, vinegar, and salt. Stir water into cornstarch; add to skillet. Cook and stir till thickened and bubbly. Add bratwurst, green pepper, and carrot, stirring to coat. Cover; cook for 5 minutes. Stir in bacon and cabbage; heat through. Spoon into pita rounds. Serves 4.

■ Total preparation time: 30 minutes

For a casual sandwich lunch or light supper, serve your friends an arranged tray of assorted breads, cheeses, and sliced fully cooked sausages. Some good choices include beerwurst (also called beer salami), blood sausage, salami, summer sausage, mortadella, and New England sausage. The meal is easy to make and quick to clean up.

Here's a great meal you can serve for a pregame picnic. Whether the sport is golf, tennis, baseball, soccer, or football, *your* "fans" will agree Poor Boy Loaf is a winner.

★ *see recipe, page 229*

Poor Boy Loaf

  1 **14-inch-long loaf Italian bread**
 ¼ **cup butter *or* margarine, softened**
  1 **tablespoon snipped parsley**
  1 **tablespoon prepared mustard**
  1 **clove garlic, minced**
 ¼ **teaspoon crushed red pepper**
  6 **ounces salami *or* pepperoni, sliced**
  6 **ounces mozzarella cheese, sliced**
  2 **medium tomatoes, thinly sliced**
  3 **pickled sweet peppers, seeded and cut into quarters**

▬▬ Cut bread into ½-inch slices, cutting to, but not through, bottom crust. Combine next 5 ingredients; spread onto bread in every other slit. Insert meat, cheese, tomatoes, and peppers into buttered slits. Wrap in heavy-duty foil. Bake in a 350° oven for 15 minutes or till warm. Makes 12 servings.

▬▬ Total preparation time: 35 minutes

Hearty Ham and Potato Soup

  1 **cup thinly sliced fresh mushrooms**
 ½ **cup thinly sliced green onion**
  2 **tablespoons butter *or* margarine**
  1 **9-ounce package frozen cut green beans**
  3 **cups milk**
  1 **cup cubed fully cooked ham**
 ¾ **cup packaged instant mashed potato flakes**
 ½ **cup shredded American cheese (2 ounces)**

▬▬ Cook mushrooms and onion in hot butter till tender. Add beans and ½ cup *water*. Bring to boiling; reduce heat. Cook, covered, about 5 minutes or till beans are crisp-tender. Add milk, ham, potato flakes, cheese, and ⅛ teaspoon *pepper*. Cook and stir till bubbly. Cover and cook for 5 minutes. Serves 6.

▬▬ Total preparation time: 25 minutes

Ham and Noodle Salad

  3 **ounces green noodles**
  3 **ounces plain noodles**
  1 **medium cucumber, seeded and chopped (about 2 cups)**
 1½ **cups cubed fully cooked ham (8 ounces)**
 ½ **cup shredded carrot (1 medium)**
 ½ **cup cubed cheddar cheese (2 ounces)**
 ½ **cup cream-style cottage cheese**
 ⅓ **cup thinly sliced green onion**
 ¼ **cup salad oil**
  3 **tablespoons vinegar**
 ¼ **teaspoon garlic salt**
 ¼ **teaspoon dried marjoram, crushed**
 ⅛ **teaspoon pepper**
     Lettuce leaves (optional)

▬▬ In a large saucepan cook the green noodles and plain noodles according to package directions; drain. Rinse with cold water; drain well. In a large mixing bowl combine the drained noodles, chopped cucumber, the ham, shredded carrot, cheddar cheese, the *undrained* cottage cheese, and sliced green onion.

▬▬ For dressing, in a screw-top jar combine salad oil, vinegar, garlic salt, marjoram, and pepper. Cover and shake well to mix. Pour dressing over noodle mixture and toss gently to coat. Cover and chill in the refrigerator for 6 hours, stirring occasionally. To serve, spoon the salad mixture onto lettuce-lined individual salad plates, if desired. Makes 4 servings.

▬▬ Preparation time: 30 minutes
▬▬ Chilling time: at least 6 hours

Lamb and Beef Pie Florentine

     1 beaten egg
     1 3-ounce package cream cheese, softened
  1½ cups soft bread crumbs (2 slices)
     ½ cup milk
  1½ teaspoons salt
     ½ teaspoon dried rosemary, crushed, *or*
          dried marjoram, crushed
     ¼ teaspoon pepper
     1 10-ounce package frozen chopped
          spinach, thawed and well drained
     1 3-ounce can chopped mushrooms, drained
     1 pound lean ground lamb *or* pork
     1 pound lean ground beef
     1 9-inch frozen unbaked deep-dish pastry
          shell, thawed
     1 beaten egg yolk
     1 tablespoon water

■ In a mixing bowl combine the beaten egg and the cream cheese; stir in bread crumbs, milk, salt, rosemary or marjoram, and pepper. Stir in spinach and mushrooms. Add ground lamb or pork and ground beef; mix well. Pat the meat mixture into a 10-inch pie plate. Invert onto a shallow baking pan; remove pie plate. Bake, uncovered, in a 375° oven for 50 to 60 minutes or till done. Drain off fat.

■ Using a small cookie cutter or an hors d'oeuvre cutter, make 4 or 5 cutouts in the pastry shell while still in foil pan. Carefully remove cutouts and set aside. Invert the foil pan over meat loaf. Loosen pastry and remove the pan. Arrange cutouts atop pastry.

■ Combine the egg yolk and water; brush onto pastry and cutouts. Return to a 375° oven for 12 to 15 minutes or till golden. Brush again with yolk mixture. To serve, carefully transfer the pie to a heated serving platter. Makes 8 servings.

■ Preparation time: 30 minutes
■ Cooking time: about 1¼ hours

Spicy Meat and Corn Bread Wedges

     1 pound ground lamb, beef, pork,
          veal, *or* turkey
     ⅓ cup catsup
     1 1¼-ounce envelope taco seasoning mix
     1 10-ounce package corn bread mix *or*
          one 8-ounce package corn muffin mix
     1 cup shredded mozzarella, Monterey Jack,
          Swiss, cheddar, *or* American cheese
          (4 ounces)
     1 10-ounce can tomatoes and green chili
          peppers, cut up
        Canned green chili peppers (optional)

■ In a large skillet cook the ground meat till brown; drain off fat. Remove from heat. Stir in the catsup and taco seasoning mix.

■ Meanwhile, in a mixing bowl prepare the corn bread mix or corn muffin mix according to package directions. Spread *half* of the batter in the bottom of a greased 8x1½-inch round baking dish. Spoon the meat mixture atop batter in pan. Sprinkle with the shredded cheese. Spread the remaining batter over cheese. Bake in a 350° oven for 25 to 35 minutes or till the corn bread is done.

■ Meanwhile, to prepare the sauce, in a saucepan heat tomatoes and chili peppers. To serve, cut the warm corn bread into 6 wedges. Spoon some of the heated sauce atop each serving; pass the remaining sauce. If desired, garnish each serving with a canned green chili pepper. Makes 6 servings.

■ Preparation time: 25 minutes
■ Cooking time: 25 to 35 minutes

Curried Turkey à la King

- 6 **frozen patty shells**
- 2 **tablespoons butter** *or* **margarine**
- 2 **tablespoons all-purpose flour**
- 1 **to 2 teaspoons curry powder**
- ½ **teaspoon salt**
- ½ **teaspoon dry mustard**
- 1½ **cups light cream**
- 1 **cup milk**
- 3 **beaten egg yolks**
- 3 **cups cubed cooked turkey** *or* **chicken**
- 1 **cup frozen peas, thawed**
- 3 **tablespoons chopped pimiento**

■ Bake the patty shells according to package directions. Meanwhile, melt butter or margarine; stir in flour, curry powder, salt, and dry mustard. Add light cream and milk all at once. Cook and stir till thickened and bubbly. Cook and stir for 1 minute more. Stir about *half* of the hot mixture into egg yolks; return all to pan. Cook and stir till thickened. Reduce heat; cook and stir for 2 minutes more. Stir in turkey or chicken, peas, and pimiento; heat through. Spoon into patty shells. Makes 6 servings.

■ Total preparation time: 25 minutes

Turkey Croissant Sandwiches

- 2 **3-ounce packages cream cheese, softened**
- ¼ **cup mayonnaise** *or* **salad dressing**
- 1 **tablespoon milk**
- ¼ **teaspoon salt**
- 3 **cups diced cooked turkey** *or* **chicken**
- 1 **cup halved seedless green grapes**
- ½ **cup chopped water chestnuts**
- ½ **cup chopped green pepper**
- 2 **tablespoons chopped pimiento**
- 6 **purchased croissants, split**

■ In a mixing bowl combine cream cheese, the mayonnaise or salad dressing, milk, and salt. Fold in turkey or chicken, grape halves, water chestnuts, green pepper, and pimiento. Cover and chill in the refrigerator for 2 hours.

■ To serve, remove about *one-third* of the soft dough inside *each* bottom croissant half. If necessary, stir additional milk (about 1 tablespoon) into turkey mixture to make of spreading consistency. Spoon *some* of the turkey mixture into bottom half of *each* croissant. Replace croissant tops. Makes 6 servings.

■ Total preparation time: 2½ hours

Cheese-Topped Turkey Roast

- 1 **2½- to 3-pound frozen boneless turkey roast (without gravy)**
- ¼ **cup chopped onion**
- ¼ **cup chopped green pepper**
- 1 **tablespoon cooking oil**
- 1 **8-ounce can tomato sauce**
- ¼ **teaspoon garlic salt**
- ¼ **teaspoon ground cumin**
- 3 **tablespoons yellow cornmeal**
- ¼ **teaspoon salt**
- ¼ **teaspoon paprika**
- ¾ **cup shredded Monterey Jack cheese with jalapeño peppers (3 ounces)**

■ Roast turkey according to package directions. Slice into ¼-inch-thick slices; arrange in a 12x7½x2-inch baking dish.

■ Cook onion and green pepper in hot cooking oil till tender. Stir in the tomato sauce, garlic salt, and cumin. Cover; simmer for 5 minutes. Pour over the sliced turkey. Bake, covered, in a 350° oven about 25 minutes or till heated through. Combine the cornmeal, salt, and paprika; stir in shredded cheese. Sprinkle over sauce. Bake, uncovered, about 5 minutes more or till cheese is melted. Makes 12 to 15 servings.

■ Total preparation time: 3 hours

Stuffed Sopaipillas

- **3 medium tomatoes, seeded and finely chopped, *or* one 16-ounce can tomatoes, drained and cut up**
- **1 4-ounce can green chili peppers, rinsed, seeded, and chopped**
- **1 medium onion, finely chopped (½ cup)**
- **1 tablespoon vinegar**
- **1 teaspoon sugar**
- **⅛ teaspoon salt**
  Chicken Filling *or* Sausage Filling
- **1 package active dry yeast**
- **¾ cup warm water (110° to 115°)**
- **1 tablespoon cooking oil**
- **2 cups all-purpose flour**
- **½ teaspoon baking powder**
- **½ teaspoon salt**
  Cooking oil *or* shortening for deep-fat frying
- **1 cup shredded cheddar *or* Monterey Jack cheese (4 ounces)**
- **½ cup sliced green onion**
- **1 medium avocado, seeded, peeled, and sliced**

■ For salsa, in a mixing bowl combine tomatoes, chili peppers, onion, vinegar, sugar, and the ⅛ teaspoon salt. Let stand at room temperature while making the filling and sopaipillas. Prepare Chicken Filling or Sausage Filling; keep warm.

■ Dissolve yeast in warm water. Add the 1 tablespoon cooking oil; set aside. In a mixing bowl stir together flour, baking powder, and the ½ teaspoon salt. Add yeast mixture; stir with a fork till moistened. Turn out onto a lightly floured surface. Knead gently for 15 to 20 strokes or till dough forms a ball. Divide dough into 12 portions and shape into balls. Place balls of dough so they do not touch. Cover and let rest for 10 minutes. On a lightly floured surface roll dough, one ball at a time, into twelve 4-inch circles. Keep remaining dough covered while working.

Fry the dough circles, one at a time, till dough rises to the surface. Immediately spoon some of the hot fat over the dough till it puffs, as shown. Continue frying, turning once, till golden. (The total cooking time should be 2 to 3 minutes.)

■ In a large saucepan or deep-fat fryer heat cooking oil or shortening to 365°. Fry dough circles, one at a time, till dough rises to surface. Immediately spoon hot fat over top till the dough puffs (see photograph above). Continue frying, turning once, till golden. (The total cooking time should be 2 to 3 minutes.) Drain the sopaipillas well on paper toweling.

■ To serve, cut off about *one-fourth* of each sopaipilla to expose the pocket. Fill with Chicken Filling or Sausage Filling. Replace the tops. Serve the stuffed sopaipillas warm with salsa, shredded cheese, sliced green onion, and avocado slices. Makes 6 servings.

Chicken Filling: In a saucepan melt 3 tablespoons *butter or margarine*; stir in ¼ cup *all-purpose flour*. Add 1 cup *chicken broth*. Cook and stir till thickened and bubbly. Cook and stir for 1 minute more. Stir in 1 tablespoon snipped *parsley*, 1 tablespoon *lemon juice*, 1 teaspoon grated *onion*, dash *paprika*, dash ground *nutmeg*, and a dash *pepper*. Stir in 1½ cups diced cooked *chicken or turkey*; heat through.

Sausage Filling: In a skillet cook 1½ pounds *chorizo or Italian sausage links*, sliced ½ inch thick, for 15 to 20 minutes or till done. Drain off fat. Add ¾ cup *taco sauce*; heat through.

■ Total preparation time: 1¼ hours

Stuffed Sopaipillas, which are based on the puffed fried bread eaten as an appetizer or dessert in the Southwest, make a savory main dish. The pockets in the bread are filled with a succulent *Chicken* or *Sausage Filling*, then these hearty sandwiches are served warm with flavorful salsa.

Chicken with Fines Herbes

Chicken with Fines Herbes

      4 **whole large chicken breasts, skinned,
         halved lengthwise, and boned**
    ¼ **cup butter *or* margarine, softened**
      1 **tablespoon snipped parsley**
    ¼ **teaspoon fines herbes**
    ¼ **teaspoon dried oregano, crushed**
    ¼ **teaspoon dried marjoram, crushed**
      2 **ounces Monterey Jack cheese, cut into
         eight strips**
      1 **beaten egg**
      1 **tablespoon water**
    ½ **teaspoon cooking oil**
    ¼ **cup all-purpose flour**
    ½ **cup fine dry bread crumbs**
    ¼ **cup dry white wine**
         Hot cooked noodles
         Lemon slices (optional)
         Parsley sprig (optional)

▬▬ Place 1 piece of chicken between 2 pieces of clear plastic wrap. Working from center to edges, pound with a meat mallet to ⅛-inch thickness. Remove plastic wrap. Repeat with remaining chicken.

▬▬ In a bowl combine butter or margarine, parsley, fines herbes, oregano, and marjoram. Using *half* of the herb mixture, dot some on each chicken breast half. Place a strip of cheese on each. Fold in sides; roll up jelly-roll style. Press edges together to seal. In a medium mixing bowl combine egg, water, and cooking oil. Roll chicken in flour to coat; dip into the egg mixture. Roll in bread crumbs to coat.

▬▬ Place chicken rolls, seam side down, in a 12x7½x2 inch baking dish. Bake, uncovered, in a 350° oven for 20 minutes. Meanwhile, melt remaining herb mixture; add wine. After 20 minutes of baking, pour wine mixture over the rolls. Bake for 20 to 25 minutes more or till chicken is tender. Drain, reserving pan juices. Serve chicken over hot cooked noodles. Garnish with lemon slices and fresh parsley, if desired. Pass reserved juices with chicken. Serves 8.

▬▬ Preparation time: 30 minutes
▬▬ Cooking time: 40 to 45 minutes

Dilled Chicken Chowder

      1 **medium onion, chopped (½ cup)**
      1 **clove garlic, minced**
      2 **tablespoons butter *or* margarine**
    ¼ **cup all-purpose flour**
      3 **cups chicken broth**
    1½ **cups shredded zucchini**
    ½ **cup shredded carrot**
      2 **cups cubed cooked chicken *or* turkey**
      1 **cup light cream**
    ¼ **cup snipped parsley**
      1 **teaspoon dried dillweed**

▬▬ Cook onion and garlic in hot butter till tender. Stir in flour, ½ teaspoon *salt,* and ¼ teaspoon *pepper.* Add broth. Cook and stir till bubbly. Add zucchini and carrot. Cover; simmer for 10 minutes. Stir in remaining ingredients. Heat through. Makes 6 servings.

▬▬ Total preparation time: 35 minutes

Chicken and Pea Pod Salad

    ½ **cup salad oil**
    ½ **cup vinegar**
      2 **tablespoons dry sherry**
      2 **tablespoons soy sauce**
      2 **teaspoons sugar**
      6 **ounces fresh pea pods *or* one 6-ounce
         package frozen pea pods, thawed**
      5 **cups torn fresh spinach**
      3 **cups cubed cooked chicken *or* turkey**
      6 **nectarines, pitted and thinly sliced**
    ½ **cup broken walnuts**

▬▬ For dressing, in a screw-top jar combine oil, vinegar, sherry, soy sauce, and sugar. Cover; shake well. Chill. Halve pea pods diagonally. Combine pea pods, spinach, chicken, nectarines, and walnuts. Shake dressing; pour atop and toss. Serves 6 to 8.

▬▬ Total preparation time: 40 minutes

MENU
**FANCY CHICKEN
SUPPER**

Chicken with Fines
Herbes

Green Beans

Hot Cooked Noodles

French Bread

Pick-a-Fruit Pie ★

Coffee

If you're longing for the flavor of country-style cooking, plan a fancy but homey supper party. Complement our great-tasting chicken main dish with your favorite family recipe for green beans.
    Fresh-baked *Pick-a-Fruit Pie* makes a delicious home-style dessert.
★ *see recipe, page 231*

If you grow basil in your garden, use this fresh, sweet herb to perk up the flavor of tomato-sauced pasta dishes, vegetables, eggs, casseroles, main dishes, salads, and soups. Before serving, add a sprig of fresh basil to make an attractive but simple garnish.

You can use dried basil instead of the fresh. To substitute, use one-third as much of the dried as you would the fresh. You need less of the dried herb because dehydration makes its flavor more concentrated.

Asparagus and Shrimp Salad

Fresh Basil Dressing
1 to 1½ pounds fresh asparagus *or* one 10-ounce package frozen cut asparagus
1 pound fresh *or* frozen shelled shrimp
¼ cup sliced green onion
2 tablespoons snipped parsley
3 medium tomatoes, cut into thin wedges
Lettuce leaves

▄▄ Prepare the Fresh Basil Dressing. Set aside. Snap off and discard the woody base of fresh asparagus stalks; wash and cut up. Cook fresh asparagus, covered, in a small amount of boiling salted water for 10 to 15 minutes or till tender. (*Or,* cook frozen asparagus according to package directions.) Drain well. Cook fresh or frozen shelled shrimp in a large amount of boiling salted water for 1 to 3 minutes or till shrimp turn pink. Drain.

▄▄ In a mixing bowl combine the cooked asparagus, cooked shrimp, green onion, and parsley. Shake the dressing; pour over shrimp mixture. Stir gently to coat. Cover and chill in the refrigerator for 6 hours, stirring mixture occasionally.

▄▄ To serve, drain the shrimp mixture, reserving dressing. Add the tomato wedges to the shrimp mixture; turn into a lettuce-lined salad bowl. Drizzle some of the reserved dressing atop. Makes 4 to 6 servings.

Fresh Basil Dressing: In screw-top jar combine 3 tablespoons *salad oil;* 3 tablespoons *white wine vinegar;* 3 tablespoons *lemon juice;* 1 tablespoon *sugar;* 1 tablespoon snipped *fresh basil or* 1 teaspoon *dried basil,* crushed; ½ teaspoon *salt;* ¼ teaspoon freshly ground *pepper;* and several dashes *bottled hot pepper sauce.* Cover and shake well to mix.

▄▄ Preparation time: 40 minutes
▄▄ Chilling time: at least 6 hours

Pasta with Sausage-Clam Sauce

½ pound bulk Italian sausage
¼ cup chopped onion
¼ cup chopped celery
1 clove garlic, minced
1 16-ounce can tomatoes, cut up
1 8-ounce can tomato sauce
¼ cup dry red wine
1 tablespoon snipped fresh basil *or* 1 teaspoon dried basil, crushed
1 teaspoon sugar
2 7½-ounce cans minced clams, drained and finely chopped
8 ounces linguine *or* other pasta
2 tablespoons butter *or* margarine
½ cup grated Parmesan cheese
3 tablespoons snipped parsley

▄▄ For the sauce, in a large saucepan or Dutch oven cook Italian sausage, onion, celery, and garlic till sausage is brown and onion is tender. Drain off fat. Stir in *undrained* tomatoes, tomato sauce, red wine, basil, and sugar. Bring to boiling; reduce heat. Simmer, uncovered, about 30 minutes or till sauce is of desired consistency, stirring occasionally. Add the clams to the sauce. Heat mixture through.

▄▄ Meanwhile, cook linguine or other pasta according to package directions; drain. Add butter or margarine to hot pasta; toss gently to coat. Add the clam sauce, Parmesan cheese, and parsley; toss to coat pasta. Serve warm. Makes 6 servings.

▄▄ Preparation time: 25 minutes
▄▄ Cooking time: 30 minutes

To serve a soufflé, insert two forks, back to back, and gently pull the soufflé apart, as shown. Cut into serving-size portions in this manner. Use a large serving spoon to transfer the portions to heated individual plates.

Tuna-Rice Brunch Squares

½ cup finely chopped onion
¼ cup finely chopped green pepper
2 tablespoons butter *or* margarine
1 8-ounce carton dairy sour cream
2 tablespoons all-purpose flour
2 beaten eggs
3 cups cooked rice
1 cup milk
¼ cup finely chopped water chestnuts
2 tablespoons snipped parsley
2 tablespoons chopped pimiento
1 teaspoon seasoned salt
1 teaspoon Worcestershire sauce
1 9¼-ounce can tuna, drained and flaked
1½ cups shredded American cheese
       (6 ounces)

▬▬ In a small skillet cook onion and green pepper in hot butter or margarine till tender but not brown. In a mixing bowl combine sour cream and flour; stir in eggs, cooked rice, milk, water chestnuts, parsley, pimiento, seasoned salt, and Worcestershire sauce. Stir in onion mixture, tuna, and cheese. Turn into a greased 12x7½x2-inch baking dish. Bake, uncovered, in a 325° oven for 35 to 40 minutes or till a knife inserted near center comes out clean. Let stand for 5 minutes; cut into squares. Makes 8 to 10 servings.

▬▬ Preparation time: 20 minutes
▬▬ Cooking time: 35 to 40 minutes
▬▬ Standing time: 5 minutes

Salmon Soufflé

¼ cup sliced green onion
3 tablespoons butter *or* margarine
¼ cup all-purpose flour
¼ teaspoon dried tarragon, crushed, *or* dried dillweed, crushed
   Dash pepper
¾ cup milk
¼ cup grated Romano *or* Parmesan cheese
1 7¾-ounce can salmon, drained and flaked
3 egg yolks
3 egg whites

▬▬ In a saucepan cook green onion in hot butter or margarine till tender but not brown. Stir in flour, tarragon or dillweed, and pepper. Add milk all at once. Cook and stir till mixture is thickened and bubbly. Stir in Romano or Parmesan cheese. Remove from heat. Stir in the drained salmon.

▬▬ In a mixing bowl beat egg yolks about 5 minutes or till thick and lemon colored. Gradually add the salmon mixture, stirring constantly. Cool about 5 minutes. Thoroughly wash beaters. In a mixing bowl beat egg whites till stiff peaks form (tips stand straight). Stir a small amount of stiff-beaten egg white into the salmon mixture. Gradually pour the salmon mixture over remaining egg white, folding gently to combine.

▬▬ Turn the mixture into an ungreased 1½-quart soufflé dish. Bake in a 325° oven for 40 to 50 minutes or till a knife inserted near the center comes out clean. Serve soufflé immediately. Makes 4 servings.

▬▬ Preparation time: 35 minutes
▬▬ Cooking time: 40 to 50 minutes

Salmon en Brioche

Salmon en Brioche is a fish within a fish. Once you seal the fish fillets and filling inside the *Brioche Dough*, shape and mark the dough to resemble your favorite catch.

Create the shape of the fish's head, using a hard-cooked egg, as shown opposite. To cook the egg, place 1 *egg* in a small saucepan and cover it with cold *water*. Bring the water to boiling, then reduce the heat to just below simmering. Cover and cook for 15 minutes. Run cold water over the egg till it is cool.

2 1½-pound fresh *or* frozen salmon fillets, skinned and boned
  Brioche Dough
3 cups finely chopped fresh mushrooms
2 shallots *or* green onions, chopped
1 tablespoon butter *or* margarine
1 beaten egg yolk
¾ cup soft bread crumbs (1 slice)
½ teaspoon dried dillweed
1 hard-cooked egg, shelled
1 beaten egg
  Thyme Sauce
  Fresh thyme (optional)
  Lime twist (optional)

▬▬▬ Thaw fish, if frozen. Prepare Brioche Dough. Trim fillets to equal sizes. Set aside. For filling, in a skillet cook mushrooms and shallots in hot butter or margarine about 10 minutes or till mixture is a thick paste, stirring constantly. Combine egg yolk, bread crumbs, dillweed, 2 tablespoons *water*, ¼ teaspoon *salt*, and ⅛ teaspoon *pepper;* stir into mushroom mixture. Cook and stir till thickened. Set aside.

▬▬▬ Cover a large baking sheet with foil; grease foil. Reserve *one-fourth* of the dough for fins. On a lightly floured surface roll *half* of the remaining dough into a rectangle 6 inches longer and 1½ inches wider than the fillets; transfer dough to baking sheet. Place one fish fillet, skinned side down, in center of dough.

Spread filling onto fillet. Top with second fish fillet, skinned side up. Place hard-cooked egg about ½ inch from wide end of fish, as shown.

▬▬▬ Combine beaten egg and 1 tablespoon *water;* brush onto edges of dough. Bring edges of dough up around egg and fillets; press. Brush with egg mixture. On a lightly floured surface roll the remaining half portion of dough into a rectangle 8 inches longer and 2 inches wider than the fillets. Place the dough rectangle atop fish; tuck edges of top layer under bottom layer. Press to seal in fillets.

▬▬▬ For head, shape dough over hard-cooked egg. For tail, shape dough at opposite end into a triangle. Prop up tail with a piece of crumpled foil, as shown. For fins, roll out the reserved dough; cut into fin shapes. Brush fins with egg mixture; press to sides of fish, as shown. Use a small spatula or table knife to mark lines for fins, tail, gills, and backbone. Use a small round cutter to mark scales and eye, as shown. (Do not cut through dough.) Brush with egg mixture. Chill in the refrigerator for 30 to 45 minutes.

▬▬▬ Brush dough with egg mixture. Bake in a 375° oven for 45 to 50 minutes or till golden, covering loosely with foil after 25 minutes. Meanwhile, prepare Thyme Sauce; serve with fish. Garnish with fresh thyme and lime twists, if desired. Makes 12 servings.

Brioche Dough: Soften 2 packages *active dry yeast* in ½ cup warm *water* (110° to 115°). Combine 3

beaten *eggs*, ⅓ cup melted *butter or margarine*, and ⅓ cup *cooking oil*. Stir in softened yeast. Stir together 1½ cups *all-purpose flour*, 3 tablespoons *sugar*, and 1 teaspoon *salt*. Add yeast mixture; beat well. Using a spoon, stir in an additional 2½ to 3 cups *all-purpose flour*. On a lightly floured surface knead in enough remaining flour to make a moderately stiff dough that is smooth and elastic (6 to 8 minutes total). Shape into a ball. Place into a greased bowl; turn once to grease surface. Cover; let rise in a warm place till double (about 1 hour). Punch down; let rest for 10 minutes.

Thyme Sauce: In a saucepan combine ⅓ cup *white wine vinegar*; 2 teaspoons finely chopped *shallots or green onion*; 1 teaspoon snipped *fresh thyme or* ¼ teaspoon *dried thyme*, crushed; and ⅛ teaspoon *white pepper*. Cook, uncovered, about 4 minutes or till volume is reduced to ¼ cup. Beat 8 *egg yolks* in the top of a double boiler. Slowly add reduced liquid. Cut 1 cup *butter or margarine* into 8 equal pieces. Add *one piece* of the butter to yolk mixture; place over boiling water (upper pan should not touch water). Cook and stir till butter melts and sauce begins to thicken. Continue adding remaining butter, *one piece* at a time, stirring constantly. Cook and stir till mixture is the consistency of thick cream. Remove from heat. Sprinkle with thinly sliced *green onion*, if desired

Preparation time: about 2 hours
Rising time: 1¼ hours
Chilling time: 30 to 45 minutes
Cooking time: 45 to 50 minutes

When marking the dough, press firmly enough to make sure the marks will appear after the dough bakes. Be careful not to press all the way through the dough to the fish fillets, or the filling may leak out and cause a soggy crust.

Souffléed Baked Eggs

Souffléed Baked Eggs

1   **10-ounce package frozen chopped broccoli**
1   **large onion, cut into thin wedges**
1   **clove garlic, minced**
2   **tablespoons butter *or* margarine**
⅓   **cup grated Parmesan cheese**
½   **teaspoon dried thyme, crushed**
1   **tablespoon butter *or* margarine**
1   **tablespoon all-purpose flour**
¼   **teaspoon salt**
    Dash pepper
½   **cup milk**
¼   **cup shredded cheddar cheese (1 ounce)**
8   **eggs**

▬ Cook broccoli according to package directions; drain well. In a skillet cook onion and garlic in the 2 tablespoons hot butter or margarine till onion is tender. Remove from heat; stir in broccoli, Parmesan cheese, and thyme. Turn into a 9- or 10-inch pie plate or quiche dish. Bake in a 325° oven for 15 minutes.

▬ Meanwhile, for soufflé mixture, in a saucepan melt the 1 tablespoon butter or margarine. Stir in flour, salt, and pepper. Add milk all at once. Cook and stir till thickened and bubbly. Add the shredded cheese, stirring till melted. Remove from heat. Separate 2 of the eggs; beat the 2 egg yolks till thick and lemon colored. Slowly add the cheese mixture to the beaten egg yolks, stirring constantly. Cool slightly. Thoroughly wash beaters. In a large mixing bowl beat the 2 egg whites till stiff peaks form (tips stand straight). Gradually pour the yolk mixture over the beaten whites, folding to combine.

▬ Using the back of a spoon, make 6 indentations in the center of hot broccoli mixture. Break remaining eggs into indentations. Spoon soufflé mixture around the edge of the pie plate. (The whole eggs should not be covered with soufflé mixture.) Bake in a 325° oven for 20 to 25 minutes or till soufflé is set and eggs in center are done. Serve immediately. Serves 6.

▬ Preparation time: 30 minutes
▬ Cooking time: 35 to 40 minutes

Oriental Omelet Bundles

2 **tablespoons dried mushrooms**
1¾ **cups water**
¾ **cup long grain rice**
¼ **cup dry white wine**
⅓ **to ½ cup cooking oil**
2 **tablespoons thinly sliced green onion**
½ **cup chopped fully cooked ham**
1 **tablespoon sweet pickle relish**
½ **teaspoon salt**
½ **teaspoon sugar**
1 **tablespoon cornstarch**
1 **tablespoon cold water**
4 **beaten eggs**
Soy sauce

■ For filling, soak mushrooms in enough warm water to cover for 30 minutes. Drain; squeeze out excess liquid. Chop mushrooms, discarding stems. In a saucepan combine the 1¾ cups water, the uncooked rice, and white wine. Bring to boiling; reduce heat. Cover and simmer over low heat for 20 to 25 minutes or till rice is done and liquid is absorbed. (The rice should be sticky.) Remove from heat.

■ Preheat a large skillet or wok over high heat; add *1 tablespoon* of the cooking oil. Stir-fry green onion in hot oil for 30 seconds. Add ham and stir-fry for 30 seconds. Add mushrooms and sweet pickle relish; stir-fry for 30 seconds. Stir in the cooked rice, salt, and sugar. Remove from heat.

■ Stir cornstarch into the 1 tablespoon cold water; stir into beaten eggs. Remove *1 tablespoon* of the egg mixture; set aside. In a 10-inch skillet with flared sides heat *1 tablespoon* of the cooking oil. Lift and tilt pan to coat sides. Remove pan from heat. Pour *about 3 tablespoons* of the egg mixture into hot pan. Lift and tilt pan to form a large, thin omelet (see top photograph at right). Return to heat. Cook for 1 to 2 minutes or till

egg is set on top, lifting sides with a spatula to loosen bottom. (The bottom should be light brown.) Carefully turn the omelet over; cook for 30 seconds more. Invert onto waxed paper. Repeat with remaining egg mixture to make 4 omelets.

■ Spoon ¾ *cup* of the rice filling across and just below the center of *one* omelet, leaving 1 inch on left and right sides; pat filling to compact. Fold in sides of omelet, then fold bottom and top over filling, forming an envelope (see lower photograph below). Brush edges with reserved egg mixture; press to seal in filling. Repeat with remaining omelets and rice filling.

■ Fry the filled omelets, seam side down, in a small amount of hot cooking oil till golden. Turn and cook till golden on the other side. Serve with soy sauce. Makes 2 servings.

■ Total preparation time: about 1¾ hours

In 10-inch skillet with flared sides heat 1 tablespoon cooking oil. Lift and tilt pan to coat sides. Remove from heat. Pour *about 3 tablespoons* of egg mixture into hot pan. Lift and tilt pan to form a large, thin omelet, as shown. Return to heat to cook omelet.

Spoon ¾ *cup* of the filling across and just below the center of omelet, leaving 1 inch on left and right sides; pat filling to compact. Fold in sides of omelet, then fold bottom and top over filling, forming an envelope, as shown. Brush with egg mixture; seal.

Savory rice-filled omelets are a delicious main dish for an Oriental meal. Or, they make the perfect appetizer for an international dinner party.

To make eight appetizer servings, first cut the fried omelet bundles in half. Then place each half on a piece of bok choy leaf.

If you do a little preparation ahead, this supper will go together in a jiffy.

Make the coleslaw, brownies, and spiced tea the morning of the big game.

After the game, while the potato casserole bakes, arrange the meat on a serving platter and pour the tea. All that remains is to set out the relishes and a basket of bakery-fresh buns on the buffet table.

Lima Beans with Apple

- 1 **medium onion, cut into thin wedges**
- 1 **small apple, coarsely chopped**
- 1 **clove garlic, minced**
- 2 **tablespoons butter *or* margarine**
- 2 **10-ounce packages frozen baby lima beans**
- 1 **8-ounce can stewed tomatoes**
- 2 **tablespoons brown sugar**
- 1 **teaspoon prepared mustard**
- 1 **teaspoon Worcestershire sauce**
  Dash ground cloves

■ Cook onion, apple, and garlic in hot butter till onion is tender. Stir in beans, tomatoes, brown sugar, mustard, Worcestershire sauce, and cloves. Bring to boiling; reduce heat. Simmer, covered, for 15 to 20 minutes or till beans are tender. Serves 6 to 8.

■ Total preparation time: 30 to 35 minutes

Oriental-Style Beans

- ⅓ **cup orange juice**
- 1 **tablespoon soy sauce**
- 1 **teaspoon cornstarch**
  Dash ground ginger
- 2 **tablespoons butter *or* margarine**
- 2 **green onions, thinly sliced**
- 2 **tablespoons slivered almonds**
- 1 **9-ounce package frozen Italian green beans, thawed**

■ Stir together orange juice, soy sauce, cornstarch, and ginger; set aside. In a wok or large skillet melt butter or margarine. Add the green onions and almonds; stir-fry for 2 minutes or till almonds are light brown. Add beans and stir-fry for 2 minutes more. Stir orange juice mixture; stir into bean mixture. Cook and stir till thickened and bubbly. Cover and cook for 1 minute more. Makes 4 servings.

■ Total preparation time: 20 minutes

Easy Cheesy Potato Bake

- 1 **24-ounce package frozen hash brown potatoes with onion and peppers**
- 1 **8-ounce jar cheese spread**
- ⅓ **cup cooked bacon pieces**
- ¼ **cup milk**

■ In a 12x7½x2-inch baking dish combine the potatoes, cheese spread, bacon pieces, and milk. Cover with foil and bake in a 350° oven for 30 minutes. Uncover; stir and bake 15 to 20 minutes more or till done. Stir before serving. Makes 6 servings.

■ Preparation time: 5 minutes
■ Cooking time: 45 to 50 minutes

Chived Potato Patties

- 3 **medium potatoes, peeled and cut up**
- 1 **slightly beaten egg**
- ½ **of a 3-ounce package cream cheese, softened**
- 2 **tablespoons snipped chives**
- ¼ **cup finely crushed rich round crackers**
- ¼ **cup butter *or* margarine**

■ Cook potatoes in boiling salted water till tender. Drain and mash. In a mixing bowl combine the egg, cream cheese, and chives; stir in potatoes. Cover and chill for 1 hour. Sprinkle *half* of the crushed crackers onto a piece of waxed paper. Spoon the potato mixture into 6 mounds atop crackers. Press down each mound to form six 1-inch-thick patties. Sprinkle the remaining crushed crackers atop potato patties.

■ In a 10-inch skillet melt butter or margarine over medium heat. Add potato patties and cook about 5 minutes on each side or till brown. Serves 6.

■ Preparation time: 30 minutes
■ Chilling time: 1 hour
■ Cooking time: 10 minutes

Blue Cheese and Brussels Sprouts Soufflé

- 1 **10-ounce package frozen brussels sprouts**
- ¼ **cup butter *or* margarine**
- ¼ **cup all-purpose flour**
- ½ **teaspoon salt**
- 1 **cup milk**
- ½ **cup shredded cheddar cheese (2 ounces)**
- ¼ **cup crumbled blue cheese (1 ounce)**
- 4 **egg yolks**
- 4 **egg whites**

■■■ In a saucepan cook the brussels sprouts according to package directions. Drain and finely chop the sprouts. Set aside.

■■■ In a saucepan melt the butter or margarine; stir in the flour and salt. Add milk all at once. Cook and stir till mixture is thickened and bubbly. Cook and stir for 1 minute more. Add the cheddar and blue cheeses; stir till cheeses are melted. Remove from heat.

■■■ In a mixer bowl beat egg yolks on high speed of electric mixer about 5 minutes or till thick and lemon colored. Slowly add the cheese mixture, stirring constantly. Stir in the chopped brussels sprouts.

■■■ Thoroughly wash the beaters. In a large mixer bowl beat egg whites till stiff peaks form (tips stand straight). Gradually pour the cheese-egg yolk mixture over beaten egg whites, gently folding to combine. Turn into an ungreased 1½-quart soufflé dish. Bake in a 350° oven for 35 to 45 minutes or till a knife inserted near center comes out clean. Makes 4 to 6 servings.

■■■ Preparation time: 25 minutes
■■■ Cooking time: 35 to 45 minutes

Pepper Cheese Tomatoes

- 2 **medium tomatoes, sliced ½ inch thick**
- 4 **ounces pepper cheese, sliced ¼ inch thick**
- 2 **tablespoons sliced pitted ripe olives**
- 1 **tablespoon sliced green onion**

■■■ In a broiler-proof shallow dish or pie plate place tomato slices, overlapping slightly if necessary. Broil 5 inches from heat for 3 to 4 minutes. Remove from broiler; top tomato slices with cheese slices. Sprinkle with olives and onion. Place under broiler for 2 minutes more or till cheese is melted. Makes 4 servings.

■■■ Preparation time: 10 minutes
■■■ Cooking time: 5 to 6 minutes

Zucchini and Onion au Gratin

- 3 **medium zucchini (about 1 pound), bias-sliced ½ inch thick**
- 1 **cup frozen small whole onions**
- 1 **11-ounce can condensed cheddar cheese soup**
- ⅓ **cup plain yogurt**
- 2 **dashes bottled hot pepper sauce**
- ⅓ **cup crushed rich round crackers**
- 1 **tablespoon butter *or* margarine, melted**

■■■ In a medium saucepan cook zucchini and the frozen onions in boiling salted water for 3 to 5 minutes or just till tender; drain well. Place the vegetables in a 10x6x2-inch baking dish.

■■■ Meanwhile, combine the condensed cheese soup, yogurt, and hot pepper sauce; pour over vegetables. For topping, combine the crushed crackers and melted butter or margarine; sprinkle over soup mixture. Bake, uncovered, in a 350° oven for 15 to 20 minutes or till heated through. Makes 6 servings.

■■■ Preparation time: 20 minutes
■■■ Cooking time: 15 to 20 minutes

Blue Cheese and Brussels Sprouts Soufflé, like all soufflés, should be served immediately after it's removed from the oven—before it has a chance to fall.

The best way to serve a soufflé is to insert two forks, back to back, into the soufflé. Then, gently pull apart into serving-size portions. (See the photograph on page 209.) Use a large serving spoon to transfer the soufflé to individual plates.

Cauliflower with Cheese Sauce,
Dilled Carrots

Cauliflower with Cheese Sauce

1 medium head cauliflower (about 1 pound)
1 1½-ounce envelope cheese sauce mix
½ cup shredded Swiss cheese (2 ounces)
1 2½-ounce jar sliced mushrooms, drained
1 to 2 tablespoons dry white wine
1 tablespoon snipped parsley (optional)

■ In a saucepan cook the head of cauliflower, covered, in a small amount of boiling salted water for 10 to 15 minutes or just till tender. Drain well.

■ Meanwhile, prepare the cheese sauce mix according to package directions. Add Swiss cheese and mushrooms; stir till cheese is melted. Stir in enough wine to make of desired consistency. Sprinkle cauliflower with parsley, if desired. Pass the cheese sauce with cauliflower. Makes 6 servings.

■ Total preparation time: 20 minutes

Dilled Carrots

20 small *or* baby carrots (1 pound)
2 tablespoons butter *or* margarine
1 tablespoon sunflower nuts
½ teaspoon snipped fresh dill
or ⅛ teaspoon dried dillweed
Fresh dill (optional)

■ Cut off all but 1 inch of the carrot tops and trim bottoms; wash thoroughly. In a saucepan cook carrots, covered, in a small amount of boiling salted water for 10 to 15 minutes or till crisp-tender; drain well.

■ Meanwhile, in a 10-inch skillet heat butter or margarine just till light brown. Stir in the sunflower nuts. Cook and stir over low heat till nuts are lightly toasted. Add carrots and dillweed; toss gently to coat. Garnish with fresh dill, if desired. Makes 6 servings.

■ Total preparation time: 30 minutes

Five-Fruit Salad with Peanut Butter Dressing

1 6-ounce can frozen pineapple juice concentrate, thawed
¼ cup creamy peanut butter
¾ cup salad oil
1 cup fresh peach slices *or* frozen loose-pack peach slices, *or* one 8-ounce can peach slices (juice pack)
Lemon juice (optional)
4 cups torn lettuce
1 cup fresh pineapple chunks *or* canned, drained pineapple chunks
¼ of a medium cantaloupe, peeled and sliced lengthwise
½ cup seedless green grapes, halved
½ cup fresh strawberries, halved

■ For dressing, in a blender container or food processor bowl place the pineapple juice concentrate and peanut butter. Cover and blend or process till smooth. With blender or processor running on high speed, gradually add the salad oil through hole in lid (*or,* tilt lid ajar); blend till smooth. Turn the dressing into a storage container. Cover and chill in the refrigerator about 2 hours or till cold.

■ Meanwhile, thaw peach slices, if frozen. (*Or,* drain canned peach slices.) If using fresh or thawed peaches, brush with lemon juice to prevent browning.

■ Before serving, place the lettuce on a serving platter; arrange the peach slices, pineapple chunks, cantaloupe slices, grape halves, and strawberry halves atop the lettuce. Stir the chilled dressing; pass with the salad. Makes 8 servings.

■ Advance preparation time: 10 minutes
■ Chilling time: at least 2 hours
■ Final preparation time: 30 minutes

To add a fun and interesting look to a casual supper party, use unconventional serving containers.

Gourmet cooking utensils—such as the steamer basket placed on a napkin-lined round baking pan or pizza pan, the au gratin pan, and the charlotte mold (all shown in photograph opposite), work well as serving dishes. Next time you plan a party, look around your house to see what you can come up with.

If small or baby carrots (as shown in the photograph opposite) are unavailable when you're ready to make *Dilled Carrots,* then substitute 6 medium *carrots* (1 pound).

Prepare the medium carrots for cooking by cutting them into ¼-inch-thick slices or julienne strips. Continue as directed in the recipe.

If you have the space in your freezer, keep cranberries on hand for a special cranberry treat, such as *Easy Fruit Salad,* when the berries are out of season.

To freeze cranberries, simply place an unopened package of fresh berries in the freezer for up to 12 months.

Just before using the cranberries, rinse them. The frozen berries need no thawing before you cook with them.

Easy Fruit Salad

- 1 11-ounce can mandarin orange sections
- 1 8¼-ounce can pineapple chunks
- 1 cup cranberries, finely chopped
- ½ cup raisins
- ½ cup chopped walnuts *or* pecans
- ½ of a 4-ounce container frozen whipped dessert topping, thawed
- ¼ cup mayonnaise *or* salad dressing
  Lettuce leaves

■■■ Drain oranges. Drain pineapple, reserving 1 tablespoon of the syrup. Combine pineapple chunks, orange sections, cranberries, raisins, and nuts. Stir together the topping, mayonnaise, and reserved pineapple syrup. Fold into fruit mixture. Chill for 2 to 3 hours. Serve in a lettuce-lined bowl. Serves 6 to 8.

■■■ Preparation time: 25 minutes
■■■ Chilling time: 2 to 3 hours

Blueberry and Banana Salad

- 3⅓ cups unsweetened pineapple juice
- 1 6-ounce package lemon-flavored gelatin
- 1 8-ounce carton dairy sour cream
- 2 cups fresh *or* frozen unsweetened blueberries
- 1 large banana, chopped
  Lettuce leaves

■■■ In a saucepan bring *1⅓ cups* of the pineapple juice to boiling. Dissolve the gelatin in boiling juice. Remove from heat. Stir in the remaining juice. Gradually stir the gelatin mixture into the sour cream. Chill to the consistency of unbeaten egg whites (partially set). Fold in the blueberries and banana. Turn into a 6½-cup mold. Chill about 6 hours or till firm. Unmold onto a lettuce-lined serving platter. Makes 12 servings.

■■■ Preparation time: 1¼ hours
■■■ Chilling time: at least 6 hours

Raspberry-Peach Salad

- 1 3-ounce package raspberry-flavored gelatin
- 1 3-ounce package orange-pineapple-flavored gelatin
- 2 cups boiling water
- 1 10-ounce package frozen red raspberries
- 1 10-ounce package frozen peach slices
- 1 8½-ounce can applesauce
- 2 tablespoons sugar
- 1 teaspoon all-purpose flour
- ½ teaspoon salt
- ⅓ cup milk
- 1 slightly beaten egg yolk
- 1 teaspoon butter *or* margarine
- 1 4-ounce container frozen whipped dessert topping, thawed
  Ground cinnamon

■■■ In a mixing bowl dissolve the raspberry- and orange-pineapple-flavored gelatins in boiling water. Add the frozen raspberries and peaches, stirring till thawed. Stir in the applesauce. Pour the gelatin mixture into a 13x9x2-inch baking dish or a 3-quart serving bowl. Cover and chill in the refrigerator about 6 hours or till the mixture is firm.

■■■ Meanwhile, for topping, in a small saucepan combine the sugar, flour, and salt. Stir in the milk. Add the egg yolk. Cook and stir till bubbly. Cook and stir for 2 minutes more. Add the butter or margarine; stir till butter is melted. Cool. Fold the egg yolk mixture into dessert topping. Cover and chill about 1 hour.

■■■ To serve, cut the gelatin mixture in the rectangular dish into squares or spoon from the serving bowl. Dollop each serving with some of the topping and sprinkle with cinnamon. Makes 12 to 15 servings.

■■■ Preparation time: 30 minutes
■■■ Chilling time: at least 6 hours

Curried Coleslaw

    3   cups shredded cabbage
    ¼   cup thinly sliced celery
    ¼   cup shredded carrot
    ¼   cup coconut
    ¼   cup currants *or* raisins
    ⅔   cup mayonnaise *or* salad dressing
    1   tablespoon lemon juice
    1   clove garlic, minced
    ½   teaspoon curry powder
    ½   cup coarsely chopped cashews

▬ In a large bowl combine the first 5 ingredients. In a small bowl combine next 4 ingredients; toss with salad. Chill. Fold in nuts before serving. Serves 6.

▬ Preparation time: 25 minutes
▬ Chilling time: at least 2 hours

Hot Watercress-Potato Salad

    1   pound unpeeled red potatoes, cut into
            1-inch cubes
    2   slices bacon
    4   teaspoons all-purpose flour
    3   tablespoons tarragon vinegar
    4   teaspoons sugar
    1½ teaspoons instant chicken bouillon
            granules
    4   cups torn watercress

▬ Cook potatoes in enough boiling salted water to cover for 12 to 15 minutes or till tender; drain. In a skillet cook bacon till crisp. Remove bacon, reserving drippings in pan. Drain bacon; crumble and set aside. Stir flour into drippings. Add vinegar, sugar, bouillon granules, ¾ cup *water,* and dash *pepper.* Cook and stir till bubbly. Add watercress; cook, stirring occasionally, for 3 minutes or till wilted. Add potatoes; heat through. Turn into a bowl; top with bacon. Serves 4.

▬ Total preparation time: 40 minutes

Garden Pasta Salad

    6   ounces spaghetti *or* fettuccine, broken up
    4   medium tomatoes, peeled, seeded, and
            coarsely chopped
    1   medium cucumber, seeded and chopped
    1   4-ounce can green chili peppers, rinsed,
            seeded, and chopped
    ¼   cup snipped parsley
    3   tablespoons chopped onion
    ¼   cup Italian salad dressing
        Several dashes bottled hot pepper sauce
    1   cup crumbled feta cheese (4 ounces)

▬ Cook pasta; drain. Rinse with cold water. Meanwhile, combine next 5 ingredients. Cover; chill. Combine dressing and hot pepper sauce. Toss with pasta. Cover; chill. To serve, turn pasta into bowl. Spoon tomato mixture and feta cheese atop; toss. Serves 6.

▬ Preparation time: 30 minutes
▬ Chilling time: at least 3 hours

Cucumber Salad

    2   medium cucumbers, peeled
    2   tablespoons vinegar
    1   tablespoon salad oil
    1   teaspoon sugar
    1   clove garlic, minced
    ⅛   to ¼ teaspoon ground red pepper
    1   tablespoon sesame seed, toasted
    1   tablespoon thinly sliced green onion

▬ Score cucumbers by running tines of fork down sides; thinly slice. Arrange on a serving platter. In a screw-top jar combine the vinegar, oil, sugar, garlic, and red pepper. Cover; shake well to mix. Drizzle over cucumbers. Sprinkle with sesame seed and green onion. Cover; chill about 2 hours. Serves 6 to 8.

▬ Preparation time: 20 minutes
▬ Chilling time: at least 2 hours

▬▬ MENU ▬▬
PICNIC SUPPER

Grilled Hamburgers
with Buns

Curried Coleslaw

Chilled Cantaloupe
Wedges

Cupcakes

Carbonated Beverage

Pack up the portable grill and tote it to the park for a casual picnic supper. Keep the coleslaw chilled on ice and remember to take along condiments for the burgers—catsup, mustard, and pickle relish.
    To make the cleanup when "dining out" simple, use paper plates, napkins, and cups, and plastic eating utensils.

Homemade Herb Linguine with Cheesy Sauce

Homemade Herb Linguine with Cheesy Sauce*

- 10 ounces Homemade Herb Linguine *or* other pasta
- 3 beaten eggs
- 3 tablespoons milk
- ¼ teaspoon ground nutmeg
- 3 tablespoons butter *or* margarine, softened
- ½ cup grated Romano *or* Parmesan cheese
- ¼ cup shredded Swiss cheese (1 ounce)

■■■ Prepare Homemade Herb Linguine; cook in boiling salted water for 10 minutes or till tender. (*Or,* cook pasta according to package directions.) Drain. Meanwhile, in a saucepan combine eggs, milk, and nutmeg; cook and stir over medium-low heat about 3 minutes or just till warm. Toss cooked pasta with butter. Add egg mixture; toss to coat. Add Romano or Parmesan and Swiss cheeses; toss gently to mix. Serve immediately. If desired, garnish with additional finely shredded Swiss cheese and fresh basil. Season to taste with salt and pepper. Makes 6 servings.

Homemade Herb Linguine: In a mixing bowl stir together 2 cups *all-purpose flour,* 1 tablespoon snipped *parsley,* 1 tablespoon chopped fresh *basil,* and ½ teaspoon *salt.* Make a well in the center. Combine 2 beaten *eggs,* ⅓ cup *water,* and 1 teaspoon *olive oil or cooking oil.* Stir into flour mixture; mix well.

■■■ Sprinkle kneading surface with ⅓ cup *all-purpose flour.* Turn dough out onto the floured surface. Knead till dough is smooth and elastic (8 to 10 minutes). Cover and let rest for 10 minutes. (Dough can be refrigerated for up to 3 days or frozen for longer storage.) Divide dough into thirds. On a lightly floured surface roll each portion into a 16x12-inch rectangle. After rolling, let dough stand about 20 minutes to dry surface slightly. To cut by hand, roll up dough loosely and cut into ¼-inch-wide slices. Lift and shake to separate pasta. (If using a pasta machine, follow the manufacturer's directions.) Makes 1 pound pasta.

■■■ Total preparation time: 1½ hours
* *pictured on the cover*

Baked Granola-Oatmeal Puff

- 1 tablespoon butter *or* margarine, softened
- ⅓ cup granola, crushed
- 2 cups apple juice
- 1 cup quick-cooking rolled oats
- ¾ teaspoon ground cinnamon
- ½ teaspoon salt
- ⅛ teaspoon ground cloves
- 3 egg yolks
- 1 teaspoon vanilla
- 3 egg whites
 Maple-flavored syrup *or* light cream

■■■ Grease an 8x8x2-inch baking dish with the butter or margarine. Turn the granola into dish; spread evenly. Press granola onto bottom and sides of dish to form a firm, even crust; set aside.

■■■ In a medium saucepan bring apple juice to boiling. Slowly add oats, cinnamon, salt, and cloves to boiling juice, stirring constantly. Cook, stirring occasionally, for 1 minute. Remove from heat; set aside.

■■■ In a mixer bowl beat egg yolks on high speed of electric mixer about 5 minutes or till thick and lemon colored. Stir in vanilla. Stir in the oatmeal mixture. Thoroughly wash the beaters. In a large mixer bowl beat egg whites till stiff peaks form (tips stand straight). Fold oatmeal mixture into egg whites.

■■■ Turn the mixture into prepared dish. Bake in a 325° oven for 35 to 40 minutes or till a knife inserted near center comes out clean. Serve warm with maple-flavored syrup or light cream. Makes 8 servings.

■■■ Preparation time: 25 minutes
■■■ Cooking time: 35 to 40 minutes

MENU
BRUNCH FOR WEEKEND GUESTS

Fruit Cup

Baked Granola-Oatmeal Puff with Maple Syrup or Cream

Crisp Bacon

Coffee

When entertaining weekend guests it's best if you can simplify menu preparations by planning to cook just a few items.
 For this brunch, save time by purchasing a chilled citrus fruit mixture, rather than sectioning the fruit yourself.

MENU
EASTER BRUNCH

Sliced Strawberries
with Powdered Sugar

Scrambled Eggs

Sausage Patties

Easter Nest
Coffee Cake

Coffee

Impress your guests with the presentation of the food. A meal always seems to taste better when it appeals to the eye as well as the palate.

Arrange the strawberries in stemmed glassware, such as wine or parfait glasses. Sprinkle them with powdered sugar just before serving and add a sprig of fresh mint for a garnish.

Feature *Easter Nest Coffee Cake* as your spectacular centerpiece. Its unusual shape will delight your friends as well as decorate your dining table.

Use two-thirds of the dough to make the "nest" for *Easter Nest Coffee Cake*. Shape this portion of dough into two 26-inch-long ropes and gently twist them together, as shown.

Wrap the twisted ropes of dough around the six "eggs" placed on the greased baking sheet, as shown. Seal the ends of the dough together.

Easter Nest Coffee Cake

2¾ **to 3¼ cups all-purpose flour**
1 **package active dry yeast**
¾ **cup milk**
¼ **cup sugar**
¼ **cup butter *or* margarine**
1 **egg**
   Shredded coconut
1 **or 2 drops green *or* yellow food coloring**
   Powdered Sugar Icing
   Small multicolored decorative candies

■■■ In a large mixer bowl combine *1½ cups* of the flour and the yeast. In a saucepan heat milk, sugar, butter or margarine, and 1 teaspoon *salt* just till warm (115° to 120°) and butter is almost melted; stir constantly. Add to flour mixture; add egg. Beat on low speed of electric mixer for ½ minute, scraping bowl. Beat 3 minutes on high speed. Using a spoon, stir in as much remaining flour as you can. Turn out onto a lightly floured surface. Knead in enough remaining flour to make a moderately stiff dough that is smooth and elastic (6 to 8 minutes total). Shape into a ball. Place into a lightly greased bowl; turn once to grease surface. Cover; let rise till double (about 1 hour).

■■■ Punch down; divide into thirds. Cover; let rest 10 minutes. Shape *one-third* of the dough into 6 "eggs"; place close together in center of a greased baking sheet. For the "nest," shape remaining dough into two 26-inch-long ropes. Twist ropes together (see top photograph at left). Wrap ropes around eggs (see lower photograph at left); seal the ends together. Cover; let rise till nearly double (about 1 hour). Bake in a 375° oven for 15 to 20 minutes or till golden. Remove from baking sheet; cool on a wire rack. Tint coconut with food coloring. Make Powdered Sugar Icing; frost coffee cake. Before icing dries, sprinkle the eggs with candies and the nest with coconut. Makes 1.

Powdered Sugar Icing: Combine 1 cup sifted *powdered sugar* and ¼ teaspoon *vanilla*. Stir in *milk* (about 1½ tablespoons) till of spreading consistency.

■■■ Total preparation time: 3½ hours

Applesauce Muffins

1 **slightly beaten egg**
½ **cup applesauce**
¼ **cup packed brown sugar**
¼ **cup milk**
2 **tablespoons cooking oil**
2 **cups packaged biscuit mix**
½ **cup chopped walnuts**
½ **cup raisins**

■■■ Combine the first 5 ingredients; add mix. Stir just till moistened but still lumpy. Stir in nuts and raisins. Grease muffin cups or line with paper bake cups; fill ⅔ full. Bake in a 400° oven for 20 minutes. Makes 12.

■■■ Total preparation time: 30 minutes

Basic Biscuits

2 cups all-purpose flour
1 tablespoon baking powder
½ teaspoon salt
½ cup shortening
¾ cup milk

In a mixing bowl stir together the flour, baking powder, and salt. Cut in shortening till mixture resembles coarse crumbs. Make a well in the center; add milk all at once. Stir just till dough clings together.

Knead dough gently on a lightly floured surface for 10 to 12 strokes. Roll or pat to ½-inch thickness. Cut with a 2½-inch biscuit cutter, dipping cutter into flour between cuts. Transfer biscuits to an ungreased baking sheet. Bake in a 450° oven for 10 to 12 minutes or till golden. Serve warm. Makes 8 or 9 biscuits.

Orange Twists: Prepare Basic Biscuits as above, *except* add 2 tablespoons *sugar* to dry ingredients in mixing bowl. On a lightly floured surface roll dough into a 15x8-inch rectangle. Combine ½ cup *orange marmalade* and ½ teaspoon *rum flavoring;* spread over dough. Sprinkle with ¼ cup *coconut.*

Fold the dough in half lengthwise to make a 15x4-inch rectangle. Cut the dough into fifteen 1-inch-wide strips. Holding a strip at both ends, twist in opposite directions twice, forming a spiral. Place onto a lightly greased baking sheet. Bake in a 450° oven for 10 to 12 minutes or till golden. Makes 15 twists.

Preparation time: 15 minutes
Cooking time: 10 to 12 minutes

Whole Wheat and Orange Coffee Cake

2 cups whole wheat flour
½ cup sugar
1 tablespoon baking powder
1 teaspoon ground cinnamon
¼ teaspoon salt
1 medium unpeeled orange, seeded and cut into chunks
2 eggs
½ cup water
¼ cup butter *or* margarine, cut up
½ cup raisins
¾ cup sifted powdered sugar
⅛ teaspoon ground cinnamon
   Orange juice

Grease a 9x1½-inch round baking pan; set aside. In a large mixing bowl combine the whole wheat flour, sugar, baking powder, the 1 teaspoon cinnamon, and the salt. In a blender container or food processor bowl combine the orange chunks, eggs, water, and butter or margarine; cover and blend or process till the orange is finely chopped.

Make a well in the center of the dry ingredients; add the orange mixture, stirring just till moistened. Stir in the raisins. Turn the batter into the prepared pan. Bake in a 350° oven about 40 minutes or till done. Cool on a wire rack.

For icing, combine the powdered sugar, the ⅛ teaspoon cinnamon, and enough orange juice (1 to 2 tablespoons) to make of drizzling consistency. Drizzle icing over cooled cake. Makes 1 coffee cake.

Preparation time: 20 minutes
Cooking time: 40 minutes
Cooling time: 30 minutes

To dress up *Basic Biscuits,* brush the tops of the unbaked biscuits with a little melted butter or margarine or milk. Then sprinkle lightly with caraway seed, sesame seed, poppy seed, dillweed, or a mixture of sugar and cinnamon. Choose a topping that complements the flavors of the other foods in your menu. Continue baking as directed in the recipe.

Fried doughnuts are a favorite any time, especially when you introduce your guests to the light texture of *Doughnut Twists*.

To eliminate any messy last-minute preparation, you can make these holeless doughnuts ahead.

Prepare and shape the dough as directed in the recipe. Place the dough twists onto a greased baking sheet. Cover and store them in the refrigerator overnight.

Before you start frying, let the dough stand at room temperature for 1 hour. Then fry the twists in deep hot fat (375°) about 2 minutes on each side or till golden. Drain the doughnuts on paper toweling and sprinkle them with powdered sugar.

Cheesy Whole Wheat Fingers

- 1 16-ounce loaf frozen whole wheat bread dough, thawed
- ¼ cup chopped onion
- 1 tablespoon butter *or* margarine
- 1 teaspoon dried oregano, crushed
- ½ teaspoon garlic salt
- ½ teaspoon celery seed
- ½ teaspoon paprika
- 2 cups shredded cheddar cheese (8 ounces)

▬▬ On a floured surface roll dough into a 13x9-inch rectangle. (If difficult to roll, cover. Let rest 10 minutes; finish rolling.) Place into a greased 13x9x2-inch baking pan. Cover; let rise till nearly double (about 1½ hours). Cook onion in butter till tender. Add seasonings; cool slightly. Stir in cheese. Spoon atop dough. Bake in a 375° oven for 20 to 25 minutes or till done. Cut into 3x1½-inch strips; serve warm. Makes 24.

▬▬ Total preparation time: 2¼ hours

Date-Walnut Ring

- 1 cup chopped pitted dates
- 1 cup cooking oil
- 3 slightly beaten eggs
- 1 teaspoon vanilla
- 3 cups all-purpose flour
- 1½ cups sugar
- 1 teaspoon baking soda
- 1 cup chopped walnuts

▬▬ In a saucepan bring 1½ cups *water* to boiling; remove from heat. Stir in dates; cool for 15 minutes. Stir in oil, eggs, and vanilla. Combine flour, sugar, soda, and ½ teaspoon *salt;* add to date mixture. Stir till combined; stir in nuts. Turn into a greased 10-inch tube pan; bake in a 350° oven for 45 to 50 minutes, covering with foil the last 15 minutes. Cool. Makes 1.

▬▬ Total preparation time: 1½ hours

Doughnut Twists

- 3 to 3½ cups all-purpose flour
- 1 package active dry yeast
- 2 teaspoons aniseed (optional)
- 1 cup milk
- ⅓ cup butter *or* margarine
- 2 tablespoons sugar
- 1 teaspoon salt
- 1 egg
   Cooking oil *or* shortening for deep-fat frying
   Powdered sugar (optional)

▬▬ In a large mixer bowl combine *1¾ cups* of the flour, the yeast, and aniseed, if desired. In a saucepan heat milk, butter or margarine, sugar, and salt just till warm (115° to 120°) and butter is almost melted; stir constantly. Add to flour mixture; add egg. Beat on low speed of electric mixer for ½ minute, scraping the sides of the bowl constantly. Beat for 3 minutes on high speed. Using a spoon, stir in as much of the remaining flour as you can.

▬▬ Turn the dough out onto a lightly floured surface. Knead in enough of the remaining flour to make a moderately soft dough that is smooth and elastic (3 to 5 minutes total). Shape into a ball. Place into a lightly greased bowl; turn once to grease surface. Cover; let rise in a warm place till double (1 to 1½ hours).

▬▬ Punch the dough down. Cover; let rest for 10 minutes. Divide the dough into 24 portions. Roll each portion into a rope 12 inches long. Fold each rope in half; twist tightly (the dough relaxes slightly as it rises). Cover and let rise in a warm place till nearly double (30 to 45 minutes).

▬▬ In a large saucepan or deep-fat fryer heat cooking oil or shortening to 375°. Fry the dough twists, a few at a time, for 2 to 3 minutes or till golden brown. Drain on paper toweling. If desired, sprinkle powdered sugar over top. Makes 24 doughnuts.

▬▬ Preparation time: 50 minutes
▬▬ Rising time: 1½ to 2¼ hours
▬▬ Cooking time: about 25 minutes

Doughnut Twists

Making delicious cakes is easy—if you follow these hints:

Preheat your oven to the correct temperature before you start to mix the cake batter.

Place the baking pans as near to the center of the oven as possible. Air should circulate freely around cakes during baking, so make sure pans do not touch each other or the sides of the oven. If the pans won't fit on one oven shelf, stagger them on two shelves, but avoid placing one directly under another.

Allow cakes to cool thoroughly on a wire rack before frosting. This will take about 1 hour.

Easy Peanut-Butterscotch Cake

¼	cup peanut butter
¼	cup butter *or* margarine
1½	cups all-purpose flour
¾	cup milk
½	cup packed brown sugar
1	egg
2½	teaspoons baking powder
1½	teaspoons vanilla
½	teaspoon salt
½	of a 6-ounce package (½ cup) butterscotch pieces
	Chocolate-Peanut Frosting

▄▄▄ Grease and lightly flour a 9x9x2-inch baking pan; set aside. In a medium mixer bowl combine the peanut butter and the butter or margarine; beat on medium speed of electric mixer for 30 seconds. Add the flour, milk, brown sugar, egg, baking powder, vanilla, and salt; beat on low speed of electric mixer till combined. Beat for 2 minutes on medium speed.

▄▄▄ Pour *half* of the batter into the prepared pan. Sprinkle *half* of the butterscotch pieces over batter in pan. Pour the remaining batter over butterscotch pieces, spreading evenly. Sprinkle the remaining butterscotch pieces atop. Bake in a 375° oven for 25 to 30 minutes or till cake tests done. Cool in the pan on a wire rack. Prepare Chocolate-Peanut Frosting; frost top of cake. Cut into squares. Makes 9 servings.

Chocolate-Peanut Frosting: In a small mixer bowl beat 3 tablespoons *peanut butter* on medium speed of electric mixer till light and fluffy. Gradually add 1 cup sifted *powdered sugar*, beating till combined. Add 1 square (1 ounce) *unsweetened chocolate,* melted and cooled; 2 tablespoons *milk;* and 1 teaspoon *vanilla;* beat till smooth. Gradually beat in an additional 1 cup sifted *powdered sugar*. Beat in additional milk (1 to 2 tablespoons), if necessary, to make of spreading consistency.

▄▄▄ Total preparation time: 2 hours

Buttery Rum Cake

¾	cup chopped pecans
½	cup coconut
1	package 2-layer-size yellow cake mix
¼	cup rum
1	cup sugar
½	cup butter *or* margarine
¼	cup water
¼	cup rum

▄▄▄ Grease and lightly flour a 10-inch fluted tube pan. Sprinkle the chopped pecans and the coconut evenly in the bottom of the pan; set aside.

▄▄▄ Prepare the cake mix according to package directions, *except* substitute ¼ cup rum for ¼ cup of the water called for in the directions. Turn batter into the prepared pan. Bake in a 350° oven for 40 to 45 minutes or till cake tests done.

▄▄▄ Meanwhile, for glaze, in a small saucepan combine the sugar, butter or margarine, and water. Bring to boiling; boil gently for 5 minutes. Remove from heat and stir in ¼ cup rum.

▄▄▄ When the cake is done, do not remove from the pan. Place on a wire rack. Prick holes over the cake's surface with tines of a fork. Slowly spoon about *half* of the glaze over hot cake. Let stand for 10 minutes, allowing the glaze to soak in. Invert onto a serving platter; remove the pan. Prick holes in the top of the cake with tines of fork. Slowly spoon the remaining glaze over cake. Cool thoroughly. Makes 12 servings.

▄▄▄ Preparation time: 35 minutes
▄▄▄ Cooking time: 40 to 45 minutes

Rhubarb Cream Torte

- 1 frozen loaf pound cake
- 1½ cups fresh *or* frozen rhubarb cut into ½-inch pieces
- ¼ cup sugar
- 2 tablespoons water
- ¼ cup cranberry-orange relish
- 1 tablespoon cornstarch
- ⅛ teaspoon pumpkin pie spice *or* ground cinnamon
  Few drops red food coloring (optional)
- 2 tablespoons crème de cacao, cranberry liqueur, *or* orange liqueur (optional)
- 1 4-ounce container frozen whipped dessert topping, thawed

■ Let the pound cake stand at room temperature to thaw. Meanwhile, for filling, in a small saucepan combine rhubarb, sugar, and water. Bring to boiling; reduce heat. Cover and simmer for 3 minutes. Combine the cranberry-orange relish, cornstarch, and pumpkin pie spice or cinnamon; add to the rhubarb mixture. Cook and stir till thickened and bubbly. Cook and stir for 2 minutes more. Add the red food coloring, if desired. Cool slightly.

■ Slice the pound cake horizontally into 3 layers. Place the bottom cake layer on a serving platter. If desired, drizzle *1 tablespoon* of the crème de cacao, cranberry liqueur, or orange liqueur over bottom layer. Reserve *¼ cup* of the rhubarb mixture. Spread *half* of the remaining rhubarb mixture over the bottom cake layer. Place the second cake layer atop. If desired, drizzle the remaining crème de cacao, cranberry liqueur, or orange liqueur over the second cake layer. Spread the remaining half of the rhubarb mixture over cake. Add the top cake layer.

■ Swirl the dessert topping over the sides and top of cake. Spoon the reserved rhubarb mixture atop. Cover and chill in the refrigerator about 3 hours or till cold. Slice to serve. Makes 8 to 10 servings.

■ Preparation time: 50 minutes
■ Chilling time: at least 3 hours

Doughnut Brunch Pudding

- 6 day-old plain cake doughnuts
- ½ cup finely snipped dried apricots
- ¼ cup toasted, slivered almonds
- 4 slightly beaten eggs
- 2 cups milk
- ½ cup sugar
- ¼ teaspoon salt
- ¼ teaspoon ground allspice
  Almond Sauce

■ Cut the doughnuts vertically into ½-inch-thick pieces. Arrange the doughnut pieces in an 8x8x2-inch baking dish or 8x1½-inch round baking dish. Sprinkle the snipped dried apricots and toasted, slivered almonds over doughnut pieces.

■ In a medium mixing bowl combine the beaten eggs, milk, sugar, salt, and allspice. Pour the egg mixture over the doughnut pieces, apricots, and almonds. Bake in a 325° oven for 50 to 55 minutes or till a knife inserted near the center comes out clean. Let stand for 5 minutes.

■ Meanwhile, prepare Almond Sauce. To serve, spoon some of the Almond Sauce over each serving. Makes 6 to 8 servings.

Almond Sauce: In a small mixing bowl combine 2 beaten *egg yolks*, ¼ cup sifted *powdered sugar*, 1 tablespoon *dry white wine or dry sherry*, several drops *almond extract*, and a dash *salt*. In a medium mixing bowl beat ½ cup *whipping cream* till soft peaks form. Gently fold the whipped cream into egg yolk mixture.

■ Preparation time: 20 minutes
■ Cooking time: 50 to 55 minutes
■ Standing time: 5 minutes

Doughnut Brunch Pudding is a delightful dessert that calls for leftover cake doughnuts. In fact, the doughnuts need to be leftover or at least a day old. If they are not dried out, the pudding will have a soggy texture.
  To make sure the doughnuts are dry enough, you may need to leave them out, uncovered, for several hours or overnight before preparing the recipe.

To give your *Almond Tea Cookies* a textured surface, flatten the balls of cookie dough with a fork. Simply press the fork tines (dipped in sugar, if desired) across the dough in a straight or a crisscross pattern. Or use a cookie stamp to press down the centers.

Pretzel Cookies

    3 cups all-purpose flour
    1 teaspoon baking powder
    1 teaspoon ground ginger
    1 teaspoon ground cinnamon
    ½ teaspoon baking soda
    ¼ teaspoon salt
    ½ cup butter *or* margarine
    ½ cup shortening
    ¾ cup packed brown sugar
    1 egg
    ¼ cup molasses
       Sugar

▬ Grease a cookie sheet. In a mixing bowl stir together the flour, baking powder, ginger, cinnamon, baking soda, and salt. In a large mixer bowl beat butter or margarine and shortening on medium speed of electric mixer for 30 seconds. Add brown sugar and beat till fluffy. Add the egg and molasses; beat well. Add the dry ingredients to the beaten mixture and beat till combined. Cover and chill in the refrigerator about 3 hours or till easy to handle.

▬ Divide the dough in half; keep one portion chilled till ready to use. On a well-floured surface roll remaining portion of dough into a 10x5-inch rectangle. Using a sharp knife, cut the rectangle into twenty 5x½-inch strips. Using hands, roll each strip into a 9-inch-long rope. To shape, form one rope of dough into a circle, overlapping about 1 inch from each end and leaving the ends free. Take one end of dough in each hand and twist at the point where dough overlaps (see photograph at upper right). Carefully lift ends across to the opposite edge of the circle. Tuck the ends under edge to make a pretzel shape. Place onto the prepared cookie sheet. Sprinkle the tops of cookies with sugar. Bake in a 375° oven for 6 to 8 minutes or till done. Cool for 1 minute before transferring to a wire rack. Repeat with remaining dough. Makes 40.

▬ Preparation time: 1 hour
▬ Chilling time: at least 3 hours
▬ Cooking time: 20 to 25 minutes

To shape a pretzel cookie, take one of the free ends of the dough circle in each hand and twist at the point where the dough overlaps, as shown. Carefully lift the ends across to the opposite edge of the circle.

Almond Tea Cookies

    1¾ cups all-purpose flour
     ½ cup ground almonds
      1 cup butter *or* margarine
     ⅓ cup packed brown sugar
     ¼ teaspoon almond extract

▬ In a mixing bowl stir together the flour and ground almonds. In a mixer bowl beat butter or margarine on medium speed of electric mixer for 30 seconds. Add brown sugar and almond extract; beat till fluffy. Stir in the dry ingredients.

▬ Shape the dough into 1-inch balls. Place 2 inches apart onto an ungreased cookie sheet. Press the centers of cookies with a cookie stamp, or crisscross with the tines of a fork. Bake in a 325° oven for 16 to 18 minutes or till done. Transfer to a wire rack; cool. Makes about 48 cookies.

▬ Preparation time: 30 minutes
▬ Cooking time: about 1 hour

Peanut Butter and Jam Bars

⅔ cup all-purpose flour
½ cup packed brown sugar
¼ teaspoon baking soda
⅛ teaspoon salt
¼ cup peanut butter
3 tablespoons shortening
¼ cup quick-cooking rolled oats
1 slightly beaten egg
1 tablespoon milk
½ teaspoon vanilla
¼ cup all-purpose flour
¼ cup quick-cooking rolled oats
2 tablespoons brown sugar
⅛ teaspoon salt
2 tablespoons butter or margarine
¼ cup raspberry jam or preserves

■■■ Grease an 8x8x2-inch baking pan; set aside. In a medium mixing bowl stir together the ⅔ cup flour, the ½ cup brown sugar, baking soda, and ⅛ teaspoon salt; cut in peanut butter and shortening till mixture resembles coarse crumbs. Add ¼ cup oats, egg, milk, and vanilla; mix well. Spread in the prepared pan. Bake in a 375° oven for 10 minutes.

■■■ Meanwhile, for topping, stir together the ¼ cup flour, ¼ cup oats, the 2 tablespoons brown sugar, and ⅛ teaspoon salt; cut in the butter or margarine till mixture resembles coarse crumbs. Set aside.

■■■ Spoon the raspberry jam or preserves evenly over the baked layer. Sprinkle the topping over jam or preserves. Bake in a 375° oven for 12 to 15 minutes more or till light brown. Cool in the pan on a wire rack. Cut into bars. Makes 18 bars.

■■■ Preparation time: 30 minutes
■■■ Cooking time: 22 to 25 minutes

Old-Fashioned Blueberry-Oatmeal Cookies

2 cups all-purpose flour
1 teaspoon baking powder
1 teaspoon salt
½ teaspoon baking soda
1 cup butter or margarine
2 cups sugar
2 eggs
1 teaspoon vanilla
¾ teaspoon finely shredded lemon peel
1 cup quick-cooking rolled oats
1 cup fresh blueberries or frozen unsweetened blueberries, thawed
½ cup chopped pecans

■■■ In a medium mixing bowl stir together the flour, baking powder, salt, and baking soda. In a mixer bowl beat butter or margarine on medium speed of electric mixer for 30 seconds. Add sugar and beat till fluffy. Add eggs, vanilla, and lemon peel; beat well. Add the dry ingredients to the beaten mixture and beat till combined. Fold in the oats, blueberries, and pecans.

■■■ Drop from a teaspoon 2 inches apart onto an ungreased cookie sheet. Bake in a 375° oven for 10 to 12 minutes or till done. Let stand about 1 minute before transferring to a wire rack; cool. Makes about 54.

■■■ Preparation time: 25 to 30 minutes
■■■ Cooking time: 40 to 50 minutes

You'll like *Old-Fashioned Blueberry-Oatmeal Cookies* so much you'll want to fix them again soon. When you do, however, try this different variation. Substitute one 6-ounce package (1 cup) *semisweet chocolate pieces* for the blueberries.

Near the end of the suggested baking time, gently touch a light brown cookie with your fingertip. If your finger leaves a barely visible imprint, the cookie is done.

After you remove one cookie batch from the cookie sheet, cool the baked cookies on a wire rack to let air circulate and prevent them from becoming soggy. For your next batch, be sure to use a cool cookie sheet to keep the cookies from spreading and becoming too thin.

beat on medium speed of electric mixer till soft peaks form (tips curl over). Gradually add the 3 tablespoons sugar, beating till stiff peaks form (tips stand straight).

■■■ Using a spoon, spread the meringue onto the bottom and sides of the prepared pie plate, building up the sides to form a shell. Bake in a 325° oven about 25 minutes or till the meringue is light brown. Cool thoroughly on a wire rack.

■■■ Meanwhile, for filling, in a small saucepan combine the eggs, the ¼ cup sugar, lemon peel, lemon juice, and the 1 tablespoon butter or margarine. Cook and stir over low heat till the mixture is slightly thickened; *do not boil*. Cool.

■■■ Prepare the dessert topping mix according to package directions. Spread *one-fourth* of the lemon filling evenly over the meringue crust. Spoon *half* of the dessert topping atop the lemon filling in the crust. Gently fold the remaining dessert topping into the remaining lemon filling. Spoon the mixture atop the dessert topping in the crust.

■■■ Cover and chill the pie in the refrigerator about 3 hours or till firm. Garnish the pie with a lemon twist, if desired. To serve, carefully cut the pie into wedges. Makes 8 servings.

■■■ Preparation time: 45 minutes
■■■ Cooking time: 25 minutes
■■■ Chilling time: at least 3 hours

A lemon twist is an easy but striking garnish for delicious *Lemon Light Pie* (pictured above).

To make a lemon twist, cut a ⅛-inch-thick slice from a lemon. Cut halfway across the slice, stopping at the center, and twist the ends of the slice in opposite directions.

Lemon Light Pie

Butter *or* margarine
2 egg whites
½ teaspoon vinegar
½ teaspoon vanilla
Dash salt
3 tablespoons sugar
2 slightly beaten eggs
¼ cup sugar
1 tablespoon finely shredded lemon peel
¼ cup lemon juice
1 tablespoon butter *or* margarine
1 1.4-ounce envelope dessert topping mix
Lemon twist (optional)

■■■ For meringue crust, grease a 9-inch pie plate with butter or margarine; set aside. In a mixer bowl combine the egg whites, vinegar, vanilla, and salt;

Galliano Pie

2 cups coconut
3 tablespoons butter *or* margarine, melted
½ cup sugar
1 envelope unflavored gelatin
¼ teaspoon salt
½ cup orange juice
¼ cup water
2 teaspoons lemon juice
3 slightly beaten egg yolks
⅓ cup Galliano *or* Neapolitan liqueur
2 tablespoons vodka
3 egg whites
¼ cup sugar
1 cup whipping cream

■■■ For the coconut crust, in a mixing bowl combine coconut and the melted butter or margarine. Turn the coconut mixture into a 9-inch pie plate. Spread the mixture evenly in pie plate. Press onto the bottom and sides to form a firm, even crust. Bake in a 325° oven about 20 minutes or till coconut is golden. Cool thoroughly on a wire rack before filling.

■■■ For filling, in a medium saucepan combine the ½ cup sugar, unflavored gelatin, and salt. Stir in orange juice, water, lemon juice, and egg yolks. Cook and stir over low heat till gelatin is dissolved and mixture is slightly thickened. Remove from heat. Stir in Galliano or Neapolitan liqueur and vodka. Chill to the consistency of corn syrup, stirring occasionally. Remove from refrigerator (gelatin will continue to set).

■■■ Immediately beat the egg whites till soft peaks form (tips curl over). Gradually add the ¼ cup sugar, beating till stiff peaks form (tips stand straight). When gelatin mixture is the consistency of unbeaten egg whites (partially set) fold in the stiff-beaten egg whites. Beat whipping cream till soft peaks form; fold into gelatin mixture. Chill till the mixture mounds when spooned. Turn into the coconut crust. Cover and chill about 6 hours or till firm. Makes 8 servings.

■■■ Preparation time: 1¼ hours
■■■ Cooking time: about 20 minutes
■■■ Chilling time: at least 6 hours

Pick-a-Fruit Pie

2 cups all-purpose flour
⅔ cup shortening *or* lard
6 to 7 tablespoons cold water
¾ to 1 cup sugar
2 tablespoons quick-cooking tapioca
¼ teaspoon ground cinnamon
¼ teaspoon ground nutmeg
2 cups desired fresh fruit
   (3 cups if apples are used)
2 to 3 oranges, peeled and sectioned (1 cup),
   or one 8-ounce can pineapple tidbits
   (juice pack), drained
1 cup halved seedless green grapes
1 tablespoon lemon juice

■■■ For pastry, in a mixing bowl stir together flour and 1 teaspoon *salt*. Cut in shortening or lard till pieces are the size of small peas. Sprinkle *1 tablespoon* of the cold water over part of mixture; gently toss with a fork. Push to side of bowl. Repeat till all is moistened. Form dough into two balls; set aside.

■■■ For filling, combine sugar, tapioca, cinnamon, nutmeg, and a dash *salt*. Add desired fruit (see suggestions in column at right), oranges or pineapple, grapes, and lemon juice; toss. Let stand 15 minutes.

■■■ On a lightly floured surface, flatten one ball of dough with hands. Roll the dough from center to edge, forming a circle about 12 inches in diameter. Ease the pastry into a 9-inch pie plate, being careful not to stretch the pastry. Turn the fruit filling into the pastry-lined pie plate.

■■■ Roll the remaining ball of dough into a 10x3-inch rectangle; cut lengthwise into six ½-inch-wide strips. Arrange the strips atop the fruit filling in a spoke fashion. Trim, seal, and flute edge. Cover edge of pie with foil to prevent overbrowning. Bake in a 375° oven for 25 minutes. Remove foil; bake for 25 to 30 minutes more or till crust is golden. Cool pie on a wire rack before serving. Makes 8 servings.

■■■ Preparation time: 55 minutes
■■■ Cooking time: 50 to 55 minutes

For a *Pick-a-Fruit Pie* with best-of-all flavor, use only ripe fruit.

Sliced, peeled apples, peaches, and pears; sliced, unpeeled nectarines and plums; and blueberries or raspberries—all are excellent choices for this pie.

If you enjoy eating fruit pies, but hate cleaning the messy spills in the oven, set the pie plate onto a shallow baking pan on the oven rack. The baking pan will catch any juice if the pie bubbles over.

Apricot Puff Ring is an elegant dessert you'll be proud to serve. It features a delicately flavored filling of whipped cream, chopped apricots, and grated chocolate.

If you've never grated chocolate before, don't worry—it's easy. Simply rub a square of unsweetened chocolate across the rough surface of a small hand grater. This makes very fine particles of grated chocolate.

You might like to keep a supply of grated chocolate on hand for garnishing desserts and using in recipes. Store the grated chocolate in a clear plastic bag in the freezer.

Apricot Puff Ring

½ **cup butter** *or* **margarine**
1 **cup water**
1 **cup all-purpose flour**
4 **eggs**
½ **cup sugar**
1 **envelope unflavored gelatin**
1 **cup apricot nectar**
2 **slightly beaten egg yolks**
1 **teaspoon vanilla**
2 **egg whites**
¼ **cup sugar**
½ **cup whipping cream**
1 **16-ounce can unpeeled apricot halves, drained and chopped**
1 **square (1 ounce) unsweetened chocolate, grated**

■■■ Line a 9x1½-inch round baking pan with foil. Grease foil; set aside. In a saucepan melt butter or margarine. Add water; bring to boiling. Add flour and ¼ teaspoon *salt*. Stir vigorously till combined. Cook and stir over medium heat till mixture forms a smooth ball that doesn't separate. Remove from heat; cool slightly, about 5 minutes. Add eggs, one at a time, beating vigorously with a wooden spoon after each addition for 1 to 2 minutes or till smooth.

■■■ For puff ring, using about *two-thirds* of the dough, spoon mounds of dough into the prepared pan ½ inch from outer edge of pan and ½ inch apart, making a ring about 1½ inches wide. Spoon the remaining dough into smaller mounds atop the first mounds of dough. Bake in a 400° oven for 30 minutes. Reduce the oven temperature to 375° and bake 20 minutes more. Using a sharp knife, make 6 slits in puff ring for escape of steam. Return to the oven; bake about 20 minutes more or till golden. Remove from the pan; cool on a wire rack.

■■■ For apricot filling, in a saucepan combine the ½ cup sugar and gelatin; stir in nectar and egg yolks. Cook and stir over low heat till gelatin is dissolved and mixture is slightly thickened. Remove from heat. Stir in vanilla. Chill to the consistency of corn syrup, stirring occasionally. Remove from the refrigerator (gelatin will continue to set).

■■■ Immediately beat the egg whites till soft peaks form (tips curl over). Gradually add the ¼ cup sugar, beating till stiff peaks form (tips stand straight). When gelatin is the consistency of unbeaten egg whites (partially set), fold in the stiff-beaten egg whites. Beat whipping cream till soft peaks form. Fold the whipped cream into the gelatin mixture. Fold in the apricots and chocolate. Chill till mixture mounds when spooned.

■■■ To assemble, cut off the top *third* of puff ring. Using a fork, scoop out soft dough from bottom (see top photograph below). If desired, scoop out the soft dough from top. Place the bottom of the ring onto a serving plate. Spoon the apricot filling into the bottom (see lower photograph below). Cover with the top of the ring. Chill in the refrigerator about 6 hours or till firm. Makes 12 servings.

■■■ Preparation time: 2¼ hours
■■■ Chilling time: at least 6 hours

Use a fork to scoop out the soft dough from the bottom of the cooled puff ring, as shown. If desired, scoop out the soft dough from the top of the ring.

Spoon the apricot filling into the bottom of the puff ring, as shown. Place the top of the puff ring atop the filling.

Strawberry Cream Squares

- 1 **cup all-purpose flour**
- ½ **cup coconut**
- ½ **cup chopped walnuts** *or* **pecans**
- ⅓ **cup butter** *or* **margarine, melted**
- ¼ **cup packed brown sugar**
- 1 **3-ounce package strawberry-, raspberry-, *or* cherry-flavored gelatin**
- ⅔ **cup boiling water**
- 1 **pint vanilla ice cream**
- 1 **8-ounce carton dairy sour cream**
- 1 **10-ounce package frozen sliced strawberries, thawed**

■ In a small mixing bowl combine the flour, coconut, walnuts or pecans, melted butter or margarine, and brown sugar. Spread the crumb mixture in an ungreased shallow baking pan. Bake in a 350° oven for 18 to 20 minutes, stirring occasionally.

■ Meanwhile, in a mixing bowl dissolve the gelatin in boiling water. Add the vanilla ice cream by spoonfuls, stirring till the ice cream is melted. Add sour cream; beat with a rotary beater till combined. Chill in the refrigerator to the consistency of unbeaten egg whites (partially set). Fold in the strawberries. Chill in the refrigerator till the mixture mounds when spooned.

■ Sprinkle *half* of the baked crumb mixture into a 9x9x2-inch baking pan. Spoon the strawberry mixture over crumbs. Sprinkle the remaining crumb mixture atop. Cover and chill about 6 hours or till firm. To serve, cut into squares. Makes 9 servings.

■ Preparation time: about 1 hour
■ Chilling time: at least 6 hours

Citrus Mousse*

- ⅓ **cup sugar**
- 1 **envelope unflavored gelatin**
- 1½ **teaspoons cornstarch**
- 2 **teaspoons finely shredded orange peel *or* tangerine peel**
- 1 **cup orange juice** *or* **tangerine juice**
- 4 **beaten eggs yolks**
- 2 **tablespoons orange liqueur**
- 6 **egg whites**
- 3 **tablespoons sugar**
- 1½ **cups whipping cream**
  Pizzelles (see recipe, page 29) (optional)
  Chocolate leaves (optional)
  Orange *or* tangerine strips (optional)

■ In a large saucepan combine the ⅓ cup sugar, the unflavored gelatin, and cornstarch. Stir in the tangerine peel or orange peel, tangerine juice or orange juice, and egg yolks. Cook and stir over low heat till the gelatin is dissolved and mixture is slightly thickened. Remove from heat. Stir in liqueur. Chill in the refrigerator to the consistency of corn syrup, stirring frequently to keep the mixture smooth. Remove from the refrigerator (gelatin mixture will continue to set).

■ Immediately beat the egg whites till soft peaks form (tips curl over). Gradually add the 3 tablespoons sugar, beating till stiff peaks form (tips stand straight). When the gelatin mixture is the consistency of unbeaten egg whites (partially set), fold in the stiff-beaten egg whites. Beat the whipping cream till soft peaks form; fold into the partially set gelatin mixture. Chill in the refrigerator till the mixture mounds when spooned. Turn into a 2-quart soufflé dish. Cover and chill about 6 hours or till firm. If desired, spoon the mousse into Pizzelle cups (see column at far right); add chocolate leaves and orange or tangerine strips. Serves 12.

■ Preparation time: about 1 hour
■ Chilling time: at least 6 hours
★ *pictured on page 12*

Show off *Citrus Mousse* by doing a simple but elegant presentation. Shape Pizzelles, lacy wafer-like cookies, into dessert cups. Then, spoon the mousse into the individual cups for an impressive dessert.

To make the Pizzelle cups, remove cookie from the iron. Immediately place the warm cookie over an inverted custard cup or a small juice glass. Press the warm cookie lightly to fit the custard cup or glass. Remove and set Pizzelle cup upright to cool.

Banana-Pecan Ice Cream, Daiquiri Ice Cream,
Frozen Berry Yogurt

Daiquiri Ice Cream

- 1　8-ounce can crushed pineapple (juice pack), drained
- 1　6-ounce can frozen daiquiri mix concentrate, thawed
- 1　4½-ounce package custard dessert mix
- ¼　cup light rum
- 1½　cups whipping cream
- Lime twist (optional)
- Lemon twist (optional)

■ In a large mixing bowl combine the pineapple, daiquiri mix, custard mix, and light rum. Beat whipping cream till soft peaks form; fold into the pineapple mixture. Turn the mixture into a 9x5x3-inch loaf pan. Cover and freeze about 6 hours or till firm. Let stand at room temperature for 10 to 15 minutes before serving. Scoop to serve. Garnish with lime twist, lemon twist, and fern leaf, if desired. Makes 8 or 9 servings.

■ Preparation time: 20 minutes
■ Freezing time: at least 6 hours
■ Standing time: 10 to 15 minutes

Frozen Berry Yogurt

- 1　10-ounce package frozen strawberries *or* red raspberries, thawed
- 2　teaspoons unflavored gelatin
- 2　cups plain yogurt
- ¼　cup sugar
- 1　teaspoon vanilla
- 2　egg whites
- ½　cup sugar

■ Drain strawberries or raspberries, reserving syrup; set berries aside. In a small saucepan soften gelatin in the reserved syrup for 5 minutes; cook and stir over low heat till gelatin dissolves. Cool. Stir together yogurt, berries, gelatin mixture, the ¼ cup sugar, and vanilla. Turn mixture into an 11x7x1½-inch baking pan. Cover and freeze about 45 minutes or till partially frozen around edges.

■ Turn the partially frozen mixture into a large mixer bowl. Beat with an electric mixer till fluffy. Wash beaters; beat the egg whites till soft peaks form (tips curl over). Gradually add the ½ cup sugar, beating till stiff peaks form (tips stand straight); fold into berry mixture. Return to pan. Cover; freeze about 6 hours or till firm. Scoop to serve. Makes 8 to 10 servings.

■ Preparation time: 1 hour
■ Freezing time: at least 6¾ hours

Banana-Pecan Ice Cream

- 2　ripe large bananas
- ⅓　cup milk
- 2　teaspoons lemon juice
- 1　teaspoon vanilla
- ¼　teaspoon salt
- 2　egg yolks
- 2　egg whites
- ¼　cup sugar
- 1　cup whipping cream
- ½　cup toasted, chopped pecans

■ In a large mixing bowl mash the bananas; add milk, lemon juice, vanilla, and salt; set aside. In a small mixer bowl beat egg yolks on high speed of electric mixer about 5 minutes or till thick and lemon colored. Add to the banana mixture.

■ Thoroughly wash beaters. Beat egg whites till soft peaks form (tips curl over). Gradually add sugar, beating till stiff peaks form (tips stand straight); fold into the banana mixture. Beat whipping cream till soft peaks form; fold into the banana mixture. Fold in the pecans. Pour into an 8x8x2-inch or 9x9x2-inch baking pan. Cover and freeze about 6 hours or till firm. Scoop to serve. Makes 8 to 10 servings.

■ Preparation time: 30 minutes
■ Freezing time: at least 6 hours

MENU
GALA OUTDOOR DINNER

Potato Chips

Garden Pasta Salad★

Grilled Ham Slice

Spicy Baked Beans

Banana-Pecan Ice Cream
Frozen Berry Yogurt
Daiquiri Ice Cream

Mint Iced Tea

When you serve several desserts—such as *Banana-Pecan Ice Cream*, *Daiquiri Ice Cream*, and *Frozen Berry Yogurt*—some of your guests may want to try all three. To satisfy everyone's tastes, serve individual scoops in pretty paper bake cups, and let the guests choose their favorites.
★ *see recipe, page 219*

Spicy gingerbread and tangy lemon sherbet are perfect flavor partners in *Frozen Lemon-Gingerbread Roll*.

The key to making this jelly-roll dessert is to roll the cake while it's still very warm. This prevents the cake from tearing.

Another important step is to sprinkle sifted powdered sugar on a towel and roll it up with the warm cake. The towel keeps the cake from sticking together as it cools, and the powdered sugar keeps the cake from sticking to the towel.

Frozen Lemon-Gingerbread Roll

½ **cup all-purpose flour**
1 **teaspoon baking powder**
1 **teaspoon ground ginger**
½ **teaspoon ground allspice**
4 **egg yolks**
⅓ **cup sugar**
¼ **cup molasses**
4 **egg whites**
⅓ **cup sugar**
½ **cup chopped walnuts**
   Powdered sugar
1 **quart lemon sherbet**

■■■ Grease and lightly flour a 15x10x1-inch jelly-roll pan; set aside. Stir together flour, baking powder, ginger, allspice, and ¼ teaspoon *salt*. In a mixer bowl beat egg yolks on high speed of electric mixer about 5 minutes or till thick and lemon colored. Gradually add ⅓ cup sugar, beating till combined. Stir in molasses. Thoroughly wash beaters. Beat egg whites till soft peaks form (tips curl over). Gradually add ⅓ cup sugar, beating till stiff peaks form (tips stand straight). Fold molasses mixture into egg whites. Sprinkle flour mixture over egg mixture; fold in gently. Spread evenly in prepared pan. Sprinkle walnuts atop. Bake in a 375° oven for 12 to 15 minutes or till done.

■■■ Using a narrow spatula, immediately loosen edges of cake from the pan. Quickly invert the pan and shake gently over a towel sprinkled with powdered sugar. Lift off the pan, being careful not to tear the cake. Starting with the narrow end, roll the warm cake and towel together. Cool on a wire rack.

■■■ Carefully unroll the cooled cake and towel. Stir sherbet just to soften; spread onto cake to within 1 inch of edges. Roll up cake. Cover and freeze about 4 hours or till firm. Slice to serve. Makes 10 servings.

■■■ Preparation time: 35 minutes
■■■ Cooking time: 12 to 15 minutes
■■■ Cooling time: 45 minutes
■■■ Freezing time: at least 4 hours

Mocha Ice-Cream Sandwiches

1 **tablespoon instant coffee crystals**
½ **cup water**
2 **cups all-purpose flour**
⅔ **cup unsweetened cocoa powder**
1 **teaspoon baking soda**
¼ **teaspoon salt**
½ **cup shortening**
1¼ **cups sugar**
2 **eggs**
¾ **cup buttermilk**
½ **cup whipping cream**
1 **quart coffee ice cream**
2 **tablespoons coffee liqueur *or*
   crème de cacao**

■■■ For the cookies, dissolve coffee crystals in water; set aside. Stir together the flour, cocoa powder, baking soda, and salt. In a mixer bowl beat shortening on medium speed of electric mixer for 30 seconds. Add sugar and beat till combined. Add the eggs; beat well. Add dry ingredients, coffee mixture, and buttermilk alternately to the beaten mixture. Beat till combined. Drop the batter from a tablespoon 2 inches apart onto an ungreased cookie sheet. Bake in a 350° oven for 8 to 10 minutes or till done. Carefully remove from cookie sheet; cool on a wire rack.

■■■ For the filling, beat the whipping cream till soft peaks form. Stir the coffee ice cream just to soften; fold in the whipped cream and the coffee liqueur or crème de cacao. For *each* sandwich, quickly spread about ⅓ cup of the filling onto the bottom side of *one* cookie; top with another cookie. Immediately place onto a baking pan in the freezer (keep the pan in the freezer to prevent cookies from softening while assembling the remaining sandwiches). Repeat with the remaining cookies and filling. Cover and freeze about 4 hours or till firm. Makes 12 sandwiches.

■■■ Preparation time: 40 minutes
■■■ Cooking time: 16 to 20 minutes
■■■ Freezing time: at least 4 hours

Frozen Ice-Cream Cones

½ cup coarsely crushed crisp rice cereal
⅛ teaspoon ground cinnamon
    Dash ground nutmeg
2 teaspoons honey
6 ice-cream cones
½ of a 6-ounce package (½ cup) semisweet
    chocolate pieces, melted
1 quart vanilla ice cream
6 maraschino cherries (optional)

■ Stir together the coarsely crushed cereal, the cinnamon, and nutmeg. Add the honey and stir just till the cereal clings together; set aside.

■ Spread the inside of *each* ice-cream cone with about *2 teaspoons* of the melted chocolate. Set in the freezer about 10 minutes or till chocolate hardens.

■ In a medium mixing bowl stir vanilla ice cream just to soften. For *each* cone, spoon in about *2 tablespoons* of the ice cream. Top with *1 tablespoon* of the cereal mixture. Spoon in another *3 tablespoons* ice cream, rounding the tops.

■ Dip the tops of the cones into the remaining cereal mixture to lightly coat. Garnish each with a maraschino cherry, if desired. Freeze about 4 hours or till firm. Makes 6 servings.

■ Preparation time: 45 minutes
■ Freezing time: at least 4 hours

Mexican Chocolate Cups

1 14-ounce can (1¼ cups) Eagle Brand
    sweetened condensed milk
⅔ cup chocolate-flavored syrup
½ cup toasted, chopped almonds
1 teaspoon vanilla
¼ teaspoon ground cinnamon
2 cups whipping cream

■ Combine the sweetened condensed milk, chocolate-flavored syrup, chopped almonds, vanilla, and cinnamon. In a large mixer bowl beat the whipping cream till soft peaks form; fold in the chocolate mixture. Line muffin pans with paper bake cups. Spoon about ⅓ cup of the chocolate mixture into *each* cup. Freeze about 4 hours or till firm. Makes 18 servings.

■ Preparation time: 20 minutes
■ Freezing time: at least 4 hours

Frosty Banana Shake

3 cups vanilla ice cream
1 small banana, sliced
½ of a 6-ounce can (⅓ cup) frozen apple juice
    concentrate *or* orange juice concentrate
¼ cup milk
⅛ teaspoon ground allspice

■ Place the vanilla ice cream in a blender container; add the banana slices, apple or orange juice concentrate, milk, and allspice. Cover and blend till smooth. To serve, pour into tall glasses. Makes about 4 (8-ounce) servings.

■ Total preparation time: 10 minutes

It's great to have something cool and refreshing stashed away in the freezer for pop-in guests—especially in the summertime. You can keep *Mocha Ice-Cream Sandwiches, Frozen Ice-Cream Cones,* and *Mexican Chocolate Cups* in your freezer for those impromptu visits.

After freezing these desserts till they are firm, wrap each individually in moisture-vaporproof wrap and return them to the freezer. You can store them for up to 1 month.

Celebration ·Party·

layered vegetable dip

chips and pretzels

assorted breads 'n spreads

festive citrus slush

celebration cake

Special occasions—such as housewarmings, anniversaries, retirements, and weddings—warrant extra-special celebrations. Don't let the thought of serving 50 people at such an event scare you off. Instead, do some detailed planning, including as much make-ahead preparation as possible.

At party time, enlist some willing guests to help serve the food and beverages. The timetable suggested for this celebration gives you an idea of what to do before the party as well as how to divide last-minute preparations among guest helpers.

Initial party planning tips: Very few homes can comfortably accommodate 50 people, but most backyards will. Other alternative locations for the large party include a town park or a rented hall. Once you decide on the location for the celebration party, start your planning.

Determine the color theme for the party decorations, then carry it through in the paper plates, cups, and napkins. If you use disposable paper and plastic items, the cleanup will be a snap.

Food and beverage service: Self-serve buffet-style is the most efficient way to serve a large group. To encourage people to circulate, arrange the food in different areas. You'll need one or two buffet tables for the *Assorted Breads 'n' Spreads*, the *Layered Vegetable Dip* and dippers, and the chips and pretzels. Use baskets or trays to hold the chips and breads, and a handled basket or picnic basket to hold the vegetables for dipping. For each spread, provide crocks or bowls and small spreaders.

Set up one or two small tables for the liquor and carbonated beverage used in the *Festive Citrus Slush*. Keep the slush the proper consistency in a large ice-filled container. A small bowl of citrus slices or wedges provides the garnish for each drink. Have plenty of plastic drink cups and cocktail stirrers on hand so guests can mix their own concoctions.

Plan to have a separate table for the cake and coffee service or use a small table for each. For the coffee service, provide small pots of coffee and replenish them from one large-capacity coffee maker. If necessary, rent a coffee maker.

Before the party, enlist about four willing guests to help with the final preparations. You also might ask them to keep an eye out for food trays or beverage containers that need replenishing during the party and to refill the items for you.

One table holds a collage of crackers, breads, spreads, dips, and dippers. If there is still room, add the chips and pretzels. Otherwise, set up another table.

TIMETABLE

1 week before: You can freeze a number of foods in advance (or make them the day before the party). Bake the cakes, then freeze (without frosting and decorations); or, order the cake from a bakery. Bake breads; wrap and freeze. Remember to prepare 2 loaves of each of the *Lemon Almond Bread* and the *Date Banana Bread*. Prepare the *Festive Citrus Slush;* freeze. Write out an instruction card for the slush telling guests how to prepare their own drinks.

3 days before: Prepare the *Chili Cheese Dip* and the *Coconut Cream Cheese Spread*. Cover; refrigerate.

1 day before: Thaw cakes. Frost and decorate; cover loosely. Prepare garnishes and dippers, except mushrooms. Chill carrots in ice water and other vegetables in separate moisture-vaporproof containers.

3 hours before: Remove the breads from freezer to thaw. Make the *Layered Vegetable Dip* and prepare mushrooms; chill until serving time. Set up serving tables. Cut pita bread into triangles; arrange on trays with crackers. Place chips and pretzels in containers.

At the party: As the host, you will supervise all the food serving activities and act as party coordinator.

One of your helpers prepares the coffee, and with the assistance of another helper arranges the beverages on the tables, setting up bowls with the slush mixture. During the party, these helpers replenish ice in the cooling bowl as necessary. Store the ice in a cooler during the party. Don't forget to provide a corkscrew and bottle opener.

A third helper slices the breads and arranges them on a serving platter. (Or, you can do this ahead of time and cover the platters with clear plastic wrap.) Serving plates are replenished during the party as needed. This person makes sure that the spreads and dip for the *Assorted Breads 'n' Spreads* are in serving containers and that they are removed from the refrigerator 30 minutes before the party begins.

A fourth helper sets out the layered dip and arranges the dippers in trays or baskets. Dippers are replenished (from the cooler) as necessary. This helper also cuts the cake at the appropriate time.

Serve a specially decorated cake for the celebration dessert. If you are short on time and your budget allows, order a fancy creation from the bakery. However, you can cut cost, and have fun doing it, by preparing and decorating the cakes.

For this size party, prepare four packages of 2-layer-size cake mixes, baking the batter in four 15x10x1-inch or 13x9x2-inch baking pans. Use canned or packaged frosting to frost the cakes. Then decorate them with a mix of small candies and mints, small multicolored decorative candies, chocolate-flavored sprinkles, and semisweet chocolate pieces.

To keep the *Layered Vegetable Dip* chilled throughout the party during hot weather, place the serving platter or board on a tray with sides, then surround the platter with crushed ice.

Also, arrange the vegetable dippers in a bed of crushed ice to keep them crisp and chilled. Suggestions for the fresh vegetable dippers include cauliflower flowerets, broccoli flowerets, cherry tomatoes, celery sticks, radishes, whole mushrooms, cucumber sticks, carrot sticks, and green onions.

Assorted Breads 'n' Spreads

Coconut Cream Cheese Spread
Chili Cheese Dip
Desired purchased cheese spread
Date-Banana Bread
Lemon-Almond Bread
Pita bread, cut into triangles
Assorted crackers

■ Let spreads and dip stand at room temperature 30 minutes before serving time. Arrange on trays with slices of Date-Banana Bread, Lemon-Almond Bread, pita bread triangles, and assorted crackers.

■ Total preparation time: 40 minutes

Festive Citrus Slush

8 **6-ounce cans frozen tangerine *or* orange juice concentrate**
½ **gallon pineapple sherbet**
 Dry white wine, champagne, rum, *or* vodka; sparkling water *or* lemon-lime carbonated beverage, chilled*
 Orange, lemon, *or* lime slices *or* wedges

■ Thaw frozen concentrate slightly. Stir sherbet to soften. Stir concentrate and 6 cups *water* into sherbet. Cover and freeze till nearly frozen; stir mixture. Freeze at least 5 hours or till firm. To serve, let mixture stand 10 minutes at room temperature. Scoop frozen mixture into a serving bowl. Fill a larger bowl with *crushed ice;* insert the bowl of slush in the ice-filled bowl.

■ For each serving, spoon 2 tablespoons slush into an 8- or 9-ounce glass; pour in choice of beverage (*if using rum or vodka, use 2 to 3 tablespoons [1 to 1½ ounces] liquor and also add carbonated beverage). Trim with a citrus slice. Makes 19 cups slush.

■ Preparation time: 40 minutes
■ Freezing time: at least 6 hours

Layered Vegetable Dip

 Lettuce leaves
2 **8-ounce containers sour cream dip with blue cheese**
1½ **cups finely shredded cheddar cheese (6 ounces)**
1 **cup chopped pitted ripe olives *or* chopped pimiento-stuffed olives**
2 **8-ounce containers sour cream dip with French onion**
1 **hard-cooked egg *or* 3 hard-cooked egg yolks, sieved**
 Sliced ripe olives *or* pimiento-stuffed olives, sliced
 Assorted fresh vegetable dippers

■ Line a 12x8-inch wooden board or a platter with lettuce leaves. Spread the sour cream dip with blue cheese to within about 1 inch of lettuce edges on the wooden board or platter. Top with a layer of the finely shredded cheddar cheese, then add a layer of the 1 cup chopped ripe or pimiento-stuffed olives.

■ Spread the sour cream dip with French onion atop the chopped olive layer. Score a lattice design atop the dip; sprinkle sieved hard-cooked egg or egg yolk over the lines. Fill in the design with sliced ripe or pimiento-stuffed olives (see photograph on page 240). Serve with fresh vegetable dippers (see suggestions in column at far left). Makes 6 cups dip.

■ Total preparation time: 40 minutes

Lemon-Almond Bread

1 beaten egg
1 8-ounce carton plain yogurt
1 package 1-layer-size yellow cake mix
2 teaspoons finely shredded lemon peel
½ cup chopped almonds

■■■ In a bowl combine egg and yogurt; add cake mix and lemon peel. Stir till combined. Stir in nuts. Turn into greased 8x4x2-inch loaf pan. Bake in a 350° oven for 35 to 45 minutes or till done. Cool in pan 10 minutes. Remove from pan; cool on rack. Makes 1.

■■■ Preparation time: 20 minutes
■■■ Cooking time: 35 to 45 minutes
■■■ Cooling time: 10 minutes

Chili Cheese Dip

3 cups cream-style cottage cheese
½ cup milk
1 tablespoon lemon juice
2 teaspoons chili powder
2 teaspoons paprika
¼ teaspoon garlic powder
⅛ teaspoon bottled hot pepper sauce
3 cups shredded sharp cheddar cheese
Paprika
Assorted crackers *or* chips

■■■ Using *half* the ingredients at a time, in a blender container combine first 7 ingredients. Cover; blend till smooth, stopping as needed to stir. Add *half* the cheddar cheese. Cover; blend till smooth. Transfer to bowl. Repeat. Cover and chill for 4 hours. To serve, allow mixture to stand at room temperature for 30 minutes. Turn into a serving container. Sprinkle with paprika. Serve with crackers or chips. Makes about 4½ cups.

■■■ Preparation time: 20 minutes
■■■ Chilling time: at least 4 hours
■■■ Standing time: 30 minutes

Date-Banana Bread

2 17-ounce packages date quick bread mix
1 cup mashed ripe banana
¾ teaspoon ground allspice
Powdered sugar (optional)

■■■ Prepare quick bread mixes according to package directions, *except* decrease water to 1⅓ cups total and add mashed banana and allspice with the water. Pour mixture into a greased 10-inch fluted tube pan or plain tube pan. Bake in a 375° oven for 50 to 60 minutes or till a wooden pick inserted in the center comes out clean. Cool in pan 15 minutes. Remove from the pan; cool thoroughly on a wire rack. Sprinkle with powdered sugar, if desired. Slice thinly to serve. Makes 1 loaf.

■■■ Preparation time: 20 minutes
■■■ Cooking time: 50 to 60 minutes
■■■ Cooling time: 15 minutes

Coconut Cream Cheese Spread

3 8-ounce packages cream cheese, softened
¾ cup flaked coconut, chopped and toasted
¼ cup honey
Milk

■■■ In a mixer bowl beat together the softened cream cheese, the coconut, and honey. If the mixture is too stiff to spread, stir in milk, 1 tablespoon at a time, until it is of spreading consistency. Spoon mixture into a serving bowl. Cover and chill for 2 hours. To serve, allow mixture to stand at room temperature for 30 minutes. Garnish with additional toasted coconut, if desired. Makes about 4 cups spread.

■■■ Preparation time: 20 minutes
■■■ Chilling time: at least 2 hours
■■■ Standing time: 30 minutes

To have enough of both breads to serve your guests, you will need to bake two loaves each of the *Date-Banana Bread* and the *Lemon-Almond Bread*.

You can mix the batter for both loaves of the *Lemon-Almond Bread* at once, divide it in half, and bake the twin loaves at the same time.

However, it's best to prepare two separate recipes of the *Date-Banana Bread*. Smaller batches are easier to mix properly and won't require such a large mixing bowl. In addition, you may not have two tube pans to bake the two loaves at once.

COCKTAIL PARTY

CREAMY CURRY DIP
WITH VEGETABLE DIPPERS
■
CRAB MINI-SANDWICHES
IN RYE LOAVES
■
SMOKY CHEESE LOG
WITH CRACKERS
■
CITRUS-VODKA PUNCH
■
STRAWBERRY SPRITZER

A cocktail party starts the evening off right, whether you're celebrating a promotion, a birthday, or an anniversary, or setting the mood for an evening with friends. The food for this party works well for any occasion, because almost all of it can be prepared ahead. Since the menu involves very little last-minute preparation, you may elect to make all of the food yourself or divide the work among several hosts. The big bonus is that all of the foods are served cold and require no attention during the party, giving everyone time to mingle.

TIMETABLE

One of the most flexible parties you can have is a cocktail party, because you can cater to any size group. Set out a variety of sensational snacks and thirst-quenchers, then let your guests serve themselves.

When planning the menu, select pickup foods and bite-size snacks that guests can conveniently handle with their fingers or spear with small wooden picks. Often guests are balancing a glass in one hand and a plate in the other, so they do appreciate food that they can eat easily in one or two bites. With this menu, you can serve about 24 people.

2 days before: Bake *Homemade Rye Bread* or order two round loaves from your baker. Prepare *Smoky Cheese Log*, wrap, and store it in the refrigerator.

1 day before: Prepare and chill *Creamy Curry Dip*. Prepare the crab filling for the sandwiches. Store the dip and filling in the refrigerator until time to set out the food for the party. Clean and prepare the vegetables for dippers. Chill the vegetable dippers in ice water to keep them crisp. Chill all the beverage ingredients that require chilling.

Several hours before: Cut the loaves of bread for the sandwiches. Assemble and arrange the sandwiches in the lettuce-lined bread shells. Cover them tightly with clear plastic wrap and store in the refrigerator till serving time. Let the strawberries used for the spritzer stand at room temperature for 30 minutes to thaw slightly.

30 minutes before: Prepare *Citrus-Vodka Punch* and *Strawberry Spritzer*. Arrange the snacks, drinks, plates, napkins, and flowers on one or two tables.

Nothing sets a party mood better than festive decorations. And you needn't go to a lot of time, effort, and expense either. A few colorful balloons, pretty napkins, and fresh flowers will add the sparkle you're after.

Whatever the reason for your cocktail party—be it business-related or social—shoot some informal snapshots of your group. Afterward distribute reprints to those who want a memento of the special event.

Smoky Cheese Log tastes just as good whether prepared and chilled several days before serving or frozen a month in advance. If you make it more than two days ahead, wait until party day to add the parsley garnish.

And if you decide to make the cheese log more than one week in advance, you'll need to freeze it. Wrap the log in a moisture-vaporproof wrap and seal it securely. Remember to label the package with the recipe title and preparation date.

To thaw the frozen cheese log, leave wrapped and let the log stand at room temperature for 2 hours or in the refrigerator for at least 24 hours.

Smoky Cheese Log

    1 **cup shredded smoked cheddar cheese**
    1 **cup shredded American cheese**
    1 **3-ounce package cream cheese with chives, softened**
    3 **tablespoons mayonnaise *or* salad dressing**
    2 **teaspoons lemon juice**
    1 **teaspoon Worcestershire sauce**
       Dash bottled hot pepper sauce
    ½ **cup finely chopped walnuts**
    ⅓ **cup snipped parsley**
       Assorted crackers

■■■ Bring cheeses to room temperature. In a mixer bowl place cream cheese, mayonnaise, lemon juice, Worcestershire sauce, and hot pepper sauce; beat till combined. Add cheddar and American cheeses; beat till combined. Stir in walnuts. Chill for 1 hour.

■■■ Shape into a log 6 to 8 inches long. Roll in parsley, pressing parsley lightly onto log. Wrap in clear plastic wrap. Chill about 3 hours or till firm. To serve, unwrap log; serve with crackers. Makes 1 log.

■■■ Preparation time: 30 minutes
■■■ Chilling time: at least 4 hours

Citrus-Vodka Punch

    1 **6-ounce can frozen pineapple juice concentrate**
    1 **6-ounce can frozen orange juice concentrate**
    2 **cups vodka**
    1 **32-ounce bottle ginger ale, chilled**
       Ice cubes

■■■ In a large pitcher combine concentrates and 3 cups *cold water*. Stir in vodka. Pour in ginger ale; stir gently to mix. Add ice. Makes 22 (4-ounce) servings.

■■■ Total preparation time: 15 minutes

Creamy Curry Dip

    1 **cup dairy sour cream**
    1 **cup mayonnaise *or* salad dressing**
    1 **tablespoon minced dried onion**
    1 **tablespoon dried parsley flakes**
    2 **teaspoons curry powder**
    1 **teaspoon lemon juice**
    ¼ **teaspoon garlic salt**
       Assorted fresh vegetable dippers

■■■ In a mixing bowl combine the sour cream, mayonnaise or salad dressing, dried onion, parsley, curry powder, lemon juice, and garlic salt. Cover and chill in the refrigerator about 3 hours or till flavors are blended. Prepare the vegetable dippers.

■■■ To serve, turn the dip into a serving bowl. Serve with fresh vegetable dippers. Makes 2 cups dip.

■■■ Preparation time: 20 minutes
■■■ Chilling time: at least 3 hours

Strawberry Spritzer

    3 **10-ounce packages frozen sliced strawberries**
    6 **cups white grape juice, chilled**
    1 **28-ounce bottle carbonated water, chilled**
       Few drops red food coloring (optional)

■■■ Let the strawberries stand at room temperature for 30 minutes. Place *2 packages* of *undrained* berries in a blender container or food processor bowl. Cover and blend or process till smooth. In a large pitcher combine blended strawberries, grape juice, and remaining *undrained* strawberries. Pour in carbonated water; stir gently to mix. Stir in red food coloring, if desired. Makes 24 (4-ounce) servings.

■■■ Standing time: 30 minutes
■■■ Preparation time: 15 minutes

Crab Mini-Sandwiches in Rye Loaves

- 2 loaves Homemade Rye Bread *or* two 16-ounce round loaves, unsliced light rye bread
- 2 8-ounce packages cream cheese, softened
- 2 6-ounce cans crab meat, drained, flaked, and cartilage removed
- ⅓ cup finely chopped green onion
- 2 teaspoons capers, chopped
  Lettuce leaves

■ Prepare Homemade Rye Bread or use purchased bread. To assemble, insert wooden picks around the edge of top of each loaf. Using the wooden picks as a guide, cut cylinders of bread from centers with a serrated knife, removing picks as you cut (see top photograph at right). Remove cylinders; slice off the bottoms and tops, and set aside. Thinly slice cylinders crosswise (see lower photograph at right).

■ For filling, in a mixing bowl combine cream cheese, crab meat, green onion, and capers. Spread filling onto *half* of the bread slices; top with remaining slices. Cut sandwiches into 2x1-inch rectangles.

■ Place the bread shells onto two serving platters; replace bottoms of loaves. Line each shell with lettuce leaves. Place the sandwiches in loaves; then replace tops of loaves, if desired. Cover and chill in the refrigerator till serving time. Makes about 54.

Homemade Rye Bread: In a large mixer bowl combine 2½ cups *all-purpose flour,* 2 packages *active dry yeast,* and 1 tablespoon *caraway seed.* In a saucepan heat 2 cups *water,* ½ cup packed *brown sugar,* 1 tablespoon *cooking oil,* and 1 teaspoon *salt* just till warm (115° to 120°); stir constantly. Add to flour mixture. Beat on low speed of electric mixer for ½ minute, scraping the bowl. Beat for 3 minutes on high speed. Using a spoon, stir in 2½ cups *rye flour* and as much of ¾ to 1¼ cups *all-purpose flour* as you can.

Insert wooden picks in a circle around the top edge of each loaf. Using the picks as a guide, make a vertical cut all the way through bread with a serrated knife. Following the picks around, cut a circle in the bread to form a cylinder, as shown. Remove the picks.

Remove the cylinder from the center of each loaf, leaving a bread shell. Slice off the bottom and top of each cylinder; set aside. Using a serrated knife, thinly slice the cylinders vertically into rectangles, as shown.

■ Turn dough out onto a lightly floured surface. Knead in enough remaining *all-purpose flour* to make a moderately stiff dough that is smooth and elastic (6 to 8 minutes total). Shape into a ball. Place in a lightly greased bowl; turn once to grease surface. Cover; let rise in a warm place till double (1 to 1¼ hours).

■ Punch dough down; divide in half. Cover and let rest for 10 minutes. Shape into two 4½-inch round loaves, pulling edges under to make a smooth top. Place onto greased baking sheets. Cover and let rise in a warm place till nearly double (30 to 40 minutes). Combine 1 beaten *egg white* and 1 tablespoon *water;* brush atop loaves. Bake in a 350° oven for 40 to 45 minutes or till done. Cool on wire racks. Seal, label, and freeze, if desired. Makes 2 loaves.

■ Advance preparation time: 35 minutes
■ Rising time: 1½ to 2 hours
■ Cooking time: 40 to 45 minutes
■ Final preparation time: 40 minutes

Holiday
Open House

Make-Ahead Fruit Canapés • Nordic Dip

Caraway-Sesame Flatbread • Swiss Cheese Bites • Rosettes

Layered Vegetable Terrine • Mincemeat Fruitcake

Coconut Tartlets • Crème de Menthe Squares • Snowflake Punch

Spiced Orange Nog

The holiday season is a time for entertaining. The cheery spirit that fills the air helps make every gathering, large or small, a party. It's a perfect time for you to have an open house. With an open house, you can entertain many people at once. Your guests can come and go as they please, within a designated time period.

If your heart is in the right place but you're on a tight budget, don't worry. With this economical but lavish menu, you can serve about 25 people and still keep costs down. And by beginning just 1 week ahead and fixing 1 or 2 dishes a day, you can make most of the food before the day of the party so all you need to do then is set the table.

You need to work very quickly to keep the *Orange Aspic* for *Make-Ahead Fruit Canapés* from becoming too firm before you finish coating all 30 slices.

If it does firm up, you can resoften it. Return the gelatin mixture to a small saucepan. Cook and stir it over low heat till softened. Chill it in the refrigerator to the consistency of unbeaten egg whites (partially set). Then begin spooning the aspic over the bread slices again.

Though you'll be busy preparing food days before the party, when the party day finally arrives you'll be ready to enjoy it too. Simply set out the food on your favorite holiday dishes. Then sit back, relax, and wait for your guests to arrive.

Since all the food is chilled or at room temperature, you'll need no warming trays or chafing dishes. Check the table during the party to see whether anything needs replenishing.

TIMETABLE

2 weeks before: Make up your guest list and invite your guests.

7 days before: Bake *Mincemeat Fruitcake* and wrap it in brandy-soaked cheesecloth and foil. Store it in a cool, dry place for at least 1 week. Prepare *Snowflake Punch* and freeze it in two portions.

6 days before: If you would like to send some holiday food gifts home with your guests, assemble the eye-catching silver gift boxes (see directions on page 257). They make attractive containers for treats.

4 days before: Shape and bake *Caraway-Sesame Flatbread.* Meanwhile, fry *Rosettes.* Store the bread and *Rosettes* in airtight containers to keep them crisp.

3 days before: Bake *Swiss Cheese Bites;* cover and store in refrigerator. Prepare *Crème de Menthe Squares;* cover and store in the refrigerator.

2 days before: Bake and chill *Layered Vegetable Terrine.* Make *Nordic Dip* and chill. Bake and glaze *Coconut Tartlets;* cover tightly to store.

1 day before: Prepare *Almond Butter* and *Orange Aspic* for *Make-Ahead Fruit Canapés.* Assemble the canapés; cover tightly and chill. Wash and cut the vegetables for dipping; store in ice water to keep crisp. Make and chill *Spiced Orange Nog.* Frost and decorate the fruitcake. Select your serving dishes and set up the buffet table.

1 hour before: If desired, prepare the eggplant boat container for serving the *Nordic Dip* (see column at far left on page 254). Let the terrine stand for 20 minutes at room temperature before unmolding; unmold and garnish with romaine. Pour the punches into punch bowls and arrange the food on the buffet table.

Inviting your guests: After you decide to host an open house, make out your guest list and set a time. Consider the number of guests you will feel comfortable hosting and how many you can handle with the space available. Keep in mind that an open house means guests will arrive and depart at staggered times, so you probably won't have all the guests assembled in your home at once. With this menu, you can serve about 25 people.

Schedule the party for a time of day and time length that suits you and most of your guests. Open houses usually are held in the afternoon or evening and generally span two to three hours.

Once you've planned the guest list and when to hold your party, invite your guests by sending homemade or purchased invitations. Or, you may prefer to extend your invitations by telephone.

Decorating your home: Since you are opening your home to your guests, have it looking its merriest. Decorate each room individually or unify several rooms with a theme—the verses to your favorite Christmas carol, for example.

If you have a centerpiece, be sure its size is in proportion to the size of the buffet table or tables. The centerpiece itself can range from a very simple arrangement of candles to a wreath of holly and evergreen. And if you don't want to make your own but still want a personal touch, ask your florist to incorporate your favorite silver bowl or Christmas decoration into a colorful arrangement.

Setting up the party: Take an inventory of your serving pieces. Buy, rent, or borrow any you may need. Polish the silver and wash the linens and dishes.

If you have a large table, arrange the refreshments on it, with the beverages at opposite ends. For two or more smaller tables, set the beverages apart.

During the party: As the host or hostess, you are in constant demand, greeting new arrivals and saying goodbye to departing guests. To free yourself for these duties, have someone watching and replenishing the food table. Also, you can ask four or five people to take turns serving the punches and coffee, or you can let guests serve themselves.

Make-Ahead Fruit Canapés

Almond Butter
Orange Aspic
30 slices firm-textured whole wheat
    or white bread
**Assorted fruit and nut toppers
    (for suggestions see column at right)**

■ Prepare Almond Butter and Orange Aspic. Cut crusts from whole wheat or white bread slices; trim slices to make square. Spread about *2 tablespoons* of the Almond Butter onto *each* slice of bread. Spoon the remaining Almond Butter into a decorating bag fitted with a star tip. For each buttered bread slice, pipe a border of Almond Butter onto 2 edges that are opposite each other.

■ Garnish each bread slice with small pieces of fruit or nuts. Slowly spoon about *2 teaspoons* of the partially set Orange Aspic over each fruit-topped slice to cover. Chill the bread slices in the refrigerator for 2 to 3 hours or till the aspic is firm. Before serving, cut each bread slice into 3 long triangles, so that the piped border is on the narrow side or base of the triangle. Makes 90 canapés.

Almond Butter: Let two 8-ounce packages *cream cheese* and 1 cup *butter or margarine* stand at room temperature about 1 hour or till softened. In a large mixer bowl beat one 8-ounce can *almond paste* on medium speed of electric mixer. Add the cream cheese and butter or margarine; beat about 6 minutes or till fluffy.

Orange Aspic: In a small saucepan soften 1 envelope *unflavored gelatin* in ⅓ cup *cold water;* let stand for 5 minutes. Cook and stir over low heat till gelatin is dissolved. Remove from heat. Stir in ⅔ cup *cold water* and ⅓ cup *orange liqueur.* Chill in the refrigerator about 1 hour or to the consistency of unbeaten egg whites (partially set).

■ Preparation time: 1½ hours
■ Chilling time: at least 3½ hours

Use small pieces of thinly sliced or cut-up fruits such as unpeeled apples or pears, red or green seedless grapes, and grapefruit, orange, or mandarin orange sections.

Treat apple and pear slices with lemon juice to prevent the fruit from browning.

For nuts, you can use broken pecans or walnuts, or sliced almonds.

Add color to your holiday buffet table with evergreen, ribbons, candles, and attractive garnishes.

For garnishes, arrange romaine leaves, carrot curls, tomato roses, and fresh coriander on the platter around *Layered Vegetable Terrine*.

Serve *Nordic Dip* in an eggplant boat instead of a serving bowl. To make the boat, slice one-third of the eggplant away from the side. Scoop out the pulp from the remaining eggplant, leaving a ½-inch shell. Spoon the dip into the shell. Save the slice and pulp for another use.

You may want to serve some crackers of various shapes with the terrine and dip, too.

Layered Vegetable Terrine

- 8 **ounces chopped carrots**
- 1 **medium head romaine**
- 1 **large onion, finely chopped (1 cup)**
- 1 **4-ounce can chopped mushrooms, drained and finely chopped**
- 1 **clove garlic, minced**
- 2 **tablespoons butter *or* margarine**
- 2 **vegetable bouillon cubes, crushed**
- 1 **15-ounce can navy beans, drained**
- 1½ **cups soft bread crumbs (2 slices)**
- 3 **beaten eggs**
- ½ **cup butter *or* margarine, softened**
- 3 **bay leaves**
- ½ **teaspoon finely shredded lemon peel**
- 1 **tablespoon lemon juice**
- 1 **teaspoon dried savory, crushed**

▪▪▪ Cook carrots in boiling water 10 to 15 minutes or till tender. Drain; set aside. Clean romaine and remove large stem. Reserve a few inner leaves; finely chop remaining. Cook in a small amount of boiling salted water about 3 minutes or till crisp-tender. Drain well; squeeze out excess liquid. Measure 1 cup romaine. Cook onion, mushrooms, and garlic in 2 tablespoons butter till tender. Remove from heat. Dissolve bouillon in 2 tablespoons *hot water*. Mash beans. Stir bouillon, beans, crumbs, and ¼ teaspoon *pepper* into onion mixture. Stir in eggs and the ½ cup butter.

▪▪▪ Place *2* bay leaves in a well-greased 8x4x2-inch loaf dish; crush remaining leaf. Divide bean mixture in half. To half, stir in carrots, lemon peel, and lemon juice; press into bottom of pan. To the remaining half, stir in cooked romaine, crushed bay leaf, and savory. Spoon atop carrot mixture; cover. Set into a 13x9x2-inch baking pan in oven. Pour hot water into pan to a depth of 1 inch. Bake in a 350° oven about 1½ hours or till set. Cool; cover and chill 2 hours. Before serving, let stand 20 minutes at room temperature. Unmold onto plate; trim with reserved romaine. Makes 1.

▪▪▪ Preparation time: 1 hour
▪▪▪ Cooking time: 1½ hours
▪▪▪ Cooling and chilling time: 2¼ hours
▪▪▪ Standing time: 20 minutes

Nordic Dip

- 1 **3¾-ounce can sardines in mustard sauce**
- 1 **3-ounce package cream cheese, softened**
- 3 **tablespoons chopped pimiento**
- 1 **teaspoon prepared horseradish**
- 1 **teaspoon Dijon-style mustard**
- ½ **teaspoon Worcestershire sauce**
- 1 **small clove garlic, minced**
- 1 **8-ounce carton plain yogurt**
  Assorted vegetable dippers

▪▪▪ In a blender container or food processor bowl combine *undrained* sardines, cream cheese, *1 tablespoon* of the pimiento, horseradish, mustard, Worcestershire, and garlic. Blend or process till smooth; stir into yogurt. Stir in remaining pimiento. Cover and chill. Serve with vegetable dippers. Makes 1½ cups.

▪▪▪ Total preparation time: 30 minutes

Caraway-Sesame Flatbread

- 1 **16-ounce loaf frozen whole wheat bread dough, thawed**
- 1 **beaten egg**
- 2 **tablespoons sesame seed**
- 2 **tablespoons caraway seed**

▪▪▪ Place thawed dough into a greased bowl; cover. Let rise till double (about 1¾ hours). Divide dough into 25 to 30 balls. Cover; let rest 5 minutes. Chill till ready to bake. To bake, on lightly floured surface roll each ball into a 4½- to 5-inch paper-thin circle; place onto a greased baking sheet. Combine egg and 1 tablespoon *water;* brush onto each. Combine sesame and caraway seed; sprinkle about ½ *teaspoon* seed atop each. Bake in a 350° oven for 8 to 10 minutes or till golden and crisp; cool on rack. Makes 25 to 30.

▪▪▪ Rising time: 1¾ hours
▪▪▪ Preparation time: 2 hours
▪▪▪ Cooking time: 8 to 10 minutes per batch

Rosettes

- 2 **beaten eggs**
- 1 **cup all-purpose flour**
- 1 **cup milk**
- 1 **tablespoon sugar**
- 1 **teaspoon vanilla**
   Cooking oil for deep-fat frying
   Powdered sugar

Combine eggs, flour, milk, sugar, vanilla, and ¼ teaspoon *salt;* beat till smooth. Heat a rosette iron in deep hot oil (375°). Dip iron into batter for 2 to 3 seconds (batter should come three-fourths of the way up side of iron). Dip iron into hot oil for 30 to 45 seconds or till golden. Lift out; tip slightly to drain. With fork, push rosette off iron onto paper toweling over a wire rack. Repeat with remaining batter, reheating iron each time. Sprinkle with powdered sugar. Makes 42.

- Preparation time: 5 minutes
- Cooking time: about 1 hour

Swiss Cheese Bites

- 3 **cups shredded process Swiss cheese**
   (12 ounces)
- ⅔ **cup shortening**
- 1½ **cups all-purpose flour**
- 3 **tablespoons cold water**

Bring cheese to room temperature. In a mixer bowl combine cheese and shortening; beat on medium speed of electric mixer till nearly smooth. Stir in flour. Sprinkle *1 tablespoon* of the water over part of the mixture; toss with a fork. Push to side of bowl. Repeat till all is moistened. Shape into 1-inch balls or 1½x½-inch sticks. Place onto a lightly greased baking sheet. Bake in a 375° oven for 20 to 25 minutes or till light brown. Cool on wire racks. Makes about 60.

- Preparation time: 30 minutes
- Cooking time: 20 to 25 minutes

Mincemeat Fruitcake

- 2 **cups prepared mincemeat**
- 2 **cups diced mixed candied fruits and peels**
   (16 ounces)
- 1 **cup chopped walnuts**
- 2½ **cups all-purpose flour**
- ½ **teaspoon baking powder**
- ½ **teaspoon baking soda**
- ¼ **teaspoon salt**
- ¼ **cup butter** *or* **margarine**
- ¾ **cup packed brown sugar**
- 1 **teaspoon vanilla**
- 2 **eggs**
   Brandy *or* **bourbon** *or* **fruit juice**
   Brandy Icing

Grease and lightly flour a 10-inch fluted tube pan; set aside. In a mixing bowl combine mincemeat, candied fruits and peels, and walnuts; set aside. Stir together flour, baking powder, baking soda, and salt.

In a large mixer bowl beat butter or margarine on medium speed of electric mixer for 30 seconds. Add the brown sugar and the vanilla; beat till fluffy. Add eggs, one at a time, beating well on medium speed. Stir the dry ingredients into beaten mixture (batter will be stiff). Stir in the fruit mixture.

Turn the batter into the prepared pan. Bake in a 325° oven about 65 minutes or till cake tests done. Cool thoroughly on a wire rack; remove from the pan. Wrap the cake in brandy-, bourbon-, or fruit juice-moistened cheesecloth. Overwrap with foil. Store in a cool, dry place for at least 1 week. Before serving, prepare Brandy Icing; drizzle over cake. Garnish with additional *candied fruit,* if desired. Slice thinly to serve. Makes 1 cake.

Brandy Icing: In a mixing bowl combine 1 cup sifted *powdered sugar,* 1 tablespoon *brandy or bourbon,* and ½ teaspoon *vanilla.* Add enough *milk* (1 to 2 tablespoons) to make of drizzling consistency.

- Advance preparation time: 1½ hours
- Standing time: at least 1 week
- Final preparation time: 15 minutes

To make *Rosettes,* you will need a special rosette iron. The iron actually is a mold mounted on the end of a long steel handle. The mold portion shapes the cookie into fancy designs, such as stars or flowers. The long handle allows you to dip the mold portion into hot fat without burning yourself.

You can purchase rosette irons in the housewares section of most department stores and in specialty cookware shops.

For an open-house party, where guests are arriving and leaving throughout, you may want to set out half of each punch at the beginning and then refill the punch bowls when necessary.

For *Spiced Orange Nog,* combine half of the chilled mixture with half of the ginger ale. For *Snowflake Punch,* freeze the ice cream mixture in two portions. Add half of the milk to each part before serving.

To prepare a *Strawberry Ice Ring,* combine one 10-ounce package frozen sliced *strawberries,* thawed, with enough *water* to fill your ring mold. Pour the berry mixture into the ring mold and freeze about 6 hours or till firm. To serve, unmold the ice ring and float it atop *Snowflake Punch.*

Spiced Orange Nog

- 6 **eggs**
- ¼ **cup sugar**
- 1 **quart vanilla ice cream, softened**
- ¼ **teaspoon ground cardamom**
- ¼ **teaspoon ground cinnamon**
- 6 **cups orange juice**
  Orange Ice Ring (optional)
- 1 **32-ounce bottle (1 quart) ginger ale, chilled**

■■■ In a mixer bowl beat eggs on low speed of electric mixer till combined. Gradually add sugar, beating on medium speed till dissolved. Add softened ice cream, cardamom, and cinnamon; beat on low speed till combined. Stir in orange juice. Cover; chill in the refrigerator till serving time. If desired, prepare Orange Ice Ring (see lower left column on page 300).

■■■ Before serving, turn the chilled mixture into a large punch bowl. Gradually add the ginger ale, stirring with an up-and-down motion. Float the ice ring atop, if desired. Makes about 22 (6-ounce) servings.

■■■ Total preparation time: 15 minutes

Snowflake Punch

- 3 **quarts vanilla ice cream**
- 2 **cups bourbon**
- 1 **cup light rum**
  Strawberry Ice Ring (optional)
- 14 **cups milk**

■■■ In a mixing bowl stir ice cream *just till softened.* Stir in bourbon and rum; freeze in 2 portions. Prepare Strawberry Ice Ring, if desired (see column at left). Before serving, turn the frozen mixture into a large punch bowl. Gradually stir in milk. Float the ice ring atop, if desired. Makes about 34 (6-ounce) servings.

■■■ Preparation time: 15 minutes
■■■ Freezing time: at least 6 hours

Coconut Tartlets

- 1⅔ **cups all-purpose flour**
- ⅓ **cup sugar**
- 1 **teaspoon finely shredded lime peel**
- ¼ **teaspoon salt**
- ½ **cup butter *or* margarine**
- 1 **slightly beaten egg**
- 2 **beaten eggs**
- ½ **cup sugar**
- ¼ **cup all-purpose flour**
- ¼ **teaspoon salt**
- ¼ **cup cream of coconut**
- 2 **tablespoons lime juice**
- 2 **tablespoons water**
- 2 **tablespoons butter *or* margarine, melted**
- 2 **cups coconut**
- ¼ **cup apple jelly *or* red currant jelly**

■■■ In a mixing bowl stir together the 1⅔ cups flour, the ⅓ cup sugar, the lime peel, and ¼ teaspoon salt. Cut in the ½ cup butter or margarine till the mixture resembles fine crumbs. Add the slightly beaten egg; stir till combined. Form dough into a ball. For *each* tartlet crust, pinch off *1 rounded teaspoon* of dough; press evenly onto bottom and sides of 1¾-inch muffin pans.

■■■ For filling, in a mixing bowl combine the 2 beaten eggs, the ½ cup sugar, the ¼ cup flour, and ¼ teaspoon salt. Add the cream of coconut, lime juice, water, and the 2 tablespoons melted butter or margarine; stir till combined. Stir in coconut.

■■■ Spoon *1 rounded teaspoon* of the filling into *each* tartlet crust. Bake in a 325° oven about 25 minutes or till the pastry is golden and filling is set.

■■■ Meanwhile, for glaze, in a small saucepan heat apple or currant jelly over low heat till melted. Brush the glaze onto hot tartlets. Cool on a wire rack; remove from pans. Makes 48 tartlets.

■■■ Preparation time: 45 minutes
■■■ Cooking time: 25 minutes per batch

Crème de Menthe Squares

1¼	cups butter *or* margarine
½	cup unsweetened cocoa powder
3½	cups sifted powdered sugar
1	beaten egg
1	teaspoon vanilla
2	cups finely crushed graham crackers
⅓	cup green crème de menthe
1½	cups semisweet chocolate pieces

▬▬ In a heavy saucepan combine ½ *cup* of the butter and the cocoa powder. Cook and stir over low heat till butter is melted. Remove from heat; stir in ½ *cup* of the powdered sugar, the egg, and vanilla. Add graham crackers; stir till combined. Press onto the bottom of an ungreased 13x9x2-inch baking pan.

▬▬ Melt ½ *cup* of the butter or margarine. In a mixer bowl combine the melted butter and crème de menthe. Gradually add the remaining powdered sugar, beating with electric mixer till smooth. Spread over the chocolate layer. Chill in the refrigerator for 1 hour. In a heavy small saucepan combine the remaining ¼ cup butter and chocolate pieces. Cook and stir over low heat till melted. Spread over mint layer. Cover and chill 1 to 2 hours or till firm. Cut into small squares. Store in refrigerator. Makes about 96 squares.

▬▬ Preparation time: 45 minutes
▬▬ Chilling time: at least 2 hours

Silver Gift Boxes: With a razor blade, cut a 10-inch square of railroad board coated with metallic paper. Draw lines on white side of square, following diagram. Cut at bold black slash marks A, B, C, and D. Score and crease all dotted lines toward the white side. Starting at slash A and working on white side, fold shaded flap behind the striped flap to dotted line 1. (The white side of the shaded flap should overlap the metallic side of the striped flap.) Glue flap down. Fold slash B over to dotted line 2; glue. Repeat with slashes C and D. Dry. Line box with tissue paper. Add treats. Fold tops down and tie with ribbon.

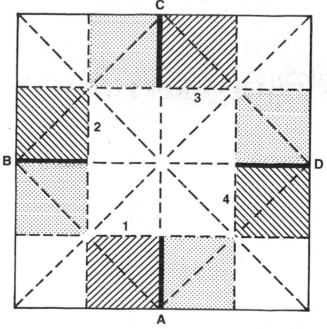

Coconut Tartlets and *Crème de Menthe Squares* make great-tasting treats to send home with guests. Wrap them in silver gift boxes as shown in the picture above.

To make the boxes, follow the directions and diagram at left. All you need is a razor blade or art knife, glue, colored tissue paper, ribbon, scaling wax, seals, and railroad board coated with metallic paper (available in most art supply stores).

SPECIAL CELEBRATION PARTIES

Any important event or occasion calls for a special celebration. Have a party to mark a birthday, wedding anniversary, family reunion, or holiday. Or, if your calendar calls for no special affair, make up something. Just wanting to see friends is reason enough.

Once you decide to throw a party, you will find the food easy to plan if you use this book. Look through this chapter for an array of food to fit the occasion you're celebrating. Many of the recipes are simple to prepare, and all are delicious to eat.

Special celebrations just are not parties unless they offer a tasty variety of snacks, sweets, and drinks. The snack recipes in this chapter include dips and spreads, nibble mixes, and attractive party appetizers. Also featured are a variety of delectable sweets.

When you invite friends over, you'll need a supply of thirst-quenching drinks. This chapter offers several refreshing punches—some with alcohol and some without. And at the end of the chapter you'll discover barmanship information, bar drink recipes, a wine guide, and beer and after-dinner drink suggestions.

Curried Nuts

　3　tablespoons butter *or* margarine
1½　teaspoons Worcestershire sauce
　1　teaspoon curry powder
1½　cups pecan halves
1½　cups raw peanuts

■■■ In a large saucepan melt the butter or margarine. Stir in the Worcestershire sauce and curry powder. Add the pecan halves and peanuts; stir well to evenly coat the nuts. Spread the mixture evenly in a shallow baking pan. Bake in a 300° oven for 15 to 20 minutes or till lightly toasted, stirring once. Remove from oven. Cool. Makes 3 cups.

■■■ Preparation time: 5 minutes
■■■ Cooking time: 15 to 20 minutes

Cocoa Sugared Peanuts

　2　cups raw peanuts
1½　cups sugar
　¾　cup water
　⅓　cup presweetened cocoa powder
　¼　cup Eagle Brand sweetened condensed
　　　milk

■■■ Spread the raw peanuts evenly in a 13x9x2-inch baking pan; bake in a 350° oven for 20 to 25 minutes or till lightly toasted.

■■■ In a small mixing bowl stir the sugar and water together till mixed. Stir sugar mixture into peanuts. Bake in a 350° oven for 35 minutes, stirring occasionally. Combine the cocoa powder and sweetened condensed milk; stir into peanut mixture. Bake about 20 minutes more or till the coating is dry and crisp, stirring frequently. Immediately transfer to another pan. Stir to separate peanuts. Cool. Makes about 6 cups.

■■■ Total preparation time: 1½ hours

Gorp

1 **cup quick-cooking rolled oats**
1 **cup cocktail peanuts**
½ **cup shredded coconut**
¼ **cup toasted wheat germ**
¼ **cup honey**
2 **tablespoons cooking oil**
1 **cup candy-coated milk chocolate pieces**
½ **cup coarsely chopped mixed dried fruit**
½ **cup raisins**

■ In a mixing bowl combine the oats, peanuts, coconut, and wheat germ. Combine honey and oil; stir into the oat mixture. Spread evenly in a 9x9x2-inch baking pan. Bake in a 300° oven for 30 to 40 minutes or till light brown, stirring every 15 minutes; remove from the oven. Transfer to a large greased pan or foil-lined pan. Cool without stirring. Break up large pieces; stir in the candy-coated chocolate pieces, mixed dried fruit, and raisins. Store in a lightly covered container or plastic bag. Makes 6 cups.

■ Preparation time: 15 minutes
■ Cooking time: 30 to 40 minutes

Cereal Brittle

3 **cups round toasted oat cereal**
2 **cups bite-size shredded corn squares**
1 **cup salted peanuts**
¾ **cup sugar**
¾ **cup apple juice *or* apple cider**
¼ **cup light corn syrup**
1 **teaspoon finely shredded orange peel**

■ Butter a large mixing bowl. In it combine the round toasted oat cereal, the bite-size shredded corn squares, and the salted peanuts. Set aside.

■ In a heavy saucepan combine the sugar, apple juice or apple cider, corn syrup, and finely shredded orange peel. Cook and stir over medium heat till the sugar dissolves and the mixture comes to boiling. Continue cooking to 290° (soft-crack stage), stirring occasionally. Immediately remove from the heat.

■ Slowly pour the sugar mixture over the cereal mixture; toss to coat. Spread evenly in a buttered shallow baking pan. Cool until hardened. To serve, break the mixture into pieces. Store in a tightly covered container or plastic bag. Makes about 6 cups.

■ Preparation time: 10 minutes
■ Cooking time: about 15 minutes

Granola*

3 **cups regular rolled oats**
¾ **cup shredded coconut**
½ **cup coarsely chopped almonds**
½ **cup toasted wheat germ**
½ **cup sunflower nuts**
⅓ **cup packed brown sugar**
⅔ **cup light corn syrup**
3 **tablespoons molasses**
½ **cup dried currants *or* raisins**
½ **cup dried banana chips**

■ In a large mixing bowl combine the oats, coconut, almonds, wheat germ, sunflower nuts, and brown sugar. Set aside. Combine corn syrup and molasses. Stir into the oat mixture. Spread evenly in a 13x9x2-inch baking pan. Bake in a 300° oven for 35 to 40 minutes, stirring after 15 minutes and stirring several times during the last 15 minutes. Remove from the oven; stir in currants or raisins and banana chips. Transfer the mixture to another pan. Cool. Stir mixture often to prevent lumps from forming. Store in a tightly covered container or plastic bag. Makes 8 cups.

■ Preparation time: 20 minutes
■ Cooking time: 35 to 40 minutes
 * *pictured on page 261*

For your costume party, have fun and dress up your refreshments, too. An unusual serving container makes these tasty treats even more appealing.

Fill baskets, clay pots, or your cookie jar with any one of these bewitching snacks. An old-fashioned cracker or cookie tin not only has character, but also can serve as a storage container after the party.

★ *see recipe, page 259*

Nutty Caramel Corn

20 cups popped popcorn (about 1 cup unpopped)
2 cups packed brown sugar
1 cup butter *or* margarine
½ cup light corn syrup
½ teaspoon salt
½ teaspoon baking soda
½ teaspoon cream of tartar
2½ cups dry roasted peanuts

■■■ Remove all unpopped kernels from the popped popcorn. Put the popcorn in a large roasting pan and keep warm in a 300° oven.

■■■ In a medium saucepan combine the brown sugar, the butter or margarine, light corn syrup, and the salt. Cook and stir over medium heat till the butter or margarine melts and the mixture comes to boiling. Cook, without stirring, for 5 minutes or till temperature reaches 260° (hard-ball stage). Remove from heat; stir in the baking soda and cream of tartar.

■■■ Slowly pour the brown sugar mixture over the warm popcorn. Gently stir to evenly coat the popcorn. Stir in the dry roasted peanuts. Bake in a 300° oven for 30 minutes, stirring the popcorn mixture after 15 minutes. Transfer the popcorn mixture to a large shallow pan. Cool. Store in tightly covered containers or plastic bags. Makes about 20 cups.

■■■ Preparation time: 30 minutes
■■■ Cooking time: 30 minutes

Party Scramble

3 cups bite-size shredded wheat biscuits
2 cups salted mixed nuts
1½ cups round toasted oat cereal
1½ cups bite-size shredded wheat squares *or* bite-size shredded corn squares
2½ cups small pretzel sticks *or* one 3-ounce can chow mein noodles
½ cup butter *or* margarine
⅓ cup grated Parmesan cheese
1½ teaspoons chili powder
⅛ teaspoon garlic powder

■■■ In a 13x9x2-inch baking pan combine the shredded wheat biscuits, mixed nuts, toasted oat cereal, bite-size shredded wheat or corn squares.

■■■ Bake the cereal mixture in a 300° oven about 5 minutes or till warm. Stir in the small pretzel sticks or the chow mein noodles.

■■■ Melt the butter or margarine; pour over cereal mixture. Combine the grated Parmesan cheese, chili powder, and garlic powder; sprinkle over the cereal mixture. Stir to coat the mixture evenly. Bake in a 300° oven for 15 to 20 minutes more or till dry and crisp, stirring twice during cooking. Remove from oven. Cool. Store in tightly covered containers or plastic bags. Makes about 10½ cups.

■■■ Preparation time: 10 minutes
■■■ Cooking time: about 25 minutes

Granola (see recipe, page 25?
Nutty Caramel Corn, Party Scramb?

Tuna-Filled Appetizer Puffs

- ¼ cup butter *or* margarine
- ½ cup water
- ½ cup all-purpose flour
- 1 cup shredded *process* Swiss cheese *or* American cheese (4 ounces)
- 2 eggs
- 1 9¼-ounce can tuna, drained and flaked
- ⅓ cup dairy sour cream
- 3 tablespoons thinly sliced green onion
- 3 tablespoons finely chopped green pepper
  Dash pepper

■■■ Grease a baking sheet; set aside. For the puffs, in a medium saucepan melt the butter or margarine. Add the water and bring to boiling. Add the flour all at once and stir vigorously. Cook and stir till the mixture forms a ball that doesn't separate. Stir in *half* of the shredded cheese. Remove from the heat and cool slightly, about 5 minutes.

■■■ Add the eggs, one at a time, beating with a wooden spoon after each addition for 1 to 2 minutes or till smooth. Drop the dough by level teaspoonfuls 2 inches apart onto the greased baking sheet. Bake in a 400° oven about 20 minutes or till golden brown and puffed. Remove from the oven and transfer the puffs to a wire rack; cool for 10 minutes. Split puffs, removing any soft dough inside.

■■■ Meanwhile, for filling, in a small mixing bowl stir together the tuna, the remaining shredded cheese, the sour cream, green onion, green pepper, and pepper; chill till serving time. Before serving, spoon a slightly rounded teaspoon of the filling into each puff. Makes about 48 appetizers.

■■■ Preparation time: about 1 hour
■■■ Cooking time: 20 minutes

Cheese-Piped Canapés

- 12 slices firm-textured white bread, whole wheat bread, *or* rye bread
- 1 8-ounce package cream cheese, softened
- 1 4½-ounce can deviled ham
- 1 tablespoon catsup *or* chili sauce
- 2 teaspoons finely chopped onion
- 1 5-ounce jar American cheese spread
- ½ cup butter *or* margarine, softened
  Jellied cranberry sauce, chilled (optional)

■■■ Remove the crusts from the white bread, whole wheat bread, or rye bread, if desired.

■■■ In a small mixing bowl combine the softened cream cheese, the deviled ham, catsup or chili sauce, and the finely chopped onion; set aside. In another bowl add the American cheese spread to the butter or margarine; beat till smooth. Place the cheese-butter mixture into a decorating bag fitted with a star tip.

■■■ For the canapés, spread about *2 tablespoons* of the deviled ham mixture on *each* slice of bread. Cut the bread slices into desired shapes (see illustrations, page 52). Pipe *some* of the cheese-butter mixture (about 1½ teaspoons) around the edges of *each* piece of bread. Cover and chill in the refrigerator about 1 hour or till cold.

■■■ Just before serving, garnish with the jellied cranberry sauce, if desired. Slice the jellied cranberry sauce; using an hors d'oeuvre cutter or a small cookie cutter, cut decorative shapes from jellied cranberry sauce. Place atop canapés. Makes 48 servings.

■■■ Preparation time: about 1 hour
■■■ Chilling time: at least 1 hour

Salmon Triangles

- 1   7¾-ounce can salmon
- 1   beaten egg
- 1   cup ricotta cheese *or* cream-style cottage cheese, drained
- ½   cup finely chopped zucchini *or* cucumber
- ½   cup grated Parmesan *or* Romano cheese
- ½   teaspoon dried marjoram, crushed, *or* dried basil, crushed
- 12 sheets phyllo dough (8 to 10 ounces)
- ¾   cup butter *or* margarine, melted

■ For the filling, drain and flake the salmon; remove the skin and bones. In a mixing bowl combine the egg, ricotta cheese or drained cottage cheese, finely chopped zucchini or cucumber, grated Parmesan or Romano cheese, and dried marjoram or basil. Gently fold in the salmon. Set aside.

■ Lightly brush *1 sheet* of the phyllo dough with *some* of the melted butter or margarine. Place another sheet of phyllo dough atop the first sheet; brush with *some* of the butter or margarine. (Cover the remaining phyllo with a damp cloth to prevent drying.)

■ Cut the stack of phyllo lengthwise into 2-inch-wide strips. For each triangle, spoon *a scant tablespoon* of the salmon filling about 1 inch from one end of *each* strip. Fold the end over the filling at a 45-degree angle. Continue folding to form a triangle that encloses the filling, using the entire strip of 2 layers (see photograph at right).

■ Repeat with the remaining sheets of phyllo dough, butter or margarine, and salmon filling. Place on a baking sheet; brush with butter or margarine. Bake in a 375° oven for 20 to 22 minutes. Serve warm. Makes about 36 appetizers.

■ Preparation time: about 1 hour
■ Cooking time: 20 to 22 minutes

Fold the end of the 2-inch-wide strip of phyllo dough over the salmon filling at a 45-degree angle. Continue folding the phyllo to form a triangle that encloses the filling, as shown.

Ham-Orange Mini-Muffins*

- 2   3-ounce packages cream cheese, softened
- 1   tablespoon milk
- ¼   teaspoon finely shredded orange peel
- ¼   teaspoon dry mustard
- ½   cup sour cream dip with chives
- ½   cup finely diced fully cooked ham
- 1   package (10) refrigerated biscuits
      Paprika

■ For the filling, in a small mixing bowl combine the softened cream cheese, milk, finely shredded orange peel, and the dry mustard; mix well. Fold in the sour cream dip and the finely diced ham.

■ Halve the unbaked biscuits horizontally. Place each biscuit half in a 1¾-inch-diameter muffin cup, pressing the biscuit dough onto the bottom and up the sides of the muffin cup. Spoon about *1 tablespoon* of the filling into *each* biscuit cup. Sprinkle with paprika. Bake in a 375° oven for 20 to 25 minutes or till golden. Remove from pans. Serve warm. Makes 20 muffins.

■ Preparation time: 25 minutes
■ Cooking time: 20 to 25 minutes
* *pictured on page 269*

Ham-Orange Mini-Muffins taste their best served warm from the oven.

To remove the baked muffins from the pan, loosen their edges by using a small metal spatula.

If you can't serve them right away, tip the muffins to one side in the pan. This lets the steam escape and keeps the muffins from becoming soggy on the bottom.

Chicken and Crab Pot Stickers

Pot stickers are savory dumplings that get their name because they stick to the skillet or "pot" during cooking.

You'll find these delicately seasoned appetizers on the menu in many Chinese restaurants. And if you've tried them there, you'll enjoy learning how to make *Chicken and Crab Pot Stickers* at home for an international party.

  1 **cup finely chopped cooked chicken**
  1 **7-ounce can crab meat, drained, flaked, and cartilage removed**
  ¾ **cup finely chopped celery**
  ¾ **cup finely chopped bok choy *or* cabbage**
  ¼ **cup finely chopped green onion**
  1 **tablespoon soy sauce**
  1 **tablespoon dry sherry**
  2 **teaspoons cornstarch**
  1 **teaspoon sesame oil *or* cooking oil**
  ½ **teaspoon sugar**
  ½ **teaspoon salt**
  3 **cups all-purpose flour**
  ½ **teaspoon salt**
  1 **cup boiling water**
  ⅓ **cup cold water**
  ¼ **cup all-purpose flour**
  9 **tablespoons cooking oil**
    Soy-Ginger Sauce
    Chinese Mustard Sauce
    Cucumber stars (optional)
    Green onion brushes (optional)

■ For the filling, in a mixing bowl combine the chopped chicken, the crab meat, celery, bok choy or cabbage, and green onion. Stir together the soy sauce, dry sherry, cornstarch, the 1 teaspoon sesame oil or cooking oil, the sugar, and ½ teaspoon salt. Add the soy mixture to the chicken-crab meat mixture; mix well. Cover and chill in the refrigerator.

■ Meanwhile, prepare the dough. In a mixing bowl stir together the 3 cups flour and ½ teaspoon salt. Slowly pour the 1 cup boiling water into the flour mixture, stirring constantly. Continue stirring till combined. Stir in the ⅓ cup cold water. Cover and set aside to cool slightly.

■ When cool enough to handle, turn the dough out onto a well-floured surface. Knead in the ¼ cup flour to make a stiff dough that is smooth and elastic (8 to 10 minutes total). Shape into a ball. Return the dough to bowl; cover with a damp towel. Let stand at room temperature for 15 to 20 minutes.

■ Turn the dough out onto a lightly floured surface. Divide dough into 4 equal portions. Roll *each* portion to ⅛-inch thickness. Using a 3-inch round cutter, cut each portion into ten rounds, as shown. Reroll the dough as necessary.

■ For the pot stickers, spoon about *1 tablespoon* of the filling into the center of one dough round, as shown. Lightly moisten the edges of dough with water. Fold the dough up around filling, as shown; pinch edges to seal. Set the pinched edge of dumpling upright and press gently to slightly flatten bottom, as shown. Transfer the dumpling to a floured baking sheet. Cover with a dry towel. Repeat with the remaining filling and the dough rounds.

In a large skillet heat *2 tablespoons* of the cooking oil about 1 minute or till very hot. Set *one-third* of the pot stickers upright in the skillet (making sure the pot stickers do not touch each other), as shown. Cook, uncovered, in hot oil about 1 minute or till bottoms are light brown.

Carefully add ⅔ cup *water* to skillet. Reduce heat; cover and cook about 10 minutes. Uncover and cook for 3 to 5 minutes more or till all the water evaporates. Add *1 tablespoon* of the cooking oil to skillet; lift and tilt the skillet to spread oil. Cook the pot stickers, uncovered, for 1 minute more. Using a wide spatula, gently remove the pot stickers from skillet. Keep the pot stickers warm in a 250° oven. Repeat with the remaining pot stickers, cooking oil, and 1⅓ cups more *water*. Prepare the Soy-Ginger Sauce and the Chinese Mustard Sauce; serve with warm pot stickers. Garnish with cucumber stars and green onion brushes, if desired. Makes 40 pot stickers.

Soy-Ginger Sauce: In a small mixing bowl combine 3 tablespoons *soy sauce*, 2 tablespoons *rice vinegar or white vinegar*, and ⅛ teaspoon *ground ginger*.

Chinese Mustard Sauce: In a small saucepan bring ¼ cup *water* to boiling. Combine ¼ cup *dry mustard*, 2 teaspoons *cooking oil*, and ½ teaspoon *salt*. Stir the boiling water into the mustard mixture

Total preparation time: 2¼ hours

To make cucumber stars, slice a cucumber into 1-inch-thick slices. Using a sharp knife, make a diagonal cut in side of each slice, cutting just to cucumber's center; remove knife. Make another cut to center on the opposite angle next to first diagonal cut. Repeat sawtooth cut all the way around. Separate halves and place, sawtooth edge up, on plate. For green onion brushes, follow directions in column at far right on page 75.

Fried Cheese Wedges (pictured above) are equally delicious made with Brie, Swiss, Camembert, Gouda, Edam, caraway, or Muenster cheese.

Make sure that the cheese pieces are well coated with the crumb-wheat germ mixture to keep the cheese from leaking out when it's fried.

Fried Cheese Wedges

16 **ounces Monterey Jack** *or* **cheddar cheese**
 1 **cup fine dry bread crumbs**
 1 **cup toasted wheat germ**
¼ **teaspoon ground red pepper**
 1 **tablespoon butter** *or* **margarine**
 1 **2-ounce can mushroom stems and pieces, drained**
 1 **8-ounce can tomato sauce**
½ **teaspoon dried oregano, crushed**
½ **teaspoon dried basil, crushed**
 4 **beaten eggs**
   Cooking oil for deep-fat frying
   Cherry tomatoes, halved (optional)
   Whole sweet pickles (optional)
   Boiled whole new potatoes (optional)

▬ Cut the cheese into 2x1½x¾-inch wedges. Cover and chill in the refrigerator. In a small mixing bowl stir together the fine dry bread crumbs, wheat germ, and ground red pepper; set aside.

▬ For the sauce, in a saucepan melt the butter or margarine. Reserve 2 mushroom pieces for garnish, if desired; chop remaining. Stir chopped mushrooms, tomato sauce, oregano, and basil into butter. Bring to boiling; reduce heat. Simmer, uncovered, about 5 minutes, stirring occasionally. Cover and keep warm.

▬ Dip the cheese wedges into the beaten eggs to coat evenly. Dip the egg-coated cheese wedges in the bread crumb mixture to coat evenly. Repeat dipping in egg and crumbs (be sure cheese is well coated with bread crumb mixture to prevent leaking).

▬ In a 3-quart saucepan or a deep-fat fryer heat 3 inches of cooking oil to 375°. Fry cheese wedges, a few at a time, in hot oil for 30 to 60 seconds or till golden brown on all sides. Remove fried cheese and drain on paper toweling. Keep warm in a 250° oven while frying remaining. Serve warm with the sauce and accompany with cherry tomatoes, sweet pickles, and new potatoes, if desired. Makes about 20.

▬ Preparation time: 30 minutes
▬ Cooking time: about 25 minutes

Broccoli-Stuffed Cheese Beignets

2 cups small broccoli flowerets
½ cup butter *or* margarine
1 cup water
1 cup all-purpose flour
⅛ teaspoon salt
4 eggs
½ cup grated Parmesan *or* Romano cheese
½ teaspoon Worcestershire sauce
Cooking oil for deep-fat frying

■ Cook the broccoli flowerets, covered, in a small amount of boiling salted water about 5 minutes or just till crisp-tender. Drain.

■ In a medium saucepan melt the butter or margarine. Add the water; bring to boiling. Add the flour and salt all at once; stir vigorously. Cook and stir till the mixture forms a ball that doesn't separate. Remove from heat; cool slightly, about 5 minutes. Add eggs, one at a time, beating with a wooden spoon after each addition for 1 to 2 minutes or till smooth. Beat in Parmesan or Romano cheese and Worcestershire sauce till combined. (Batter should appear smooth, thick, and be slightly sticky to the touch.)

■ For beignets, using half of the batter, drop by heaping teaspoonfuls (about 40) onto waxed paper. Place a broccoli floweret atop each. Pipe or spoon some of the remaining batter atop each floweret (see photograph at right).

■ In a 3-quart saucepan or a deep-fat fryer heat 3 inches of cooking oil to 375°. Lift beignets one at a time with a slotted spoon; place in the hot oil. Fry beignets, a few at a time, for 5 to 6 minutes or till crisp and golden. Remove from oil using a slotted spoon; drain on paper toweling. Sprinkle with additional Parmesan or Romano cheese, if desired. Keep warm in a 250° oven while frying remaining beignets. Serve warm. Makes about 40.

■ Preparation time: 40 minutes
■ Cooking time: about 50 minutes

If desired, use a decorating bag fitted with a star tip to pipe some of the batter (about 1 teaspoon) atop the broccoli till flowerets are partially covered. The batter will puff and fully cover the broccoli during frying.

Petite Beef Bundles with Sour Cream-Chili Sauce

¼ pound ground beef
2 tablespoons sliced green onion
⅓ cup chili sauce
¼ cup finely chopped celery
1 package (8) refrigerated crescent rolls
½ cup dairy sour cream
2 tablespoons chili sauce
½ teaspoon dry mustard

■ In a medium skillet brown the ground beef and sliced green onion; drain well. Stir in the ⅓ cup chili sauce and the chopped celery. Cool slightly.

■ Unroll crescent rolls; separate into 4 rectangles, sealing the perforations between triangles of dough. Press each to about 7x4½ inches. Spread *each* with about *one-fourth* of the meat mixture. Roll up, jelly-roll style, starting from shortest side. Cut crosswise into fourths, forming a total of 16 pieces. Place, seam side down, onto a lightly greased baking sheet. Bake in a 375° oven about 10 minutes or till golden.

■ To make the sour cream sauce, in a small mixing bowl combine sour cream, the 2 tablespoons chili sauce, and the dry mustard. To serve, dip the warm beef bundles in sauce. Makes 16 appetizers.

■ Preparation time: 25 minutes
■ Cooking time: 10 minutes

To make a fancy version of *Broccoli-Stuffed Cheese Beignets,* instead of spooning the batter atop the broccoli flowerets, pipe it on. This may take you just a little longer, but piping is really quite easy, and the results are spectacular. Keep these helpful hints in mind as you prepare to pipe:

Fill the decorating bag by folding back the top of the bag about 1½ inches. Next, spoon the batter into the bag, filling it only about two-thirds full. Unfold the top of the bag, twist it closed, and squeeze the bag to release the batter.

This party menu features several make-ahead recipes just so you can relax and join your guests at the party.

Sake Cheese Ball gets its name from one of the ingredients, sake (sa-KEE), a clear Japanese rice wine. The sake adds a distinctive flavor to the cheese ball.

★ *see recipe, page 263*

Appetizer Frittata

- ¼ **cup chopped celery**
- ¼ **cup chopped onion**
- 2 **tablespoons butter** *or* **margarine**
- 8 **beaten eggs**
- ½ **cup dairy sour cream**
- ½ **cup grated Parmesan cheese**
- 1 **3½-ounce package sliced pepperoni**
  Sliced green onion (optional)

■■■ In a 10-inch skillet with an oven-proof handle, cook the chopped celery and chopped onion in hot butter or margarine till tender. In a mixing bowl combine the eggs, sour cream, and grated Parmesan cheese. Chop *half* of the sliced pepperoni and add to the egg mixture. Pour the egg mixture into the skillet and cook over medium heat, lifting the edges occasionally to allow the uncooked portion to flow underneath. Cook for 8 to 10 minutes or till almost set.

■■■ Arrange the remaining sliced pepperoni around the edge of the cooked egg mixture. Broil 5 inches from heat for 1 to 2 minutes or till eggs are set. Sprinkle the sliced green onion atop, if desired. To serve, cut into wedges. Makes 12 servings.

■■■ Total preparation time: 30 minutes

Sake Cheese Ball

- 1 **8-ounce package cream cheese, softened**
- 1 **cup shredded Monterey Jack cheese (4 ounces)**
- ¼ **cup sake**
- ¾ **cup coarsely crushed glazed sesame crackers**
- 2 **tablespoons snipped parsley**
  Party rye bread

■■■ In a small mixer bowl combine the cheeses; beat on medium speed of electric mixer till nearly smooth. Gradually beat in the sake. Cover and chill about 1 hour or till slightly firm.

■■■ Combine the crushed crackers and snipped parsley. Shape the cheese mixture into a ball. Roll in the cracker-parsley mixture. Wrap in clear plastic wrap and store in the refrigerator till serving time. Serve with party rye bread. Makes 1 cheese ball.

■■■ Preparation time: 30 minutes
■■■ Chilling time: at least 1 hour

Bacon-Tomato Dip

- 6 **slices bacon**
- 1 **8-ounce package cream cheese, softened**
- 2 **teaspoons prepared mustard**
- ½ **teaspoon celery salt**
- 1 **medium tomato, peeled, seeded, and finely chopped**
- ¼ **cup finely chopped green pepper**
  Assorted fresh vegetable dippers

■■■ In a skillet cook the bacon till crisp; remove. Drain on paper toweling and crumble. In a mixing bowl combine the softened cream cheese, prepared mustard, and celery salt. Stir in the crumbled bacon, the finely chopped tomato, and the finely chopped green pepper. Transfer to a serving bowl. Cover and chill in the refrigerator till cold. Serve with vegetable dippers. Makes 2 cups.

■■■ Preparation time: 30 minutes
■■■ Chilling time: at least 2 hours

Appetizer Frittata, Sake Cheese Ball, Bacon-Tomato Dip, Ham-Orange Mini-Muffins (see recipe, page 263)

You can serve a variety of dippers with *Cheese and Beer Fondue.* Bread—either French or Italian—and warm boiled potatoes are two delicious possibilities. As a general guideline, allow 10 to 12 pieces per serving for appetizer fondues.

Cut the French or Italian bread into cubes so each piece has one crust.

Wash tiny new or medium potatoes. Leave tiny potatoes whole; cut medium potatoes into quarters. Cook, covered, in boiling salted water till tender. Allow 10 to 15 minutes for tiny new potatoes or 20 to 25 minutes for quartered potatoes.

Cheese and Beer Fondue

      3 **cups shredded cheddar cheese (12 ounces)**
      2 **tablespoons all-purpose flour**
      1 **small clove garlic, halved**
      1 **cup beer**
    ¼ **cup water**
    ¼ **cup mayonnaise** *or* **salad dressing**
      1 **teaspoon Worcestershire sauce**
    ½ **teaspoon dry mustard**
    ½ **teaspoon prepared horseradish**
      2 **tablespoons snipped chives (optional)**
        French or Italian bread, cut into bite-size cubes
        Warm boiled potatoes, cut up

████ In a mixing bowl combine the shredded cheddar cheese and flour; toss to coat. Rub the bottom and sides of a heavy saucepan with the cut surface of garlic; discard garlic. Add beer and water to the saucepan. Heat the beer mixture over low heat just till warm. Gradually add small amounts of the cheese mixture, *stirring constantly* over low heat till the cheese is melted. (Make sure each addition of cheese has melted before adding more.) Stir in the mayonnaise or salad dressing, Worcestershire sauce, dry mustard, and prepared horseradish. Cook and stir the mixture till heated through.

████ Transfer the hot cheese mixture to a fondue pot; place over fondue burner. Garnish with snipped chives, if desired. Serve immediately with bread cubes or warm boiled potatoes. Spear the bread cubes or the warm boiled potatoes with fondue forks. Dip into the cheese mixture, swirling to coat the bread or potatoes. (The swirling is important to keep the hot cheese mixture in motion so it doesn't set up.) If the cheese mixture thickens while standing, stir in some additional warmed beer. Makes about 6 servings.

████ Total preparation time: about 25 minutes

Cheesy Hot Bean Dip

      3 **slices bacon, cut up**
      1 **cup finely chopped celery**
      1 **cup finely chopped onion**
      2 **cloves garlic, minced**
    ½ **of a 16-ounce can (1 cup) refried beans**
      1 **8-ounce bottle taco sauce**
      1 **4-ounce can green chili peppers, rinsed, seeded, and chopped**
    ½ **teaspoon chili powder**
      2 **cups shredded cheddar** *or* **Monterey Jack cheese (8 ounces)**
        Tortilla chips, corn chips, *or* **celery sticks**

████ In a medium skillet partially cook the bacon; stir in the celery, the onion, and the minced garlic. Cook over medium heat till the celery and onion are tender but not brown; drain off fat.

████ Stir in the refried beans, taco sauce, green chili peppers, and chili powder. Bring the mixture to boiling; reduce heat. Cover and simmer for 5 minutes.

████ Gradually add small amounts of the shredded cheese to the refried bean mixture, *stirring constantly* over low heat till the cheese is melted. (Make sure each addition of cheese has melted before adding more.) Transfer the hot cheese-bean mixture to a fondue pot or chafing dish; place over burner and keep mixture warm. Serve with tortilla chips, corn chips, or celery sticks as dippers. Makes 6 servings.

████ Total preparation time: 25 minutes

Fresh Fruit Dip

1 8-ounce package cream cheese, softened
½ cup lemon yogurt
1 tablespoon honey
½ teaspoon vanilla
½ cup coconut, toasted
3 tablespoons milk
  Assorted fruit dippers

■ In a small mixer bowl beat together the cream cheese, lemon yogurt, honey, and vanilla till smooth. Stir in the coconut and milk. Turn into a serving bowl. Cover and chill in the refrigerator till cold. Serve with fruit dippers. Makes about 2 cups dip.

■ Preparation time: 15 minutes
■ Chilling time: at least 2 hours

Pineapple-Cheese Spread

1 cup shredded Swiss cheese
  (4 ounces)
1 5-ounce jar Neufchâtel cheese spread
  with pineapple
½ cup cream-style cottage cheese
¼ cup chopped walnuts
  Assorted fruits

■ In a blender container or food processor bowl place the shredded Swiss cheese, cheese spread, and cottage cheese. Cover and blend or process till smooth. Line a small bowl with clear plastic wrap. Press the cheese mixture into the bowl. Cover and chill in the refrigerator about 1 hour or till firm.

■ To serve, unmold onto a serving plate. Remove the clear plastic wrap. Press the chopped walnuts onto the cheese to coat. Serve with assorted fruits. Makes 1⅓ cups spread.

■ Preparation time: 20 minutes
■ Chilling time: at least 1 hour

Honey-Cheese Spread

1 cup ricotta cheese
½ cup plain yogurt
2 tablespoons honey
½ cup whipping cream
  Sliced apples or pears

■ In a bowl combine the cheese, yogurt, and honey; beat well. In a small mixer bowl beat the whipping cream on medium speed of electric mixer till soft peaks form; fold into the ricotta cheese mixture. Turn into a serving bowl. Cover and chill in the refrigerator till cold. Serve with apples or pears. Makes 2½ cups.

■ Preparation time: 15 minutes
■ Chilling time: at least 2 hours

Apple and Wheat Germ Spread

1 cup shredded cheddar cheese
⅓ cup mayonnaise or salad dressing
1 teaspoon lemon juice
1 teaspoon Worcestershire sauce
½ cup finely chopped apple
½ cup finely shredded carrot
¼ cup finely chopped celery
¼ cup chopped walnuts
2 tablespoons chopped raisins
1 tablespoon finely chopped green pepper
1 tablespoon toasted wheat germ
  Party rye bread slices

■ Bring cheese to room temperature. In a mixer bowl combine the cheese, mayonnaise, lemon juice, and Worcestershire sauce. Beat on medium speed of electric mixer till nearly smooth. Fold in the apple, carrot, celery, walnuts, raisins, green pepper, and wheat germ. Cover and chill in refrigerator till cold. Stir before serving. Serve with rye bread. Makes 2 cups.

■ Preparation time: 20 minutes
■ Chilling time: at least 2 hours

Layered Taco Spread

Layered Taco Spread

2 8-ounce packages cream cheese, softened
¼ cup dairy sour cream
3 tablespoons mayonnaise *or* salad dressing
¼ teaspoon garlic powder
1 16-ounce can refried beans
   Several dashes bottled hot pepper sauce
   (optional)
   Taco sauce
1 large avocado, seeded, peeled, and cut up
1 medium onion, cut up
1 tablespoon lemon juice
   Lettuce leaves
2 cups shredded lettuce
1½ cups shredded cheddar cheese (6 ounces)
2 medium tomatoes, seeded and chopped
½ cup chopped pitted ripe olives
   Tortilla chips *or* crackers

In a mixer bowl combine the softened cream cheese, sour cream, mayonnaise or salad dressing, and garlic powder; beat on medium speed of electric mixer till smooth. Set aside.

Combine the refried beans, hot pepper sauce, if desired, and enough of the taco sauce (about ½ cup) to make of spreading consistency. In a blender container or food processor bowl place the avocado, onion, and lemon juice. Cover and blend or process till mixture is combined.

Line a large serving platter with lettuce leaves. Spread the cream cheese mixture over the lettuce on the serving platter, making a layer about ¼ inch thick. Spread the avocado mixture evenly over the cream cheese layer. Spread the refried bean mixture atop the avocado layer. Top with the shredded lettuce and shredded cheddar cheese. Sprinkle the chopped tomatoes and chopped olives atop. Cover and chill in the refrigerator till serving time. Serve with tortilla chips or crackers. Makes 12 servings.

Preparation time: 15 minutes
Chilling time: at least 1 hour

Mustard-Cheese Dip

1 cup cream-style cottage cheese
¼ cup butter *or* margarine, softened
¼ cup dairy sour cream
1 tablespoon drained capers
2 teaspoons paprika
1 teaspoon finely chopped green onion
1 teaspoon Dijon-style mustard
   Assorted fresh vegetable dippers

Place cottage cheese in a blender container or food processor bowl. Cover and blend or process till smooth, stopping to scrape sides as necessary. Add butter, sour cream, capers, paprika, onion, and mustard; cover and blend or process till combined. Turn into a small bowl. Cover and chill in refrigerator till cold. Serve with vegetable dippers. Makes 1½ cups.

Preparation time: 15 minutes
Chilling time: at least 1 hour

Lima-Chili Dip

1 10-ounce package frozen lima beans
½ cup chopped onion
½ teaspoon dried oregano, crushed
¼ teaspoon garlic salt
1 8-ounce carton dairy sour cream
¼ cup chopped, seeded canned green
   chili peppers
   Tortilla chips

Cook beans and onion according to package directions for beans, *except* omit salt. Drain, reserving ¼ cup liquid. In a blender container place bean mixture, reserved liquid, oregano, and garlic salt. Cover; blend till smooth. Turn into a bowl; stir in sour cream and peppers. Transfer to a serving bowl. Cover; chill till cold. Serve with tortilla chips. Makes 2⅔ cups.

Preparation time: 20 minutes
Chilling time: at least 2 hours

MENU
BACHELOR PARTY

Layered Taco Spread
Tortilla Chips

Tossed Green Salad

Broiled Steaks

Baked Potatoes

French Bread

Chocolate Cake

Cold Beer

To keep *Layered Taco Spread* chilled for as long as possible, serve it on two small platters, rather than on one large platter. That way, you can keep part of this tasty appetizer in the refrigerator until your guests finish the first platter.

The avocado is a special ingredient in this recipe, simply because you may need to let it ripen. If the avocado feels firm and doesn't yield to gentle pressure, let it ripen at room temperature till no feeling of firmness remains. Ripening may take a few days.

Curried Cheese Spread

- 1   8-ounce carton dairy sour cream
- 1   3-ounce package cream cheese, softened
- ¼   cup finely chopped pimiento-stuffed olives
- ¼   cup finely chopped celery
- 2   tablespoons finely chopped green pepper
- 1   tablespoon finely chopped green onion
- 1   tablespoon lemon juice
- 2   teaspoons curry powder
- ¼   teaspoon Worcestershire sauce
      Dash bottled hot pepper sauce
- ⅓   cup finely crushed rich round crackers
      (8 crackers)
- 1   tablespoon butter *or* margarine, melted
      Sliced pimiento-stuffed olives
      Assorted crackers *or* vegetable dippers

■ Line a 3-cup mold or bowl with clear plastic wrap; set aside. In a mixing bowl combine sour cream, cream cheese, the ¼ cup finely chopped olives, celery, green pepper, green onion, lemon juice, curry powder, Worcestershire sauce, and bottled hot pepper sauce. In another bowl combine the ⅓ cup crushed crackers and melted butter or margarine.

■ Spoon about *one-third* of the sour cream mixture into the lined mold or bowl; sprinkle with *half* of the crumb mixture. Repeat the layers, ending with the sour cream mixture. Cover and chill in the refrigerator at least 4 hours or till firm.

■ To serve, unmold onto a serving plate; remove the plastic wrap. Garnish with the olive slices. Serve with crackers or vegetable dippers. Makes 1⅔ cups.

■ Preparation time: 30 minutes
■ Chilling time: at least 4 hours

Cheddar Vegetable Dip

- 1   8-ounce package cream cheese, softened
- ½   cup mayonnaise *or* salad dressing
- ¼   cup milk
- ½   teaspoon Worcestershire sauce
- ⅓   cup shredded cheddar cheese
      Assorted vegetable dippers

■ In a small mixer bowl combine cream cheese, mayonnaise or salad dressing, milk, and Worcestershire sauce; beat with an electric mixer till smooth. Stir in the cheddar cheese. Cover and chill in the refrigerator about 2 hours or till cold. Serve with vegetable dippers. Makes about 1¾ cups.

Blue Cheese Vegetable Dip: Prepare the Cheddar Vegetable Dip as above, *except* omit cheddar cheese and stir in ¼ cup crumbled *blue cheese* and 2 tablespoons sliced *green onion*.

■ Preparation time: 20 minutes
■ Chilling time: at least 2 hours

Artichoke-Chili Dip

- 1   14-ounce can artichoke hearts, drained
      and chopped
- 1   cup grated Parmesan cheese
- 1   cup mayonnaise *or* salad dressing
- 1   4-ounce can green chili peppers, rinsed,
      seeded, and chopped
      Tortilla chips

■ In a mixing bowl combine the artichoke hearts, Parmesan cheese, mayonnaise or salad dressing, and chili peppers. Turn the mixture into an 8x1½-inch round baking dish. Bake in a 350° oven about 20 minutes or till heated through. Serve warm with tortilla chips. Makes about 2⅔ cups.

■ Preparation time: 10 minutes
■ Cooking time: 20 minutes

Braunschweiger Pâté

 8 **ounces braunschweiger** *or* **liverwurst**
 ½ **cup cream-style cottage cheese**
 ⅓ **cup chopped walnuts**
 ⅓ **cup milk**
 ¼ **cup crumbled blue cheese (1 ounce)**
 2 **3-ounce packages cream cheese, softened**
 Watercress *or* **parsley (optional)**
 Assorted crackers

■ Line a 3-cup bowl with clear plastic wrap; set aside. Place braunschweiger or liverwurst, cottage cheese, walnuts, milk, and blue cheese in a blender container or food processor bowl. Cover and blend or process till smooth, stopping to scrape sides as necessary. Add cream cheese; blend till smooth. Turn the mixture into the prepared bowl; cover and chill in the refrigerator about 2 hours or till firm.

■ To serve, unmold onto a serving plate; remove the plastic wrap. Garnish with watercress or parsley, if desired. Serve with crackers. Makes 2¼ cups.

■ Preparation time: 20 minutes
■ Chilling time: at least 2 hours

Smoked-Oyster Cheese Ball

 2 **4½-ounce packages Camembert cheese, softened**
 1 **8-ounce package cream cheese, softened**
 ¼ **cup butter** *or* **margarine**
 1 **tablespoon brandy**
 1 **3¾-ounce can smoked oysters, rinsed, drained, and chopped**
 8 **to 12 pickled grape leaves** *or*
 1½ cups finely chopped pecans

■ In a mixer bowl combine Camembert cheese, cream cheese, and butter or margarine; beat with an electric mixer till smooth. Add brandy; beat well. Stir in the oysters. Cover and chill in the refrigerator about 1 hour or till firm enough to shape.

■ Meanwhile, if using grape leaves, separate leaves. Soak in cold water for 30 minutes. Drain; pat dry with paper toweling. Divide the chilled cheese mixture into 3 or 4 portions; shape each into a ball. Wrap grape leaves around each ball. (*Or,* roll balls in chopped pecans on waxed paper.)

■ Wrap each ball in clear plastic wrap and chill about 2 hours or till cold. To serve, peel back the pickled grape leaves, if used. Serve with unsalted crackers. Makes 3 or 4 cheese balls.

■ Preparation time: 30 minutes
■ Chilling time: at least 2 hours

For a unique edible present, give someone a *Smoked-Oyster Cheese Ball* (pictured above).

To wrap, place the chilled cheese ball and an assortment of unsalted crackers in a box trimmed with colorful ribbon.

For a special celebration party, bring out a very special sweet—*Orange Petits Fours*. To give them added interest, cut the cake into various shapes and sizes. Use small cookie cutters to cut pieces out of the cake. If you have no cutters, then use a small sharp knife. Cut diamonds, circles, rectangles, or create your own shapes.

Orange Petits Fours

1½ cups all-purpose flour
1½ teaspoons baking powder
¼ teaspoon salt
3 eggs
1½ cups sugar
¾ cup milk
3 tablespoons butter *or* margarine
1 teaspoon finely shredded orange peel
Petits Fours Icing

■ Grease a 13x9x2-inch baking pan; set aside. Stir together the flour, baking powder, and salt. In a large mixer bowl beat eggs on high speed of electric mixer 4 minutes or till thick. Gradually add the sugar; beat at medium speed 4 to 5 minutes or till sugar dissolves. Add the dry ingredients to egg mixture; stir just till combined.

■ In a small saucepan heat the milk with the butter or margarine and the shredded orange peel till the butter melts; stir into the batter and mix well. Turn the batter into the prepared pan.

■ Bake in a 350° oven for 20 to 25 minutes or till cake tests done. Place the baking pan on a wire rack; cool for 10 minutes. Remove cake from the pan; cool thoroughly on the wire rack.

■ Trim the sides of cake to make a smooth and straight edge. Cut the cake into 1½-inch diamonds, squares, circles, or desired shapes. Set a large wire rack (or two small racks) over waxed paper. If necessary, with fingertips gently brush the excess crumbs from the cake pieces.

■ Prepare the Petits Fours Icing. Insert a 3-prong long-handled fork into the side of one piece of cake. Hold the cake over the icing and spoon on enough icing to cover the sides and top. Place the cake piece on wire rack, making sure the pieces do not touch each other. Repeat with the remaining cake pieces. Let the icing dry 15 minutes.

■ Spoon on a second coat of icing. For this coat, place the piece of cake on the tines of the long-handled fork. (Do not spear.) Again, hold the cake over the icing and spoon on enough icing to cover the sides and top. Let dry 15 minutes on rack. Spoon on a third coat of icing, following the directions for second coat. (If necessary, reuse the icing. Scrape the icing off waxed paper and into a small bowl. Beat in a few drops of warm water to make frosting drizzling consistency.) Makes about 40.

Petits Fours Icing: In a 2-quart saucepan combine 3 cups *sugar,* 1½ cups hot *water,* and ¼ teaspoon *cream of tartar.* Bring the mixture to boiling, over medium-high heat for 5 to 9 minutes, stirring to scrape sides of saucepan. Clip a candy thermometer to side of saucepan. Continue cooking over medium-low heat for 18 to 20 minutes to 226°, stirring only as necessary to prevent sticking. Remove saucepan from heat. Cool, without stirring, to lukewarm (110°), about 1 hour. Stir in enough sifted *powdered sugar* (about 4 cups) to make of drizzling consistency. If desired, stir in a few drops of *food coloring.* If necessary, beat the mixture with rotary beater or wire whisk to remove the lumps. Makes about 3½ cups.

■ Preparation time: 1½ hours
■ Cooking time: 25 to 30 minutes
■ Cooling time: 1 hour

Individual Orange Savarins

1 cup Sourdough Starter
2½ cups all-purpose flour
1½ teaspoons baking soda
½ teaspoon baking powder
½ cup butter *or* margarine
1⅓ cups sugar
3 tablespoons finely shredded orange peel
3 eggs
⅔ cup orange juice
¾ cup sugar
¼ cup orange liqueur

■ Bring Sourdough Starter to room temperature. Grease and flour muffin pans. Stir together flour, soda, baking powder, and ½ teaspoon *salt*. Beat butter with electric mixer for 30 seconds. Add the 1⅓ cups sugar and *2 tablespoons* of the orange peel; beat till combined. Add eggs, one at a time, beating well on medium speed. Stir in Sourdough Starter. Add dry ingredients and orange juice alternately to beaten mixture, beating after each addition till combined. Fill the prepared pans with a generous *2 tablespoons* batter. Bake in a 350° oven for 16 to 18 minutes or till done. Remove from pans to wire rack.

■ Combine the ¾ cup sugar, remaining orange peel, and ¾ cup *water*. Bring to boiling; reduce heat. Simmer, uncovered, for 2 minutes. Cool 10 minutes. Stir in orange liqueur. Place wire rack with savarins in shallow pan. Spoon warm syrup slowly over savarins; repeat till all syrup is absorbed. Cool. Makes 40.

Sourdough Starter: Soften 1 package *active dry yeast* in ½ cup warm *water* (110° to 115°). Stir in 2 cups warm *water,* 2 cups *all-purpose flour,* and 1 tablespoon *sugar.* Beat till smooth. Cover bowl with cheesecloth. (Do *not* place in tightly closed container.) Let stand at room temperature for 5 to 10 days or till bubbly, stirring 2 to 3 times a day. Chill.

■ Advance preparation time: 15 minutes
■ Standing time: 5 to 10 days
■ Preparation time: 50 minutes
■ Cooking time: 16 to 18 minutes
■ Cooling time: 10 minutes

Broiled Coconut-Topped Gingerbread

1 14½-ounce package gingerbread mix
1 cup coconut
½ cup packed brown sugar
½ cup chopped pecans *or* walnuts
½ cup toasted wheat germ
¼ cup butter *or* margarine, melted
¼ cup milk
1 teaspoon vanilla

■ Prepare the gingerbread mix according to package directions. Turn the batter into an ungreased 9x9x2-inch baking pan. Bake gingerbread according to package directions.

■ Meanwhile, for topping, in a medium mixing bowl stir together the coconut, brown sugar, chopped pecans or walnuts, and wheat germ. Add the melted butter or margarine, milk, and vanilla; stir till combined. Using the back of a spoon or a small spatula, quickly spread the coconut topping over the hot gingerbread in baking pan.

■ Broil the gingerbread 4 to 5 inches from heat for 2 to 3 minutes or till the coconut topping is golden brown. Serve warm or cool. Cut into squares to serve. Makes 9 servings.

■ Preparation time: 15 minutes
■ Cooking time: about 35 minutes

Let the *Sourdough Starter* come to room temperature before using it. After removing the amount of starter needed for your recipe, add ¾ cup *water,* ¾ cup *all-purpose flour,* and 1 teaspoon *sugar* to the remaining starter. Let it stand at room temperature at least 1 day or till bubbly.

Cover the remaining starter with cheesecloth and refrigerate it for later use. *Do not* place starter in a tightly closed container because the pressure of the gases generated during fermentation may pop the lid off.

If you don't use the starter within 10 days, add 1 teaspoon *sugar;* repeat every 10 days until used.

The starter will last for months if you replenish it after every use and feed it every 10 days if it is unused.

For a festive look, sprinkle powdered sugar on the top of an unfrosted cake. For example, *Cheesy Carrot-Zucchini Cake* (pictured above) is decorated with a crisscross pattern. Try this or any other pattern.

Simply cut out the pattern from a sheet of stiff paper. Place the paper on the cake and sift the powdered sugar atop. Carefully remove the paper after sifting.

Cheesy Carrot-Zucchini Cake

    2 3-ounce packages cream cheese,
         softened
    ⅓ cup sugar
    1 egg
  1⅓ cups packaged biscuit mix
    ⅓ cup sugar
    2 teaspoons pumpkin pie spice
    ½ cup shredded carrot
    ½ cup shredded zucchini
    ¼ cup cooking oil
    2 eggs
    1 teaspoon vanilla
         Powdered sugar (optional)

■■■ Grease and lightly flour an 8x8x2-inch baking pan; set aside. For the filling, in a small mixer bowl combine cream cheese and ⅓ cup sugar. Beat on medium speed of electric mixer till fluffy. Add 1 egg and beat mixture till smooth; set aside.

■■■ In a large mixer bowl stir together the biscuit mix, ⅓ cup sugar, and pumpkin pie spice. Add the shredded carrot, zucchini, cooking oil, the 2 eggs, and vanilla. Beat on low speed of electric mixer for 30 seconds. Beat on medium speed for 2 minutes.

■■■ Pour *half* of the batter into the prepared baking pan. Spoon the filling atop. Spoon the remaining batter over filling. Bake in a 350° oven for 35 to 40 minutes or till done. Cool on a wire rack.

■■■ To serve, sift powdered sugar over the top of the cake, if desired. Cut the cake into diamonds or squares. Makes 9 servings.

■■■ Preparation time: 30 minutes
■■■ Cooking time: 35 to 40 minutes

Minted Cake Squares

    1 package 2-layer-size white cake mix
    ¼ cup green crème de menthe
    1 16-ounce jar fudge topping
    1 8-ounce container frozen whipped
         dessert topping, thawed

■■■ Grease and lightly flour a 13x9x2-inch baking pan; set aside. Prepare the cake mix according to package directions, *except* substitute *2 tablespoons* of the crème de menthe for 2 tablespoons of the water called for in package directions. Turn batter into the prepared pan. Bake in a 350° oven for 25 to 35 minutes or till done. Cool cake on a wire rack for 1 hour.

■■■ Spread the fudge topping over cake. Fold the remaining crème de menthe into thawed dessert topping; spread over fudge topping. Cover and chill in the refrigerator about 2 hours or till serving time. Cut into squares to serve. Makes 12 to 15 servings.

■■■ Preparation time: 25 minutes
■■■ Cooking time: 25 to 35 minutes
■■■ Cooling time: 1 hour
■■■ Chilling time: at least 2 hours

Apple Streusel Squares

    2 cups all-purpose flour
    ½ cup sugar
    ½ teaspoon baking powder
    ½ teaspoon salt
    1 cup butter *or* margarine
    1 slightly beaten egg
    ¾ cup sugar
    ¼ cup all-purpose flour
    1 teaspoon ground cinnamon
    4 medium apples, peeled, cored, and sliced
       (about 4 cups)
    1 cup sifted powdered sugar
       Milk

■ In a medium mixing bowl stir together the 2 cups flour, the ½ cup sugar, the baking powder, and salt. Cut in the butter or margarine till the pieces are the size of small peas. Stir in the beaten egg; gently toss with a fork to combine. Divide the flour mixture in half. Turn *half* of the mixture into an ungreased 13x9x2-inch baking pan; spread evenly. Press onto the bottom of pan to form a firm, even crust.

■ In a large mixing bowl combine the ¾ cup sugar, the ¼ cup flour, and the cinnamon; add apple slices and toss to mix. Arrange apple mixture over crust. Sprinkle remaining flour mixture over apple layer. Bake in a 350° oven for 40 to 45 minutes or till done. Cool for 1 hour.

■ For icing, in a mixing bowl stir together the powdered sugar and enough milk (1 to 2 tablespoons) to make of drizzling consistency. Drizzle the icing atop the cooled streusel. Cut into squares to serve. Makes 16 to 20 servings.

■ Preparation time: 30 minutes
■ Cooking time: 40 to 45 minutes
■ Cooling time: 1 hour

Easy Brownie Cupcakes

    4 squares (4 ounces) semisweet chocolate
    ¾ cup butter *or* margarine
    1⅓ cups sugar
    1¼ cups all-purpose flour
    ¼ teaspoon ground cinnamon (optional)
    4 slightly beaten eggs
    1 teaspoon vanilla
    1 cup chopped walnuts
       Chocolate-Sour Cream Frosting

■ Grease and lightly flour muffin pans or line with paper bake cups; set aside. In a small heavy saucepan melt the semisweet chocolate squares and butter or margarine over low heat, stirring often. Cool the mixture slightly, about 5 minutes.

■ In a mixing bowl stir together sugar, flour, and, if desired, cinnamon. Add the eggs, vanilla, and the cooled chocolate-butter mixture. Stir just till combined. Stir in the chopped walnuts.

■ Fill each muffin cup half full. Bake in a 350° oven for 18 to 20 minutes or till done. Remove cupcakes from the pans. Cool for 1 hour on a wire rack. Meanwhile, prepare Chocolate-Sour Cream Frosting; frost cupcakes. Makes 24 servings.

Chocolate-Sour Cream Frosting: In a small heavy saucepan melt ½ cup *semisweet chocolate pieces* and 2 tablespoons *butter or margarine* over low heat, stirring often. Cool for 10 minutes. Stir in ¼ cup *dairy sour cream,* ½ teaspoon *vanilla,* and ⅛ teaspoon *salt.* Gradually add 1¼ cups sifted *powdered sugar,* beating by hand till the frosting is smooth and of spreading consistency.

■ Preparation time: 55 minutes
■ Cooking time: 18 to 20 minutes
■ Cooling time: 1 hour

■■ **MENU** ■■
SHAMROCK TEA

Tea Sandwiches

Cheesy Carrot-
Zucchini Cake

Crème de Menthe
Squares

Tea

Invite some close friends over for a relaxing afternoon of tea and talk.
    The mint-green cake is perfect for a Saint Patrick's Day tea, or serve this same menu for any spring gathering.

Fudge-making is fun—and the fudge is guaranteed to turn out just right—when you follow this step-by-step detailed recipe. The key to success is using an accurate thermometer and taking care not to stir the fudge during cooling.

Either let the fudge set in a pan or choose among the several shape variations pictured here. You may find shaping the *Fudge Balls, Molded Fudge,* and *Fudge Cutouts* easier if you leave out the optional nuts.

Basic Fudge

    Butter *or* margarine
 2 **cups sugar**
 ¾ **cup milk**
 2 **squares (2 ounces) unsweetened chocolate**
 1 **tablespoon light corn syrup**
    Dash salt
 2 **tablespoons butter *or* margarine**
 1 **teaspoon vanilla**
 ½ **cup chopped nuts (optional)**

■ Lightly grease the bottom and sides of an 8x8x2-inch baking pan with butter or margarine, or if thicker fudge is desired, a 9x5x3-inch loaf pan. Do not butter too heavily, or fudge will feel greasy. Set aside.

■ Butter the sides of a heavy, high-sided, 2-quart saucepan. In saucepan combine the sugar, milk, chocolate, corn syrup, and salt. Cook and stir over medium heat till the sugar is dissolved and mixture comes to boiling. Stir gently to avoid splashing syrup on sides of pan, which causes graininess. Use medium rather than high heat to prevent the mixture from sticking or boiling over. The mixture will begin to bubble vigorously and will rise close to the pan rim.

■ Clip candy thermometer to side of pan, making sure the bulb is covered by the mixture, but not touching the bottom of the pan. Continue cooking the mixture, stirring only as necessary to prevent sticking, till

the thermometer registers 234°, soft-ball stage (a few drops of the mixture, dropped from a teaspoon into *cold* water, form a soft ball that flattens when removed from the water). Watch the thermometer closely; the temperature rises quickly above 220°.

■ Immediately remove pan from heat; add the 2 tablespoons butter or margarine, but *do not stir.* Stirring or moving the mixture can result in coarse, grainy candy. Cool mixture, without stirring or moving pan, till thermometer registers 110°. At this temperature bottom of pan should feel comfortably warm to the touch.

■ Remove the thermometer. Stir in vanilla; beat mixture with a wooden spoon, lifting candy with an up-and-over motion. *Do not use an electric mixer.* Continue beating for 7 to 10 minutes or till fudge becomes very thick, starts to lose its gloss, and doesn't stream back into the pan when the spoon is lifted. (*Or,* till a small amount of the mixture holds its shape when dropped onto waxed paper.)

■ Immediately stir in nuts, if desired. Quickly pour mixture into a prepared pan or follow one of the shape variations. Do not scrape saucepan, as the scrapings will have a less creamy texture. Decorate with additional chopped nuts or nut halves, if desired. Score into squares with a sharp knife; cool. Cut into squares. Store, tightly covered, in a cool, dry place. *Do not store in refrigerator.* Makes about 1¼ pounds.

Fudge Balls: With buttered fingers, shape fudge into 1-inch balls and roll in finely crushed *hard peppermint candies,* as shown, *or* finely chopped *nuts.*

Molded Fudge: Butter small individual molds or sheet molds; press fudge into molds. Unmold, using wooden picks to loosen corners, as shown.

Fudge Cutouts: Spread fudge ½ inch thick on a buttered baking sheet; cut into shapes with hors d'oeuvre or small cookie cutters, as shown.

Fudge Ring: Butter a 2-cup ring mold. Turn fudge into mold; cool. Loosen sides; unmold onto plate. If desired, garnish with sliced *almonds,* as shown.

Fudge Log: With buttered fingers, shape fudge into a log; roll in finely chopped *coconut or nuts,* as shown. Cool; cut into ⅜-inch-thick slices.

▬ Total preparation time: 1¼ to 1½ hours

Chocolate-Mint Candies

- 1 6-ounce package (1 cup) semisweet chocolate pieces
- 1 teaspoon shortening
- 1 egg
- ½ cup sifted powdered sugar
- 2 drops oil of peppermint

▪ In a heavy medium saucepan melt chocolate pieces and shortening over low heat, stirring constantly. Cool till lukewarm, about 15 minutes. Add egg; beat with a spoon till smooth and glossy. Add powdered sugar and oil of peppermint; mix well. Spoon into tiny paper or foil bake cups (about 1¼ inches in diameter), using a scant tablespoon for each. Chill in the refrigerator about 1 hour or till firm. Store in an airtight container in a cool, dry place. Makes about 18.

▪ Preparation time: 35 minutes
▪ Chilling time: at least 1 hour

Chocolate Chip Sandies

- ¾ cup butter *or* margarine
- ⅓ cup sugar
- 1 teaspoon vanilla
- 1¾ cups all-purpose flour
- ½ cup toasted, chopped pecans
- ½ of a 6-ounce package (½ cup) semisweet chocolate pieces

▪ Beat butter with electric mixer for 30 seconds. Add sugar; beat till fluffy. Add vanilla and 3 tablespoons *water*; beat well. Add flour; beat till combined. Stir in pecans and chocolate. Shape into balls, using about 2 teaspoons of dough for each. Place onto an ungreased cookie sheet. Bake in a 325° oven for 15 to 20 minutes or till done. Transfer to a wire rack. Sprinkle with powdered sugar, if desired. Makes 48.

▪ Preparation time: 20 minutes
▪ Cooking time: 15 to 20 minutes

Mocha Diamonds

- 6 squares (6 ounces) semisweet chocolate, cut up
- 1 tablespoon rum
- 1 teaspoon instant coffee crystals
- ½ cup butter *or* margarine
- 2 tablespoons light corn syrup
- 1¼ cups sifted powdered sugar
- ¼ cup finely crushed chocolate wafers

▪ Line a 9x9x2-inch baking pan with clear plastic wrap; set aside. In a small heavy saucepan melt the chocolate over low heat, stirring often. Cool slightly, about 5 minutes. Combine rum and coffee crystals; set aside till coffee crystals are dissolved.

▪ In a small mixer bowl beat butter or margarine on medium speed of electric mixer for 30 seconds or till softened. Beat in corn syrup; add powdered sugar and beat till combined. Stir in melted chocolate and rum-coffee mixture till combined.

▪ Turn the mixture into the prepared pan; spread evenly over bottom. Sprinkle with crushed chocolate wafers. Cover and chill in the refrigerator about 1 hour or till mixture is firm.

▪ Remove from pan by lifting plastic wrap; remove wrap. Using a sharp knife, cut into 2x1-inch diamonds. Store, covered, in the refrigerator. Makes 23.

▪ Preparation time: 30 minutes
▪ Chilling time: at least 1 hour

Festive Butter Cookies

- 3½ cups all-purpose flour
- 1 teaspoon baking powder
- 1 cup butter *or* margarine
- 1 8-ounce package cream cheese, softened
- 1½ cups sugar
- 1 egg
- 1 teaspoon vanilla
- ½ teaspoon almond extract
  Food coloring
- 2 squares (2 ounces) semisweet chocolate, melted and cooled
- 1 slightly beaten egg white
  Colored sugar crystals
  Almond Icing
  Milk
  Small multicolored decorative candies

■ Stir together flour and baking powder. In a mixer bowl beat butter and cream cheese with electric mixer for 30 seconds. Add sugar; beat till fluffy. Add egg, vanilla, and almond extract; beat well. Add dry ingredients to beaten mixture; beat till combined. Divide dough into thirds. To one portion, add food coloring; set aside. Stir chocolate into a second portion. Chill chocolate and plain portions for 1½ hours or till firm.

■ Meanwhile, force unchilled colored cookie dough through cookie press onto an ungreased cookie sheet. Bake in a 375° oven for 8 to 10 minutes or till done. Transfer to a wire rack; cool for 30 minutes. Brush with egg white; sprinkle with colored sugar.

■ Shape the chilled chocolate dough into 1-inch balls using about 1 teaspoon dough for each; shape into logs about 2½ inches long. Place onto an ungreased cookie sheet; bake in a 375° oven for 8 to 10 minutes or till done. Transfer to a wire rack; cool 30 minutes. Prepare Almond Icing; divide in half. Thin half by adding enough milk to make of dipping consistency; set aside remaining icing. Dip chocolate cookie ends into thinned Almond Icing, then into candies.

■ On a lightly floured surface roll remaining portion of chilled dough to ⅛-inch thickness. Cut with cookie cutters; place onto an ungreased cookie sheet. Bake in a 375° oven for 8 to 10 minutes or till done. Cool on a wire rack for 30 minutes. Frost with Almond Icing; sprinkle with colored sugar. Makes 96.

Almond Icing: Combine 1 cup sifted *powdered sugar*, 1 tablespoon softened *butter or margarine*, and several drops *almond extract*. Add enough *milk* (1 to 2 tablespoons) to make of spreading consistency.

■ Preparation time: 40 minutes
■ Chilling time: at least 1½ hours
■ Cooking time: about 40 minutes
■ Cooling time: 1½ hours

Mincemeat-Filled Cookies

- 3 cups all-purpose flour
- 1 cup butter *or* margarine
- 1 cup sugar
- 1 egg
- 2 tablespoons milk
- 1 teaspoon vanilla
- ¾ cup prepared mincemeat

■ Stir together flour and ½ teaspoon *salt*. Beat butter with electric mixer for 30 seconds. Add sugar; beat till fluffy. Add egg, milk, and vanilla; beat well. Add dry ingredients; beat till combined.

■ On a lightly floured surface roll dough, half at a time, to ⅛-inch thickness. Cut with a floured 2½-inch scalloped cookie cutter, dipping cutter into flour between cuts. Reroll dough as necessary. Spread *1 teaspoon* mincemeat onto the centers of *half* of the dough circles. Using a thimble or hors d'oeuvre cutter, cut out small shapes in the centers of remaining circles. Place dough circles over mincemeat-topped circles. Press the edges of dough gently with a fork to seal. Place onto an ungreased cookie sheet. Bake in a 350° oven for 12 to 15 minutes or till golden. Cool on a wire rack. Makes 36 cookies.

■ Preparation time: 25 minutes
■ Cooking time: 50 minutes

The recipe for *Festive Butter Cookies* gives you three different cookies from one batch of dough.
Make colorful sugar-topped spritz cookies from one portion and candy-dipped chocolate logs with another. Cut the third portion into shaped cookies, using a variety of cookie cutters. Frost the cutouts with *Almond Icing,* then make them sparkle with colored sugar crystals.

Pastel Ribbon Bavarian

Pastel Ribbon Bavarian

- 1 envelope unflavored gelatin
- ¾ cup sugar
- ¾ cup water
- 4 slightly beaten egg yolks
- 1½ cups frozen loose-pack unsweetened red raspberries, thawed
- 1 cup frozen loose-pack unsweetened peach slices, thawed
- 4 egg whites
- 1½ cups whipping cream
- 2 tablespoons lime juice
  Few drops green food coloring (optional)
  Whipped cream
  Rolled cookies (optional)

■ In a saucepan combine the unflavored gelatin and sugar; stir in water. Stir in egg yolks. Cook and stir over low heat till gelatin is dissolved and mixture is slightly thickened. Cool to room temperature.

■ In a blender container or food processor bowl puree raspberries (you should have about ¾ cup); remove and set aside. Rinse container; puree peaches (you should have about ½ cup). Set aside.

■ Beat egg whites till stiff peaks form (tips stand straight); fold into gelatin mixture. Beat the 1½ cups whipping cream till soft peaks form; fold into gelatin mixture. Divide the mixture into three portions (about 2 cups each). Fold the pureed raspberries into one portion; set aside. Fold the pureed peaches into another portion; set aside. Fold the lime juice and, if desired, green food coloring into the remaining portion.

■ Pour the lime mixture into a 6½- or 7-cup glass bowl. Carefully spoon peach mixture atop lime layer. Carefully spoon raspberry mixture atop peach layer. Cover and chill about 4 hours or till firm.

■ Before serving, spoon whipped cream into a decorating bag fitted with a large tip; pipe atop dessert. Garnish with cookies, if desired. Serves 12.

■ Preparation time: 1¼ hours
■ Chilling time: at least 4 hours

Banana Split Dessert

- 1 cup finely crushed graham cracker crumbs
- 3 tablespoons sugar
- ¼ teaspoon ground cinnamon
- ¼ cup butter or margarine, melted
- 1 cup sugar
- ¾ cup butter (do not use margarine)
- 3 squares (3 ounces) unsweetened chocolate, melted and cooled
- 1½ teaspoons vanilla
- 3 eggs
- 2 medium bananas, sliced
- 1 15½-ounce can crushed pineapple, drained
- 1 cup whipping cream
- 6 maraschino cherries, halved
- ¼ cup toasted, chopped almonds

■ For crust, in a mixing bowl combine the graham cracker crumbs, the 3 tablespoons sugar, and the cinnamon. Add ¼ cup melted butter or margarine; toss to combine. Turn the crumb mixture into an 8x8x2-inch baking dish; spread evenly. Press onto bottom to form a firm crust. Bake in a 350° oven for 8 to 10 minutes or till edges are brown. Cool.

■ Meanwhile, in a small mixer bowl combine the 1 cup sugar and the ¾ cup butter. (Some brands of margarine may produce a nonfluffy, sticky mixture when used in a recipe of this type. Therefore, we recommend using only butter.) Beat about 4 minutes or till light. Stir in the cooled chocolate and the vanilla. Add eggs, one at a time, beating on medium speed of electric mixer for 2 minutes after each addition; scrape sides of bowl constantly.

■ Arrange banana slices in a single layer over the cooled crust. Spread chocolate mixture over banana slices. Spread pineapple over chocolate layer. Beat whipping cream till soft peaks form; spread over pineapple layer. Top with maraschino cherry halves and toasted, chopped almonds. Chill about 3 hours or till cold. Makes 12 servings.

■ Preparation time: 1 hour
■ Chilling time: at least 3 hours

MENU
WEDDING SHOWER

Party Wine Punch or Citrus Punch ★

Pastel Ribbon Bavarian

Assortment of Fancy Cookies

Nuts and Mints

Coffee

Invite friends of the soon-to-be bride and groom over to your home and honor them with a wedding shower.

Plan refreshments around *Pastel Ribbon Bavarian,* a billowy make-ahead dessert rich with whipped cream. To show off the pastel colors of this elegant, layered dessert, prepare it in a glass serving bowl, as shown opposite.

Select colors for the napkins, plates, candles, and flowers to pick up the pastel pink, yellow, and green tints of the dessert.

★ see recipe, page 300

When fresh fruit and warm weather are both at their seasonal best, invite a group of people over for an outdoor party.

Make-Your-Own Fruit Bowls is a refreshing dessert, and it serves a crowd. Prepare the fruit and the toppings ahead of time, then set them out to let guests create their own dessert.

Liven up your serving table by using fresh-fruit containers to hold the fruit. Hollow out and artfully cut the edges of a watermelon or other melon and fill it with melon chunks or balls. (Make sure that the melon has a flat enough bottom for a stable base.)

You can also halve a fresh pineapple, leaving the top intact. Remove the fruit and use the hollowed-out pineapple shells to hold fruit pieces.

Make-Your-Own Fruit Bowls

- 4 17½-ounce cans vanilla pudding, chilled
- 4 16-ounce cartons dairy sour cream
  Assorted fruit such as pineapple chunks, strawberries, blueberries, mandarin orange sections, banana chunks, melon chunks, *or* seedless grapes
- 2 to 3 cups granola
- 2 cups toasted, shredded coconut
- 2 cups chopped nuts
- 1 16-ounce container frozen whipped dessert topping, thawed
- 1 16-ounce can chocolate-flavored syrup
- 1 16-ounce jar maraschino cherries with stems, drained

■ In a large bowl combine pudding and sour cream; cover and chill while preparing fruit. (Toss banana chunks with lemon juice to preserve color.) Arrange fruit on a platter. Place pudding mixture, granola, coconut, nuts, whipped topping, chocolate syrup, and cherries into separate containers. Assemble in individual bowls, as desired. Serves 25 to 30.

■ Total preparation time: 1½ to 2 hours

Rich Vanilla Ice Cream

- 4 cups whipping cream
- 2 cups sugar
- 6 well-beaten eggs
- 1 tablespoon vanilla
- 4 cups milk

■ In a large saucepan combine whipping cream and sugar. Cook and stir over medium heat till sugar is dissolved. Stir about *half* of the hot mixture into the beaten eggs. Return all to saucepan. Cook and stir about 5 minutes more or till mixture is slightly thickened and coats a metal spoon. Cool; stir in vanilla. Cover and chill for at least 2 hours. Stir in milk; pour into a 5-quart ice cream feeezer. Freeze according to manufacturer's directions. Makes about 4 quarts.

Strawberries-and-Cream Ice Cream: Combine 3½ cups *sliced strawberries,* slightly crushed, and ¼ cup *sugar.* Prepare Rich Vanilla Ice Cream as above, *except* stir the strawberries into chilled mixture. Pour into a 5-quart ice cream freezer. Freeze according to manufacturer's directions. Makes about 4 quarts.

■ Preparation time: 30 minutes
■ Chilling time: at least 2 hours
■ Freezing time: 30 minutes
■ Ripening time: 4 hours

Coffee Angel Pie

  Meringue Shell
- 1 package 4-serving-size *regular* vanilla pudding mix
- 1 teaspoon unflavored gelatin
- 1½ cups milk
- ½ cup coffee liqueur
- 1 cup whipping cream

■ Prepare Meringue Shell and cool. In a saucepan combine vanilla pudding mix and gelatin. Stir in milk. Cook and stir over medium heat till thickened and bubbly. Remove from heat. Stir in coffee liqueur. Cover; cool thoroughly. Beat whipping cream till soft peaks form; fold into pudding mixture. Pile into Meringue Shell. Chill in the refrigerator about 4 hours or till firm. To serve, cut into wedges. Makes 8 servings.

Meringue Shell: In a mixer bowl bring 3 *egg whites* to room temperature; add 1 teaspoon *vanilla,* ¼ teaspoon *cream of tartar,* and a dash *salt.* Beat till soft peaks form (tips curl over). Gradually add 1 cup *sugar,* beating till stiff peaks form (tips stand straight). Spread onto bottom and sides of a lightly buttered 9-inch pie plate, forming a shell. Bake in a 300° oven for 45 minutes. Turn off heat; let dry in oven with door closed for 2 hours. Cool thoroughly on a wire rack.

■ Preparation time: 4½ hours
■ Chilling time: at least 4 hours

Cranberry and Apple Pizza

1¼ cups all-purpose flour
1 tablespoon sugar
1 teaspoon baking powder
½ teaspoon salt
½ teaspoon ground cinnamon
⅓ cup milk
2 tablespoons cooking oil
2 teaspoons lemon juice
1 8-ounce can whole cranberry sauce
1 20-ounce can sliced apples, drained
3 tablespoons sugar
1 teaspoon ground cinnamon
4 slices American cheese, halved diagonally (4 ounces)

■■■ For crust, in a mixing bowl combine the flour, the 1 tablespoon sugar, the baking powder, salt, and the ½ teaspoon cinnamon. Combine milk, cooking oil, and lemon juice; add all at once to dry ingredients. Stir just till dough clings together. Turn out onto a lightly floured surface; knead gently for 10 to 12 strokes.

■■■ Roll dough into a circle about 13 inches in diameter. Fit dough into a greased 12-inch pizza pan, forming a rim around the edge. Bake in a 425° oven for 10 minutes. Remove from the oven.

■■■ Spread the cranberry sauce over dough; arrange the apple slices atop. Combine the 3 tablespoons sugar and the 1 teaspoon cinnamon; sprinkle over apples. Return to oven and bake about 10 minutes more or till apples are heated through. Arrange cheese triangles around outer edge of pizza; bake about 3 minutes more or till cheese is melted. Serve warm. Makes 10 to 12 servings.

■■■ Preparation time: 20 minutes
■■■ Cooking time: 25 minutes

Chocolate-Strawberry Puffs

½ of a 17¼-ounce package (1 sheet) frozen puff pastry
⅓ cup strawberry jelly
1 cup whipping cream
3 tablespoons sugar
2 tablespoons unsweetened cocoa powder
2 tablespoons butter or margarine
⅔ cup sifted powdered sugar
2 tablespoons unsweetened cocoa powder
½ teaspoon vanilla
Sliced strawberries (optional)

■■■ Thaw pastry according to package directions. Unroll the thawed pastry and cut into twenty-eight 2½x1¼-inch rectangles. Transfer to an ungreased baking sheet. Bake in a 350° oven for 18 to 20 minutes or till done. Cool thoroughly on a wire rack.

■■■ Split each rectangle in half horizontally. In a small saucepan heat jelly just enough to soften, do not melt. Spoon the jelly over the bottom halves of pastry rectangles. Set aside to cool slightly.

■■■ Meanwhile, in a mixer bowl combine the whipping cream, sugar, and 2 tablespoons cocoa powder; beat till soft peaks form. Cover and chill in the refrigerator till ready to use.

■■■ For glaze, in a saucepan melt the butter or margarine; remove from heat. Stir in the powdered sugar and 2 tablespoons cocoa powder. Stir in the vanilla and enough hot water (about 1 tablespoon) to make of glazing consistency.

■■■ Drizzle the chocolate glaze over jelly on bottom halves. Replace top halves of pastry rectangles. Pipe or dollop chocolate whipped cream on top of pastry. Garnish with sliced strawberries, if desired. Chill, if not served immediately. Makes 28 servings.

■■■ Total preparation time: 2 hours

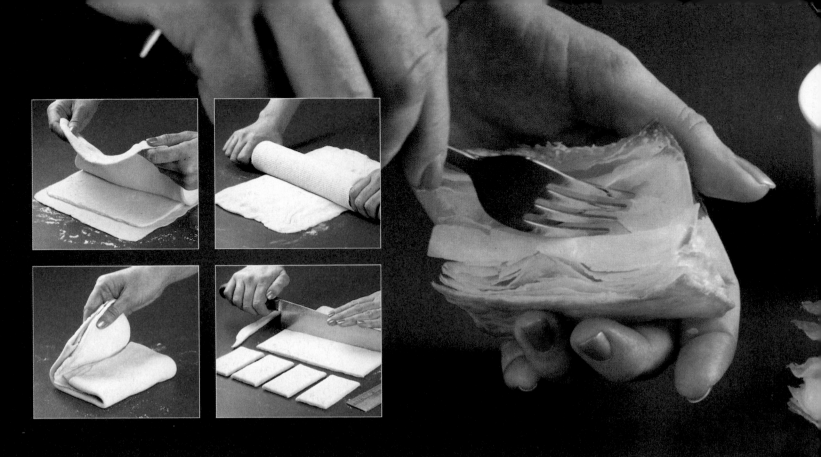

Interested in making *Napoleons* but not in making the pastry from scratch? If so, try substituting one 17¼-ounce package (2 sheets) frozen *puff pastry* for the butter, flour, and ½ cup ice water.

Prepare and bake the thawed pastry according to package directions. Fill between the pastry layers with *Napoleon Filling*. Spread the tops with *Vanilla Glaze*, then drizzle with *Chocolate Icing*.

You will have the same delicious results without all the rolling and chilling that the homemade pastry requires.

Napoleons

- **1 cup butter *or* margarine, chilled**
- **1¾ cups all-purpose flour**
- **½ cup ice water**
- **1 slightly beaten egg white**
- **1 tablespoon water**
- **Napoleon Filling**
- **Vanilla Glaze**
- **Chocolate Icing**

▬ For pastry, reserve *2 tablespoons* of the butter or margarine; chill. In a mixing bowl work remaining butter with back of wooden spoon or with electric mixer just till pliable. Pat or roll out butter between two sheets of waxed paper into an 8x6-inch rectangle. Chill in the refrigerator for 1 hour. (*Or,* chill in the freezer for 20 minutes.) Chill utensils before each use.

▬ Using a pastry blender, cut reserved 2 table-spoons butter into flour till mixture resembles coarse crumbs. Gradually add the ½ cup ice water, tossing with a fork to make a stiff dough. Shape into a ball. On a lightly floured surface knead for 5 minutes or till smooth and elastic. Cover; let rest for 10 minutes.

▬ On a lightly floured surface roll the dough into a 15x9-inch rectangle. Remove the top sheet of waxed paper from chilled rectangle of butter; invert the butter onto half of the pastry. Remove waxed paper. Fold other half of the pastry over butter (see upper left inset photograph). Seal edges by pressing with heel of hand. Wrap in waxed paper; chill in the refrigerator for 1 hour. (*Or,* chill in the freezer for 20 minutes.)

▬ Unwrap pastry. On a lightly floured surface roll pastry into a 15x9-inch rectangle, starting from center and rolling just to edges (see upper right inset photograph). Do not flatten edges; pastry should be of even thickness. Brush excess flour from pastry.

▬ Fold pastry into thirds; then turn and fold into thirds again (see lower left inset photograph). The pastry now has nine layers. Seal edges with heel of hand. Wrap in waxed paper; chill in the refrigerator for 1 hour (*Or,* chill in the freezer for 20 minutes.) Repeat rolling, folding, and chilling two more times. Meanwhile, prepare Napoleon Filling; cover and chill.

Roll into a 15x9-inch rectangle. Using a floured sharp knife, cut off ¼ to ½ inch on all four sides to make a 14x8-inch rectangle. Prick dough with a fork. Cut into sixteen 3½x2-inch rectangles (see lower right inset photograph). Cover baking sheets with 3 or 4 thicknesses of white paper toweling; place pastry rectangles on paper toweling. Chill pastry in the refrigerator for 1 hour. (Or, chill in the freezer for 20 minutes.) Combine egg white and the 1 tablespoon water; brush onto rectangles. (Do not remove toweling.)

Bake on the baking sheet lined with paper toweling in a 450° oven for 6 minutes. Reduce the oven temperature to 300°; bake for 25 to 30 minutes more or till light brown and crisp. Transfer to a wire rack; cool. Prepare Vanilla Glaze and Chocolate Icing.

Separate each rectangle horizontally into 3 layers (see photograph above left). Fill between the layers with Napoleon Filling; spread Vanilla Glaze onto tops. Drizzle Chocolate Icing atop. Makes 16 pastries.

Napoleon Filling: In a saucepan combine 1 cup *sugar*, ¼ cup all-purpose *flour*, ¼ cup *cornstarch*, and ½ teaspoon *salt*. Stir in 3 cups *milk*. Cook and stir till thickened and bubbly. Cook and stir for 2 minutes more. Remove from heat. Gradually stir about *1 cup* hot mixture into 4 beaten *egg yolks*. Return all to pan; cook and stir till bubbly. Cook and stir for 2 minutes more. Remove from heat. Cool; stir in 2 teaspoons *vanilla*. Chill. Beat till smooth just before using.

Vanilla Glaze: In a mixing bowl combine 2 cups sifted *powdered sugar*, ¼ teaspoon *vanilla*, and a dash *salt*. Stir in enough *boiling water* (2 to 3 tablespoons) to make of spreading consistency.

Chocolate Icing: Melt 1 square (1 ounce) *unsweetened chocolate* and 1 teaspoon *butter or margarine*. Cool. Add 3 tablespoons sifted *powdered sugar* and a dash *salt*; stir till smooth. Stir in enough *boiling water* (about 4 teaspoons) to make of drizzling consistency.

Preparation time: 2½ hours
Chilling time (refrigerator): 6 hours
Cooking time: 31 to 36 minutes

Garnish a plate of *Napoleons* with strawberry fans. To make strawberry fans, use fresh berries with the green tops attached. Slice the berries from the tips almost all the way to the stem ends; fan out the berry slices.

Tea makes an ideal beverage to serve guests in cold or hot weather. Choose from a variety of tea products including tea bags and loose tea in regular and special blends.

On cold days, brew flavored teas the same as regular tea, either by the cup or by the pot. For each cup of tea, place 1 to 1½ teaspoons *loose tea or 1 tea bag* into a teapot or infuser, and add ¾ cup *boiling water*. Cover and steep for 3 to 5 minutes. Strain the loose tea or remove the tea bag.

To make iced tea on warmer days, steep the tea for 1 or 2 minutes more than hot tea before straining or removing bags. Keep the brewed tea at room temperature to prevent clouding.

For an iced tea surprise, add ice cubes with fresh mint leaves or citrus slices frozen inside.

Spiced Percolator Punch

- 3 24-ounce bottles unsweetened white grape juice
- 1 46-ounce can unsweetened pineapple juice
- 1 6-ounce can frozen lemonade concentrate, thawed
- ½ cup sugar
- 12 inches stick cinnamon, broken
- 4 teaspoons whole cloves
- 2 teaspoons whole allspice
  Peel of 1 lemon, cut into strips

In a 24-cup electric percolator combine white grape juice, pineapple juice, thawed lemonade concentrate, and sugar. Place cinnamon, cloves, allspice, and lemon peel into coffee maker basket. Prepare according to the manufacturer's directions. To serve, pour into heat-proof glasses or cups. Makes about 32 (4-ounce) servings.

Total preparation time: 30 minutes

Hot and Spicy Berry Cider

- 8 cups apple cider *or* apple juice
- 1 10-ounce package frozen unsweetened red raspberries *or* frozen unsweetened sliced strawberries
- 4 inches stick cinnamon
- 1½ teaspoons whole cloves
- 1 medium apple, cut into 8 wedges

In a large saucepan combine apple cider or juice, berries, cinnamon, and cloves. Bring to boiling; reduce heat. Cover and simmer for 10 minutes. Strain through a sieve lined with cheesecloth. To serve, pour the cider into 8 heat-proof glasses or cups; float an apple wedge in each. Makes 8 (8-ounce) servings.

Total preparation time: 25 minutes

Lemon-Mint Tea

- 1 cup instant tea powder
- ¾ cup sugar-sweetened lemonade mix
- 1 to 2 teaspoons dried mint, crushed

Stir together tea powder, lemonade mix, and mint; store in a tightly covered container till ready to use. Stir before using. To use, for *each* serving, stir *1 tablespoon* of the mix into 1 cup *boiling water or cold water*. Makes enough for 28 (8-ounce) servings.

Advance preparation time: 5 minutes
Final preparation time: about 10 minutes

Spicy Coffee Brew

- 2 cups ground coffee
- 9 inches stick cinnamon, broken
- 6 whole cloves
- 1 vanilla bean, split lengthwise and cut up

Stir together ground coffee, cinnamon, cloves, and vanilla bean. Store in a tightly covered container in the refrigerator for at least 2 weeks.

Stir the mix before using. To use, for *each* serving, measure *1 tablespoon* of the coffee mix into coffee maker basket and add ¾ cup *cold water*. Prepare drip or percolator coffee according to the manufacturer's directions. Pour into heat-proof glasses or cups. Makes enough for 32 (6-ounce) servings.

Advance preparation time: 10 minutes
Standing time: at least 2 weeks
Final preparation time: about 20 minutes

Hot Buttered Lemonade Mix

1 cup butter *or* margarine, softened
½ cup sifted powdered sugar
½ cup sugar-sweetened lemonade mix
½ teaspoon ground cinnamon
1 pint vanilla ice cream (2 cups), softened
Ground nutmeg (optional)

■■■ In a mixer bowl place butter or margarine, powdered sugar, lemonade mix, and cinnamon; beat on low speed of electric mixer till combined. Add ice cream; beat just till combined. Turn into a 4-cup freezer container. Seal, label, and freeze about 7 hours.

■■■ To use, for *each* serving, spoon about ⅓ cup of the ice cream mixture into a mug. Add ½ cup *boiling water.* Stir to combine. If desired, sprinkle nutmeg atop. Makes enough for 10 (6-ounce) servings.

■■■ Advance preparation time: 10 minutes
■■■ Freezing time: at least 7 hours
■■■ Final preparation time: about 10 minutes

Orange Nog

½ of a 6-ounce can (⅓ cup) frozen orange
    juice concentrate
1 cup vanilla ice cream
1 cup milk
2 eggs
1 tablespoon sugar
Ground nutmeg

■■■ Let the orange juice concentrate stand at room temperature for 10 minutes. In a blender container place the orange juice concentrate, ice cream, milk, eggs, and sugar. Cover and blend just till combined. Blend about 30 seconds or till foamy. Pour into chilled tall glasses. Sprinkle nutmeg atop each. Serve immediately. Makes 3 (8-ounce) servings.

■■■ Total preparation time: 15 minutes

Polynesian Smoothie

½ cup buttermilk
¼ cup cream of coconut
1 cup vanilla ice cream
    Pineapple spears (optional)

■■■ In a blender container combine buttermilk and cream of coconut. Add ice cream by spoonfuls. Cover and blend till smooth. Pour into 3 chilled glasses. If desired, garnish each serving with a pineapple spear. Serve immediately. Makes 3 (4-ounce) servings.

■■■ Total preparation time: 5 minutes

Frosty Hawaiian Buttermilk Nog

3 cups buttermilk
1 8-ounce can crushed pineapple
    (juice pack), chilled
¼ cup sugar *or* honey
1 teaspoon vanilla
¼ teaspoon salt
5 ice cubes
    Fresh mint sprigs (optional)

■■■ In a blender container place buttermilk, *undrained* pineapple, sugar or honey, vanilla, and salt. Cover and blend about 30 seconds or till combined. With blender running, add ice cubes, one at a time, through opening in lid. Blend till mixture is nearly smooth and frothy. Pour into 6 chilled mugs or tall glasses. If desired, garnish each serving with a sprig of mint. Makes about 6 (8-ounce) servings.

■■■ Total preparation time: 10 minutes

Lemon-Mint Tea, Spicy Coffee Brew, and *Hot Buttered Lemonade Mix* are three prepared mixes you can keep on hand for drop-in guests. All you need to do when you hear the doorbell ring is boil some water.

Creamy Yogurt Fizz is an easy-to-make versatile recipe. You and your guests can use any fruit-flavored yogurt you prefer. Besides tasting great, it's also a nutritious drink. You'll want to remember it for after-school snacks.

Creamy Yogurt Fizz

2 **cups light cream**
1 **8-ounce carton fruit-flavored yogurt**
¼ **cup dry instant eggnog**
¼ **cup sifted powdered sugar**
1 **10-ounce bottle carbonated water, chilled**
  Ice cubes

■■■ In a pitcher or mixing bowl combine light cream, fruit-flavored yogurt, instant eggnog, and powdered sugar. Stir till eggnog is dissolved. In *each* of 4 tall glasses combine *one-fourth* of the yogurt mixture and *one-fourth* of the carbonated water; stir gently with an up-and-down motion to mix. Add ice cubes. Makes 4 (8-ounce) servings.

■■■ Total preparation time: 10 minutes

Dreamy Coconut Shake

1 **cup coconut ice cream**
1 **8¼-ounce can crushed pineapple, chilled**
¾ **cup light cream *or* milk**
½ **of a 6-ounce can (⅓ cup) frozen tangerine *or* orange juice concentrate**
1 **small banana, cut into chunks**
3 ***or* 4 ice cubes**
  Toasted coconut (optional)

■■■ In a blender container place the coconut ice cream, *undrained* pineapple, light cream or milk, frozen juice concentrate, and banana chunks. Cover and blend just till combined. With blender running, add ice cubes, one at a time, through opening in lid. Blend till mixture is thick and foamy. Pour into 6 chilled glasses. If desired, sprinkle coconut atop each serving. Serve immediately. Makes 6 (5-ounce) servings.

■■■ Total preparation time: 10 minutes

Sparkling Peaches and Cream

1 **16-ounce can peach slices, chilled**
½ **cup unsweetened pineapple juice, chilled**
1 **egg**
1 **tablespoon sugar**
1 **tablespoon lemon juice**
1 **teaspoon vanilla**
4 **ice cubes**
⅓ **cup light cream**
⅔ **cup sparkling mineral water *or* carbonated water, chilled**
  Sliced almonds (optional)

■■■ In a blender container combine the *undrained* peach slices, pineapple juice, egg, sugar, lemon juice, vanilla, and ice cubes. Cover and blend till smooth. Stir in cream; slowly pour sparkling water down the side of the container. Stir gently with an up-and-down motion to mix. Pour into 4 chilled glasses. If desired, garnish each serving with sliced almonds. Makes 4 (7-ounce) servings.

■■■ Total preparation time: 10 minutes

Apricot Soda

1 **12-ounce can apricot nectar *or* 1½ cups orange juice, chilled**
⅓ **cup presweetened cocoa powder**
  Vanilla ice cream *or* ice milk
  Carbonated water *or* ginger ale, chilled

■■■ Stir together the apricot nectar or orange juice and presweetened cocoa powder; pour into 3 chilled tall glasses. To each glass, add *1 or 2 scoops* of ice cream or ice milk; stir gently to mix. Slowly pour about *½ cup* carbonated water or ginger ale down the side of each glass. Serve immediately with straws. Makes 3 (10- to 12-ounce) servings.

■■■ Total preparation time: 10 minutes

Orange-Chocolate Drink Mix

1 tablespoon finely shredded orange peel
5½ cups nonfat dry milk powder
3 cups sifted powdered sugar
1 cup unsweetened cocoa powder
½ cup powdered non-dairy creamer
¼ teaspoon ground cinnamon
¼ teaspoon ground allspice

▰ Place the orange peel into a shallow baking pan. Bake, uncovered, in a 350° oven about 6 minutes or till peel is dried, stirring every 2 minutes.

▰ Stir together dry milk powder, powdered sugar, unsweetened cocoa powder, non-dairy creamer, cinnamon, allspice, and dried orange peel. Store in a tightly covered container till ready to use.

▰ Stir the mix before using. To use, for *each* serving, spoon ⅓ cup of the mix into a cup or mug. Add ¾ cup *boiling water*. Stir till dissolved. Makes enough for 30 (6-ounce) servings.

▰ Advance preparation time: 20 minutes
▰ Final preparation time: about 10 minutes

Butterscotch Cocoa

¼ cup semisweet chocolate pieces
¼ cup butterscotch pieces
4 cups milk
½ teaspoon vanilla

▰ In a 2-quart heavy saucepan melt chocolate and butterscotch pieces over low heat, stirring often. Stir in the milk; heat mixture almost to boiling, but *do not boil*. Remove from heat; stir in vanilla. If desired, beat the mixture with a rotary beater till frothy. To serve, pour into 4 cups or mugs. Makes 4 (8-ounce) servings.

▰ Total preparation time: 15 minutes

Choose-a-Milkshake

1 tablespoon Spicy Mocha Milkshake Mix *or* Citrus Milkshake Mix
1 pint vanilla ice cream (2 cups)
1 cup milk

▰ Prepare desired milkshake mix. In a blender container place ice cream, milk, and mix. Cover; blend just till smooth. Pour into 2 chilled tall glasses; serve immediately. Makes 2 (8-ounce) servings.

Spicy Mocha Milkshake Mix: Mix one 8-ounce can *instant Swiss-style coffee powder,* ½ cup *presweetened cocoa powder,* 1 teaspoon ground *cinnamon,* ½ teaspoon ground *cloves,* and ¼ teaspoon ground *allspice.* Store in a tightly covered container. Stir before using. Makes enough for 68 (8-ounce) servings.

Citrus Milkshake Mix: Combine 1 cup *sugar-sweetened lemonade mix,* ¼ cup *orange-flavored instant breakfast drink powder,* and ¼ teaspoon ground *nutmeg.* Store in a tightly covered container. Stir before using. Makes enough for 40 (8-ounce) servings.

▰ Advance preparation time: 5 minutes
▰ Final preparation time: 10 minutes

Chocolate Malt

1 pint vanilla ice cream (2 cups)
¾ cup milk
¼ cup instant malted milk powder
3 tablespoons chocolate-flavored syrup, chilled
Chocolate ice cream (optional)

▰ In a blender container place vanilla ice cream, milk, milk powder, and syrup. Cover and blend just till smooth. Pour into 2 chilled tall glasses. Add chocolate ice cream, if desired. Makes 2 (10-ounce) servings.

▰ Total preparation time: 10 minutes

MENU
ROLLER SKATING PARTY

Choose-a-Milkshake *or* Chocolate Malt

Peanut Butter Cookies

Invite a group of youngsters or adults to go on a roller skating party. When you return from skating, treat the hungry group to some simple refreshments.
Besides peanut butter cookies, offer your friends a choice of a *Chocolate Malt* or the citrus version of *Choose-a-Milkshake.* (Be sure to prepare the milkshake mix ahead of time.)

Frosted Lemonade Punch

Frothy Apple Punch

       3 **cups apple juice** *or* **apple cider, chilled**
       ⅓ **cup orange juice, chilled**
       2 **cups light cream**
       3 **egg whites**
       ⅓ **cup sugar**
          Ground cinnamon

▰▰▰ In a large mixing bowl combine apple juice or cider and orange juice. Add cream. Beat with a rotary beater till frothy. In a small mixer bowl beat egg whites on high speed of electric mixer till soft peaks form (tips curl over). Gradually add sugar, beating till stiff peaks form (tips stand straight). Gently fold egg whites into cider-cream mixture, leaving a few fluffs of egg white. Pour into a punch bowl. Sprinkle cinnamon atop. To serve, ladle into punch cups. Serve immediately. Makes 8 (6-ounce) servings.

▰▰▰ Total preparation time: 20 minutes

Lemon Berry Apple Cooler

       6 **tea bags**
       3 **cups boiling water**
       2 **32-ounce bottles (8 cups) cranberry juice cocktail, chilled**
       1 **32-ounce bottle (4 cups) apple juice, chilled**
       1 **28-ounce bottle (3½ cups) lemon-lime carbonated beverage, chilled**
       1 **quart lemon sherbet (4 cups)**

▰▰▰ Steep tea bags in boiling water for 5 minutes. Remove bags; chill tea for 3 hours. In a punch bowl combine tea, cranberry juice cocktail, and apple juice. Slowly pour carbonated beverage down side. Stir gently with an up-and-down motion. Add small scoops of sherbet. Ladle into punch cups. Serve immediately. Makes about 44 (4-ounce) servings.

▰▰▰ Preparation time: 20 minutes
▰▰▰ Chilling time: at least 3 hours

Strawberry Slush

       2 **15½-ounce cans crushed pineapple (juice pack)**
       1 **20-ounce package frozen unsweetened strawberries, thawed**
       3 **cups orange juice**
          Lemon-lime carbonated beverage, chilled

▰▰▰ In a blender container combine *one can* of *undrained* pineapple, *half* of the strawberries, and *half* of the orange juice. Cover; blend till smooth. Pour into ice cube trays. Repeat with remaining pineapple, strawberries, and orange juice; pour into additional ice cube trays. Cover; freeze about 6 hours or till firm.

▰▰▰ At serving time, remove frozen cubes from the freezer trays. Place the cubes into a large ice bucket or bowl. To serve, place two or three cubes into glasses. Add carbonated beverage; stir gently to make a slush. Makes enough frozen cubes for 30 servings.

▰▰▰ Preparation time: 20 minutes
▰▰▰ Freezing time: at least 6 hours

Frosted Lemonade Punch

       4 **cups cold water**
       1 **6.7-ounce envelope (1 cup) sugar-sweetened lemonade mix**
       2 **cups unsweetened pineapple juice, chilled**
       1 **quart lemon sherbet (4 cups)**
       2 **16-ounce bottles (4 cups) grapefruit carbonated beverage, chilled**

▰▰▰ In a punch bowl combine water and lemonade mix; stir till dissolved. Stir in juice. Stir *half* of the sherbet to soften; stir into mixture. Scoop remaining sherbet atop. Slowly pour carbonated beverage down side of bowl; stir gently. Ladle into punch cups. Serve immediately. Makes 28 (4-ounce) servings.

▰▰▰ Total preparation time: 20 minutes

When making *Strawberry Slush* you'll need about five ice cube trays to freeze the beverage base. If you don't have that many trays, freeze half of the mixture and keep the remaining mixture in the refrigerator.

After the first batch freezes, transfer the cubes to a plastic bag and place them in the freezer. Then freeze the remaining strawberry mixture in the ice cube trays.

For an ice ring on the outside of the punch bowl—such as one pictured—start with a large bowl. In it, place a container the same size as the punch bowl and weight it down. Freeze water in layers around the weighted container, adding lemon leaves and citrus slices. After freezing, remove the duplicate container. Unmold the ice ring onto a tray and place the punch bowl into the center.

For a different flavor combination, vary the *Apricot-Banana Spritzer* by using peach nectar instead of the apricot nectar.

An if you're trimming calories, substitute a low-calorie carbonated beverage for the regular carbonated beverage.

You'll like *Apricot-Lemon Frappé* so much, you'll want to serve it other ways. Try these variations:

For a truly fruity slush, spoon some of the slushy apricot mixture atop a cantaloupe half that is filled with bite-size chunks of fruit.

Or, for a punch, place the slushy mixture into a tall glass and carefully stir in chilled lemon-lime carbonated beverage.

Apricot-Banana Spritzer

1 12-ounce can apricot nectar
1 medium banana, cut up
2 16-ounce bottles lemon-lime carbonated beverage, chilled
   Mint sprigs (optional)

▪ In a blender container combine apricot nectar and banana pieces. Cover and blend till smooth. Turn the mixture into a shallow baking pan and freeze about 2 to 3 hours or till partially frozen and slushy.

▪ Before serving, in a blender container combine *half* of the frozen mixture and *one bottle* of the chilled carbonated beverage. Cover and blend till smooth. Pour into 3 chilled tall glasses. Repeat with the remaining frozen mixture and carbonated beverage. Garnish each serving with a mint sprig, if desired. Serve immediately. Makes 6 (8-ounce) servings.

▪ Preparation time: 20 minutes
▪ Freezing time: 2 to 3 hours

Grape Pizzazz

4 cups unsweetened grape juice, chilled
2 cups pineapple-orange juice, chilled
1 16-ounce bottle lemon-lime carbonated beverage, chilled
   Ice cubes

▪ In a large pitcher or bowl stir together grape juice and pineapple-orange juice. Slowly pour the carbonated beverage down the side. Stir gently with an up-and-down motion to mix. To serve, fill 8 tall glasses with ice cubes, then pour in grape juice mixture. Serve immediately. Makes 8 (8-ounce) servings.

▪ Total preparation time: 10 minutes

Apple-Grenadine Sipper

8 cups apple juice *or* apple cider, chilled
⅓ cup lime juice, chilled
⅓ cup grenadine syrup, chilled
   Ice cubes

▪ In a large pitcher or bowl stir together apple juice or apple cider, lime juice, and grenadine syrup. To serve, fill 8 tall glasses with ice cubes, then pour in the apple juice mixture. Makes 8 (8-ounce) servings.

▪ Total preparation time: 10 minutes

Apricot-Lemon Frappé

¾ cup water
¼ cup sugar
1 12-ounce can apricot nectar
½ of a 6-ounce can (⅓ cup) frozen lemonade concentrate
   Lemon *or* orange wedges *or* mint sprigs (optional)

▪ In a small saucepan combine the water and sugar. Bring to boiling; reduce heat and simmer, uncovered, for 5 minutes. Cool slightly. Stir in apricot nectar and lemonade concentrate; pour into an 8x4x2-inch loaf pan. Cover the pan with foil and freeze about 3 hours or till mixture is firm.

▪ To serve, scrape the mixture with a spoon till slushy. Spoon into 6 chilled sherbet glasses. If desired, garnish each serving with a lemon or orange wedge or a mint sprig. Makes 6 (3-ounce) servings.

▪ Preparation time: 20 minutes
▪ Freezing time: at least 3 hours

Banana Jupiter

1 medium banana, cut into small pieces
⅔ cup milk
½ cup cold water
½ of a 6-ounce can (⅓ cup) frozen pineapple
   or orange juice concentrate
1 tablespoon sugar *or* honey
½ teaspoon vanilla
6 to 8 ice cubes
   Ground cinnamon

■■■ In a blender container combine banana, milk, cold water, juice concentrate, sugar or honey, and vanilla. With blender running, add ice cubes, one at a time, through opening in lid. Blend till smooth. Pour into 3 chilled tall glasses. Sprinkle cinnamon atop each serving. Makes 3 (8-ounce) servings.

■■■ Total preparation time: 10 minutes

Strawberry Cooler

½ of a 16-ounce package (2 cups) frozen
   whole unsweetened strawberries
½ of a 6-ounce can (⅓ cup) frozen lemonade
   concentrate
1 cup unsweetened orange juice, chilled
½ cup ice cubes
¾ cup lemon-lime carbonated beverage,
   chilled

■■■ Let strawberries and lemonade stand at room temperature about 20 minutes or till partially thawed. In a blender container combine strawberries, lemonade, and orange juice. Cover and blend till smooth. With blender running, add ice cubes, one at a time, through opening in lid. Blend till slushy. Transfer to a pitcher. Slowly pour the carbonated beverage down the side; stir gently with an up-and-down motion. Pour into 5 chilled glasses. Makes 5 (6-ounce) servings.

■■■ Total preparation time: 30 minutes

Citrus Punch

2 cups cold water
1 6-ounce can grapefruit juice, chilled
⅓ cup sugar-sweetened lemonade mix
2 tablespoons grenadine syrup
   Ice cubes

■■■ In a pitcher or bowl combine cold water, grapefruit juice, lemonade mix, and grenadine syrup; stir till mix is dissolved. To serve, fill 3 tall glasses with ice cubes, then pour in the grapefruit juice mixture. Makes 3 (8-ounce) servings.

■■■ Total preparation time: 10 minutes

Berry Frappé

3 cups frozen loose-pack strawberries *or*
   raspberries
1 12-ounce can carbonated creme soda
1 8-ounce carton plain yogurt
½ of a 6-ounce can (⅓ cup) frozen
   lemonade concentrate, thawed
¼ cup sugar
2 cups carbonated water, chilled

■■■ In a blender container place *half* of the following ingredients: strawberries or raspberries, creme soda, yogurt, lemonade concentrate, and sugar. Cover and blend till berries are pureed and sugar is dissolved. Pour into a 13x9x2-inch baking pan. Repeat with remaining ingredients except carbonated water. Cover and freeze about 3 hours or till firm.

■■■ To serve, using a fork, break up the frozen mixture. Place *half* of the mixture and *1 cup* of the carbonated water into a chilled blender container; cover and blend till frothy. Pour into 4 chilled glasses. Makes 4 (6-ounce) servings.

■■■ Preparation time: 25 minutes
■■■ Freezing time: at least 3 hours

Keep the few ingredients it takes to make *Citrus Punch* on hand. That way you will have a great-tasting punch for spur-of-the-moment entertaining. You can easily double or even triple the recipe to serve up to nine people.

If you haven't tried any of the bottled waters available, you're in for a pleasant surprise.

Experiment with several types and brands of bottled water since they vary considerably—no two are exactly alike.

Add sparkling water to wine for a bubbling spritzer. For nonalcoholic beverages, drink bottled water on the rocks with a twist of lime or a slice of lemon. Or, use spring or mineral water to prepare coffee, tea, fruit-flavored drink mixes, and fruit juice concentrates.

Hot Buttered Pineapple Punch

    1 **46-ounce can unsweetened pineapple juice**
    ½ **cup sugar**
    ¼ **cup lime juice**
    ¼ **teaspoon ground nutmeg**
    1 **750-milliliter bottle dry white wine**
       Butter
   12 **cinnamon sticks (optional)**

■■■ In a large saucepan combine pineapple juice, sugar, lime juice, and nutmeg; bring to boiling, stirring till sugar dissolves. Reduce heat; stir in white wine. Heat through, but *do not boil.* To serve, pour punch into 12 heat-proof glasses or mugs; float a pat of butter on each serving. If desired, serve each with a cinnamon stick stirrer. Makes 12 (6-ounce) servings.

■■■ Total preparation time: 15 minutes

Banana Punch

    2 **cups milk**
    ½ **cup rum**
    1 **egg white**
    1 **tablespoon sugar**
    ½ **teaspoon vanilla**
    2 **bananas, peeled, sliced, and frozen**

■■■ In a blender container place milk, rum, egg white, sugar, and vanilla. Cover and blend just till combined. Add frozen banana slices; cover and blend till smooth. Pour into 6 chilled stemmed glasses or wineglasses. If desired, garnish each serving with a fresh fruit kabob or sprinkle with a ground spice. Makes 6 (6-ounce) servings.

■■■ Total preparation time: 10 minutes

Spiced Wassail*

    3 **small cooking apples**
    ½ **cup brandy**
    ¼ **cup packed brown sugar**
    6 **inches stick cinnamon, broken**
    ½ **teaspoon whole cloves**
    ½ **teaspoon whole allspice, crushed**
   3¼ **cups dry red wine**
   1½ **cups dry sherry**

■■■ Core apples; peel strips around tops. Place into an 8x8x2-inch baking dish. Combine brandy and brown sugar. Bring to boiling. Pour over apples. Cover with foil. Bake in a 350° oven for 35 to 40 minutes or till tender. Drain, reserving ¾ cup of the syrup.

■■■ In a saucepan combine reserved syrup and ½ cup *water.* Tie spices in cheesecloth bag; add to pan. Bring to boiling; reduce heat. Cover; simmer for 10 minutes. Stir in wine and sherry. Heat through. Remove spice bag. Pour mixture into a heat-proof punch bowl. Float apples atop. Pour into 12 heat-proof glasses or cups. Garnish each serving with a cinnamon stick, if desired. Makes 12 (4-ounce) servings.

■■■ Total preparation time: 1¼ hours
  ★ *pictured on page 301*

Scarlett O'Hara Punch

    2 **cups Southern Comfort**
    1 **12-ounce can frozen cranberry juice cocktail concentrate, thawed**
   1½ **cups cold water**
       Cracked ice
       Lime slices

■■■ Combine the Southern Comfort, thawed juice concentrate, and water. Pour over ice in punch bowl. Float lime slices atop. Makes 6 (6-ounce) servings.

■■■ Total preparation time: 5 minutes

Sangria Blanco

- ½ **lemon, chilled and thinly sliced**
- ½ **orange, chilled and thinly sliced**
- ½ **apple, chilled and thinly sliced**
- 1 **750-milliliter bottle dry white wine, chilled**
- ¼ **cup brandy**
- 1 **tablespoon sugar**
- 1 **12-ounce can lemon-lime carbonated beverage, chilled**

■ In a 1½-quart pitcher combine lemon, orange, and apple slices. Add wine, brandy, and sugar; stir till sugar is dissolved. Slowly pour the carbonated beverage down the side of the pitcher. Stir gently with an up-and-down motion to mix. Pour into 8 chilled glasses. Serve immediately. Makes 8 (6-ounce) servings.

■ Total preparation time: 10 minutes

Spicy Apple Eggnog*

- 2 **beaten eggs**
- 3 **cups milk**
- 2 **cups light cream**
- ⅓ **cup sugar**
- ½ **teaspoon ground cinnamon**
  Dash salt
- ¾ **cup apple brandy**
  Ground nutmeg

■ In a saucepan combine beaten eggs, milk, light cream, sugar, cinnamon, and salt. Cook and stir over medium heat till mixture is slightly thickened and heated through, but *do not boil.* Remove from heat; stir in apple brandy. To serve, pour into 12 heat-proof glasses or cups. Sprinkle each serving with nutmeg. Serve warm. Makes 12 (4-ounce) servings.

■ Total preparation time: 25 minutes
★ *pictured on page 301*

Espresso Alexander*

- 6 **cups cold water**
- ¾ **cup ground espresso coffee**
- 8 **inches stick cinnamon, broken**
- ½ **cup crème de cacao**
- ¼ **cup brandy**
- 1 **cup whipping cream**
  Chocolate curls *or* grated chocolate

■ Pour the cold water into an electric percolator. Place ground espresso and stick cinnamon into the coffee maker basket. (If using an electric drip coffee maker, pour cold water into upper compartment. Place ground espresso and cinnamon into filter.) Brew according to the manufacturer's directions, using the strongest setting. Remove the basket or filter; stir the crème de cacao and brandy into coffee.

■ Meanwhile, in a mixer bowl beat the whipping cream till soft peaks form. To serve, pour the coffee mixture into 12 to 14 heat-proof glasses or cups, filling two-thirds full. Top each serving with whipped cream and chocolate curls or grated chocolate. Makes 12 to 14 (4 ounce) servings.

■ Total preparation time: 25 minutes
★ *pictured on page 301*

Golden Apple*

- ½ **cup apple juice *or* apple cider, chilled**
- 1½ **ounces vermouth**
  Few drops lemon juice
- 1 **thin apple slice (optional)**

■ In a chilled wineglass stir together apple juice or cider, vermouth, and lemon juice. Garnish with a thin apple slice, if desired. Makes 1 (6-ounce) serving.

■ Total preparation time: 5 minutes
★ *pictured on page 301*

Espresso Alexander calls for ground espresso coffee. Look for it in specialty coffee shops, in stores that sell espresso coffee makers, or in the coffee section of large supermarkets.

For special guests, add a special touch: Serve them a cold drink, such as the *Golden Apple,* in a prechilled wineglass.
Prechill the wineglasses by placing them in the freezer just before your guests arrive. Or, chill the glasses by filling them with ice cubes; empty just before mixing the drink.

The unique flavor and color of *Kir Champagne Punch* come from crème de cassis (black currant liqueur) and from raspberries.

After adding the chilled champagne, remember to gently stir the punch with an up-and-down motion. This mixes the ingredients together without destroying the carbonation of the champagne.

Keep punches chilled by floating an ice ring in the punch bowl. An ice ring is easy to make. Fill a ring mold with water and freeze till firm.

Or, perhaps you prefer a fruit-filled ice ring. First, line the bottom of the ring mold with citrus slices, berries, or melon balls. Add enough water to cover and freeze till firm. Then fill the mold with water and freeze till firm.

Kir Champagne Punch

- 2 10-ounce packages frozen red raspberries
- 4 cups carbonated water, chilled
- 1 cup crème de cassis
- 3 750-milliliter bottles champagne, chilled

■■■ Let raspberries stand at room temperature about 20 minutes or till partially thawed. Place *one package* of the raspberries into a blender container or food processor bowl; cover and blend or process till berries are smooth. Strain the mixture to remove seeds. Pour puree, carbonated water, and crème de cassis into a punch bowl; stir gently to combine.

■■■ Using a fork, break up the remaining raspberries; add to punch bowl. Slowly pour the champagne down side of punch bowl; stir gently with an up-and-down motion to mix. To serve, ladle into punch cups. Serve immediately. Makes 30 (4-ounce) servings.

■■■ Total preparation time: 20 minutes

Creamy Mocha-Cacao Punch

- 1 quart coffee ice cream (4 cups)
- 1 cup milk
- ½ cup bourbon
- ¼ cup light rum
- ¼ cup crème de cacao
  Chocolate curls (optional)

■■■ In a blender container combine *half* of the ice cream with the milk, bourbon, rum, and crème de cacao. Cover and blend just till smooth. Pour the mixture into 6 chilled glasses. Top each serving with a scoop of the remaining coffee ice cream. If desired, garnish each with chocolate curls. Serve immediately. Makes 6 (6-ounce) servings.

■■■ Total preparation time: 10 minutes

Party Punch Base

- ½ cup water
- ⅓ cup sugar
- 12 inches stick cinnamon, broken
- ½ teaspoon whole cloves
- 3 cups apple juice, chilled
- 1 12-ounce can apricot nectar, chilled
- ¼ cup lemon juice

■■■ For syrup, in a small saucepan combine the water, sugar, cinnamon, and cloves. Bring to boiling; reduce heat. Cover and simmer for 10 minutes. Strain and discard spices. Chill in the refrigerator for 1 hour.

■■■ Combine the chilled syrup, apple juice, apricot nectar, and lemon juice. Makes 5 cups Party Punch Base. Use in the following party punches:

Party Wine Punch: Prepare Party Punch Base as above. In a punch bowl combine Party Punch Base and two 750-milliliter bottles of chilled *dry white wine*. Stir to mix. To serve, ladle into punch cups. If desired, garnish each serving with a maraschino cherry. Makes 23 (4-ounce) servings.

Citrus Punch: Prepare Party Punch Base as above. In a punch bowl combine Party Punch Base and two 28-ounce bottles chilled *lemon-lime or grapefruit carbonated beverage*. Stir gently with an up-and-down motion to mix. To serve, ladle into punch cups. Serve immediately. Makes 22 (4-ounce) servings.

Individual Cocktails: Prepare Party Punch Base as above. For each serving, pour 3 tablespoons *vodka, bourbon, brandy, or rum* over ice cubes in a glass. Add about ½ *cup* of the Party Punch Base to the glass; stir. If desired, garnish with an apple slice. Makes 10 (4-ounce) cocktails.

■■■ Advance preparation time: 20 minutes
■■■ Chilling time: at least 1 hour
■■■ Final preparation time: 5 minutes

Clockwise from back left: Kir Champagne Punch, Party Wine Punch, Spicy Apple Eggnog (see recipe, page 299), Golden Apple (see recipe, page 299), Ice Cream Grasshopper (see recipe, page 304), Espresso Alexander (see recipe, page 299), Creamy Mocha-Cacao Punch, Spiced Wassail (see recipe, page 298)

BARMANSHIP

Before hosting a party where you will serve drinks, you need to know a few of the basics. What kinds of beverages will you serve and what quantities of ingredients should you buy? How can you make your own bar drinks? What kinds of glasses will you need?

If you plan to offer bar drinks to your guests, refer to the recipes on pages 303, 304, and 305. Check the recipes for the ingredients you need and stock up. You should also purchase a variety of liquors and beverage mixers. And remember to buy plenty of ice.

When planning amounts of liquor for bar drinks, you can generally expect your guests to drink anywhere from one to three drinks an hour. If you use 1½ ounces of liquor for each drink, you'll get about 16 drinks from each 750-milliliter bottle (fifth) of liquor.

For wine and beer information, turn to pages 306, 307, and 308. These guidelines will help you match beverage quantities to the number of your guests.

Remember to make a variety of nonalcoholic beverages available to guests who don't care to drink alcoholic beverages. For these guests, try serving some of the recipes on this page or use carbonated beverages, fruit and vegetable juices, bottled water, iced tea, or hot coffee or tea.

It's unnecessary to buy a wide selection of bar glasses. A supply of 10- or 12-ounce all-purpose glasses and 9- or 10-ounce stemmed wineglasses will suit nearly every drink and occasion that may arise. If you'd like, you can rent old-fashioned glasses, highball glasses, brandy snifters, and cordial glasses for your party. Disposable plastic glasses, available in various sizes, are convenient to use, especially for a big party.

Bar Drinks Without Alcohol

Prepare these refreshing and tasty individual drinks for those guests who want to forgo alcohol.

Florida Freeze: In a blender container combine ½ cup *orange sherbet*, 3 tablespoons chilled *lemon-lime carbonated beverage*, 2 tablespoons *lime juice*, and ¼ cup *cracked ice*. Cover and blend till smooth. Pour into a chilled tall glass. Makes 1 serving.

Grape Fizz: Combine ½ cup chilled *unsweetened grape juice*, 2 tablespoons *grenadine syrup*, and 1 tablespoon *lemon juice*. Pour over *cracked ice* in a tall glass. Pour chilled *carbonated water* down the side of the glass to fill; stir gently with an up-and-down motion to mix. Makes 1 serving.

Lime and Tonic: Place *ice cubes* into a tall glass. Add 2 teaspoons *lime juice*. Pour 1 cup chilled *tonic water* (quinine water) down the side of the glass; stir gently with an up-and-down motion to mix. Garnish with a *lime wedge*. Makes 1 serving.

Orange Collins: Squeeze the juice from 1 medium *orange* (about ⅓ cup). Combine the freshly squeezed orange juice and ¼ cup chilled *collins mixer*. Pour over *ice cubes* in a tall glass. Pour chilled *carbonated water* (about ½ cup) down the side of the glass to fill; stir gently with an up-and-down motion to mix. Garnish with an *orange slice* and a *maraschino cherry*. Makes 1 serving.

Rum-Flavored Cola: Place *ice cubes* into a tall glass. Add 1 teaspoon *lime juice* and ½ teaspoon *rum flavoring*. Pour one chilled 12-ounce can *cola* down the side of the glass; stir gently with an up-and-down motion to mix. Garnish with a lime wedge, if desired. Makes 1 serving.

Zippy Tomato Cocktail: In a cocktail shaker combine several *ice cubes*, one chilled 6-ounce can *vegetable juice cocktail*, ½ teaspoon *lemon juice*, ¼ teaspoon *Worcestershire sauce*, a dash *bottled hot pepper sauce*, and a dash *celery salt*. Shake well to mix. Strain over *ice cubes* in a tall glass. Garnish with a *celery stalk*. Makes 1 serving.

Bar Drinks with Alcohol

Amaretto Sour: In a cocktail shaker combine *ice cubes*, ¼ cup *Amaretto*, and 2 tablespoons *lemon or lime juice*. Shake well to mix. Strain into a chilled glass. Pour 2 tablespoons chilled *grapefruit carbonated beverage* down the side of glass; stir gently. Add ice cubes, if desired. Garnish with an *orange twist* and a *maraschino cherry* on a skewer. Makes 1 serving.

Black Russian: In a cocktail glass combine ¼ cup *vodka* and 2 tablespoons *coffee liqueur*. Add ice cubes, if desired. Makes 1 serving.

White Russian: In a cocktail glass combine ¼ cup *vodka* and 2 tablespoons *coffee liqueur;* stir in 3 tablespoons *light cream*. Add *ice cubes*. Makes 1 serving.

Bloody Mary: In a cocktail shaker combine *ice cubes*, ⅓ cup chilled *tomato juice*, 3 tablespoons *vodka*, 1 tablespoon *lemon juice*, dash *Worcestershire sauce*, dash *celery salt*, and a dash *pepper or bottled hot pepper sauce*. Shake well to mix. Pour into a chilled glass; add ice cubes, if desired. Garnish with a *celery stalk*. Makes 1 serving.

Note: You may prefer to make Bloody Marys ahead and chill for flavors to blend. Stir before serving.

Bourbon Sour: In a cocktail shaker combine *ice cubes;* ¼ cup *bourbon, Scotch whisky, or rye whiskey;* 2 tablespoons *lemon juice or lime juice;* and 2 teaspoons *powdered sugar*. Shake well to mix. Strain into a chilled glass. Pour 2 tablespoons chilled *grapefruit carbonated beverage* down the side of the glass; stir gently to mix. Add ice cubes, if desired. Garnish with an *orange twist* and a *maraschino cherry* on a skewer. Makes 1 serving.

Vodka Sour: Prepare Bourbon Sour as above, *except* substitute ¼ cup *vodka* for the bourbon.

Brandy Alexander: In a cocktail shaker combine 3 *ice cubes*, ¼ cup *brandy*, 2 tablespoons *crème de cacao*, and 2 tablespoons *whipping cream*. Shake vigorously till frothy. Strain into a chilled cocktail glass. Sprinkle with ground *nutmeg*. Makes 1 serving.

Ice Cream Alexander: In a blender container combine ½ cup *vanilla ice cream*, 2 tablespoons *brandy*, and 1 tablespoon *crème de cacao*. Cover and blend just till smooth. Pour into a glass. Makes 1 serving.

Champagne Cocktail: In a chilled champagne glass combine 1 tablespoon *Southern Comfort*, ½ teaspoon *lemon juice*, and 1 drop *aromatic bitters*. Pour in ½ cup chilled *champagne;* stir gently with an up-and-down motion to mix. Makes 1 serving.

Collins: In a tall glass stir together 2 tablespoons *lemon juice* and 1½ teaspoons *sugar or Simple Syrup* (see column at right). Stir in 3 tablespoons *gin, vodka, or light rum*. Add *ice cubes*. Pour ¾ cup chilled *carbonated water* down the side of the glass. Garnish with an *orange slice* and a *maraschino cherry*. Makes 1 serving.

Daiquiri: In a cocktail shaker combine *cracked ice*, 3 tablespoons *light rum*, 2 tablespoons *lime juice*, 1 teaspoon *powdered sugar*, and 1 teaspoon *orange liqueur*. Shake well to mix; strain into a chilled cocktail glass. Makes 1 serving.

Frozen Daiquiris: In a blender container combine ⅓ cup *light rum*, ¼ cup *lime juice*, 1 tablespoon *powdered sugar*, and 2 teaspoons *orange liqueur*. With blender running, add 11 or 12 *ice cubes*, one at a time, through opening in lid. Blend till slushy. Pour into 2 chilled wineglasses. Makes 2 (6-ounce) servings.

Peach Daiquiris: In a blender container combine about 3 cups frozen unsweetened *peach slices*, ¾ cup *light rum*, ½ cup frozen *lemonade concentrate*, and ⅓ cup sifted *powdered sugar*. Cover and blend till smooth. With blender running, add 20 to 24 *ice cubes*, one at a time, through the opening in the lid. Blend till slushy. (If the mixture becomes too thick, add a little water.) Pour into 4 chilled wineglasses. Makes 4 (10-ounce) servings.

Strawberry Daiquiris: In a blender container combine one 10-ounce package frozen sliced *strawberries*, broken up, with ¾ cup *light rum* and ½ cup frozen *lemonade concentrate*. Cover and blend till smooth. With blender running, add 20 to 24 *ice cubes*, one at a time, through the opening in the lid. Blend till slushy. (If the mixture becomes too thick, add a little water.) Pour into 4 chilled wineglasses. Makes 4 (10-ounce) servings.

Gimlet: In a cocktail shaker combine *ice cubes*, 3 tablespoons *gin or vodka*, and 1 tablespoon *bottled sweetened lime juice*. Shake well to mix. Strain into a chilled cocktail glass. Makes 1 serving.

For sweetness, mixed drinks often call for *Simple Syrup*. To prepare it, pour 1 cup *boiling water* over 1 cup *sugar;* stir till sugar dissolves. Thoroughly chill the syrup before using it.

Keep *Simple Syrup* stored in the refrigerator until it's time to mix the drinks.

Aromatic bitters is an ingredient used in several different bar drinks, such as a *Manhattan* and an *Old-Fashioned*.

This liquid ingredient is made from an aromatic blend of herbs and spices and has been used for decades as an ingredient in cocktail beverages.

Here's a handy guide to help you choose the correct glassware for your party beverages. When a tall glass is specified in the recipe, use a 10- or 12-ounce highball glass.

The size of an old-fashioned glass ranges between 6 and 10 ounces. A cocktail glass is a 4- to 4½-ounce glass, and a liqueur glass holds about 1 or 2 ounces.

Bar Drinks with Alcohol (continued)

Gin and Tonic: Place *ice cubes* into a glass. Add ¼ cup *gin*. Pour ½ cup chilled *tonic water* (quinine water) down the side. Squeeze a *lime wedge* into glass; stir gently. Add wedge to drink. Makes 1 serving.

Golden Cadillac: In a blender container combine ¼ cup *light cream*, 2 tablespoons *white crème de cacao*, and 2 tablespoons *Galliano*. Add ⅓ cup *cracked ice*. Cover and blend till mixed. Pour into a chilled champagne glass or wineglass. Makes 1 serving.

Ice Cream Golden Cadillac: In a blender container combine ½ cup *vanilla ice cream*, 2 tablespoons *white crème de cacao*, and 2 tablespoons *Galliano*. Cover and blend just till smooth. Pour into a chilled champagne or wineglass. Makes 1 serving.

Grasshopper: In a cocktail shaker combine *ice cubes*, 2 tablespoons *white crème de cacao*, 2 tablespoons *green crème de menthe*, and 2 tablespoons *whipping cream*. Shake vigorously till frothy. Strain into a chilled cocktail glass. Makes 1 serving.

Ice Cream Grasshopper (pictured on page 301): In a blender container combine ½ cup *vanilla ice cream*, 2 tablespoons *white crème de cacao*, and 2 tablespoons *green crème de menthe*. Cover and blend just till smooth. Pour into a chilled champagne glass or wineglass. Garnish with a mint sprig, if desired. Makes 1 serving.

Harvey Wallbanger: Place *ice cubes* into a tall glass. Add 2 tablespoons *vodka*, 1 tablespoon *Galliano*, and ¾ cup *orange juice*. Stir. Makes 1 serving.

Kir: Pour ¾ cup chilled *dry white wine* into a chilled wineglass. Add 1 tablespoon *crème de cassis*; stir gently to mix. If desired, add ice cubes. Garnish with a *lemon twist*, if desired. Makes 1 serving.

Mai Tai: Place *cracked ice* into a tall glass. Add 2 tablespoons *light rum*, 2 tablespoons *dark rum*, 1 tablespoon *orange liqueur*, 3 tablespoons chilled *orange juice*, 3 tablespoons chilled *unsweetened pineapple juice*, and 2 tablespoons *bottled sweetened lime juice*; stir. Garnish with a *pineapple chunk* and a *maraschino cherry* on a skewer. Makes 1 serving.

Manhattan: In a cocktail shaker combine *cracked ice*, 3 tablespoons *blended whiskey*, 1 tablespoon *sweet vermouth*, and a dash *aromatic bitters*; shake well to mix. Strain into a chilled cocktail glass. Garnish with a *maraschino cherry*. Makes 1 serving.

Dry Manhattan: Prepare Manhattan as above, *except* substitute *dry vermouth* for the sweet vermouth. Garnish with a *green olive*. Makes 1 serving.

Margarita: In a cocktail shaker combine *ice cubes*, 3 tablespoons *tequila*, 2 tablespoons *orange liqueur*, and 2 tablespoons *lime juice*. Shake well to mix. For a salt-rimmed glass, rub the rim of a chilled cocktail glass with a *lime wedge*; invert into a dish of *coarse salt*. Strain drink into glass. Makes 1 serving.

Frozen Margaritas: In a blender container combine ¾ cup *tequila*, ½ cup *lime juice*, and ½ cup *orange liqueur*. Cover and blend till smooth. With blender running, add 20 to 24 *ice cubes*, one at a time, through the opening in the lid. Blend till slushy. Serve in salt-rimmed glasses. Makes 4 (8-ounce) servings.

Martini: In a cocktail shaker combine *cracked ice*, ¼ cup *gin*, 1 tablespoon *dry vermouth*. Shake well to mix. Strain into a chilled cocktail glass. Garnish with a *green olive*. Makes 1 serving.

Mint Julep: Pour 1 tablespoon *Simple Syrup* (see column, far right, page 303) into a tall glass. Add 2 to 4 sprigs *mint* and crush with back of spoon. Fill glass with *crushed ice*. Stir in ⅓ cup *bourbon*. Add *crushed ice* to fill the glass. Sprinkle with *powdered sugar*. Garnish with a mint sprig. Makes 1 serving.

Old-Fashioned: Pour 1 tablespoon *Simple Syrup* (see column, far right, page 303) into an old-fashioned glass. Stir in a dash *aromatic bitters*. Add *ice cubes* and 3 tablespoons *bourbon, brandy, Scotch whisky, or Southern Comfort*. Pour in 3 tablespoons chilled *carbonated water*; stir gently to mix. Garnish with an *orange twist* and a *maraschino cherry* on a skewer. Makes 1 serving.

Orange Champagne: Thinly peel ½ of a medium *orange* into a spiral of peel about 12 inches long; place into a chilled champagne glass. Add 2 teaspoons *orange liqueur*; pour in ½ cup chilled *champagne*. Stir gently to mix. Makes 1 serving.

Piña Colada: In a blender container combine ¼ cup chilled *unsweetened pineapple juice or undrained canned crushed pineapple (juice pack)*, 3 tablespoons *rum*, 2 tablespoons *cream of coconut*, and ¼ cup *cracked ice*. Cover and blend. Pour into a chilled cocktail glass. Add a *pineapple spear*. Makes 1.

Pink Lady: In a cocktail shaker combine *cracked ice*, 3 tablespoons *gin*, 1 tablespoon *grenadine syrup*, 1 tablespoon *light cream*, 1 *egg white*, and 1 teaspoon *lemon juice*. Shake. Strain into a glass. Makes 1.

Planter's Punch: In a cocktail shaker combine *ice cubes*, 3 tablespoons *dark rum*, 3 tablespoons chilled *unsweetened pineapple juice*, 3 tablespoons chilled *orange juice*, 1 tablespoon *lemon or lime juice*, 1 tablespoon *Simple Syrup* (see column, far right, page 303), and a dash *grenadine syrup*. Shake well. Strain over *ice cubes* in a tall glass. Garnish with an *orange slice* and a *maraschino cherry*. Makes 1 serving.

Pousse-Café: Into a pousse-café glass or liqueur glass, slowly pour the following ingredients in the order listed so each floats on the one below: 1½ teaspoons *grenadine syrup*, 1½ teaspoons *green crème de menthe*, 1½ teaspoons *apricot brandy*, and 1½ teaspoons *whipping cream*. Makes 1 serving.

It takes a little practice to prepare the layered after-dinner drink, *Pousse-Café*. Carefully spoon each liquid over the back of a small spoon, as shown. Be sure to add the ingredients in the order listed so that they will stay in separate layers.

Ramos Gin Fizz: In a cocktail shaker combine *cracked ice*, 3 tablespoons *gin*, 2 tablespoons *light cream*, 1 tablespoon *Simple Syrup* (see column, far right, page 303), 1 tablespoon *lemon juice*, 1 tablespoon *lime juice*, ¼ to ½ teaspoon *orange flower water*, and 1 *egg white*. Shake. Strain into a glass. Stir in ½ cup chilled *carbonated water*. Makes 1.

Rusty Nail: Place 2 *ice cubes* into a cocktail glass. Pour in ¼ cup *Scotch whisky* and 2 tablespoons *Drambuie*; stir to mix. Makes 1 serving.

Salty Dog: In a pitcher combine one chilled 18-ounce can *unsweetened grapefruit juice* and ¾ cup *vodka or gin*. For salt-rimmed glasses, rub the rim of 4 tall glasses with a *lime wedge or* dip into *lime juice* to moisten; invert into a dish of *coarse salt*. Fill each glass with *ice cubes*. Pour in the grapefruit mixture. Makes 4 (6-ounce) servings.

Screwdriver: Place 3 or 4 *ice cubes* into a tall glass. Add 3 tablespoons *vodka* and, if desired, 1 tablespoon *orange liqueur*. Add ½ to ¾ cup *orange juice* to fill the glass; stir to mix. Makes 1 serving.

Smith and Kerns: Place *ice cubes* into a tall glass. Add ¼ cup *dark crème de cacao or coffee liqueur* and ¼ cup *light cream*. Pour in 2 tablespoons chilled *carbonated water*; stir gently. Makes 1 serving.

Tequila Sunrise: Place *crushed ice* into a tall glass. Add 3 tablespoons *tequila* and 1 tablespoon *lime juice*. Slowly pour in ⅓ cup *orange juice*. Pour in 1½ teaspoons *grenadine syrup*. Stir before drinking. Makes 1 serving.

Velvet Hammer: In a blender container combine 1 cup *vanilla ice cream*, 3 tablespoons *white crème de cacao*, and 3 tablespoons *orange liqueur*. Cover and blend just till smooth. Pour into a chilled champagne glass. Makes 2 (5-ounce) servings.

Whiskey Sour: In a cocktail shaker combine *cracked ice*, 3 tablespoons *bourbon or blended whiskey*, 2 tablespoons *lemon juice*, and 2 tablespoons *Simple Syrup* (see column, far right, page 303). Shake well to mix. Strain into a chilled cocktail glass. If desired, add cracked ice. Garnish with an *orange twist* and a *maraschino cherry* on a skewer. Makes 1 serving.

Wine Spritzer: Place a *lemon twist* into a tall glass. Add *ice cubes or Fruited Ice Cubes*. Pour in ½ cup chilled *dry white wine* and ¼ cup chilled *carbonated water*; stir gently to mix. Makes 1 serving.
Fruited Ice Cubes: Freeze a *strawberry or* a *lemon twist* in *water* in each compartment of ice cube tray.

Grenadine syrup, used in beverages and desserts, is a bright red syrup that adds both color and flavor to recipes.
Look for this ingredient with the beverage mixers at the supermarket.

Sometimes a garnish makes the drink. A martini is not a martini if it does not have a green olive. If you substitute a cocktail onion for the olive, you will have a *Gibson*.
A flag is the typical garnish for a *Whiskey Sour, Amaretto Sour, Bourbon Sour*, and *Vodka Sour*. It is an orange twist and a maraschino cherry on a cocktail skewer. The *Bloody Mary, Gin and Tonic*, and *Manhattan* are other examples of drinks that call for a traditional garnish, be it a celery stalk, a lime wedge, or a maraschino cherry. Ice cream drinks and daiquiris usually have no garnish. When you make them at home, you can please yourself.

Selecting Wine: If you feel a little unsure about which wine to serve with a particular part of the meal, relax. You'll find that there aren't any absolute rules you *must* follow. Instead, let your personal tastes dictate what wines to serve. To get you started with your selection of wine, however, here are some guidelines.

Appetizer wines are served before the meal or as a cocktail to sharpen the appetite. Dry sherries are referred to as dry sherry, flor sherry, or cocktail sherry. Chilled dry (white) vermouth also can be an appetizer wine. Serve with any type of appetizer.

Table or dinner wines include the red, white, and rosé wines served at meals. Red wines are usually dry and rich, sometimes with a tart or astringent quality. White wines are lighter in body and flavor and can be dry and tart or sweet and fragrant. Rosé wines are pale red wines that can be either dry or sweet.

Red dinner wines include Burgundy, Pinot Noir, Cabernet Sauvignon, Zinfandel, Gamay, Chianti, Petite Sirah, Barbera, and Baco Noir. Serve these red wines with hearty or highly seasoned foods, such as beef, pork, game, duck, goose, and pasta dishes.

White dinner wines include Chablis, Dry Sauterne, Rhine, Chardonnay, Chenin Blanc, White Riesling, French Colombard, Sauvignon Blanc, and Seyval Blanc. Serve these white wines with light foods, such as chicken, turkey, fish, shellfish, ham, and veal.

Rosé dinner wines include Grenache Rosé, Rosé of Cabernet Sauvignon, Zinfandel Rosé, and Rosé of Pinot Noir. Serve rosé wines with ham, fried chicken, shellfish, cold beef, picnic foods, and buffet foods.

Dessert wines are heavier and sweeter than dinner wines. Also, their alcohol content is usually greater than that of the dinner wines. A few examples of dessert wines include Golden Sherry, Cream Sherry, Ruby Port, Tawny Port, White Port, Madeira, Marsala, Muscatel, Catawba, Tokay, and Sweet Sauterne. Serve dessert wines alone or with items such as fruits, nuts, pies, dessert cheeses, cakes, and cookies.

Sparkling wines can be served before, during, or after a meal. Champagne is the most popular sparkling wine. Check the label on the bottle since several varieties are available. Brut is the driest champagne; extra sec or extra dry is slightly sweeter than brut, but still fairly dry. Sec or dry is of medium sweetness, demi sec is quite sweet, and doux is very sweet. Other effervescent wines include Cold Duck, Sparkling Burgundy, and Sparkling Rosé.

APPEARANCE

To get the most enjoyment from a fine wine you need to follow just a few simple steps. The look-smell-taste process takes but a few seconds and can be done with little fuss. It serves to eliminate a bad wine—and there are wines that have been badly made or kept too long or poorly.

First, pour a small amount of wine into a wineglass. Then, hold the glass by the stem. Hold the glass to the light or against a white tablecloth. Now, look at the wine to admire its brilliance and color.

Buying Wine: Start with a good retail wine shop that carries a wide range of wines; then look for an informed store employee who will help you make a selection. Consider your tastes and the food you will serve with the wine. Will you be serving the wine before the meal, with the meal, or with dessert?

Generally you'll find wines in the 750-milliliter-size bottle. Some wines are also available in the larger 1.5-liter size, ideal when entertaining a group. You can sample a smaller bottle to ensure a good choice before investing in the larger bottle. Plan on one 750-milliliter-size bottle for every two guests (one bottle for every 3 to 4 guests if wine is served only during the meal); plan on one 1.5-liter bottle of wine for every four guests (6 to 8 guests if the wine will be served only during a meal). A 750-milliliter bottle of sparkling wine provides six generous glassfuls.

Serving Wine: To serve a bottle of wine, all you need to do is open the bottle and pour. Most wines don't need to "breathe," and they don't need decanting (pouring the wine into a fancy container). If you have purchased a larger 1.5-liter bottle of wine, to make serving easier you might want to pour the wine into a decanter and serve from it.

One set of well-shaped, fairly long-stemmed, clear "tulip" glasses (9 or 10 ounces in size) will do for any wine, even when you're serving guests sparkling wines, sherry, or a dessert wine. However, it's nice if you can serve sherry and dessert wines in smaller glasses. Fill wineglasses one-half to two-thirds full so you can capture the wine's aroma. For appetizer and dessert wines, serve smaller portions.

If a wine label has any suggstions about the wine's serving temperature, be sure to follow the suggestion. If none is suggested, here are some guidelines you can follow: Red wine should be served at a cool room temperature (around 65°F); white wines should be somewhat cooler (around 50°F). Sparkling wines should always be served chilled (somewhere between 40°F and 50°F).

Be sure to take care when opening a bottle of sparkling wine. Handle the bottle gently to minimize pressure buildup. Hold the bottle in one hand and untwist the wire loop with the other. Wrap the cork with a hand towel or cloth napkin. Then, hold the cork with one hand and tilt the bottle to a 45° angle away from you (or anyone else). Twist the bottle while gently pulling out the cork with the other hand. The wine may overflow—that's when you use the towel.

AROMA

Next, smell the wine. Don't be shy. Get your nose into the glass. This is the crucial test—if the wine smells good, it will taste good. If it's a red wine or a fragrant white wine, swirl the wine about in the glass (this is one reason for not filling the glass too close to the top) to catch all the nuances of its bouquet.

FLAVOR

Finally, of course, begin to drink the wine and enjoy its flavor. Wine tasters often hold a sip of wine in their mouths and note the consistency and mouth feel. After swallowing the wine, note any lingering aftertaste from the wine.

MOUNT
VEEDER
WINERY

There's a certain technique to pouring beer. Some people like a high foamy head; others, however, prefer a short one. By varying the distance between the can or bottle and the glass as well as the angle of the glass, you can vary the height of the head. Pouring too fast may cause overfoaming. To keep the head, use a glass with a narrower bottom than top.

You may not realize that sparkling clean glasses are also important. A smudge of grease on a glass will ruin even the frothiest head.

■■■■ BEER GUIDE ■■■■

If you're going to serve beer to your guests, you'll find more than one type of beer to choose from when you go to purchase it. Among the many choices are lager beer, pilsner or light lager beer, light beer, premium beer, imported beer, dark lager or Munich-type beer, bock beer, and keg beer.

Most beers produced in the United States are lager beers. They usually range between 3.2 and 4.0 percent alcohol. Pilsner or light lager beers are lighter in color than regular lager beer.

Do not confuse the term "light lager beer" with "light beer," which usually has fewer calories than the average beer and is made with a reduced amount of malt and grain. The alcohol content of light beer is a few tenths of a percent less than that of regular beer. Premium beer often simply refers to a particular brewer's best beer.

Imported beers are often more bitter than American beers. Dark lager or Munich-type beers are heavy and rich tasting. They're chocolate brown in color. Bock beer is a special brew of heavy beer, somewhat darker and sweeter than regular beer. It's made in the winter especially for the six-week-long bock beer season that beer lovers date as the beginning of spring. The alcohol content may be more than double that of lager beers.

You can buy both domestic and imported beers in either cans or bottles. Some of beers kinds also come in kegs. Keg beer offers a fresher flavor than bottle or can beer since the keg beer hasn't been pasteurized to kill the yeast.

When ordering beer for a party, allow about 12 ounces per guest for every half hour to an hour. For a large crowd you might want to buy a keg.

Proper storage of beer is important since beer is perishable. Keep bottled beer in a dark, cool place, out of direct sunlight. Canned beer also needs cool surroundings, but is unaffected by light. Keg beer must be kept constantly around 45° F so the yeast won't start working again.

Beer is best served at about 45° F for the lighter varieties and about 50° F for the heavier varieties. For quick chilling, place the beer containers in a deep tub of ice cubes.

Beer Drinks

For a change of pace from plain beer, try one of these cocktails made from beer.

Beer Buster: Add 3 tablespoons *gin or vodka* to a chilled tall glass of chilled *beer.* Makes 1 serving.

Bloody Bull on Ice: Combine 3 cups *tomato juice,* 2 teaspoons *Worcestershire sauce,* and several dashes *bottled hot pepper sauce;* pour into ice cube trays. Slice 1 medium *lemon;* cut slices into quarters. Place one quarter-slice into each cube section of tray. Freeze till firm (makes about 24 frozen cubes). To serve, fill a tall glass with about 4 frozen tomato juice cubes; add chilled *beer.* Makes 6 servings.

Boilermaker: Serve a jigger of *rye whiskey* with a chilled tall glass of chilled *beer.* Makes 1 serving.

Calgary Red: Fill a tall glass with equal amounts of chilled *beer* and chilled *tomato juice.* Makes 1.

Hot Calgary Red: Prepare Calgary Red as above *except* substitute chilled *hot-style tomato juice* for the tomato juice; stir gently to mix. If desired, add a green onion stirrer. Makes 1 serving.

Gold Cup: Fill a chilled tall glass with chilled *beer.* Add 3 tablespoons *gin or vodka,* 2 tablespoons *lime juice,* and ½ teaspoon *extra fine granulated sugar.* Stir gently to mix. Makes 1 serving.

Indibeer: Fill a chilled tall glass with equal amounts of chilled *beer* and chilled *orange juice.* Stir in a dash *curry powder.* Makes 1 serving.

Lager and Lime: Pour one 12-ounce bottle *lager beer* into a chilled tall glass. Stir in 1 tablespoon *lime juice.* If desired, add a lime slice. Makes 1 serving.

Sangaree: In a chilled tall glass combine 1 tablespoon *water* and 1 teaspoon *sugar;* stir till sugar is dissolved. Add chilled *beer* to fill glass; stir gently to mix. Sprinkle with ground *nutmeg.* Makes 1 serving.

Shandygaff: Fill a tall glass with equal amounts of chilled *beer* and chilled *ginger ale.* Makes 1 serving.

For after-dinner drinks, you can choose from a wide assortment of brandies, liqueurs, dessert wines, and dessert coffees.

Brandies come in many flavors, ranging from heavily sweetened brandy-based liqueurs to fiery unaged brandies. Regular brandy is made from distilled grape wines and is aged. Cognac, the king of the brandy family, comes from wines produced in the Cognac region of France. Other imported brandies include Grappa (an Italian brandy usually not aged before bottling), Metaxa (a Greek brandy), and Pisco (a Peruvian brandy). Brandy blends include B&B (a mixture of Benedictine and brandy), and Chartreuse (a green or yellow brandy flavored with herbs, plants, and extracts).

Fruit brandies are made from a wide variety of fruits other than grapes and may or may not be aged. Some fruit-based or fruit-flavored brandies include apple brandy (calvados is the French version; applejack, the American version), apricot brandy (also called abricotine), blackberry brandy, cherry brandy (the German version is called kirschwasser), peach brandy, pear brandy, plum brandy (called slivovitz by central Europeans), and raspberry brandy (also known as Framboise).

Liqueurs are also referred to as cordials. The flavorings are derived not only from fruits, but also from fruit stones and peels, flowers, herbs, seeds, barks, roots, and vegetable extracts. The basis for liqueurs can be brandy, whiskey, rum, gin, or another spirit mixed or redistilled with flavoring materials. A sugar syrup is added, then the liqueur is aged. Crèmes are extra sweet and smooth liqueurs.

Some of the many interesting liqueurs and their flavors include advocaat (eggnog), Amaretto (almond-flavored), crème de cassis (black currant), crème de cacao (coffee), crème de menthe (mint), Curaçao (orange), Kummel (caraway seed), Pimiento (spicy), rock and rye (an American invention based on rye whiskey and rock candy syrup with fruit flavorings), Sambuca (anise), Cherry Heering (cherry), Kahlua (coffee), and Galliano (anise).

To read about dessert wines, turn to pages 306 and 307. For coffees, see the recipes at right.

Dessert Coffee Drinks

½ **cup hot strong coffee**
Desired coffee flavoring
(see choices below)
Whipped cream
Ground cinnamon *or* nutmeg

■ In a coffee cup or mug stir together hot coffee and the desired coffee flavoring. Top with a dollop of whipped cream; sprinkle with cinnamon or nutmeg. Makes 1 (6-ounce) serving.

Café Alexander: Stir 1 tablespoon *crème de cacao* and 1 tablespoon *brandy* into the hot coffee.

Café Benedictine: Stir 2 tablespoons *Benedictine* and 2 tablespoons *light cream* into the hot coffee.

Café-Caribe: Stir 1 tablespoon *coffee liqueur* and 1 tablespoon *rum* into the hot coffee.

Café Columbian: Stir 2 tablespoons *coffee liqueur* and 1 tablespoon *chocolate-flavored syrup* into the hot coffee.

Café Israel: Stir 2 tablespoons *chocolate-flavored syrup* and 2 tablespoons *orange liqueur* into coffee.

Café Nut: Stir 2 tablespoons *Amaretto or hazelnut liqueur* into the hot coffee.

Dutch Coffee: Stir 2 tablespoons *chocolate-mint liqueur* into the hot coffee.

Irish Coffee: Stir 1 tablespoon *Irish whiskey* and 2 teaspoons *sugar* into the hot coffee.

Orange-Brandy Coffee: Stir 1 tablespoon *orange liqueur* and 1 tablespoon *brandy* into the hot coffee. If desired, sprinkle finely shredded orange peel atop whipped cream instead of cinnamon or nutmeg.

Spicy Coffee Brew (see recipe, page 290) and espresso coffee also make delightful after-dinner beverages. Use finely ground espresso roast coffee and brew in an ordinary coffeepot. Or, prepare instant espresso coffee powder according to package directions.

For a special treat make *Cappuccino*. Beat together ½ cup *whipping cream* and 1 tablespoon *powdered sugar* till stiff peaks form. Pour 2 cups hot *espresso coffee* into 6 small cups, filling cups half full. Add a large spoonful of whipped cream to each cup. Sprinkle with finely shredded *orange peel*. Gently stir the whipped cream into espresso coffee till it is melted. You will have 6 servings.

INDEX

INDEX

INDEX

INDEX

INDEX

INDEX

Have BETTER HOMES AND
GARDENS® magazine delivered
to your door. For information,
write to:
MR. ROBERT AUSTIN
P.O. BOX 4536
DES MOINES, IA 50336